Penguin Education
Studies in Applied Statistics
General Editor: I. R. Vesselo

Statistics for the Social Scientist: 2
Applied Statistics

K. A. Yeomans

Statistics for the Social Scientist: 2
Applied Statistics

K. A. Yeomans

Penguin Books

Penguin Books Ltd, Harmondsworth,
Middlesex, England
Penguin Books Inc., 7110 Ambassador Road,
Baltimore, Maryland 21207, U.S.A.
Penguin Books Australia Ltd, Ringwood,
Victoria, Australia

First published 1968
Reprinted 1970
Copyright © K. A. Yeomans, 1968

Made and printed in Great Britain by
Western Printing Services Ltd, Bristol
Set in Monotype Times

To my parents

Contents

8   Contents

9 Contents

Editorial foreword

In *Statistics for the Social Scientist: 2 Applied Statistics* the author extends further the study he commenced in Volume 1 (*Introducing Statistics*). This second book investigates in greater detail the aspects of statistical practice that have a particular application for the social scientist, with numerous illustrations based on practical experience.

The principles and usages of sampling are subjected to a detailed analysis, together with an exposition of regression and correlation and a study of trend curves. Non-parametric methods have been made the subject of special treatment in view of their rapidly increasing importance, and the final chapter is devoted to further developments of statistical techniques such as econometrics and operational research.

Volume 1 covers the mathematical fundamentals of statistics and will be useful to refresh the reader's memory of basic techniques whilst Volume 2 is being studied.

The author is especially well qualified to present the subject of statistics to social scientists as he is lecturer in economic and social statistics at the University of Aston in Birmingham. He is also conscious of the difficulties non-mathematical readers find in assimilating statistical theory and his text has therefore been written with this problem very much in mind.

I should like to acknowledge the valuable help of Mr Arthur Tulip, Miss Angela Powell and Miss Jacqueline Smith, all of Honeywell Controls Limited, in connexion with the computation of tables.

I. R. V.

Preface

The processing, analysis and presentation of raw empirical data were dealt with in *Statistics for the Social Scientist: 1 Introducing Statistics*. This second volume discusses inductive statistics, a term which may perhaps require some explanation.

Induction may be defined as the making of general inferences from particular instances. In the context of statistical method, the particular instances will be the results obtained from sample evidence in the form of arithmetic means, standard deviations, proportions, regression and correlation coefficients, etc. The general inferences will be made about the corresponding parameters of the statistical population from which the sample has been drawn. Thus methods will be discussed by which estimates of population parameters are obtainable from no more than a knowledge of sample measures. In an analogous manner we shall consider that aspect of decision theory concerned with the testing of hypotheses about population parameters when only sample evidence is available. In both cases it is impossible to be certain that the correct conclusions have been drawn. Estimates will be made with defined levels of confidence (or probability), and the acceptance of any hypothesis about a population parameter will involve a risk (or probability) of being wrong. The whole emphasis in inductive statistics will be on the quantification of the probability aspects of sampling methods and the basic concepts of probability and of probability distributions will be examined at an early stage.

Although the main emphasis in this volume will be on the problems of estimation and the testing of hypotheses, together with associated topics and applications such as sample design and statistical quality control, the opportunity has been taken to develop some of the areas introduced in volume 1 and to indicate the specific extensions and uses of statistical and mathematical methods in economics and management. All these discussions are necessarily of a more complex nature than those considered earlier, but the same basic method of approach that was used in volume 1 has been maintained. As far as possible topics have been explored by illustration and demonstration rather than by rigorous proof. For instance, in the principles of statistical sampling we develop the general situation first and progress deductively to the particular case so that the logical sequencing of thought involved in practice (where the steps are in the reverse direction) may be clearly appreciated.

Mathematical notes have again been included at the end of most chapters so that for the student so inclined the more rigorous proofs and derivations are available. It must be pointed out that these notes are by no means exhaustive and do not provide an integrated whole: they have been selected as the result of experience with students' queries and requests in lectures and seminars.

K. A. YEOMANS
January 1968

Acknowledgements

I should like to express my indebtedness and gratitude to the many people who have given their advice and encouragement unstintingly. At both the Lanchester College of Technology and the Birmingham College of Commerce my colleagues were always ready to listen to and discuss difficulties. To mention a few is an injustice to the rest. Nevertheless, I feel that Mr R. B. Goudie of the College of Commerce and Dr C. Sharp of the University of Leicester should be given my special thanks. Mr Goudie has read the majority of the book at manuscript stage and has provided considerable technical and administrative assistance throughout its production. Many mistakes and ambiguities would have gone unnoticed but for his vigilance. Dr Sharp also kindly read much of the manuscript and the majority of his valuable suggestions have been incorporated in the following chapters. Last but no means least I thank my wife, Merle, who has so often provided the encouragement which has lifted my flagging spirits, and who has somehow managed to fit into the most hectic day of looking after a young active family the typing of the manuscript.

I would also like to acknowledge permission given to publish the following copyright material:

(i) Her Majesty's Stationery Office for permission to use Crown copyright material taken from the *Annual Abstract of Statistics*, *National Income and Expenditure*, *Monthly Digest of Statistics*, *U.K. Balance of Payments* and *Regional Statistics*.

(ii) The Universities of Birmingham, Bristol and London for permission to use questions from their examination papers; I would point out that these bodies are in no way committed to approval of the answers given in this book.

(iii) Barclays Bank for permission to use series taken from *Barclays Bank Review*.

I am indebted to the literary executor of the late Sir Ronald A. Fisher, F.R.S., Cambridge, to Dr Frank Yates, F.R.S., Rothamsted, and to Messrs Oliver & Boyd Ltd, Edinburgh, for permission to reprint tables from their book *Statistical tables for biological, agricultural and medical research*; to D. V. Lindley, J. C. P. Miller and the Cambridge University Press for permission to reprint table 3 from *Cambridge elementary statistical tables*; to S. Siegel and the McGraw-Hill Publishing Company Ltd for permission to reprint tables 6 to 8 from *Nonparametric statistics for the behavioral sciences*; and to W. Z. Hirsch and the Macmillan Company of New York for permission to reprint table 2 from *Introduction to modern statistics*.

Chapter 1
The principles of statistical sampling

In *Statistics for the Social Scientist: 1 Introducing Statistics* we considered various methods of describing numerical data, partly because numerical values are able to provide more analytical detail than graphical representations, and partly because comparisons over time and space can be made more precisely and definitely.

While straightforward analysis is extremely valuable, we have neglected a vital qualification. We must consider the type of data we are using.

1.1 The value of sampling

1.1.1 If we have every value of the variable in a given situation, then direct comparisons are perfectly adequate. This is not the case if we are dealing with only a sample or subset of values on the assumption that the characteristics of the sample will adequately reflect the characteristics of the aggregate, or statistical population, from which it has been drawn. In these circumstances, we must make certain reservations.

Samples are by definition only part of the parent population and therefore cannot have exactly the same qualities or characteristics as the population from which they have been drawn. Experience shows, however, that in many circumstances the loss of precision does not assume large proportions. The cocoa merchant in Ghana pays the farmer according to the quality of a sample of one hundred cocoa beans taken from a sack; the doctor accepts the findings of a small sample of blood in making his diagnosis.

The assumption that the part can adequately, though not completely, reflect the whole seems to have logical foundations. Similarly, the realization that the larger the sample the more likely it is to represent the population has obvious validity when one considers the limiting case of the sample which consists of the entire population.

1.1.2   Statistical sampling seeks to determine how accurate a description of the population the sample and its properties will provide. For instance, will a sample mean or standard deviation be a good estimate of the population mean or standard deviation? The same problem is posed by any other 'average' or measure of dispersion.

We should first consider briefly different types of statistical populations and the ways in which samples can be taken from them.

1.2 Populations

A statistical population is every member of a group possessing the same basic and defined characteristic, but varying in amount or quality from one member to another. The ratepayers of Birmingham, the I.Q.s of all children in the U.K., the barometric pressure at different places in the world, the possible outcomes from the throw of a die all provide examples of statistical populations. They are, however, different sorts of population.

1.2.1   The number of Birmingham ratepayers is a known integer. A population of this type we define as being finite. The barometric pressure at different places in the world is an example of an infinite population, because there are an indefinitely large number of points on the surface of the earth. Many statistical populations involving measurements are of this type. Also many finite populations are so large that they can be treated as effectively infinite: the year's production of washers by an engineering firm, or a flight of migrating ducks in Canada, illustrates this point.

1.2.2   Finally, we should be aware of hypothetical, as opposed to existent, populations. All the possible outcomes from the throw of a die are a concept which has no existence in reality, for however long we throw the die and record the results, we could always continue to do so for a still longer period. Yule and Kendall, in their book *Introduction to the Theory of Statistics*, define a hypothetical population as 'the aggregate of all the conceivable ways in which a specified event can happen'.

Looking at a hypothetical population in this way, it is obvious that it must often necessarily be an infinite population. It should not be imagined that only games of chance provide illustrations of hypothetical populations. Whenever one knows all the possible outcomes of a situation which will take place in the future, one is dealing with a hypothetical and infinite population. Such a case is the number of ways in which a football team of eleven players can be selected from the sixteen possible members named by the club manager.

Having outlined these different populations, we must now look at the problems of drawing samples from them.

1.3 Random sampling

1.3.1 The theory of statistical sampling rests upon the assumption that the selection of the sample units has been carried out in a random manner. Random sampling indicates that the chance of any one member of the parent population being included in the sample should be the same as for any other population member; by extension, it follows that the chance of any particularly constituted sample appearing should be the same as for any other.

1.3.2 There may at first sight appear to be no difficulty in choosing a sample randomly. A haphazard method would seem to be all that is required. For instance, a clerk selecting a sample of invoices for detailed checking by sorting through a pile and taking one every now and then may be thought of as choosing randomly. Equally, a market research interviewer selecting women shoppers to find their attitude to brand X by stopping one and then another as they pass along a busy shopping precinct, must certainly seem to be practising random methods. In both cases, however, there is a strong possibility that bias is present in the selection of the sample.

1.3.3 The clerk's eye may well be drawn to invoices with elaborate printed headings, or he may pass over invoices containing many items. The market researcher may tend to ask his questions of young attractive women rather than older housewives, or he may stop women who have packets of brand X prominently on show in their shopping bags, rather than those with packets exhibiting the competitor's label.

1.3.4 There is no suggestion that biased samples are being drawn intentionally or maliciously in these two examples. From experience, it is known that the human being is a poor random selector who is very subject to bias; fundamental psychological traits prevent complete objectivity in these circumstances, and no amount of training or conscious effort can eradicate them. How then can the necessary objectivity be achieved for the sampling to be random? The answer depends to a large extent on the type of population being considered.

1.3.5 Where it is possible to identify and give a number to every population member (i.e. a finite population), lottery methods or tables of random numbers can be used. Suppose that a sample of five hundred members of a trade union was required. A list of all members of this union would be needed (called the sampling frame), and a numerical value would be placed against every name on the list. If lottery sampling is being used, correspondingly numbered slips of paper will be placed in identical metal containers which are then well mixed in a drum. Five hundred of these containers would then be selected and the members of the trade union corresponding to the numbers selected would constitute the sample.

1.3.6   When tables of random numbers are being used, the technique is somewhat faster. The tables, containing five-, six- or seven-digit numbers, are constructed according to certain mathematical principles so that each digit has the same chance of selection.

This can be achieved with a set of two dice, one black and one red. The two are thrown simultaneously. If the black turns up 1, 2 or 3, then the red die value gives the random number from 0 to 4 as shown in the table below. A red 6 is ignored and a rethrow of the red die takes place. Similarly if the black is 4, 5 or 6, then the value on the red die indicates the random digit between 5 and 9 (again a red 6 is ignored and a rethrow follows).

Black		1	2	3		4	5	6
Red	1	2	3	4	5	1	2	3	4	5
Random number	0	1	2	3	4	5	6	7	8	9

For example, if we want to construct a five-digit random number, the dice will be thrown five times. Suppose the results are as follows:

Throw	Black	Red	Random number
1	4	3	7
2	5	1	5
3	5	6 (rethrow)	
		4	8
4	2	1	0
5	3	4	3

The random number is therefore   7 5 8 0 3.

The randomness can also be achieved electronically, as in the case of the British computer ERNIE which selects the winning national premium bonds each month.

Tables of random numbers are compiled in the following form:

7	8	3	6	2		2	7	3	3	1		5	6	0	0	2
5	0	1	2	9		4	3	1	0	2		5	1	9	2	7
8	6	3	0	0		1	1	2	2	1		4	3	8	1	6
0	1	5	8	3		3	9	9	8	3		6	0	3	1	9

If the population in question contains 10,000 members, then only the first four digits in each number will be used. In our trade union survey, members numbered 7836, 5012, 8630, 158 etc. (up to five hundred members) would constitute the sample.

1.3.7   It will not always be possible or practical to identify every population member: if a sample from a churn of milk is required, it is obviously impossible to distinguish every molecule. This is an example of an infinite population, and the treatment must necessarily be different. All that can be done is to divide an infinite population into arbitrarily sized parts and select one part or several parts to make up the sample. In selecting the sample of milk, we might split the churn into 100 c.c. units and then take one of these as the sample. In this case, the selection can follow the procedure established above for randomness.

In practice, it would be unusual to go to such lengths when dealing with sampling from continuous substances such as milk, oil, and wheat flour. It is more likely that after the batch in question has been well mixed a certain prescribed quantity will be taken from the middle. The same applies to sampling from very large finite populations, such as quality inspection of batches of components bought in by a firm. In both cases, the short-cut approach is considered to yield a random sample because of the homogeneous nature of the population.

1.3.8   The problem of identifying the population members becomes particularly difficult when a hypothetical situation is considered. Here it is not possible to number all the population members because there are an infinitely large number of them which have an existence only in the future. All that can be done is to observe the population members which have occurred and to deduce that these give an indication of the nature of the entire population. One must deduce, in fact, that a random sample has been drawn. Such is the case when a card is drawn from a well-shuffled pack 5000 times or bank rate is observed daily for five years.

1.3.9   Having looked at certain basic problems of sampling, we can now return to the fundamental task of deciding how likely it is that the sample pattern will be a true reflection of the parent population. In order to demonstrate the logical sequence of thoughts involved, we will seek to establish what sort of estimate of the population mean is provided by a sample mean.

Before doing this, we should introduce a modification to our earlier notation. Previously we have used $\bar{x}$ as the symbol of the arithmetic mean. Now we will specify that $\bar{x}$ is a sample mean while μ (mu) is the corresponding population parameter. In the same way s is now confined to being a sample standard deviation and σ (sigma) is the population standard deviation.

1.4 Estimating μ from $\bar{x}$

1.4.1 Let us examine the case of a yearly Ministry of Transport test to which all cars, irrespective of age, have to be submitted. The test looks for faults in brakes, steering, lights and suspension, and it is discovered after the first year that approximately the same number of cars have 0, 1, 2, 3 or 4 faults. The mean number of faults was therefore 2, with a standard deviation of 1·414 (the mean and standard deviation of 0, 1, 2, 3, 4).

1.4.2 These results are obtained from a 100 per cent check of cars and therefore are population results. What must be considered are the estimates that could have been obtained if only a sample of vehicles had been tested during the year. For the sake of convenience, we shall consider the situation when only two cars are tested after being selected at the roadside by a mobile testing station.

1.4.3 It is conceivably possible to derive an average of two faults per car from such a sample. For instance, both cars could have two faults, one could have one fault and the other three faults, or one could be perfect whilst the second is in very poor condition with brakes, lights, steering and suspension all defective. It is also possible, however, for the average number of faults to be 0 or 4 or any of the values in between. Let us therefore consider all the hypothetically possible results:

The samples

	Items faulty	Second car 0	1	2	3	4
	0	0:0	0:1	0:2	0:3	0:4
	1	1:0	1:1	1:2	1:3	1:4
First car	2	2:0	2:1	2:2	2:3	2:4
	3	3:0	3:1	3:2	3:3	3:4
	4	4:0	4:1	4:2	4:3	4:4

1.4.4 From this list we can work out all the possible sample means by dividing the total number of faulty items in each sample by 2:

The sample means

	Items faulty	Second car 0	1	2	3	4
	0	0·0	0·5	1·0	1·5	2·0
	1	0·5	1·0	1·5	2·0	2·5
First car	2	1·0	1·5	2·0	2·5	3·0
	3	1·5	2·0	2·5	3·0	3·5
	4	2·0	2·5	3·0	3·5	4·0

It is immediately evident that some of these possible sample averages occur several times. In view of this, it would seem reasonable and sensible to construct a frequency distribution from the sample means. This will be referred to as the sampling distribution of means:

Sampling distribution

Sample mean	Number of samples	fx
0·0	1	0·0
0·5	2	1·0
1·0	3	3·0
1·5	4	6·0
2·0	5	10·0
2·5	4	10·0
3·0	3	9·0
3·5	2	7·0
4·0	1	4·0
	25	50

1.4.5   What emerges immediately from this sampling distribution is that a sample mean of 2, which is the same as the population mean μ, is more likely to occur than any other sample mean. This is evident because there are five ways in which an average of 2 can occur, while there are less than five ways in which any other sample mean can occur. What is more, the mean of the sampling distribution is also 2 (from the sampling distribution table $\dfrac{\Sigma fx}{N} = \dfrac{50}{25} = 2$) and this enables us to say that on average a sample mean provides an unbiased estimate of the population mean. It will always be the case that the mean of the means, or $\mu_{\bar{x}}$, will be identical with μ the population mean, regardless of the sample size. This result is of the utmost importance to the theory of sampling.

1.4.6   Also from the sampling distribution it can be seen that a particular sample mean is more likely to be close to the population mean than a long way away from it. From the universe of sample means we find that 19 out of 25 are in the range 1·0 to 3·0 inclusive. The particular sample taken in practice will have an arithmetic mean which is one of this universe, and therefore there is approximately a three-quarters or 75 per cent chance that it will not differ from the population mean of 2 by more than one item faulty.

23   The principles of statistical sampling

This approximation is possible because in this case we have a knowledge of the characteristics of the sampling distribution and the population mean in front of us. What is required is a more general method of ascertaining the chances of a sample mean being out by a prescribed amount, without a knowledge of either the population mean or the actual form of the sampling distribution. In practice, of course, it is completely impossible to know either of these facts, and indeed one of them, μ, we are trying to estimate.

We have talked about the 'likelihood' or 'chance' of something happening several times in this chapter. We must now digress and consider more specifically what is meant by these terms: we must look at the concept of the probability.

1.5 Probability

1.5.1 The probability of a given event (A) occurring lies between two extremes, 0 and 1. If we are absolutely certain that event A cannot occur, then the probability of A occurring is zero, $P(A) = 0$. If, on the other hand, it is completely certain that it will occur, then $P(A) = 1$. The majority of probabilities which we will look at have a fractional value between these limits.

1.5.2 There are two approaches to the problem of calculating the probability of an event. If one knows all the possible outcomes in a set of circumstances, it is possible to evaluate the probability of one of the outcomes occurring. This is known as *a priori* probability and is found most commonly in games of chance. The key point is that the probability can be obtained in advance, before the event takes place.

The other approach rests upon experience of the past. This 'empirical' probability simply asks how many times event A occurred in the past, out of a known number of possible outcomes. It is then assumed that the same proportion will continue into the future. All insurance policies are based upon this type of probability.

1.5.3 In general the probability of A occurring is the number x of success cases (A happens) divided by n, the number of all cases ($n = x + f$, where f = cases where A does not occur).

$$P(A) = \frac{x}{n} = \frac{x}{x+f}$$

1.5.4 *Mutually exclusive events*

If two events A and B are possible outcomes from n occurrences but cannot take place at one and the same time, then the probability that A or B

will occur is the sum of the probabilities that each will occur. For instance, the probability of getting a six when throwing an unbiased die is $\frac{1}{6}$. Similarly for the appearance of a five. Therefore the probability of obtaining either a six or a five is $\frac{1}{6}+\frac{1}{6} = \frac{1}{3}$. Another example could be found in the sampling distribution on page 23: the probability of a sample mean of 2·0 defective items occurring is $5/25 = 1/5$ and the probability of a sample mean of 2·5 is 4/25, so that the probability of 2·0 or 2·5 occurring is 9/25 or 0·36.

In general $P(A \text{ or } B) = P(A)+P(B)$.

Similarly, if events A and B are the exhaustive events in a mutually exclusive set, the probability of A occurring is 1 minus the probability of B occurring, as the following two illustrations will demonstrate:

(i) During a period of six months a train arrives late on 16 days. The chance of it being on time is $1-16/182 = 166/182 = 83/91$.

(ii) In the sampling distribution, the probability of a particular sample mean being outside 1·0 or 3·0 items defective is $1-19/25 = 6/25$ or 0·24.

In general $P(A) = 1-P(B)$

These two principles apply equally well to three or more events.

1.5.5 *Independent events*

If two events A and B are independent of each other, i.e. the outcome of one does not affect the outcome of the other, then the probability that they will both occur is the product of the probabilities that each will occur. Let us again consider two examples:

(i) A firm's stores must fill orders within one week of receipt or lose the order. On average, there are only three weeks in the year when orders are so great as to exhaust current stock. Similarly, from experience there is an average of five weeks in the year when stocks are not replenished within the week. What are the chances in a particular week of (a) receiving orders which are greater than the stock held, and (b) not receiving replacements within the week? In other words, what is the probability of losing orders?

Using the rule for independent events, we find the probability of (a) equals 3/52 and the probability of (b) equals 5/52, so that the probability of both occurring is $3/52 \times 5/52 = 15/2704$. The risk, slightly over 1 in 200, would be considered negligible in this case.

(ii) The Ministry of Transport sample vehicle test can be thought of as being taken from a hypothetical or effectively infinite population, so that if two roadside samples were taken on consecutive days, the result of the one would not affect the result of the other. This indicates that the chances of getting two sample averages of two items defective is $5/25 \times 5/25 = 25/625 = 1/25$.

In general $P(A \text{ and } B) = P(A) \times P(B)$.

1.5.6 Dependent events

If two events A and B are related in such a way that the probability of B taking place depends upon the probability of A having occurred, then the probability of both A and B occurring is the product of the unconditional probability of A occurring and the conditional probability of B occurring. Once again examples will be the best way of demonstrating this:
(i) Among a group of twenty people selected for jury service there are by chance two men who are neighbours. What is the probability of the neighbours being the first two selected for one of the trials being heard that day? As there are two neighbours in a group of twenty jurors, the chance of one of the two being chosen first is $2/20 = 1/10$. If one of the two is chosen there is one neighbour left out of 19 men, so that his chance is one in 19 of being called next $= 1/19$.

The chances of both being called is therefore $1/10 \times 1/19 = 1/190$.
(ii) A random sample is to be taken from a group of 100 houses on a new estate to ascertain the standard of workmanship. One house is selected randomly and carefully surveyed. Then a second is selected and so on, until the required sample size is achieved.

It is evident that the chance of a particular house being chosen as the first to be surveyed is 1 in 100 or $1/100$. Having selected one, however, the chances of a second house being included in the sample have changed to $1/99$, for there are only 99 unsurveyed houses left. If a sample of five were taken the chances of any particular five being in the sample would be $1/100 \times 1/99 \times 1/98 \times 1/97 \times 1/96 = 1/9,034,502,400$.

In general $P(A \text{ and } B) = P(A) \times P_A(B)$.

1.5.7 Non-mutually exclusive events

If two events, A and B, may occur separately or together then the probability that either A or B will occur is the sum of the probabilities of each occurring minus the probability of both A and B occurring. For instance if we select a playing card from a well-shuffled pack the probability of picking either a spade or a queen will be found from

$$P \text{ (spade)} + P \text{ (queen)} - P \text{ (queen of spades)}$$

giving

$$\tfrac{13}{52} + \tfrac{4}{52} - \tfrac{1}{52} = \tfrac{16}{52} = \tfrac{4}{13}$$

In general for non-mutually exclusive events

$$P(A \text{ or } B) = P(A) + P(B) - P(A \text{ and } B)$$

1.6 Arrangements

1.6.1   Associated with the problems of probability is the concept of arrangements. In many cases, before the probability of an event can be evaluated, it is necessary to work out the total number of events which could result from the circumstances in question. A few examples will illustrate the point:

(i) the probability of accidentally finding the combination to a safe which is fitted with a lock possessing eight digits depends upon the number of arrangements of eight digits when each digit can take 10 different values from 0 to 9 inclusive.

(ii) The probability of guesswork giving an examination candidate the right answer to a geography question asking for five countries to be put in an order of magnitude according to size of population will depend upon the number of ways of arranging the figures 1 to 5.

(iii) The probability of winning a football pool first dividend on the treble chance when there are 50 teams on the coupon and there are only 8 drawn games, depends upon the number of possible ways of selecting 8 from 50 teams.

1.6.2   It may seem to the reader that these examples are unnecessarily repetitious. In fact, while they all involve arrangements, different techniques are needed to establish the three answers.

1.6.3 *Multiple choice*

The problem relating to the combination lock on the safe requires the concept of multiple choice. We want to know how many ways there are of arranging x items from n in such a way that a particular item can occur up to x times, remembering that the order of items is important. This concept indicates that in our example 8 zeroes, 8 ones, 8 twos etc. could occur, and that 7 fives followed by 1 three is different from 1 three followed by 7 fives.

The logical way to look at this is to see that for a given value on the other seven rings of the lock, there are 10 possible figures on the first ring. For any possible figure on the first ring there are 10 possible figures on the second, etc.

Thus there are 10^8 or 100,000,000 possible eight-digit numbers, only one of which will open the safe. The probability of this number being found accidentally is 1/100,000,000. Incidentally, it is a misnomer to call a number lock a 'combination' lock, as you will see in due course.

In general, the number of choices of x from n can be found from $^nM_x = n^x$.

It should be noticed that we could have found the total number of possible samples in the vehicle test situation by using the principle of multiple choice. The number of samples size 2 from a population of 5 is:

$$5^2 = 25.$$

1.6.4 Permutations

The geography examination problem differs from the safe and its lock only in so far as repetition of digits is impossible. Assuming that there is a different number of inhabitants in the five countries it is not feasible that two or more countries can be given the same order of magnitude. Where order is important but duplication is impossible we invoke the concept of permutations. The number of permutations of n items taken x at a time equals:

$$^np_x = n(n-1)\ldots(n-x+1),$$

i.e. the product is taken over x terms. This is the same as

$$\frac{n!}{(n-x)!}$$

NOTE: The factorial notation, !, indicates that the product is taken over n terms where the magnitude of the terms decreases from n by units to 1. We define $(1-1)! = 0! = 1$, and $1!/1 = 1$.

In our case both n and x equal 5. The total number of possible answers to the question is

$$5 \times 4 \times 3 \times 2 \times 1 = 120$$
or
$$5!/0! = 120$$

The probability of guesswork achieving the correct answer is therefore 1/120.

In certain practical sampling conditions, duplication is not found. If a sample is to be taken randomly from a population of mothers of twins, it would be extremely unusual for the same mother to be interviewed twice. The random sampling here will be qualified so that any duplication which occurs will be ignored. To ascertain the size of the universe of possible samples in this case, the permutations formula would be preferred to that for multiple choice procedure.

1.6.5 *Combinations*

Finally, we have to evaluate the chances of winning the football pools in the circumstances mentioned earlier. Once again, duplication is not relevant as it is impossible to select a given match more than once in a single entry. But there is a second limiting factor. Order no longer matters. As long as the eight drawn matches are predicted correctly, it is immaterial in what order they are itemized on the entry coupon. Whatever the order, the result must be a first dividend.

To determine the number of arrangements of 8 from 50 teams we require the combinations concept. The number of ways of combining x items from n is given by

$$ {}^nC_x = \frac{n(n-1)\ldots(n-x+1)}{x!} $$

or

$$ \frac{n!}{(n-x)!\,x!} $$

NOTE: Sometimes a combination is symbolized by $\binom{n}{x}$.
This proves to be

$$ \frac{50!}{42!\,8!} = 536{,}878{,}700 $$

so that the chance of winning is 1/536,878,700. It may be noticed in passing that the football pool punter's 'perm' is the statistician's combination.

Again, circumstances can be envisaged where order is irrelevant in sampling, and where the conceivable number of samples will be determined by the rule for combinations. If a quality control inspector takes a handful of components from a bin to check the number defective, he has selected his sample in one fell swoop. There is no question of the order of selection here because all the sample units have been taken simultaneously.

These two sections on probability (1.5) and arrangements (1.6) have sought to show both the practical aspects of the concepts and also their uses in the theory of statistical sampling. This second aspect will be extended later in the chapter.

1.7 The standard error

1.7.1 Because the mean of the sample means is always the same as the population mean, we have been able to say that a particular sample mean offers an unbiased estimate of the population mean. We have also indicated something about the quality of this estimate: how likely the estimate is to be out and by how much. These themes must now be developed further.

1.7.2   If in the car tests instead of taking samples of 2 we had taken samples of 3 or 4, our sampling distributions would contain 125 and 625 sample means respectively (i.e. 5^3 and 5^4) and they would be in the following form:

Sampling distributions for samples of 3 and 4

Sample size: 3		Sample size: 4	
$\bar{x}$	Number of samples	$\bar{x}$	Number of samples
0·00	1	0·00	1
0·33	3	0·25	4
0·67	6	0·50	10
1·00	10	0·75	20
1·33	15	1·00	35
1·67	18	1·25	52
2·00	19	1·50	68
2·33	18	1·75	80
2·67	15	2·00	85
3·00	10	2·25	80
3·33	6	2·50	68
3·67	3	2·75	52
4·00	1	3·00	35
	125	3·25	20
		3·50	10
		3·75	4
		4·00	1
			625

Both of these distributions have a mean of 2 items defective, so that our first proposition is justified. What about the quality?

1.7.3   In the sampling distribution from samples of 3 it can be seen that there are 105 out of 125 samples within the range 1 to 3 inclusive. The probability of a particular sample mean being out by more than 1 item faulty is therefore $1·0 - 0·84 = 0·16$, or there is an 84 per cent chance that a sample mean will not differ from the population mean by more than 1 defective item.

Where samples of 4 are considered, the chance is 88·8 per cent, for 555 out of 625 sample means lie in the 1 to 3 range.

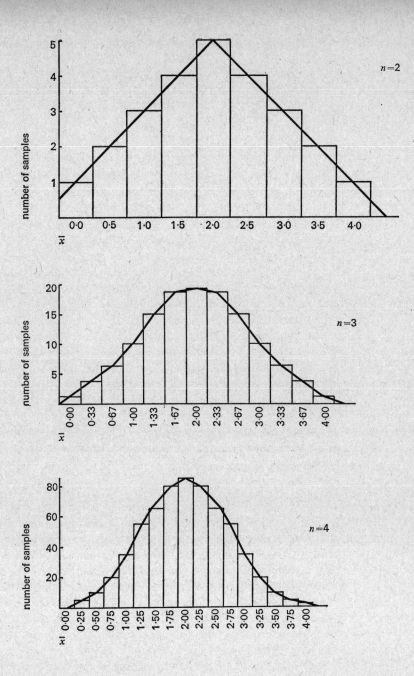

Fig. 1 Sampling distributions of $\bar{x}$.

31 The principles of statistical sampling

Summarizing the three situations, we find that:

Sample size	Chance of $\bar{x}$ being within 1 of μ
2	76%
3	84%
4	88·8%

1.7.4   It is apparent that as the sample size increases, the certainty or confidence of an estimate being within given limits also increases. This is a point that was made in a general form earlier in the chapter.

1.7.5   It is further apparent from fig. 1 that as larger samples are taken, so the shape of the histogram of the sampling distribution undergoes discernible changes. In all three cases the histograms are symmetrical, but as the sample size increases the overall configuration changes from a triangular distribution to a bell-shaped distribution. When relatively large samples are taken this bell-shaped distribution assumes the form of a 'normal' or 'Gaussian' distribution, irrespective of the form of the parent population, e.g. the population of defective items in a car is rectangular. From a knowledge of the mathematical properties of the normal distribution, it is possible to make certain quantitative probability statements based upon its standard deviation.

    If the standard deviation of the 'normal' sampling distribution can be found, these probability statements can be used in assessing the reliability of an estimate based upon a sample result. The standard deviation of a sampling distribution is termed its *standard error* and is given the symbol $\sigma_{\bar{x}}$.

1.8   The normal distribution

1.8.1   It should not be thought that the normal distribution occurs only in sampling theory. Many natural phenomena are distributed approximately normally. The I.Q.s of children, the yield of a large number of plots planted with potatoes, the weights of females in the United Kingdom, and the length of screws produced by a machine, all have the characteristic bell-shaped distribution. In fact it can be shown mathematically that whenever a measurement is affected by a large number of small independent factors, no one of which predominates, the distribution of observations will be normal.

1.8.2   Notice we have not suggested that all normal distributions are identical. Some will be broad with a wide range, others tall with a narrow range, but

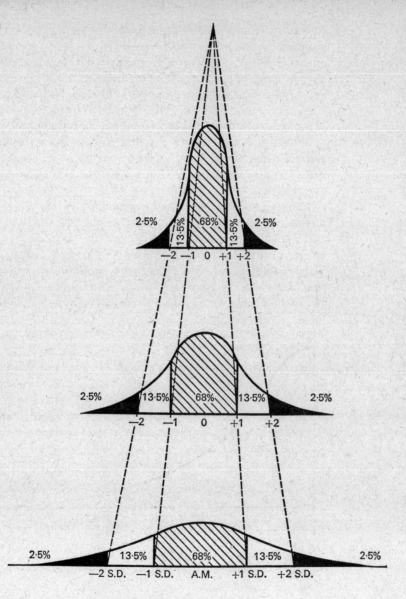

Fig. 2   Normal distributions with different spreads.

33   The principles of statistical sampling

they all share one valuable property: with a knowledge of the mean and standard deviation every other characteristic can be determined. More important even than this from our standpoint is the fact that the measurement of standard deviations from the mean establishes positions between and beyond which known proportions of the total frequency lie.

An illustration showing three normal distributions with standard deviations (spreads) of different size will demonstrate this (fig. 2).

1.8.3   In each case, $\mu \pm 1\sigma$ partitions off a range of the variable comprising approximately 68 per cent of all the frequencies. $\mu \pm 2\sigma$ encloses approximately 95 per cent of the frequencies and the whole of the distribution is effectively enclosed by $\mu \pm 3\sigma$.

These generalizations should be modified in two ways. Firstly, the figures used are approximations and while being perfectly adequate in many practical situations in applied statistics, the more exact values can be found from table 1 (page 374). This table relates to only half of the normal distribution, as the distribution is symmetrical; it shows the proportion of the area (i.e. frequency) which lies outside a specified number of standard deviations away from the mean, e.g. $2\sigma = 0.02275$ (fig. 3).

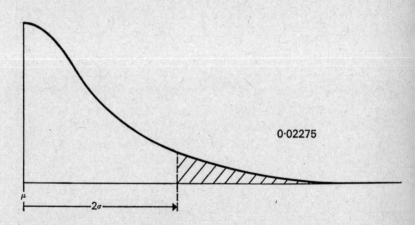

Fig. 3   The interpretation of the normal deviate.

Simple arithmetic will enable the percentage outside and inside any number of standard deviations to be found. Notice that not only integer numbers of standard deviations are given.

Secondly, it is never theoretically possible to enclose 100 per cent of the area under the frequency curve, no matter how many standard deviations are measured on either side of the mean. The mathematical equation of the normal curve

$$y = \frac{1}{\sigma\sqrt{2\pi}} . e^{-\frac{(x-\mu)^2}{2\sigma^2}}$$

is such that while the curve gets closer and closer to the x axis it never actually touches it.

1.8.4   As an example of the use of the normal curve tables, consider an electrical engineering firm which produces, among other things, neon lights. From experience, it is found that these have a life which is normally distributed with a mean of 828 hours and a standard deviation of 120 hours. The firm places a minimum life guarantee of 600 hours on its product. What proportion of output can the firm expect to have to replace?

To solve the problem, it is necessary to convert the absolute magnitudes in the situation into a relative form. Specifically, we must express the difference between the mean of 828 hours and the guarantee figure of 600 hours in standard deviations, for then we can make use of the table. To do this, the mean is subtracted from the value of the variable in question, and the answer divided by the standard deviation.

$$z = \frac{x-\mu}{\sigma} = \frac{600-828}{120} = -1 \cdot 9$$

This deviation from the mean given in terms of the standard deviation is usually known as the 'normal deviate' (z).

From the table, we find that the proportion corresponding to a deviate figure of $1 \cdot 9$ is $0 \cdot 02872$, so that the firm can expect to replace less than 3 per cent of its output.

Supposing it is decided, for the sake of improving the guarantee, that they are prepared to replace 5 per cent of output. What figure can be placed on the guarantee?

Here, we must reverse the previous process. Looking in table 1 we find that 5 per cent of the frequencies lie outside a normal deviate of $1 \cdot 64$.

Therefore,
$$-1 \cdot 64 = \frac{x-828}{120}$$

$$(-1 \cdot 64 \times 120) + 828 = x$$

$$= 631 \cdot 2 \text{ hours.}$$

The guarantee would be set at 630 hours.

35   The principles of statistical sampling

1.9 Applying the standard error

1.9.1 If the standard deviations (i.e. standard errors) are calculated from the sampling distributions, we get the following results:

Sample size: 2

Calculations for the standard error

Sample mean	Number	fx	fx^2
0·0	1	0·0	0·0
0·5	2	1·0	0·5
1·0	3	3·0	3·0
1·5	4	6·0	9·0
2·0	5	10·0	20·0
2·5	4	10·0	25·0
3·0	3	9·0	27·0
3·5	2	7·0	24·5
4·0	1	4·0	16·0
	25	50·0	125·0

$$\sigma_{\bar{x}} = \sqrt{\left\{ \frac{\Sigma fx^2}{N} - \left(\frac{\Sigma fx}{N}\right)^2 \right\}} = \sqrt{\left\{ \frac{125}{25} - \left(\frac{50}{25}\right)^2 \right\}}$$

$$= \sqrt{1} = 1$$

Sample size: 3

Here $N = 125$, $\Sigma fx = 250$, $\Sigma fx^2 = 583\cdot33$

$$\sigma_{\bar{x}} = \sqrt{\left\{ \frac{583\cdot33}{125} - \left(\frac{250}{125}\right)^2 \right\}} = \sqrt{0\cdot66}$$

$$= 0\cdot816$$

Sample size: 4

$N = 625$, $\Sigma fx = 1250$, $\Sigma fx^2 = 2812\cdot5$

$$\sigma_{\bar{x}} = \sqrt{\left\{ \frac{2812\cdot5}{625} - \left(\frac{1250}{625}\right)^2 \right\}} = \sqrt{0\cdot5}$$

$$= 0\cdot707$$

It is noticeable that once again, as the samples become larger, the standard errors decrease. It will be found that this continues to the limiting case of the sample of the entire population which has a standard error equal to zero.

1.9.2   The reader probably feels at this point that no useful purpose has been served by calculating these standard errors, for in practice we can have no detailed knowledge of the sampling distribution. However, these calculations enable us to point out a most important relationship: the variance of the population divided by the variance of the sampling distribution always equals the sample size.

$$\frac{\sigma^2}{\sigma_{\bar{x}}^2} = n$$

Algebraic manipulation therefore enables us to show that

$$\sigma_{\bar{x}} = \frac{\sigma}{\sqrt{n}}$$

1.9.3   The standard error equals the population standard deviation divided by the square root of the sample size. In other words, we do not need to calculate the standard error in the conventional way from the full sampling distribution, so long as we know the population standard deviation.

The standard errors calculated could have been obtained from:

$$n = 2 \qquad \frac{1 \cdot 414}{\sqrt{2}} = 1$$

$$n = 3 \qquad \frac{1 \cdot 414}{\sqrt{3}} = 0 \cdot 816$$

$$n = 4 \qquad \frac{1 \cdot 414}{\sqrt{4}} = 0 \cdot 707$$

1.9.4   It is important to notice at this point that the standard error does not decrease proportionately with the increase in the sample size. This is due to the fact that we divide σ by the square root of n. Thus to halve the standard error, we have to quadruple the sample size, not double it.

1.9.5   The reader is perhaps wondering why we have still not succeeded in finding a general method of arriving at the standard error. Although we no longer need the full sampling distribution, we still need the population standard deviation, σ, and this in practice will be unknown.

To answer this point, it is necessary to return to the sampling distribution so that the variances of all the samples can be calculated. We shall use the following formula, employing $n-1$ rather than n because in small samples it gives a more accurate answer; the reasons for this will be looked at in Chapter 2, page 98.

$$s^2 = \frac{\Sigma(x-\bar{x})^2}{n-1}$$

Sample size: 2

	Items	*Second car*				
	defective	0	1	2	3	4
	0	0·0	0·5	2·0	4·5	8·0
	1	0·5	0·0	0·5	2·0	4·5
First car	2	2·0	0·5	0·0	0·5	2·0
	3	4·5	2·0	0·5	0·0	0·5
	4	8·0	4·5	2·0	0·5	0·0

1.9.6   If the average sample variance is calculated from $\dfrac{\Sigma s^2}{n}$ we get $\dfrac{50}{25} = 2$

(corresponding results can be obtained from the situations where the sample size is 3 and 4).

This is the same as the population variance $(1\cdot414)^2$ and it can be stated that on the average a sample variance offers an unbiased estimate of the population variance.

In the context of the standard error formula, we can therefore use s, a sample standard deviation, as the best single estimate of σ, the population standard deviation, giving

$$\sigma_{\bar{x}} = \frac{s}{\sqrt{n}}$$

1.10   Confidence intervals

1.10.1   Two key principles have now been established:

(i) The sampling distribution of means is a normal distribution in a practical sampling situation (where the sample size is relatively large). It has a mean equal to the population mean.

(ii) The standard error of the distribution can be estimated from a sample standard deviation and the sample size. Both are found without any knowledge of the parent populations.

1.10.2   These principles can be used to estimate the unknown population mean with a defined degree of confidence. Let a sample of size n be taken randomly and let its mean $\bar{x}$ and standard deviation s be calculated. This particular $\bar{x}$ is one of the many which could have occurred; it could lie anywhere in the range of $\bar{x}$s.

If the estimate of μ is to be made with 95 per cent confidence, the important positions on the sampling distribution are $\mu + 1 \cdot 96 \dfrac{s}{\sqrt{n}}$ and $\mu - 1 \cdot 96 \dfrac{s}{\sqrt{n}}$.

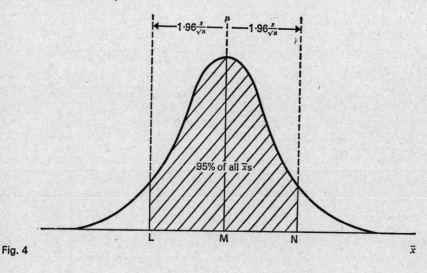

Fig. 4

In fig. 4, $\mu = M$, $\mu - 1 \cdot 96 \dfrac{s}{\sqrt{n}} = L$ and $\mu + 1 \cdot 96 \dfrac{s}{\sqrt{n}} = N$. Now if the $\bar{x}$ calculated lies between L and M and we add $1 \cdot 96$ standard errors to $\bar{x}$ we have obtained an interval into which μ must fall (the shaded area in fig. 5a).

In the same way if $\bar{x}$ lies between M and N, by subtracting $1 \cdot 96$ standard errors from $\bar{x}$ we will again enclose μ (fig. 5b).

In fact, because 95 per cent of all $\bar{x}$s lie between $\mu \pm 1 \cdot 96$ standard errors, there is a 95 per cent chance that μ will be enclosed by adding to and subtracting from the sample mean $1 \cdot 96 \dfrac{s}{\sqrt{n}}$. Only if $\bar{x}$ lies outside L or N will this process not enclose μ (figs. 5c and 5d). However, only 5 per cent of $\bar{x}$s lie outside L or N so that there is only a 5 per cent chance of this procedure not giving two limits inside which μ lies.

The main thing to remember throughout is that we do not know in

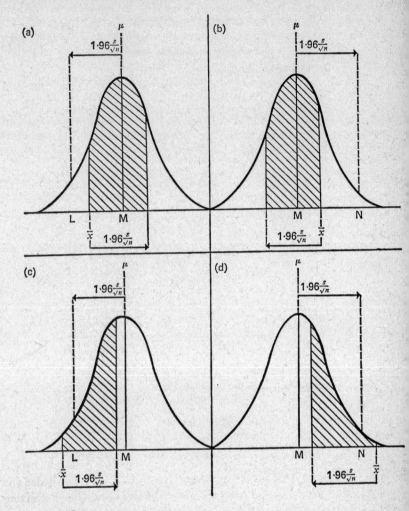

Fig. 5(a) $\bar{x} + 1.96\dfrac{s}{\sqrt{n}}$ (μ enclosed).

(b) $\bar{x} - 1.96\dfrac{s}{\sqrt{n}}$ (μ enclosed).

(c) $\bar{x} + 1.96\dfrac{s}{\sqrt{n}}$ (μ not enclosed).

(d) $\bar{x} - 1.96\dfrac{s}{\sqrt{n}}$ (μ not enclosed).

practice in which position $\bar{x}$ lies. It is only possible to assess the probabilit
of it lying in certain positions and from this assessment to establish with
given probability two limits within which μ falls.

The limits (the confidence interval) are given by

$$\underline{\mu} = \bar{x} \pm z \frac{s}{\sqrt{n}}$$

where $\underline{\mu}$ indicates the upper and lower confidence limits of the estimate of μ and $\bar{z}$ indicates the confidence level (1·96 in the case of 95 per cent confidence). The confidence level can, of course, be varied to suit the circumstances, depending upon the consequences of the estimate being incorrect. If the estimate is of the average television viewing hours per person, it hardly matters whether the probability of the estimate being correct is very high or not. However, suppose that the Ministry of Labour is trying to ascertain what income is needed to maintain a basic standard of living, with the object of setting national assistance levels. If its estimate from a sample personal expenditure survey is wrong, it will either result in hardship to people receiving national assistance benefits (if too low) or in unnecessary government expenditure (if too high).

The two main confidence levels used in practice are 95 per cent ($z = 1·96$) and 99 per cent ($z = 2·58$), which are satisfactory for a majority of purposes.

1.10.3   Consider a car assembly plant employing something over 25,000 men. In planning its future labour requirements the management wants an estimate of the number of days lost per man each year due to illness or absenteeism. A random sample of five hundred employment records shows the following situation:

Number of days lost	Number of employees
None	48
1 or 2	43
3 or 4	90
5 or 6	186
7 or 8	78
9 to 12	34
13 to 20	21
	500

$\bar{x} = 5·38$ days, $s = 3·53$ days, μ will be estimated as lying between $5·38 + \dfrac{1·96 \times 3·53}{\sqrt{500}}$ and $5·38 - \dfrac{1·96 \times 3·53}{\sqrt{500}}$ or $5·38 \pm 0·31 = 5·07$ days to $5·69$ days with 95 per cent confidence.

1.10.4   Notice that (a) if the sample size had been increased, a more precise estimate of μ could have been achieved with the same confidence level, or alternatively the same precision could be had with increased confidence; (b) if a lower confidence level were satisfactory either the sample size could have been reduced or the estimate made more precise; (c) if less precision in the estimate had been required either the sample size could have been reduced or the confidence level of the estimate increased.

In general, there are three unknowns in the equation: the precision of the estimate itself, the confidence level, and the sample data. Should two of these be available then the third can be found.

1.10.5 From the general formula $\underline{\mu} = \bar{x} \pm z \dfrac{s}{\sqrt{n}}$ we can find the degree of confidence given by z and the sample size n.

(i)
$$z = \frac{(\bar{\mu} - \bar{x})\sqrt{n}}{s}$$

(ii)
$$n = \frac{z^2 . s^2}{(\bar{\mu} - \bar{x})^2}$$

In both of these formulae $\bar{x} - \underline{\mu}$ is half the confidence interval width, so that if the precision is stated as ± 0.25 then $\underline{\mu} - \bar{x} = 0.25$. $\bar{x}$ and $\underline{\mu}$ are not specifically needed.

1.10.6 In the example in 1.10.3 suppose that the management would be satisfied if the estimate is precise to ± 0.5 of a day. With what degree of confidence can the estimate be made?

$$z = \frac{0.5\sqrt{500}}{3.53}$$

$$= 3.17$$

Consulting table 1 we find a value of 3.17 has a corresponding entry of 0.00076. Doubling to take into account both halves of the distribution, converting to a percentage and subtracting from 100, we get a 99.85 per cent confidence level. Effectively, the management can feel certain that the average number of days lost is between 4.88 and 5.88 days per annum.

1.10.7 Before undertaking this investigation, the management had before it certain information from another plant showing the average number of days lost there to be 5.6 with a standard deviation of 3.1 days. This information could have been used in establishing the sample size required to obtain an estimate precision of ± 0.5 of a day with a confidence level of 95 per cent.

$$n = \frac{1.96^2 \times 3.1^2}{0.5^2}$$

$$= 148 \text{ to nearest whole number above.}$$

Given these specifications, a sample of only 150 needs to be taken giving a speedier answer at less cost to the firm.

1.10.8　　In many cases information from an earlier survey or a similar situation can be used to estimate s, for while the mean may change over time or space the spread tends to remain more constant. If no evidence about s is available, a pilot sample can always be taken; this may also serve the purpose, where applicable, of pre-testing a questionnaire.

1.10.9　　The logic involved in making an estimate of μ from $\bar{x}$ is the logic which by and large applies to all estimates of population parameters from sample statistics. An assumption must be made about the form of the sampling distribution; often it will be normal, but having made this assumption knowledge is required of the standard error. This must be estimated from the sample data alone.

As a further illustration, but in rather different circumstances, the problem of estimating π (pi, a population proportion or percentage) from p (the proportion thrown up from the sample) will be considered.

1.11　Estimating π from p

In the preceding sections, observations have been considered which differ from one unit to the next according to the magnitude of their variable characteristic. Consequently it has been possible to talk about average values of the variable and the spread of values of the variable.

Not all statistical data are in variable form. Often observations can only be classified according to the presence or absence of a specified attribute. Examples of dichotomous observations are easily found. A man charged with drunken driving may or may not have previous convictions for the same offence; a student seeking admission to a university has or has not gained the minimum numbers of 'O' and 'A' level G.C.E. subjects; a shirt produced in a clothing factory does or does not possess a full complement of buttons when it is inspected. In all these cases, we are dealing with a clear-cut yes/no situation; borderline cases or compromises do not exist. When a group of observations of this type are considered, it is impossible to calculate a mean or standard deviation; it can only be stated that a certain percentage or proportion of the observations possess the attribute in question and a certain proportion do not.

1.12　The binomial expansion

1.12.1　　A modification to the earlier technique is evidently required when the problem of estimating a population proportion from a sample result is tackled.

Consider an airline which discovers in a detailed analysis of its operations during 1964 that 3/10 of its scheduled flights have been undertaken with less than a full payload. The directors of the company, worried about this high figure, require to keep a check on the situation in 1965 but without involving the time and expense of a full investigation. What sort of information can be provided by the statistician from a sample survey of flights?

Taking 1964, the population proportion π is known to be 3/10. Supposing that a sample of five flights is investigated: the sample proportion p could be 0, 1/5, 2/5, 3/5, 4/5 or 1 for out of the five flights 0, 1, 2, 3, 4, or 5 could have been operated with empty seats (the number of possible outcomes will always be one more than the sample size). Once again it is required to discover the likelihood or probability of each of these sample proportions occurring.

1.12.2   The probability of any one flight operating without a full payload is 3/10. If a random sample of five flights is taken we shall assume that this figure remains unaltered from the selection of one sample unit to the next. This is a reasonable assumption if the population is very large.

1.12.3   This means, of course, that these probabilities are independent of each other. Thus to ascertain the chances of all five flights having been operated with empty seats, the multiplication 'law' of independent events must be used. The probability that the sample proportion is equal to one, i.e. P (five flights with empty seats), is:

$$3/10 \times 3/10 \times 3/10 \times 3/10 \times 3/10 = (3/10)^5$$

$$= 0 \cdot 00243.$$

The probability of $p = 4/5$, i.e. P (four flights with empty seats and one full), seems to be $(3/10)^4$ multiplied by the probability of a full plane, which is $1 - 3/10 = 7/10$.

$$(3/10)^4 \times 7/10 = 0 \cdot 00567$$

In the same way, the probabilities of $p = 3/5, 2/5, 1/5$ and 0 are apparently $0 \cdot 01323, 0 \cdot 03087, 0 \cdot 07203$ and $0 \cdot 16807$ respectively.

1.12.4   It is to be expected that these six probabilities add up to one, as the six outcomes considered are exhaustive. They are mutually exclusive events, so it is certain that one or the other will occur. In fact, if the probabilities are summed, the answer is only $0 \cdot 29230$. Something, it would appear, has been omitted.

1.12.5   What we have forgotton to take into account is that some of these sample proportions could have turned up in different ways. A $p = 1/5$ can occur if the first of the sample units has the characteristic of being a flight

Sample with	Apparent probability
5 full flights and 0 with empty seats	0·16807
4 ,, ,, ,, 1 ,, ,, ,,	0·07203
3 ,, ,, ,, 2 ,, ,, ,,	0·03087
2 ,, ,, ,, 3 ,, ,, ,,	0·01323
1 ,, ,, ,, 4 ,, ,, ,,	0·00567
0 ,, ,, ,, 5 ,, ,, ,,	0·00243
	0·29230

with empty seats, or if the second, third, fourth or fifth of the sample units is of this type. It is apparent that one flight with empty seats and four with a full payload can occur in five different ways. In the same way, two unsatisfactory and three satisfactory flights can occur in ten different ways. It seems that the probabilities shown above must be multiplied by the number of ways in which each sample proportion can feasibly occur.

Having done this, we find that the sum of the probabilities is unity and this provides a justification for our logic. It may not, however, be entirely convincing to the reader, so we will approach from a different standpoint the problem of the number of ways in which a certain sample proportion can occur.

Sample proportion p	Probability of p occurring in one way	Number of ways p can occur	Probability of p
0	0·16807	1	0·16807
$\frac{1}{5}$	0·07203	5	0·36015
$\frac{2}{5}$	0·03087	10	0·30870
$\frac{3}{5}$	0·01323	10	0·13230
$\frac{4}{5}$	0·00567	5	0·02835
1	0·00243	1	0·00243
			1·00000

1.12.6 When a flight is selected randomly and observed, it either has empty seats or it has not. The probability of one or the other is 1.

$$\pi+(1-\pi)=1$$

The same applies when a second flight is observed because of the independent nature of these events. However, once two flights are considered together, there are more than the two outcomes which were originally possible. There are three, these being that both flights do or do not contain unoccupied seats and that one flight does while the other does not. The probabilities of these three outcomes must be given by the product of the possible outcomes for each sample unit drawn.

$$[\pi+(1-\pi)][\pi+(1-\pi)] = [\pi+(1-\pi)]^2$$

Expanding this gives:

$$\pi^2+2\pi(1-\pi)+(1-\pi)^2$$

The three terms of the expansion give the probabilities of the three outcomes so long as π is known. In general it will be found that the probabilities of the possible outcomes generated by samples of size n is equal to:

$$[\pi+(1-\pi)]^n$$

The expansion of $[\pi+(1-\pi)]^n$ is known as the *binomial expansion*. When $n=3$ it gives:

$$\pi^3+3\pi^2(1-\pi)+3\pi(1-\pi)^2+(1-\pi)^3$$

When $n=4$:

$$\pi^4+4\pi^3(1-\pi)+6\pi^2(1-\pi)^2+4\pi(1-\pi)^3+(1-\pi)^4$$

Finally, when $n=5$ as in the case under consideration, the expansion gives:

$$\pi^5+5\pi^4(1-\pi)+10\pi^3(1-\pi)^2+10\pi^2(1-\pi)^3+5\pi(1-\pi)^4+(1-\pi)^5$$

Substituting the known values of π and $(1-\pi)$, i.e. 0·3 and 0·7 respectively, we get the answers previously tabulated:

$$0·3^5+(5\times0·3^4\times0·7)+(10\times0·3^3\times0·7^2)+(10\times0·3^2\times0·7^3)$$

$$+(5\times0·3\times0·7^4)+0·7^5=1$$

1.12.7   The number of ways in which each sample proportion can occur has been arrived at by algebraic multiplication. Mathematical logic has shown that the order in which sample results are discovered is important when common-sense reasoning may have suggested it to be immaterial.

1.12.8   The number of ways in which each sample proportion can occur are known as *binomial coefficients*. For $n=2$, 3, 4, and 5 these binomial coefficients were 1, 2, 1; 1, 3, 3, 1; 1, 4, 6, 4, 1; 1, 5, 10, 10, 5, 1. We should consider the question of obtaining these without the necessity for fully expanding the basic equation, since in the case of a large n this may be a tedious operation.

Each one can be calculated by using the formula for combinations:

$$^nC_x = \frac{n!}{x!(n-x)!}$$

As an illustration, consider the ways of getting a sample result of 3/5. To achieve this, three out of five flights have to be operated with less than a full payload, so $x = 3$ and $n = 5$.

$$^nC_x = \frac{5!}{3!\,2!} = \frac{20}{2} = 10$$

Alternatively, Pascal's triangle can be used. This was devised over 300 years ago and enables all the binomial coefficients for any n to be read off at a glance.

n				Binomial coefficients				
1				1	1			
2				1	2	1		
3			1	3	3	1		
4		1	4	6	4	1		
5		1	5	10	10	5	1	
6	1	6	15	20	15	6	1	
7	1	7	21	35	35	21	7	1

It should be noticed that any coefficient may be obtained by adding together the values of the two coefficients on either side in the preceding row, e.g. $15 = 10 + 5$; $21 = 6 + 15$ etc. etc.

1.12.9   Having provided the groundwork, we can now give the general form of the binomial expansion (as a check notice that in each term the sum of the powers to which π and $(1-\pi)$ are raised must equal n). Each term of the expansion can be found from

$$P(x) = {^nC_x}\,\pi^x\,(1-\pi)^{n-x}$$

where x, in our case, is the number of flights possessing the attribute which has probability π, i.e. the number of flights with a full payload. This is easily converted into a sample proportion by dividing x by n.

1.12.10   The binomial expansion has considerable use outside sampling theory and can be applied directly to many practical problems. It is particularly useful in quality control experiments where a process is known to produce a certain proportion of defective items and it is required to estimate the number of samples one would expect to find with different numbers of defective components, over say a period of one week. In any circumstances where we know the chance of the attribute appearing in a single observation the probability of any possible outcome from a group of observations can be ascertained.

1.12.11   As an example of the use of the binomial distribution, let us look at the Seeds Act of 1920. All packets of seed sold are subject to its provisions. In the case of peas the seed has been tested before packeting and 75 per cent have been found to germinate. If a gardener plants 100 rows with 10 seeds in each, we can estimate the number of rows we would expect to find with 0, 1, 2, . . . 9, 10 plants in each.

Number of plants in a row x	$P(x) = {}^nC_x \pi^x(1 - \pi)^{n-x}$	Number of rows $P(x) \times 100$
0	0·0000	0
1	0·0000	0
2	0·0004	0
3	0·0031	0
4	0·0162	1
5	0·0584	6
6	0·1460	15
7	0·2503	25
8	0·2816	28
9	0·1877	19
10	0·0563	6
		100

It is evident that in general we would be surprised if any rows contained less than 4 plants and the majority will be found to have 6, 7, 8 or 9 plants per row.

1.13   The binomial sampling distribution of proportions

1.13.1   We have now found the probability of each possible sample proportion occurring. How can this be converted into a sampling distribution? The theoretically correct thing to do is simply to talk about a probability distribution instead of a frequency distribution. However, for the sake of consistency we will assume that the total possible number of samples of five flights from this population is 1000. If the individual probabilities are multiplied by 1000, we will have an approximation of the numbers of flights we would expect to find with each sample proportion.

Sampling distribution of sample proportions

Sample proportion p	P(p)	Number of samples P(p) × 1000	fx
0	0·16807	168	0
$\frac{1}{5}$	0·36015	360	72
$\frac{2}{5}$	0·30870	309	124
$\frac{3}{5}$	0·13230	132	79
$\frac{4}{5}$	0·02835	28	22
1	0·00243	3	3
		1000	300

1.13.2   Two things emerge from this sampling distribution. The first is that the mean proportion of flights flown with empty seats is $\frac{3}{10}$ $\left(\text{i.e. } \frac{\Sigma fx}{N} = \frac{300}{1000}\right)$ which is the same as the population proportion; once again we can say that on the average a sample proportion offers an unbiased estimate of the population proportion, so there is a justification for using p in estimating π. The second is that sampling distribution is badly skewed and far from normal. Fig. 6(a) shows how non-normal the distribution is: it will be

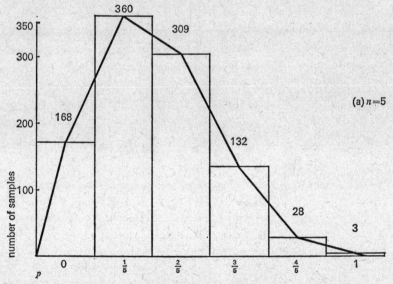

Fig. 6(a)   Sampling distribution of p (determined from the binomial expansion) (a) $n=5$

49   The principles of statistical sampling

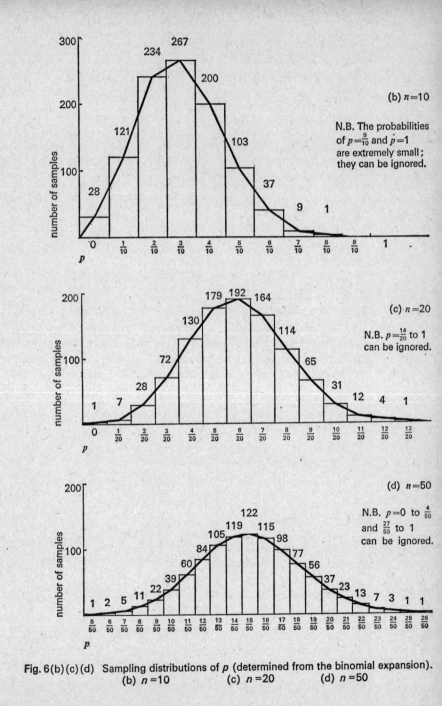

Fig. 6(b)(c)(d) Sampling distributions of *p* (determined from the binomial expansion).
(b) *n* =10 (c) *n* =20 (d) *n* =50

seen from figs. 6(b), (c) and (d) that as the sample size is increased so the sampling distribution becomes less skewed and more normal in shape.

1.13.3   The same result would be found if π was getting closer to 0.5; generally speaking, if $n\pi$ is 5 or more when $\pi < 0.5$ the binomial distribution is a close approximation to the normal form. In practice, therefore, if a knowledge of the normal curve is to be used our sample size must usually be larger than it was when we were estimating means.

1.14   The standard error of p

1.14.1   As before, we can use the sample statistic p as the basic estimate of π. We also know that as long as n is large the sampling distribution is normal. We must now look at the standard error of proportions, σ_p.

Let us calculate the standard error of the sampling distributions for samples of 5, 10, 20 and 50.

For $n = 5$:

Sample proportion	Number of samples	fx	fx^2
0	168	0	0
$\frac{1}{5}$	360	72	14·4
$\frac{2}{5}$	309	124	49·6
$\frac{3}{5}$	132	79	47·4
$\frac{4}{5}$	28	22	17·6
1	3	3	3·0
		300	132·0

$$\sigma_p = \sqrt{\left\{ \frac{\Sigma fx^2}{N} - \left(\frac{\Sigma fx}{N}\right)^2 \right\}}$$

$$\sqrt{\left\{ \frac{132}{1000} - \left(\frac{300}{1000}\right)^2 \right\}} = \sqrt{0.042}$$

$$= 0.2049$$

For $n = 10$:

$\Sigma fx = 300$, $\Sigma fx^2 = 111$, $N = 1000$

$$\sigma_p = \sqrt{\left\{ \frac{111}{1000} - \left(\frac{300}{1000}\right)^2 \right\}} = \sqrt{0.021}$$

$$= 0.1449$$

51   **The principles of statistical sampling**

For $n = 20$:

$$\Sigma fx = 300, \Sigma fx^2 = 100 \cdot 5, N = 1000$$

$$\sigma_p = \sqrt{\left\{ \frac{100 \cdot 5}{1000} - \left(\frac{300}{1000} \right)^2 \right\}} = \sqrt{0 \cdot 0105}$$

$$= 0 \cdot 1025$$

For $n = 50$:

$$\Sigma fx = 300, \Sigma fx^2 = 94 \cdot 2, N = 1000$$

$$\sigma_p = \sqrt{\left\{ \frac{94 \cdot 2}{1000} - \left(\frac{300}{1000} \right)^2 \right\}} = \sqrt{0 \cdot 0042}$$

$$= 0 \cdot 0648$$

Summarizing:

n	Standard error
5	0·2049
10	0·1449
20	0·1025
50	0·0648

1.14.2   It is again apparent that as the sample size increases, so the standard error is reduced, but we have not as yet shown how these standard errors can be achieved without a knowledge of the full sampling distribution. All we shall say at this point (but see 1.18.4) is that the correct answers can easily be found by using the following formula:

$$\sigma_p = \sqrt{\frac{\pi(1 - \pi)}{n}}$$

For $n = 5$ the standard error is $\sqrt{\dfrac{0 \cdot 3 \times 0 \cdot 7}{5}} = \sqrt{\dfrac{0 \cdot 21}{5}} = \sqrt{0 \cdot 042} = 0 \cdot 2049$.

Likewise, when $n = 10, 20, 50$ the standard error will be

$$\sqrt{\frac{0 \cdot 21}{10}} = 0 \cdot 1449, \sqrt{\frac{0 \cdot 21}{20}} = 0 \cdot 1025, \text{ and } \sqrt{\frac{0 \cdot 21}{50}} = 0 \cdot 0648.$$

In practice p will be substituted for π so that the standard error of proportions is

$$\sigma = \sqrt{\frac{p(1 - p)}{n}}$$

1.15 Confidence intervals

1.15.1 To estimate π in practice, a confidence interval (see 1.10) will be constructed from

$$\underline{\pi} = p \pm z \sqrt{\frac{p(1-p)}{n}}$$

where $\underline{\pi}$ indicates the upper and lower limits of the confidence interval. Any level of confidence can be used by changing z (the number of standard errors which will be added to and subtracted from p).

1.15.2 If z or n is required, manipulation of the above will give

$$z = \frac{\underline{\pi} - p}{\sqrt{\dfrac{p(1-p)}{n}}}$$

$$n = \frac{p(1-p)z^2}{(\underline{\pi} - p)^2}$$

1.15.3 This section has dealt with the problem of proportions, but the same methods could be used in relationship to percentages, where the standard error would be

$$\sqrt{\frac{100p(100 - 100p)}{n}}$$

1.15.4 As a practical illustration, let us look at a survey of children who have appeared in a juvenile court three times or more. A sample of 634 of these shows that 291 are orphans (one or both parents dead). What proportion of all children with three or more appearances in court are orphans? The estimate is to be made with 99 per cent confidence.

$$p = 291/634 = 0.459, \ 1 - p = 0.541, \ n = 634$$

$$\underline{\pi} = 0.459 \pm 2.58 \sqrt{\frac{0.459 \times 0.541}{634}}$$

$$= 0.459 \pm 0.051$$

$$= 0.408 \text{ and } 0.510$$

We estimate that the percentage of children of this type who are orphans lies between 40·8 per cent and 51·0 per cent.

53   The principles of statistical sampling

1.16 The normal–binomial relationship

1.16.1 It has been shown in fig. 6 that when $n\pi$ or np is equal to 5 or more (i.e. n is large or π or $p \to 0{\cdot}5$) the binomial distribution becomes a very close approximation to the normal distribution. This fact can often be used to save considerable time and effort in applied statistical problems.

1.16.2 A university economics department can take in approximately 30 students in the forthcoming academic session. Most of the applicants for these places can only be given provisional acceptances as they have yet to take the necessary G.C.E. subjects and obtain the stipulated number of passes. The problem which the department faces is how many provisional places to offer. If too many are offered, they may have more students than can be catered for; if too few, they will have idle resources. From experience of previous years, roughly 65 per cent of students given provisional places have either failed to qualify or have preferred offers from other institutions.

After consideration, the departmental head feels that he would rather be over-committed than under-committed, and he decides to offer 100 provisional places in the hope that not less than 28 and not more than 40 students will eventually be taken.

1.16.3 The statistician can take this professor's hopes and qualify them in the form of a probability statement. He can estimate the likelihood of the number of students finally taken being between 28 and 40 inclusive when the total possible number is 100 and the probability of each student qualifying and taking his place is 0·35.

It is a problem for the binomial expansion. In this case, however, it is arithmetically a difficult problem. With $n = 100$, $x = 28, 29, \ldots, 40$ and $\pi = 0{\cdot}35$:

$$P(28) = \frac{100!}{28!\,72!}\,0{\cdot}35^{28}\,0{\cdot}65^{72} = 0{\cdot}0290$$

$$P(29) = \frac{100!}{29!\,71!}\,0{\cdot}35^{29}\,0{\cdot}65^{71} = 0{\cdot}0388$$

$$P(30) = \text{etc.}$$

It can readily be seen that these 13 terms of the expansion will only be rationalized after much tedious arithmetic. If this is carried out, however, the probability of any number of students between 28 and 40 taking places in the department will be found to be 0·819 (the sum of $P(28)$ to $P(40)$ inclusive). In other words, there is only an 18·1 per cent chance that less than 28 or more than 40 out of the 100 students given provisional places will materialize. The professor will probably be happy.

1.16.4   It is very unlikely that the statistician will be satisfied after calculating these probabilities. He would much prefer to have used a simpler method in arriving at his answer. It has been established that in circumstances like these ($n\pi = 35$) the binomial distribution is approximately normal, so if we can find the mean and standard deviation surely it would be possible to apply the techniques used in 1.8.4?

1.16.5   The mean proportion of students who will take up provisional places (π) is 0·35, so that the mean number of students we will expect to find out of 100 provisional places offered is

$$n\pi = 100 \times 0.35 = 35 \text{ students.}$$

The standard deviation proportion is

$$\sqrt{\frac{\pi(1-\pi)}{n}}$$

so that the standard deviation number of students is

$$n\sqrt{\frac{\pi(1-\pi)}{n}} = \sqrt{n\pi(1-\pi)}$$
$$= \sqrt{100 \times 0.35 \times 0.65}$$
$$= 4.769 \text{ students.}$$

1.16.6   Having found $\mu = 35$, $\sigma = 4.769$ and $x = 28$ and 40, it would seem that all that remains is to use the formula

$$\frac{x-\mu}{\sigma} = z$$

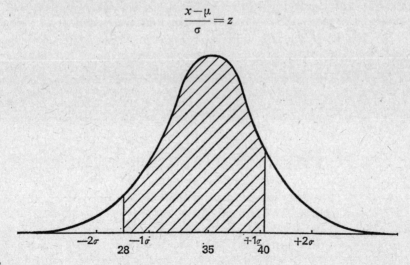

Fig. 7

55   The principles of statistical sampling

and the normal deviate table. Unfortunately it is not quite as simple as this. In this case it seems to be just a question of finding the shaded area in fig. 7 as a percentage of the total area, but consider how we would determine the probability of only 28 students attending.

It is obviously impossible, as 28 is indicated by a point, not an area under the curve. The conflict is caused by the fact that the normal distribution involves a continuous variable, whilst the binomial distribution deals only with discrete variables taking integer values.

To overcome this difficulty we shall make use of a device for converting the discrete values in the binomial to the continuous values in the normal distribution. We shall spread 28 over the range 27·5 to 28·5, and similarly with every other value of x.

Therefore in 1.16.6 $x = 27·5$ and 40·5, not 28 and 40.
Substituting $x = 27·5$:

$$z = \frac{27·5 - 35}{4·769} = -1·57$$

Substituting $x = 40·5$:

$$z = \frac{40·5 - 35}{4·769} = 1·15$$

From the normal deviate table we find that 5·8 per cent of the area lies to the left of $\mu - 1·57\sigma$ and 12·5 per cent of the area lies to the right of $\mu + 1·15\sigma$. In other words, there is only an 18·3 per cent chance that less than 28 or more than 40 students will get their department places. This is very close to the figure achieved by the binomial method (i.e. 18·1 per cent), but has been obtained in a very much more straightforward manner.

1.17 Finite population correction factor

1.17.1 In the foregoing sections, the theory of sampling has been based on the existence of a large or an infinite population. Because of this, it has been possible to contend that the withdrawal of a sample has had no appreciable effect upon the composition of the population.

However, if the sample drawn is large relative to the parent population, and no one population unit can be included in two or more samples, then the form of the parent population will be altered after the random selection of the sample units.

What is more, the shape of the sampling distribution and its standard error will have changed.

1.17.2 Suppose that a bag contains five tokens, each having a number from

1 to 5. A sample of two tokens is taken out, the sample units being drawn simultaneously; $\mu = 3$ and $\sigma = 1\cdot414$ are the population parameters. The possible sample results are

Results

1:2	1:3	1:4	1:5
2:3	2:4	2:5	
3:4	3:5		
4:5			

Sample means

1·5	2·0	2·5	3·0
2·5	3·0	3·5	
3·5	4·0		
4·5			

The sampling distribution of means has the following form:

x	f	fx	fx^2
1·5	1	1·5	2·25
2·0	1	2·0	4·00
2·5	2	5·0	12·5
3·0	2	6·0	18·0
3·5	2	7·0	24·5
4·0	1	4·0	16·0
4·5	1	4·5	20·25
	10	30	97·5

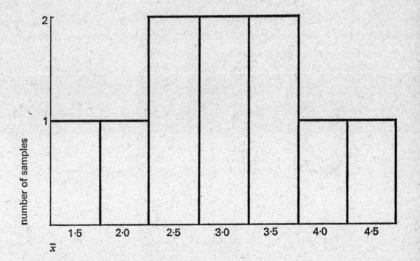

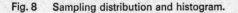

Fig. 8 Sampling distribution and histogram.

While $\mu_{\bar{x}}$ still gives μ $\left(\text{i.e. } \dfrac{\Sigma fx}{N} = \dfrac{30}{10} = 3\right)$, the standard error

$$\sqrt{\left\{\frac{97\cdot5}{10} - \left(\frac{30}{10}\right)^2\right\}} = 0\cdot866$$

is no longer obtainable from $\sigma/\sqrt{n}$ which in this case equals $1\cdot414/\sqrt{2} = 1$.

1.17.3   To get the standard error in these circumstances $\dfrac{\sigma}{\sqrt{n}}$ must be multiplied by the Finite Population Correction Factor (F.P.C.F.)

$$= \sqrt{\frac{N-n}{N-1}}$$

(where $N =$ population size and $n =$ sample size) giving

$$\frac{1\cdot414}{\sqrt{2}} \cdot \sqrt{\frac{5-2}{5-1}}$$
$$= 0\cdot866$$

In practical estimation problems s will be substituted for σ giving

$$\sigma_{\bar{x}} = \frac{s}{\sqrt{n}}\sqrt{\frac{N-n}{N-1}}.$$

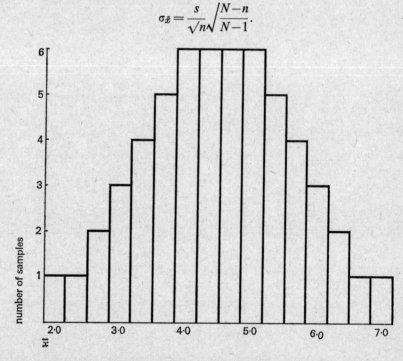

Fig. 9

1.17.4   Although the sampling distribution in this case is not normal, it can again be shown that it approaches the normal form as N and n increase. Referring once more to the experiment described in 1.17.2, if $N = 8$ and $n = 3$ there would be 56 samples possible with the sample mean histogram in the form shown in fig. 9.

1.17.5   In general, the F.P.C.F. need only be applied where the sample is more than 10 per cent of the population size, for only if this is the case does it significantly influence the standard error obtained from $s/\sqrt{n}$ alone (if $n < 10$ per cent of N the error in $s/\sqrt{n}$ is < 5 per cent).

The F.P.C.F. in the case of a sample of 450 taken from a population of 5000 is

$$\sqrt{\frac{4550}{4999}} = 0 \cdot 954.$$

If $s/\sqrt{n}$ had been $0 \cdot 43$, the F.P.C.F. would reduce it to $0 \cdot 41$, or a reduction of $4 \cdot 6$ per cent.

1.17.6   The same correction should also be made to σ_p, where the population size is small enough to justify it.

$$\sigma_p = \sqrt{\frac{p(1-p)}{n}} \sqrt{\frac{N-n}{N-1}}$$

1.18   Mathematical notes

1.18.1   This chapter has sought to examine the basic tenets of statistical sampling in such a way that readers with only a basic mathematical knowledge will have been able to follow the major steps. Generally speaking no proofs have been given of the concepts put forward, since this has not been one of the primary objectives, but at this point certain aspects will be treated more rigorously.

1.18.2   *Expected value*

Suppose that a variable x has n exhaustive values x_i; each value of the variable has a certain probability p_i of occurring. Then the group of values x_i with their respective probabilities p_i is called a *probability distribution*.

The mean of this distribution is called the *expected value* of the variate (a variable possessing a probability distribution is called a *variate*), and is shown by

$$E(x) = \Sigma p_i x_i$$

(NOTE: $\Sigma p_i = 1$, so that the denominator of $\dfrac{\Sigma p_i x_i}{\Sigma p_i}$ can be ignored.)

The standard deviation is given by

$$\sqrt{(E[\{x - E(x)\}^2])}$$

As mentioned in 1.13.1 sampling distributions are probability distributions. In fact any theoretical distribution such as the normal or binomial is of this type.

1.18.3 *The mean and standard error of the sampling distribution of $\bar{x}$*

Consider a population in which the relative frequency of x_i is p_i ($i = 1, 2, 3, \ldots, k$).

$$\mu = \Sigma p_i x_i$$
$$\sigma^2 = \Sigma p_i (x_i - \mu)^2$$

Let samples of size one be taken. Obviously the sampling distribution of means is identical with the population distribution. The mean of the sample means [$E(\bar{x})$] equals the population mean μ; similarly, the standard error squared is the population variance σ^2.

Now if a sample of n values x_j is taken, the mean is

$$\bar{x} = \frac{\Sigma x_j}{n} \qquad (j = 1, 2, 3, \ldots n)$$

so that

$$n\bar{x} = \Sigma x_j$$

Therefore the mean of the means is $E(n\bar{x}) = E(\Sigma x_j)$, taking the mean of both sides of the equation.

Now $E(\Sigma x_j) = \Sigma \Sigma x_j = \Sigma E(x_j)$, the sum of the probabilities of each possible sample total occurring once again being equal to unity,

and

$$E(x_j) = \mu$$

so that

$$\Sigma E(x_j) = \Sigma \mu = n\mu$$

Hence

$$E(n\bar{x}) = n\mu$$

and

$$E(\bar{x}) = \mu$$

Because random sampling has been used the values of the variate in the sample are independent, having as their sum $n\bar{x}$. Now if two independent variates x and y are measured from their means (i.e. $E[x] = E[y] = 0$) the variance of their sum is given by

$$E(x+y)^2 = E(x^2+2xy+y^2)$$
$$= E(x^2)+E(y^2) \qquad (E[xy] = 0)$$

which equals the sum of the variances of x and y.

Using this result, the variance of $n\bar{x}$ is the sum of the variances of the separate values in the samples. But the distribution of the sample values has a variance σ^2.

Consequently the variance of $n\bar{x}$ is given by $n\sigma^2$ and the standard deviation by $\sigma\sqrt{n}$. The standard error of $\bar{x}$ is therefore

$$\frac{\sigma\sqrt{n}}{n} = \frac{\sigma}{\sqrt{n}}$$

1.18.4 *The mean and standard error of the sampling distribution of p*

The general expression for each term in the binomial expansion is

$$P(x) = {}^nC_x p^x q^{n-x} \qquad (q = 1-p)$$

This gives the probability of x sample units (the total possible is n) possessing the attribute with probability of occurrence p. The number of samples with x (i.e. the frequency) is obtained by multiplying the general expression above by N, the total number of possible samples.

Number of sample units with attribute x	(a) Number of samples with x f	(b) fx	(c) fx^2
x	$N{}^nC_x p^x q^{n-x}$	$Nx{}^nC_x p^x q^{n-x}$	$Nx^2{}^nC_x p^x q^{n-x}$
Sum	N	Nnp	$Nnp[1+(n-1)p]$

The expansion of columns (a), (b) and (c) will give the sums shown above ($x = 0, 1, 2, \ldots n$). From these

$$\mu = \frac{Nnp}{N} = np$$

$$\sigma = \sqrt{\left\{\frac{\Sigma f x^2}{N} - \left(\frac{\Sigma f x}{N}\right)^2\right\}} = \sqrt{\left\{\frac{Nnp[1+(n-1)p]}{N} - \left(\frac{Nnp}{N}\right)^2\right\}}$$

$$= \sqrt{\{np+(np)^2-np^2-(np)^2\}} = \sqrt{\{np(1-p)\}}$$

$$= \sqrt{(npq)}$$

Now np and $\sqrt{(npq)}$ are the mean and standard deviation number of sample units possessing the attribute looked for. The mean and standard deviation (i.e. standard error) proportion possessing the attribute will be found by dividing by n

$$\text{Mean} = \frac{np}{n} = p$$

$$\text{Standard error} = \frac{\sqrt{npq}}{n} = \sqrt{\frac{pq}{n}}$$

(a) $\Sigma f = N(q^n + {}^nC_1 pq^{n-1} + {}^nC_2 p^2 q^{n-2} + {}^nC_3 p^3 q^{n-3} + \ldots + p^n)$

$\quad = N(p+q)^n \qquad [(p+q)^n = 1]$

$\quad = N$

(b) $\Sigma f x = N(0 \cdot {}^nC_0 p^0 q^n + 1 \cdot {}^nC_1 pq^{n-1} + 2 \cdot {}^nC_2 p^2 q^{n-2} + 3 \cdot {}^nC_3 p^3 q^{n-3} + \ldots$

$\qquad + n \cdot {}^nC_n p^n q^{n-n})$

$$= N\left(npq^{n-1} + \frac{2n(n-1)}{2.1}p^2 q^{n-2} + \frac{3n(n-1)(n-2)}{3.2.1}p^3 q^{n-3}\right.$$

$$\left. + \ldots + np^n\right)$$

Taking np outside the bracket

$$= Nnp\left(q^{n-1} + (n-1)pq^{n-2} + \frac{(n-1)(n-2)}{2.1}p^2 q^{n-3}\right.$$

$$\left. + \ldots + p^{n-1}\right)$$

$\quad = Nnp(p+q)^{n-1}$

$\quad = Nnp$

(c) $\Sigma f x^2 = N(0^2 \cdot {}^nC_0 p^0 q^n + 1^2 \cdot {}^nC_1 pq^{n-1} + 2^2 \cdot {}^nC_2 p^2 q^{n-2}$

$\qquad + 3^2 \cdot {}^nC_3 p^3 q^{n-3} + \ldots + n^2 \cdot {}^nC_n p^n q^{n-n})$

$$\Sigma fx^2 = N \left\{ npq^{n-1} + 2n(n-1)p^2q^{n-2} + \frac{3n(n-1)(n-2)}{2.1} p^3q^{n-3} + \ldots \right.$$
$$\left. + n^2p^n \right\}$$

Taking np outside the bracket gives

$$Nnp \left\{ q^{n-1} + 2(n-1)pq^{n-2} + \frac{3(n-1)(n-2)}{2.1} p^2q^{n-3} + \ldots + np^{n-1} \right\}$$

Expressing this as two sums gives

$$Nnp \left\{ q^{n-1} + (n-1)pq^{n-2} + \frac{(n-1)(n-2)}{2.1} p^2q^{n-3} + \ldots + p^{n-1} \right\}$$

$$+ Nnp \left\{ 0 + (n-1)pq^{n-2} + (n-1)(n-2)p^2q^{n-3} + \ldots \right.$$

$$\left. + (n-1)p^{n-1} \right\}$$

The first bracket equals $(p+q)^{n-1} = 1$. Taking $(n-1)p$ out of the second gives

$$\Sigma fx^2 = Nnp + Nn(n-1)p^2 \{ q^{n-2} + (n-2)pq^{n-3} + \ldots + p^{n-2} \}$$

The expression in the second bracket equals $(p+q)^{n-2} = 1$, leaving

$$Nnp + Nn(n-1)p^2$$

$$= Nnp[1 + (n-1)p]$$

1.19 Examples

1.19.1 *Probability*

(a) It is estimated from a viewing survey that between 7.30 and 8.00 p.m. on Mondays 58 per cent of television sets are tuned to the independent networks and 26 per cent to B.B.C. 1 and B.B.C. 2. A man visits two friends between these hours. What is the probability that the sets in the two houses are both switched off?

(b) A '999' switchboard can deal with 10 calls per minute. On average there are 25 emergency calls made each hour. What is the likelihood of emergency callers having to wait for attention?

(c) An office file is required urgently. It could be on the desk of the office manager M, or on the desks of any of his three assistants X, Y and Z.

All four men have 8 files on their desks and since last seeing the file M has passed 3 files to X, X has passed 3 to Y, Y 3 to Z and Z has returned 3 to M. What are the chances of the file being (i) on M's desk and (ii) on Y's desk?

(d) A sixth-former tries to assess his chances of being admitted to a faculty of his local university. He knows that last year only 67 applicants out of 193 were successful, although 104 had the minimum entrance requirements of two 'A' level G.C.E. subjects. His 'A' level subjects are history, geography and economics in which the results last year were as follows:

Subject	Candidates	Passes
History	2450	1056
Geography	1400	875
Economics	730	212

What seem to be his chances of getting a place?

(e) From the statistics below, what would be the probability in 1960 of a particular person in the U.K. dying from other than natural causes?

United Kingdom mortality figures, 1959

Total number of deaths	606115
Deaths from natural causes	579885
Deaths from accidents	20171
Deaths from suicide and murder	6059
Average mortality rate	11 per 1000

(f) Traffic lights control a three-way intersection. The lights sequence is as follows:

(i) North to south, south to north and south to west   25 seconds
(ii) North to west and west to north   15 seconds
(iii) West to south   10 seconds

What is the probability of having to wait when travelling from west to south? A bus travels from north to south on its outward journey and from south to north on its return. What is the probability of it going straight across on both occasions?

1.19.2 *Arrangements*

(a) A motor licensing authority finds that it has exhausted its vehicle licence numbers made up of three letters and three numbers. How many cars has the authority licensed in the past?

(b) A neon advertisement is made up of five words. How many different phases in the cycle of lights are possible so that at least two of the words are always illuminated?

(c) A rowing-club coach is dissatisfied with his uncoxed eight and feels that a rearrangement of the crew might prove beneficial. He is not prepared to move his number 1 stroke crewman. Of the rest two can only row bow side and one can only row stroke side. The other four are flexible. In how many ways may the coach have to try the crew before he finds the best formation?

(d) A square field is divided into 100 equal plots. Ten different varieties of potato are to be planted to test the yield. In how many ways can the planting be carried out in such a way that adjacent plots cannot contain the same variety?

(e) A student must select 5 courses out of 8 offered by his college. How many subject combinations can the college expect to be offered?

1.19.3 *Normal and binomial distributions*

(a) Mr Brown, a travelling salesman, has a record which shows that at 63 per cent of his calls he makes a sale. This is considerably better than any of his colleagues. Consequently the sales manager decides to accompany Brown to study his technique. Unfortunately for Brown, only three out of twenty calls produce a sale. What is the probability of this happening?

(b) An engineering company produces compression springs. The percentage of defective springs is approximately 10 per cent (the test is to compress the springs and see whether they return to the original length). Samples of 20 springs are tested every hour. In three consecutive samples the number of defectives is found to be 4, 6 and 3. What can be concluded from these results?

(c) A city education authority carries out a survey of the I.Q.s of the children in its schools at all ages, testing 150,000 children. The distribution of I.Q.s was normal, with a mean of 100, but $3\frac{1}{2}$ per cent of the children were found to be educationally sub-normal with I.Q.s of less than 70. What is the standard deviation of this distribution?

(d) Only 2 per cent of the dwelling houses insured in the United Kingdom have fire damage claims each year. What is the likelihood of one small insurance company finding that of 2000 houses insured there are claims on 50? Use the normal–binomial relationship.

(e) A nation-wide dairy company finds that the average number of pints of milk sold per roundsman per day is 1050 with a standard deviation of 380 pints. The distribution is normal.

65   The principles of statistical sampling

(i) What proportion of delivery men are selling less than 300 pints?

(ii) How many pints are sold by the top 10 per cent of delivery men?

(iii) What are the sales of the middle 50 per cent of the firm's employees?

(f) A labour exchange finds that three-quarters of the men who are found jobs as building labourers return to the exchange within one month. A construction firm informs the exchange that it requires a labour gang of 50 men. As a certain amount of training is to be given to those employed the firm's personnel manager wants to know the chances of keeping 30 per cent of those employed for more than one month. What is the labour exchange to say?

(g) It is estimated that $\frac{1}{5}$ of old age pensioners are suffering from some form of dietary deficiency. Out of a group of 20, what is the probability of at least 15 being in this category?

1.19.4 *Sampling*

(a) Using any convenient list of names (e.g. a class list) select a random sample of 10 people using tables of random numbers. What would the F.P.C.F. be in this case?

(b) A random sample of salaries paid to the administrative staff of a firm is as follows:

Salary (£p.a.)	Number
500–599	18
600–699	23
700–799	15
800–999	42
1000–1199	29
1200–1599	13
1600–1999	6
2000–3000	4

What is the standard error of the mean in this case? How is it used to estimate the average salary of administrators in the firm?

(c) In an election, a sample survey of constituents shows that 83 out of 155 intend to vote for candidate A. What sample size should be taken to convince Mr A that he has a 99 per cent chance of being elected?

(d) A national daily newspaper tells its advertisers that a recent audit shows that over 2 million copies were sold and that they were read by $3\frac{1}{2}$

million people. One of the major advertisers in the paper undertakes his own survey and finds that out of 300 people taking the paper on a particular day, only 203 had noticed his advertisement. Estimate, with 90 per cent confidence, how many people altogether are reading this advertisement.

(e) A random sample of 450 workers shows the average working week to be 46 hours, with a standard deviation of $7\frac{1}{2}$ hours. With what degree of confidence can a population mean of between 45 and 47 hours be given?

(f) A college refectory wants information on the number of student meals to prepare. A detailed analysis of meals served on 25 days shows the following results:

Cost of meal	Average number of meals per day	S.D. number of meals
2s. 6d.	325	52
3s. 6d.	260	27
4s. 6d.	93	29

It is decided to prepare 10 per cent more than the average in each case. With 95 per cent confidence, what would you estimate the maximum possible loss of money through waste to be? How many students may the refectory have to turn away altogether on a particular day?

(g) A manufacturer of refrigerators asks a consumer research group to test a sample of refrigerators. It particularly wants to show that there is a 99 per cent chance of the temperatures in one of their refrigerators being within ± 1 deg. F. They know from experience that the average temperature is 36 deg. F. with a standard deviation of $1 \cdot 5$ deg. F. What sample size should the researchers be recommended to take?

Chapter 2
Testing hypotheses

2.1 Fundamental considerations

2.1.1 Emphasis has been placed on the contribution of statistical method to the decision-making process. Both the presentation and description of numerical data supply evidence about the situation faced: this is the first step, since before decisions can be taken the facts must be known. Similarly, it is necessary to ascertain whether the facts are derived from sample surveys or full investigations. In the former case, certain reservations about the precision of the results must be made, because random sampling variation is a factor to be taken into account. In consequence, one should have equal reservations about the validity of the decisions taken on this basis. It is the expression of these reservations which will concern us in this chapter.

2.1.2 Whenever a decision is taken, whether it is one of the thousands of decisions made by any one of us in the course of our everyday lives or a decision of great financial or national importance taken by a businessman or a politician, there is the possibility of it being correct or incorrect. Specifically there are two ways in which a correct decision and two ways in which an incorrect decision may be taken.

A pedestrian waiting to cross a busy street decides either that there is a sufficient break in the traffic to enable him to cross safely, or that he should not cross for the opposite reason. If there is a satisfactory break in the traffic and he crosses, then a correct decision has been taken. Equally, if the traffic is so dense that he is prevented from crossing safely and he decides to wait, he has again taken a correct decision. But if he tries to cross without having enough time to do so, he will either be run down or cause an accident between vehicles swerving to avoid him, and if he fails to cross when a true opportunity to do so has presented itself he has wasted his own time. The four outcomes may be summarized as follows:

Decision	Situation	
	Unsafe	Safe
Wait	Correct	Incorrect
Cross	Incorrect	Correct

2.1.3   Another decision situation will throw further light on this problem. In continuous statistical quality control samples of the output from a machine or process are inspected in detail at regular intervals. The object of the inspection is to decide whether the process is operating within its inherent limits of variability (i.e. is in a state of control) or whether the quality of the output has strayed outside these limits due to some assignable defect in the machine, the raw materials fed to it, or the operator controlling it (in other words, the process is out of statistical control).

In the first case the process is allowed to continue unaltered at least until the next inspection. In the second, the machine or process is stopped so that the cause of the unsatisfactory quality can be discovered and rectified. However, it is possible for the process to be out of control even though the inspected output sample indicates a satisfactory position, or the sample may suggest a need for remedial action even though there is nothing amiss. Both of these possibilities suggest themselves because of sampling error. The decision pattern under these circumstances will be:

Decision	Situation	
	Process in control	Process out of control
Continue production	Correct	Error (type II)
Stop production	Error (type I)	Correct

2.1.4   The reader will notice that we have designated the two incorrect decisions as type I and II errors. As has been observed, they are fundamentally different. In both the pedestrian's decision and in the context of quality control a type I error occurs when action is taken incorrectly or unnecessarily. Thus a type I error can be thought of as 'an error of commission'. Conversely, the type II error occurs when one fails to take some necessary course of action, and is termed an 'error of omission'. In the field of quality control a type I error rebounds on to the producer, production being held up while attempts are made to locate non-existent faults; a 'producers' error' results, with a loss of output and therefore a loss in revenue to the manufacturer who is using statistical quality control. A type II error results in sub-standard output being passed and supplied to the consumer, who will be the immediate sufferer ('consumers' error'); admittedly this will eventually cause a loss to the producer, in the form of replacement under guarantee or loss of contracts and goodwill, but the consumer is nevertheless the first to be affected (hence the name).

2.1.5   Having discussed the different types of error, we must now turn to the risks associated with each. The pedestrian will want to minimize the risk of being run down (type I error), but he may be quite happy to accept a high probability of committing a type II error by waiting at the kerb unnecessarily. He prefers to err on the side of safety when balancing his life against a minute or two of his time.

A manufacturer must similarly weigh up the odds. The level of risks which he finds acceptable will depend upon the relative monetary costs of the two mistakes. If he is subject to penalty payments and the loss of large contracts in sending out sub-standard merchandise, then presumably the risk of a type II error will be minimized in comparison with that of the producers' error. One can also envisage circumstances when the opposite is true.

2.1.6   We shall denote the risk level associated with a type I error as α (alpha) and with a type II error as β (beta). Our task in general should be to balance α and β so that they reflect the consequences of the two wrong decisions. Within the limits of this requirement we would obviously like to minimize both, and the best situation that can be envisaged is where $\alpha = \beta = 0$. If decisions are based upon sample data, however, this can only be achieved when a sample of the entire population is taken.

2.2 z Tests: $\bar{x} - \mu$

2.2.1   Let us now think of the sort of decision problem for which sampling theory can be a help. A manufacturer of television sets buys large quantities of valves packed in cartons of twelve. It is known from experience that however carefully packed they are, some valves are damaged in transit. Because of this the supplier allows a 16·67 per cent discount (two valves out of twelve are not paid for). Nevertheless, the user decides to keep a periodic check on his supplies, by taking a random sample of 400 cartons. Having worked out the average number of defective valves per box and the standard deviation, he needs some criterion for deciding whether (i) the average number of damaged valves (for all boxes) has changed; (ii) the quality has deteriorated (he is getting more damaged than the discount allows for); or (iii) the quality has improved (he is getting less damaged than the discount allows for).

2.2.2   What is wanted is some form of test. The hypothesis that there has been a change in average number of damaged valves (in one direction or the other) is to be tested against the hypothesis that the average damage rate is unaltered. A 'test of hypotheses' lays down these two possibilities in a standardized form. The 'null hypothesis', abbreviated to H_0, states that there is no change or no difference. In this case

$$H_0 : \mu = 2 \ .$$

The 'alternative hypothesis', denoted by H_A, specifies that there has been a change in the population mean (the mean number of damaged valves):

$$H_A : \mu \neq 2 \quad \text{or} \quad H_A : \mu > 2 \quad \text{or} \quad H_A : \mu < 2$$

Only one of these alternative hypotheses can be tested at a time, the one chosen in practice depending on the objective of the test; in this chapter we shall examine each in turn. Before doing so, however, let us once again look at the decision situation in terms of H_0 and H_A.

| | Situation | |
Decision	H_0 correct	H_A correct
Accept H_0	✓	Type II error (risk β)
Reject H_0	Type I error (risk α)	✓

We see that it is basically the same as before. However, it should be explicitly stated that the rejection of a null hypothesis implies the automatic acceptance of the particular alternative hypothesis. Tests of significance are always set up in such a form that one first assumes no change or difference and then one looks for evidence to the contrary: the onus of proof rests with the hypothesis of change.

The quantification of α will be considered first and then we shall return to the risk associated with the type II error.

2.2.3   *Two-tail tests* $(H_A : \mu \neq 2)$

2.2.3.1   Having formalized the test, the decision criteria can be stated. The first sample of 400 cartons has shown the average number of damaged valves to be 2·25 with a standard deviation of 1·80 (i.e. $\bar{x} = 2 \cdot 25$ and $s = 1 \cdot 80$). While realizing that random sampling can produce samples with means which are different from the population mean, it is also known that 95 per cent of all sample means should lie within 1·96 standard errors of the population mean. Thus, if the null hypothesis is true (i.e. $\mu = 2 \cdot 0$) then 95 per cent of sample means should lie between

$$\mu - 1 \cdot 96 \frac{s}{\sqrt{n}} \text{ and } \mu + 1 \cdot 96 \frac{s}{\sqrt{n}}$$

In this example, we find the limits to be $2 \cdot 0 - (1 \cdot 96 \times 1 \cdot 8 / \sqrt{400}) = 1 \cdot 82$ and $2 \cdot 0 + (1 \cdot 96 \times 1 \cdot 8 / \sqrt{400}) = 2 \cdot 18$. These will be the decision criteria.

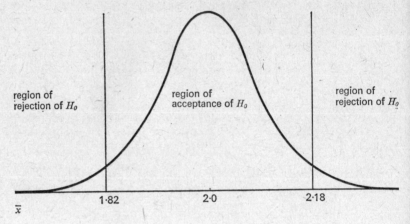

region of
rejection of H_0

region of
acceptance of H_0

region of
rejection of H_0

1·82   2·0   2·18

$\bar{x}$

Fig. 10

Any $\bar{x}$ which is less than 1·82 or greater than 2·18 will cause the H_0 to be rejected; any $\bar{x}$ between 1·82 and 2·18 will cause H_0 to be accepted (see fig. 10).

The probability (0·05) of a sample mean of less than 1·82 or greater than 2·18 having been generated when $\mu = 2$ is so small that it is preferable to conclude it has been generated from the alternative hypothesis ($\mu \neq 2$). There is nevertheless a one-in-twenty chance that $1 \cdot 82 > \bar{x}$ or $\bar{x} > 2 \cdot 18$ could occur when $\mu = 2$ so that in rejecting H_0 there is a 5 per cent risk of being wrong. This is the risk associated with a type I error of commission, so that $\alpha = 0 \cdot 05$ or 5 per cent.

2.2.3.2   The mean number of damaged valves found from the sample of 400 cartons was 2·25, which is greater than 2·18. Therefore we reject H_0 and accept H_A, the alternative hypothesis, which infers that there has been a change in the universe average number of valves damaged. The word 'change' should be stressed once more, for the two-tail test is concerned with the possibility of differences in μ in both directions. Just because 2·25 is greater than 2, no inference should be made about the average rate of damaged valves having increased. Only if the H_A had been stated as $\mu > 2\cdot0$ could this conclusion be drawn from the test.

2.2.3.3   Using the appropriate terminology, we state that the difference between $\bar{x}$ and μ is 'significant at a 5 per cent level' (tests are conventionally carried out at stated levels of significance rather than at complementary levels of confidence). It is preferable to include in the title of the test the probability of incorrectly rejecting H_0, rather than the probability of correctly accepting it.

We have developed the discussion in terms of $\alpha = 0\cdot05$ because the reader is familiar with the z value, $1\cdot96$, and because this is a widely accepted significance level. We should make the point, however, that this can and should be varied to suit the circumstances behind the test. More will be said about this in 2.2.5.5.

2.2.3.4   The reader may well wonder why this section is called 'z tests'. So far the decision criteria have been calculated as specific values of $\bar{x}$ lying z standard error units from μ. Instead we might use the z value as the critical value. Then any actual difference $\bar{x} - \mu$ less than $-z$ standard errors or greater than $+z$ standard errors would be significant, while $\bar{x} - \mu > -z$ or $\bar{x} - \mu < +z$ would cause H_0 to be accepted.

We convert the actual difference $\bar{x} - \mu$ into standard error units by dividing by $s/\sqrt{n}$ so that

$$z \text{ (calculated)} = \frac{\bar{x} - \mu}{s/\sqrt{n}}$$

It will be noted that this formula is identical with that given in Chapter 1 for use with any normal distribution, i.e. $z = \dfrac{x - \mu}{\sigma}$; here the value of

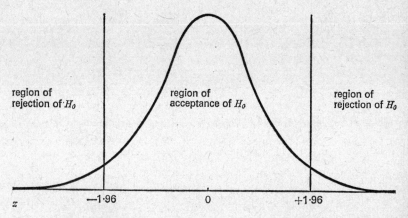

region of
rejection of H_0 region of
acceptance of H_0 region of
rejection of H_0

z $-1\cdot96$ 0 $+1\cdot96$

Fig. 11

the variable is a sample mean and the standard deviation is the standard error of the mean. The use of the z value as the critical value will generally be adopted in the rest of this chapter because of its greater inherent convenience. It can be demonstrated using our earlier data:

$$z \text{ (calculated)} = \frac{2 \cdot 25 - 2 \cdot 0}{1 \cdot 8 / \sqrt{400}} = \frac{0 \cdot 25}{0 \cdot 09} = 2 \cdot 78$$

This is greater than $1 \cdot 96$, which is the critical value of $z_{0 \cdot 05}$ for a 5 per cent significance level, and so we reject H_0 as before (see fig. 11).

2.2.4 One-tail tests ($H_A : \mu > 2 \cdot 0$ or $\mu < 2 \cdot 0$)

2.2.4.1   In taking $H_A : \mu \neq 2 \cdot 0$, we had a region of rejection of H_0 in both tails of the sampling distribution in order to cover the occurrence of a change in μ in either direction. When $H_A : \mu > 2 \cdot 0$ or $\mu < 2 \cdot 0$ the region of rejection is located at only one end of the sampling distribution. On one hand common sense will tell us we are unlikely to accept that $\mu > 2 \cdot 0$ if $\bar{x} < 2 \cdot 0$.

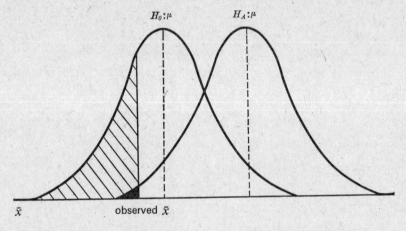

Fig. 12

Statistically it can also be shown that a $\bar{x} < 2 \cdot 0$ will always have a higher probability of occurrence under the H_0 assumption than under the H_A assumption that $\mu > 2$ (fig. 12).

The probability of $\bar{x}$ less than or equal to that is shown in fig. 12 under the H_0 as that area shaded with diagonal lines, while under H_A it is that area blocked out in black.

2.2.4.2   Although the region of rejection is located solely at one end of the sampling distribution, the level of significance (α) with which the test is conducted will generally be the same. Therefore to establish the decision criterion in terms of z one needs to know how many standard error units measured to the right or left of the population mean excludes 5 per cent of the area. This 5 per cent is now concentrated at one end and is not divided equally between the two tails. The relevant z value is 1·64 (found from table 1, page 374); this situation is shown in fig. 13.

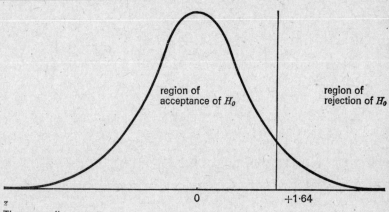

region of
acceptance of H_0

region of
rejection of H_0

z

0   +1·64

Fig. 13   The one-tail test.

2.2.4.3   Let us now suppose that our manufacturer of television sets (2.2.1) had indeed carried out a one-tail test. This is more likely, for if the average damage rate of valves has increased then he is suffering an unnecessary financial loss.

With
$$H_0 : \mu = 2 \cdot 0$$
$$H_A : \mu > 2 \cdot 0$$
$$\alpha = 0 \cdot 05$$
$$z_{0.05} = 1 \cdot 64$$

and an observed value of $\bar{x}$ of 2·25, he will obviously reject H_0 once again and accept H_A.

$$z \text{ (calc.)} = \frac{2 \cdot 25 - 2 \cdot 0}{1 \cdot 80 / \sqrt{400}} = \frac{0 \cdot 25}{0 \cdot 09} = 2 \cdot 78$$

z (calc.) = 2·78 is greater than $z_{0.05}$ = 1·64 so that his conclusion is that there has been an increase in the average number of damaged valves per box.

2.2.4.4   It would be repetitive to consider the situation for $H_A : \mu < 2 \cdot 0$. All that need be mentioned is that the critical value of $z_{0.05}$ would be −1·64; any calculated value of z which is less than −1·64 causes H_0 to be rejected.

75   Testing hypotheses

2.2.5 β and the power of the test

2.2.5.1 Although in both the two- and one-tail tests we decided to reject H_0 on the basis of a $\bar{x}$ of 2·25, we might just as easily have encountered a smaller sample mean, which would have produced the opposite decision. The risk (β) associated with this possible decision (accepting H_0 incorrectly) must be taken into account. If the observed $\bar{x}$ had fallen into the region of acceptance (either in terms of $\bar{x}$ or z values), and μ had actually changed, then an incorrect decision would have been made. The probability of making this type of mistake depends entirely upon the magnitude of the actual change in μ. If this is unknown then β can never be quantified.

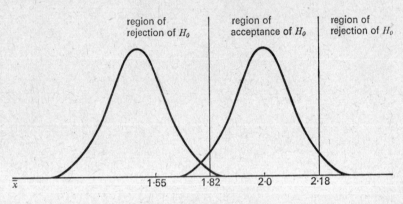

region of rejection of H_0 region of acceptance of H_0 region of rejection of H_0

$\bar{x}$ 1·55   1·82   2·0   2·18

Fig. 14

In our two-tail test imagine that H_0 has been accepted even though μ = 1·55. The situation is shown in fig. 14.

It can be seen at a glance that very little of the sampling distribution with μ = 1·55 falls into the region of acceptance of H_0. In other words, the probability of a $\bar{x}$ value which will lead to the acceptance of H_0 having been generated from a population with mean 1·55 is very slight. β is therefore very small. Its magnitude is found by calculating

$$z_\beta = \frac{\text{Critical value of } \bar{x} - \text{actual } \mu}{\text{Standard error}}$$

$$= \frac{1\cdot82 - 1\cdot55}{1\cdot8/\sqrt{400}} = \frac{0\cdot27}{0\cdot09} = 3\cdot0$$

The beginning of the region of acceptance of H_0 is therefore 3 standard error units away from μ = 1·55. Table 1 tells us that the proportion of the area under a normal curve lying outside 3 standard deviations from

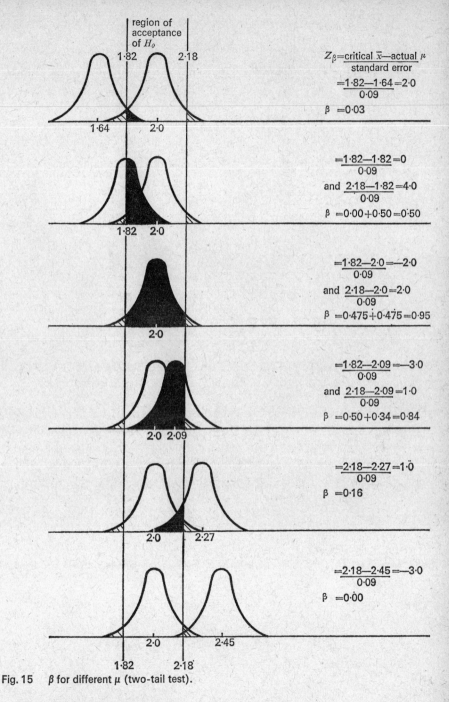

Fig. 15   β for different μ (two-tail test).

the mean is 0·00 (two significant figures). β is effectively 0·00. By repeating this procedure for different hypothetical values of μ we find the values of β shown in fig. 15.

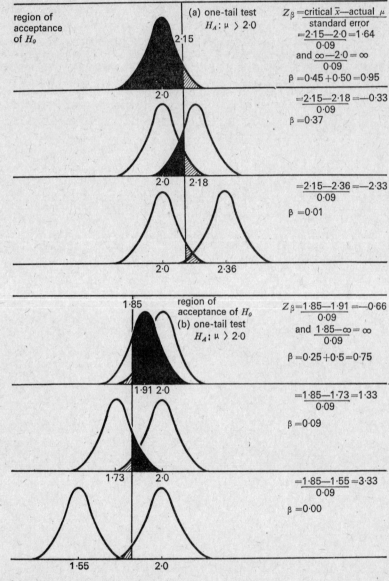

region of acceptance of H_0

(a) one-tail test
$H_A: \mu > 2\cdot0$

$$Z_\beta = \frac{\text{critical } \bar{x} - \text{actual } \mu}{\text{standard error}}$$
$$= \frac{2\cdot15 - 2\cdot0}{0\cdot09} = 1\cdot64$$
and $\frac{\infty - 2\cdot0}{0\cdot09} = \infty$
β $= 0\cdot45 + 0\cdot50 = 0\cdot95$

$$= \frac{2\cdot15 - 2\cdot18}{0\cdot09} = -0\cdot33$$
β $= 0\cdot37$

$$= \frac{2\cdot15 - 2\cdot36}{0\cdot09} = -2\cdot33$$
β $= 0\cdot01$

region of acceptance of H_0
(b) one-tail test
$H_A: \mu > 2\cdot0$

$$Z_\beta = \frac{1\cdot85 - 1\cdot91}{0\cdot09} = -0\cdot66$$
and $\frac{1\cdot85 - \infty}{0\cdot09} = \infty$
β $= 0\cdot25 + 0\cdot5 = 0\cdot75$

$$= \frac{1\cdot85 - 1\cdot73}{0\cdot09} = 1\cdot33$$
β $= 0\cdot09$

$$= \frac{1\cdot85 - 1\cdot55}{0\cdot09} = 3\cdot33$$
β $= 0\cdot00$

Fig. 16   β for different μ.

2.2.5.2   It is found that the closer the actual mean to the H_0 mean, the greater the probability of committing a type II error. The limiting case is when the actual mean is exactly the same as the H_0 mean: then $\beta = 0.95$. This may appear nonsensical to the reader at first sight. In fact one has to take into account not only the risk level, β, but also the magnitude of the difference between the actual mean and the null hypothesis mean. If this difference were large and the probability of not detecting it high, then this would be an intolerable situation. If the difference is small, however, with the same probability of it going undetected, then the consequence of the mistake assumes far smaller proportions.

2.2.5.3   When considering the β risk levels in a one-tail test there is only one departure from the above procedure, due to the fact that only actual means are considered which are either greater than 2.0 ($H_A: \mu > 2.0$) or less than 2.0 ($H_A: \mu < 2.0$). Of course, the region of acceptance has also changed, and now lies to the left or right of $1.64\ s/\sqrt{n}$ from μ. The two situations are shown schematically in figs. 16(a) and 16(b).

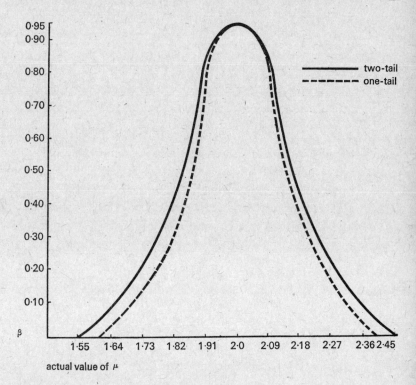

Fig. 17   The performance function ($\alpha = 0.05$ and $n = 400$).

The main point of interest is in comparing the levels for the two-tail and one-tail tests (fig. 17).

β (when $\alpha = 0.05$ and $n = 400$)

Actual value of μ	Two-tail	One-tail
1·55	0·00	0·00
1·64	0·03	0·01
1·73	0·16	0·09
1·82	0·50	0·37
1·91	0·84	0·75
2·00	0·95	0·95
2·09	0·84	0·75
2·18	0·50	0·37
2·27	0·16	0·09
2·36	0·03	0·01
2·45	0·00	0·00

If we plot these values, we produce what is called the *performance function* or *operating characteristic curve* of the test.

It can be seen that the general level of β is always smaller in a one-tail than in a two-tail test carried out at the same level of significance and with the same sample size. Wherever possible a one-tail test should therefore be employed. As a further consideration, it should also be noticed that a decision based upon a larger sample size will always be subject to a smaller β level. The following figures have been derived for the two-tail test, assuming $n = 900$ with s and α remaining unaltered.

β (when $\alpha = 0.05$ and $n = 900$)

Actual value of μ	Two-tail
1·55	0·00
1·64	0·00
1·73	0·01
1·82	0·16
1·91	0·81
2·00	0·95
2·09	0·81
2·18	0·16
2·27	0·01
2·36	0·00
2·45	0·00

The reader is recommended to check these figures in order to gain familiarity with the method.

2.2.5.4   For simplicity we have talked about β and the performance function of a test. Statisticians generally prefer to discuss the power of a test, where

$$\text{Power} = 1 - \beta.$$

The power of a test shows the probability of correctly rejecting H_0 and is evidently the complement of β. The principal reason for the predominant usage of this term is that it enables us to state whether one test is more or less powerful than another. A one-tail test is more powerful than a two-tail test; a test based upon a larger sample size is more powerful than one based upon a smaller sample size, and so on. The inference in each case is that the probability of correctly rejecting H_0 is higher (i.e. the probability of incorrectly accepting H_0 is lower).

2.2.5.5   All the developments in this section will now be consolidated by looking at an experimental test. A research economist is concerned with the increasing traffic congestion in a large city. From the work of his predecessor, who invited the co-operation of all motorists with vehicles registered in the city, he knows that in 1960 the mean time per journey between the city centre and the suburbs during the peak hours was 29·50 minutes with a standard deviation of 15·80 minutes, i.e. $\mu = 29\cdot50$ and $\sigma = 15\cdot80$.

In 1965 a random sample of 120 motorists keep detailed records of the travelling time to and from the city centre during these hours. The transport economist is to use the results of their records to test the hypothesis that congestion has increased by 10 per cent, i.e. $\mu = 32\cdot50$.

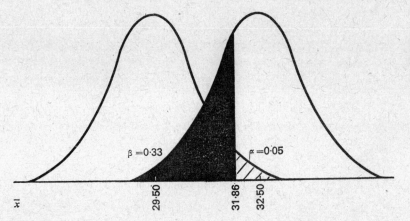

Fig. 18

However, before calculating the mean travelling time of 120 motorists he evaluates the α and β risk levels, using the previously established population standard deviation in his standard error formula. The situation which faces him, using $\alpha = 0.05$, is shown in fig. 18.

With $\sigma_{\bar{x}} = \dfrac{15\cdot80}{\sqrt{120}} = 1\cdot44$, the critical value of $\bar{x}$ (for a one-tail test) is $29\cdot5 + (1\cdot64 \times 1\cdot44) = 31\cdot86$ minutes.

Therefore

$$z_\beta = \frac{31\cdot86 - 32\cdot5}{1\cdot44} = -0\cdot44$$

and

$$\beta = 0\cdot33$$

This risk ratio of 5 to 33 the economist considers unsatisfactory. He would prefer to establish the parity of α and β. This he can do by positioning the critical value of $\bar{x}$ halfway between the null and alternative hypothesis means, i.e. $\dfrac{29\cdot50 + 32\cdot50}{2} = 31\cdot00$.

Then

$$z_\alpha = \frac{31\cdot00 - 29\cdot5}{1\cdot44} = 1\cdot04$$

and

$$z_\beta = \frac{31\cdot00 - 32\cdot5}{1\cdot44} = -1\cdot04$$

Both α and β equal $0\cdot15$. Having formalized the test to his satisfaction the researcher collects the required data from the motorists and calculates the sample mean, which turns out to be $31\cdot95$ minutes. For $\alpha = \beta = 0\cdot15$ this falls into the region of rejection of the null hypothesis, so that he has evidence to support the claim that congestion has increased by 10 per cent.

2.2.5.6   The purpose of this example is to demonstrate the precise methodological approach which must always be employed in testing hypotheses. The decision criterion should, as far as possible, be fixed in advance of the sample results becoming available. Then it will be known that this value is such as to reflect the consequences of the two possible incorrect decisions, and has not been manipulated in order to produce a conclusion satisfactory to the tester.

2.3   z Tests: $\bar{x}_1 - \bar{x}_2$

2.3.1   The preceding section has looked at differences between a known population parameter (μ) and a sample statistic $(\bar{x})$. Although this is one decision situation in which sampling theory can be of assistance, it is far from being the only one. It is frequently necessary to deal with the results of two sample surveys, conducted either in different places or at different times. The problem is to decide whether the means of the samples, $\bar{x}_1$ and $\bar{x}_2$, are drawn from populations with the same mean, i.e. $\mu_1 = \mu_2$, or whether they are drawn from populations with different means, i.e. $\mu_1 \neq \mu_2$. The point is that μ_1 and μ_2 are unknown.

2.3.2   The test is set up in exactly the same way as before, with

$$H_0 : \mu_1 = \mu_2$$

$$H_A : \mu_1 \neq \mu_2$$

$$\alpha = 0.05.$$

The difficulty appears when an appropriate sampling distribution is sought. Evidently one cannot look at the relationship between the sampling distributions of $\bar{x}_1$ and $\bar{x}_2$. Because μ_1 and μ_2 are unknown, there

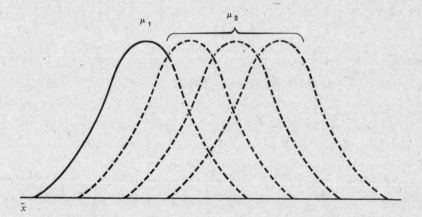

Fig. 19

is no way of deciding whether these sampling distributions are close together or a long way apart (fig. 19).

Fortunately one can construct a sampling distribution of the statistic $\bar{x}_1 - \bar{x}_2$. All possible pairs of sample means are found and one of each pair is subtracted from the other. The resulting answers, when grouped, produce a distribution which is normal. In addition, the mean of this distribution $(\mu_{\bar{x}_1 - \bar{x}_2})$ is zero when the samples are drawn under the null hypothesis assumption that $\mu_1 = \mu_2$.

83   Testing hypotheses

2.3.3 *The sampling distribution of $\bar{x}_1 - \bar{x}_2$*

To demonstrate this, let us look at a simple and hypothetical population possessing the following variable values:

x	
8	
9	The population mean, μ, is 10 and
10	the standard deviation, σ, is 1·414.
11	
12	

When two samples of size 2 are drawn from this population their means, $\bar{x}_1$ and $\bar{x}_2$ form part of the following universes or sampling distributions (notice that in this case sampling without replacement has been used):

$\bar{x}_1$	f	$\bar{x}_2$	f
8·5	1	8·5	1
9·0	1	9·0	1
9·5	2	9·5	2
10·0	2	10·0	2
10·5	2	10·5	2
11·0	1	11·0	1
11·5	1	11·5	1

These sampling distributions are identical because the two samples have been drawn from identical populations (i.e. $\mu_1 = \mu_2$). Let us now tabulate in part the pairs of $\bar{x}_1$ and $\bar{x}_2$ values and calculate the differences, $\bar{x}_1 - \bar{x}_2$.

$\bar{x}_1 - \bar{x}_2 =$	$\bar{x}_1 - \bar{x}_2 =$	$\bar{x}_1 - \bar{x}_2 =$
$8\cdot5 - 8\cdot5 = 0\cdot0$	$9\cdot0 - 8\cdot5 = 0\cdot5$	$11\cdot5 - 8\cdot5 = 3\cdot0$
$8\cdot5 - 9\cdot0 = -0\cdot5$	$9\cdot0 - 9\cdot0 = 0\cdot0$	$11\cdot5 - 9\cdot0 = 2\cdot5$
$8\cdot5 - 9\cdot5 = -1\cdot0$	$9\cdot0 - 9\cdot5 = -0\cdot5$	$11\cdot5 - 9\cdot5 = 2\cdot0$
$8\cdot5 - 9\cdot5 = -1\cdot0$	$9\cdot0 - 9\cdot5 = -0\cdot5$	$11\cdot5 - 9\cdot5 = 2\cdot0$
$8\cdot5 - 10\cdot0 = -1\cdot5$	$9\cdot0 - 10\cdot0 = -1\cdot0$	$11\cdot5 - 10\cdot0 = 1\cdot5$
$8\cdot5 - 10\cdot0 = -1\cdot5$	$9\cdot0 - 10\cdot0 = -1\cdot0$	$11\cdot5 - 10\cdot0 = 1\cdot5$
$8\cdot5 - 10\cdot5 = -2\cdot0$	$9\cdot0 - 10\cdot5 = -1\cdot5$	$11\cdot5 - 10\cdot5 = 1\cdot0$
$8\cdot5 - 10\cdot5 = -2\cdot0$	$9\cdot0 - 10\cdot5 = -1\cdot5$	$11\cdot5 - 10\cdot5 = 1\cdot0$
$8\cdot5 - 11\cdot0 = -2\cdot5$	$9\cdot0 - 11\cdot0 = -2\cdot0$	$11\cdot5 - 11\cdot0 = 0\cdot5$
$8\cdot5 - 11\cdot5 = -3\cdot0$	$9\cdot0 - 11\cdot5 = -2\cdot5$	$11\cdot5 - 11\cdot5 = 0\cdot0$

Collecting similar differences together produces the required sampling distribution, which is seen to be symmetrical and approximately normal

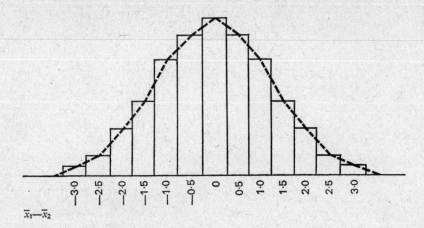

$\bar{x}_1 - \bar{x}_2$

Fig. 20   The sampling distribution of $\bar{x}_1 - \bar{x}_2$.

(fig. 20). In more realistic circumstances (a large population and sample size) the distribution is perfectly normal. The mean of the sampling distribution, $\mu_{\bar{x}_1 - \bar{x}_2}$ is zero, as expected.

$\bar{x}_1 - \bar{x}_2$	f
-3.0	1
-2.5	2
-2.0	5
-1.5	8
-1.0	12
-0.5	14
0.0	16
0.5	14
1.0	12
1.5	8
2.0	5
2.5	2
3.0	1
	100

85   Testing hypotheses

2.3.4 The standard error

2.3.4.1 We now need to establish the standard error of this sampling distribution. It can be shown that the variance of the sum or difference of two independent series is equal to the sum of the variances of these series (see 2.10.1). Now the sampling distributions of $\bar{x}_1$ and $\bar{x}_2$ constitute independent series, and it is the difference between each possible pair of values from these series that we have been concerned with. Therefore the calculation of $\sigma_{\bar{x}}^2$ and $\sigma_{\bar{x}_1-\bar{x}_2}^2$ should bear out this rule.

In the sampling distribution of both $\bar{x}_1$ and $\bar{x}_2$, $\Sigma f = 10$, $\Sigma fx = 100$ and $\Sigma fx^2 = 1007 \cdot 5$, so that in both

$$\sigma_{\bar{x}}^2 = \frac{1007 \cdot 5}{10} - \left(\frac{100}{10}\right)^2 = 0 \cdot 75$$

In the sampling distribution of $\bar{x}_1 - \bar{x}_2$, $\Sigma f = 100$, $\Sigma fx = 0$ and $\Sigma fx^2 = 150$, giving

$$\sigma_{\bar{x}-\bar{x}_2}^2 = \left\{\frac{150}{100} - \left(\frac{0}{100}\right)^2\right\} = 1 \cdot 5$$

$1 \cdot 5 = 0 \cdot 75 + 0 \cdot 75$ and therefore $\sigma_{\bar{x}_1-\bar{x}_2}^2 = \sigma_{\bar{x}_1}^2 + \sigma_{\bar{x}_2}^2$ and the standard error of the difference is given by

$$\sigma_{\bar{x}_1-\bar{x}_2} = \sqrt{\{\sigma_{\bar{x}_1}^2 + \sigma_{\bar{x}_2}^2\}}$$

Now the standard error of the mean $\sigma/\sqrt{n}$ is estimated by $s/\sqrt{n}$ when the sample size is large, and variance by s^2/n. This variance may be substituted above so that

$$\sigma_{\bar{x}_1-\bar{x}_2} = \sqrt{\left(\frac{s_1^2}{n_1} + \frac{s_2^2}{n_2}\right)}$$

Notice that the simplified example used to develop the argument involved the F.P.C.F. so that the standard error of the difference is found from

$$\sqrt{\left(\frac{s_1^2}{n_1} \cdot \frac{N_1 - n_1}{N_1 - 1} + \frac{s_2^2}{n_2} \cdot \frac{N_2 - n_2}{N_2 - 1}\right)}$$

The reader may check this for himself.

2.3.4.2 A normal sampling distribution has been derived and its mean and standard error discovered. The test may now proceed on the conventional lines established in 2.2.3.4. The critical values of z are $-1 \cdot 96$ and $+1 \cdot 96$; any difference between $\bar{x}_1$ and $\bar{x}_2$ less than or greater than these in terms of standard error units will result in the H_0 being rejected in favour of the H_A. The actual z value will be found from

$$z = \frac{\bar{x}_1 - \bar{x}_2}{\sqrt{\left(\frac{s_1{}^2}{n_1} + \frac{s_2{}^2}{n_2} \right)}}$$

To conform with $z = \dfrac{x - \mu}{\sigma}$ this should strictly read

$$\frac{(\bar{x}_1 - \bar{x}_2) - \mu_{\bar{x}_1 - \bar{x}_2}}{\sqrt{\left(\frac{s_1{}^2}{n_1} + \frac{s_2{}^2}{n_2} \right)}}$$

Under H_0, however, $\mu_{\bar{x}_1 - \bar{x}_2} = 0$ and can be ignored.

As an illustration of the method, consider an investigation undertaken in a maternity home to find whether there is any difference in the mean age of mothers whose confinement leads to a single birth as opposed to those leading to multiple births (twins, triplets, etc.). By checking admission cards over a number of years, it is found that the mean age of the first category of mothers is 26·52 years with a standard deviation of 5·32 years ($n = 825$), while for the second $\bar{x} = 31·80$ years and $s = 4·35$ years ($n = 296$).

Using a 5 per cent significance level ($\alpha = 0·05$) we must decide to reject H_0.

$$z \text{ (calc.)} = \frac{26·52 - 31·80}{\sqrt{\left(\frac{5·32^2}{825} + \frac{4·35^2}{296} \right)}} = \frac{-5·28}{0·3132} = -16·86$$

This is much less than $z_{0·05} = -1·96$. The difference in this case is highly significant.

2.3.4.3   Although the decision, based upon these sample results, has led to the conclusive rejection of H_0, the design of the test must also take into

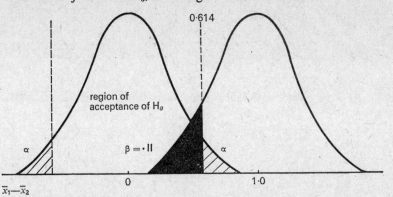

Fig. 21 $\bar{x}_1 - \bar{x}_2$

account the probability of incorrectly accepting the H_0. Again β probability levels can only be ascertained if the magnitude of the suspected difference between μ_1 and μ_2 is specified.

If the difference between μ_1 and μ_2 is not zero but $1 \cdot 0$ then it is possible to quantify the risk associated with accepting the null hypothesis. The schematic position is shown in fig. 21.

$$z_\beta = \frac{(1 \cdot 96 \times 0 \cdot 3132) - 1 \cdot 0}{0 \cdot 3132}$$

$$= -1 \cdot 23$$

$$\beta = 0 \cdot 11$$

By considering the following hypothetical values of $\mu_1 - \mu_2$ we obtain the performance function (β values) as shown in fig. 22.

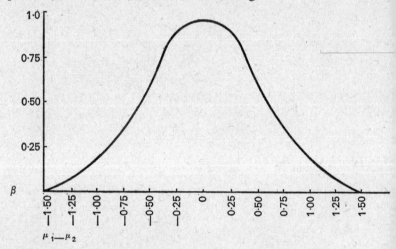

Fig. 22   The performance function for $\alpha = 0 \cdot 05$.

β (when $n_1 = 825$, $n_2 = 296$ and $\alpha = 0 \cdot 05$)

Actual value of $\mu_1 - \mu_2$	β	Actual value of $\mu_1 - \mu_2$	β
$-1 \cdot 50$	$0 \cdot 00$	$+0 \cdot 25$	$0 \cdot 88$
$-1 \cdot 25$	$0 \cdot 02$	$+0 \cdot 50$	$0 \cdot 64$
$-1 \cdot 00$	$0 \cdot 11$	$+0 \cdot 75$	$0 \cdot 33$
$-0 \cdot 75$	$0 \cdot 33$	$+1 \cdot 00$	$0 \cdot 11$
$-0 \cdot 50$	$0 \cdot 64$	$+1 \cdot 25$	$0 \cdot 02$
$-0 \cdot 25$	$0 \cdot 88$	$+1 \cdot 50$	$0 \cdot 00$
$0 \cdot 00$	$0 \cdot 95$		

This performance function relates only to the magnitude of the difference between the population parameters. It says nothing about the absolute value of these parameters.

2.3.4.4 Tests of significance between sample means are usually based upon an alternative hypothesis that the means of the populations from which the samples have been drawn are different ($H_A : \mu_1 \neq \mu_2$). There is no reason, however, for neglecting the possibility of a one-tail test being undertaken. Although less common, a null hypothesis that μ_1 is greater than or equal to μ_2 is sometimes employed ($H_0 : \mu_1 \geqslant \mu_2$). If this hypothesis is rejected (this will occur only if $\bar{x}_1$ is smaller than $\bar{x}_2$) then the alternative hypothesis that μ_1 is less than μ_2 is accepted ($H_A : \mu_1 < \mu_2$).

2.4 z Tests: $p - \pi$

2.4.1 Just as we developed arguments for estimating both μ and π in Chapter 1, so we should explore the testing of hypothesis about proportions as well as means.

Suppose a firm manufacturing margarine has developed a new product. The firm's research department considers the taste of this new line to be indistinguishable from that of butter, but before marketing on a large scale takes place it is decided to invite the co-operation of housewives from different parts of the country. Tasting sessions are held in which each participant is asked to decide which of six biscuits is spread with margarine (the rest are spread with butter). Now the firm's statistician recognizes that in the long run and by guesswork alone, one sixth of the tasters will select the biscuit spread with margarine. Therefore if any statistically valid conclusion is to be drawn the difference between 1/6 (the population proportion, π) and p (the observed sample proportion) must be significant. If no significant difference is found then the firm faces an inconclusive situation.

2.4.2 Out of 800 housewives, let us suppose that 128 correctly selected the biscuit spread with margarine (i.e. $p = 0 \cdot 16$). The statistician analysing this result may firstly seek to establish whether this indicates a significant difference from the assumption that chance alone is at work. In other words, he is undertaking a two-tail test, where

$$H_0 : \pi = 1/6 \text{ or } 0 \cdot 167$$
$$H_A : \pi \neq 1/6 \text{ or } 0 \cdot 167$$

Using a significance level of 5 per cent ($\alpha = 0 \cdot 05$) he has to establish his decision criteria. Remembering that the binomial sampling distribution of proportions is approximated by the normal distribution when the sample size is large, and that the standard error is given by $\sqrt{\left\{\dfrac{\pi(1-\pi)}{n}\right\}}$, the critical values of p will be set at

$$\pi-1\cdot96\sqrt{\left\{\frac{\pi(1-\pi)}{n}\right\}} \text{ and } \pi+1\cdot96\sqrt{\left\{\frac{\pi(1-\pi)}{n}\right\}}$$

i.e. $\qquad 0\cdot167-1\cdot96\sqrt{\left\{\dfrac{0\cdot167\times0\cdot833}{800}\right\}}=0\cdot141$

and $\qquad 0\cdot167+1\cdot96\sqrt{\left\{\dfrac{0\cdot167\times0\cdot833}{800}\right\}}=0\cdot193$

In other words any sample proportion of tasters between 0·141 and 0·193 has a 0·95 probability of occurrence when chance alone has directed their selection. If, however, p is less than 0·141 or greater than 0·193 then there is strong evidence that either the tasters can or cannot distinguish this margarine from butter. Because the sample proportion in this case was 0·16 the H_0 that $\pi \doteq 1/6$ has to be accepted.

2.4.3   In no way deterred, the research department goes to work again, and by slightly altering the blend of vegetable oils used, produces a variant of the same margarine which it is felt may commend itself more readily to the average palate. The tasting sessions are repeated, and on this occasion the firm's statistician decides to restrict his test. He employs a one-tail version with

$$H_0 : \pi = 0\cdot167$$
$$H_A : \pi < 0\cdot167$$
$$\alpha = 0\cdot05$$

If the H_0 can be rejected under these circumstances, then he has evidence suggesting that the new variety is, to a large extent, indistinguishable from butter.

Thus the region of rejection of the H_0 is now confined to the lower half of the sampling distribution and the critical value of p is found from

$$\pi-1\cdot64\sqrt{\left\{\frac{\pi(1-\pi)}{n}\right\}}$$

Giving $\qquad 0\cdot167-1\cdot64\sqrt{\left\{\dfrac{0\cdot167\times0\cdot833}{800}\right\}}=0\cdot145$

On this occasion only 105 out of the 800 housewives select the biscuit spread with the margarine, i.e. $p=0\cdot131$. This is less than 0·145 and therefore the H_A is accepted. The research department seems to have developed a product in which they can have considerable pride (although the firm's statistician should remind them that there is still a 5 per cent chance that this is false pride).

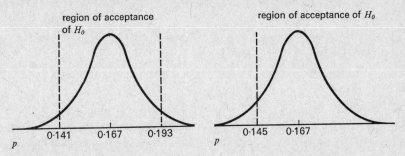

Fig. 23 The two- and one-tail tests.

2.4.4   Finally, as a means of convincing the directors of the company that this latest research work has resulted in a product which is superior to that currently marketed, the tasting sessions are once more instituted, but using the current blend of margarine. The one-tail test of hypotheses is set up in the opposite direction with

$$H_0 : \pi = 0.167$$

$$H_A : \pi > 0.167$$

$$\alpha = 0.05$$

The critical value of p is now

$$\pi + 1.64 \sqrt{\left\{ \frac{\pi(1-\pi)}{n} \right\}}$$

i.e. 0.189. The actual value of p is $\dfrac{160}{800} = 0.20$, showing that 20 per cent of the tasters detected the margarine-spread biscuit. The difference between 0.167 and 0.200 is significant, indicating that the current blend can definitely be distinguished from butter. These experiments must convince the firm that it would be advisable to market the new brand. In addition, it has statistical evidence to support an advertising campaign that 'new brand X' is not only nutritionally as good as butter, but actually tastes like butter.

2.4.5   The conversion of a test of hypotheses in terms of critical values of p into one using critical values of z follows the principle established in 2.2.3.4. Instead of asking which value(s) of p exclude 5 per cent of the area under the normal sampling distribution, we ask how many standard error units measured from the mean (in this case π) achieve the same result. Specifically we divide the difference between p and π by the standard error:

$$z \text{ (calc.)} = \frac{p - \pi}{\sqrt{\left\{\frac{\pi(1-\pi)}{n}\right\}}}$$

In the two-tail test any calculated z less than $z_{0.05} = -1.96$ or greater than $z_{0.05} = 1.96$ causes H_0 to be rejected. In the one-tail test the appropriate critical value will be either $z_{0.05} = -1.64$ or 1.64.

2.4.6   Finally, we should consider the β level and the power of the test. The performance functions for the three tests discussed above are shown in

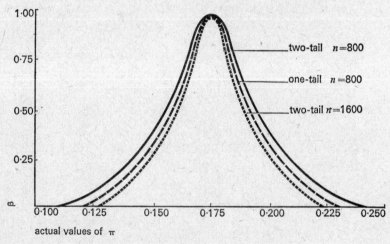

Fig. 24

fig. 24, together with the performance function for a two-tail test based upon a sample size of 1600. The one-tail tests are again shown to be subject to a lower level of β (the power of the test is higher), as is a test based upon a larger sample size.

β (when $\alpha = 0.05$ and $n = 800$ and 1600)

Actual values of π	$n = 800$ Two-tail $H_A:\pi \neq 0.167$	One-tail $H_A:\pi > 0.167$	One-tail $H_A:\pi < 0.167$	$n = 1600$ Two-tail $H_A:\pi \neq 0.167$
0.100	0.00		0.00	0.00
0.125	0.08		0.04	0.00
0.150	0.76		0.54	0.56
0.167	0.95	0.95	0.95	0.95
0.175	0.91	0.84		0.86
0.200	0.32	0.21		0.07
0.225	0.01	0.01		0.00
0.250	0.00	0.00		0.00

2.4.7   One very important divergence in principle from the previous development of performance functions should be noticed here. When looking at problems involving means, the standard error (either $\sigma_{\bar{x}}$ or $\sigma_{\bar{x}_1 - \bar{x}_2}$) was the same regardless of the value of μ or the magnitude of the difference between μ_1 and μ_2. The reason was that the standard errors are independent of the parameters central to the test. $\sigma_{\bar{x}}$ does not require a knowledge of μ, and $\sigma_{\bar{x}_1 - \bar{x}_2}$ does not require a knowledge of μ_1 and μ_2. However σ_p (the standard error of proportions) is based upon the population parameter π. Consequently when calculating β (the probability of accepting the H_0 incorrectly) the sampling distribution for the actual value of π will have a different standard error. For example, the standard error under the null hypothesis assumption ($\pi = 0.167$) was

$$\sigma_p = \sqrt{\frac{0.167 \times 0.833}{800}} = 0.0132$$

With a hypothetical π value of 0.125 the standard error is

$$\sqrt{\frac{0.125 \times 0.875}{800}} = 0.0117$$

Thus in working out β for this value of π, 0.125 was subtracted from the critical value of p (0.141) and the difference converted into standard error units by dividing by σ_p (0.0117).

$$z_\beta = \frac{0.141 - 0.125}{0.0117} = 1.37$$

Using table 1, page 374, the area to the right of $1 \cdot 37$ standard deviations measured from the mean is $0 \cdot 08$ of the total; β therefore equals $0 \cdot 08$. If the assumption of a constant standard error had been employed we would have found

$$z_\beta = \frac{0 \cdot 141 - 0 \cdot 125}{0 \cdot 0132} = 1 \cdot 21$$

and $\beta = 0 \cdot 11$ which is 3 per cent higher.

Another difference which can be observed from fig. 24 is that the performance function in the case of proportions is slightly skewed round the null-hypothesis proportion. Only if $H_0 : \pi = 0 \cdot 5$ will this function be symmetrical.

2.5　z Tests: $p_1 - p_2$

2.5.1　The final discussion of z tests concerns the difference between sample proportions. For instance, a clinical experiment to evaluate the merits of two treatments for a certain illness showed that the proportion of patients suffering side-effects differed. Out of 200 patients treated with drug A, 65 were subject to side-effects, whilst of 250 treated with drug B, 75 were affected in this way. Is the difference between $p_1 = \dfrac{65}{200} = 0 \cdot 325$ and $p_2 = \dfrac{75}{250} = 0 \cdot 300$ significant, or is it due to chance and caused by sampling variation?

2.5.2　Statistically, the test is parallel to that looked at in 2.3.1, when the difference between $\bar{x}_1$ and $\bar{x}_2$ was discussed. Formally,

$$H_0 : \pi_1 = \pi_2$$

$$H_A : \pi_1 \neq \pi_2$$

$$\alpha = 0 \cdot 01$$

Notice that we have specified an α level of $0 \cdot 01$ in this case rather than the more conventional $0 \cdot 05$. A doctor will need very strong evidence that the treatments are different (i.e. one is better than the other), because the consequences of an incorrect decision on his part could be serious and cause unnecessary suffering to the patients.

The sampling distribution of the statistic $p_1 - p_2$ is normal in circumstances where n is large. It has a zero mean when $\pi_1 = \pi_2$ (the H_0 assumption) and a standard error given by the following expression (using the theorem that the variance of the difference is equal to the sum of the variances):

$$\sigma_{p_1 - p_2} = \sqrt{\left\{\frac{\pi_1(1-\pi_1)}{n_1} + \frac{\pi_2(1-\pi_2)}{n_2}\right\}}$$

Because in the null hypothesis $\pi_1 = \pi_2$ this reduces to

$$\sqrt{\left\{\pi(1-\pi)\left(\frac{1}{n_1} + \frac{1}{n_2}\right)\right\}}$$

so that an estimate of π (the common population proportion) is required (this estimate will be designated π'). The best estimate of π is given by the weighted mean of the sample proportions. The word 'weighted' is used to indicate that the proportion based upon the larger sample is considered more accurate than that based upon the small sample. Thus, if $p_1 = 0\cdot25$ with $n_1 = 300$, and $p_2 = 0\cdot20$ with $n_2 = 750$, then π' is given by

$$\pi' = \frac{p_1 n_1 + p_2 n_2}{n_1 + n_2} = \frac{0\cdot25 \times 300 + 0\cdot20 \times 750}{300 + 750}$$

$$= 0\cdot214$$

2.5.3   In the context of the clinical experiment discussed earlier, we need to know whether the difference between p_1 and p_2 is less than $-2\cdot58\,\sigma_{p_1 - p_2}$ or greater than $2\cdot58\,\sigma_{p_1 - p_2}$.

The critical value of $z_{0\cdot01}$ is $2\cdot58$ in this example because we have specified an $\alpha = 0\cdot01$. The calculated z value which will lead either to the acceptance or rejection of the null hypothesis is found from

$$z\,(\text{calc.}) = \frac{p_1 - p_2}{\sqrt{\left\{\pi'(1-\pi')\left(\frac{1}{n_1} + \frac{1}{n_2}\right)\right\}}}$$

With $$\pi' = \frac{0\cdot325 \times 200 + 0\cdot300 \times 250}{200 + 250} = 0\cdot311$$

$$z\,(\text{calc.}) = \frac{0\cdot325 - 0\cdot300}{\sqrt{0\cdot311\,(0\cdot689)\left(\frac{1}{200} + \frac{1}{250}\right)}} = \frac{0\cdot025}{0\cdot044} = 0\cdot57$$

Thus the null hypothesis is accepted; we conclude that the two treatments produce the same proportion of patients suffering side-effects, the difference between $0\cdot325$ and $0\cdot300$ being due to chance alone.

2.5.4   Of course, in drawing this conclusion we are as usual subject to a type II error. If one of the drugs actually produces adverse side-effects in 10 per cent less patients than the other, we need to know the probability of this difference being undetected (i.e. β). We must find what proportion of the area of the sampling distribution with mean $\pi_1 - \pi_2 = 0.10$ lies in the region of acceptance of H_0 ($\pi_1 - \pi_2 = 0$), as shown in fig. 25.

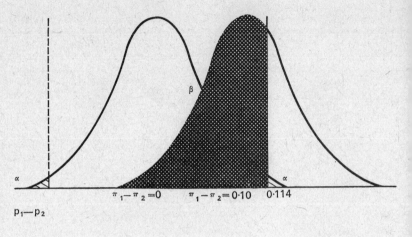

Fig. 25

The critical values of $p_1 - p_2$ are $0 \pm 2 \cdot 58 \; \sigma_{p_1 - p_2} = 0 \pm 2 \cdot 58 \times 0 \cdot 044 = -0 \cdot 114$, and $0 \cdot 114$.

$$z_\beta = \frac{-0 \cdot 114 - (-0 \cdot 10)}{0 \cdot 044} = -\frac{0 \cdot 014}{0 \cdot 044} = -0 \cdot 32$$

and
$$\frac{0 \cdot 114 - (-0 \cdot 10)}{0 \cdot 044} = \frac{0 \cdot 214}{0 \cdot 044} = 4 \cdot 86$$

The proportion of the area between $\pi_1 - \pi_2 = 0 \cdot 10$ and $-0 \cdot 32$ standard errors from it is $0 \cdot 13$, whilst the area between $\pi_1 - \pi_2 = 0 \cdot 10$ and $4 \cdot 86$ standard errors from it is $0 \cdot 50$. β is the sum of these, namely $0 \cdot 63$. In view of this high risk level it would probably be deemed wise to undertake further research and another clinical experiment before deciding that the two drugs are similar in effect.

The complete performance function is shown in fig. 26. Because the actual values of π_1 and π_2 are unknown, we have been unable to recompute the standard errors for each value of $\pi_1 - \pi_2$; the principle established in 2.4.7 cannot, therefore, be repeated.

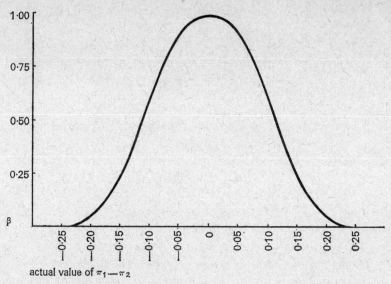

actual value of $\pi_1 - \pi_2$

Fig. 26   The performance function.

2.6   *t* Tests

2.6.1   In sections 2.2 and 2.3 tests of hypotheses about means were conducted using the evidence of large samples, Chapter 1 having already indicated that the sampling distribution of $\bar{x}$ is truly normal only on the basis of this assumption. However, there are many circumstances in the social sciences when it is not possible to take large samples, and where the sampling distributions cease to be normal, so we shall consider at this point the

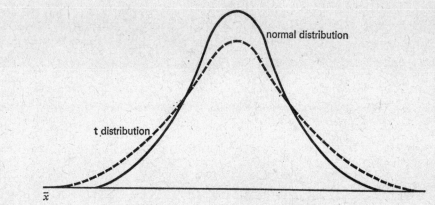

Fig. 27

amendments to our earlier theory which will be necessary in dealing with small samples.

2.6.2   A major divergence occurs when $n < 30$, in which case the sampling distribution of $\bar{x}$ conforms to a theoretical distribution known as the t or Student t distribution (the properties of this distribution were developed by W.S. Gosset who published under the pen-name of Student). The t distribution resembles the normal distribution in being symmetrical, but it is flatter and its shape alters with changes in the sample size; as larger and larger samples are considered, so the t distribution becomes more and more normal. The t distribution appears only if the population distribution is normal or approximately so; the difference between a normal and a t distribution is shown in fig. 27.

2.6.3   While as a general statement it is still true that the variance of this t sampling distribution is given by $\dfrac{\sigma^2}{n}$ it is not true that $s^2 = \dfrac{\Sigma(x-\bar{x})^2}{n}$ may be used as an unbiased estimate of σ^2. In 1.9.5 we stated that for small samples the sample variance is better estimated by

$$s^2 = \frac{\Sigma(x-\bar{x})^2}{n-1}$$

The reasons for this will now be explored. It was shown in *Statistics for the Social Scientist: 1 Introducing Statistics* that $\Sigma(x-\bar{x}) = 0$; it can also be shown that, for $a \neq \bar{x}$ (see 2.10.2), $\Sigma(x-\bar{x})^2$ is smaller than $\Sigma(x-a)^2$. Now if we knew the population mean, μ, the sum of the squared deviations of the sample values round the mean would be found from $\Sigma(x-\mu)^2$. But this will be greater than $\Sigma(x-\bar{x})^2$ unless $\mu = \bar{x}$. Therefore $\dfrac{\Sigma(x-\bar{x})^2}{n}$ as an estimate of $\dfrac{\Sigma(x-\mu)^2}{n}$ will on average be too small. If, however, $\Sigma(x-\bar{x})^2$ is divided by $n-1$, s^2 is increased and it can be shown that on average $s^2 = \sigma^2$ (see 2.10.3).

The reader may wonder why this has not been emphasized earlier. Why have variances and standard deviations been calculated from a formula using a divisor of n? Firstly, remember that the use of $n-1$ is confined to sample data and is not applicable to the variances and standard deviations of universes. Secondly, consider the effect of using $n-1$ rather than n in large samples. Suppose that from a sample of 200 observations $\Sigma(x-\bar{x})^2 = 550$. Using n, the variance is $\dfrac{550}{200} = 2 \cdot 75$. Using $n-1$ the variance is $\dfrac{550}{199} = 2 \cdot 76$ which is only slightly different. If, however,

$n = 20$ with $\Sigma(x-\bar{x})^2 = 55$, the first version gives $\dfrac{55}{20} = 2\cdot75$ while the second produces $\dfrac{55}{19} = 2\cdot89$ which is very much higher. It seems that for large sample sizes it is quite adequate to use n, but for small samples the divisor should be $n-1$.

2.6.4   Another way of looking at this problem is to notice that because $\Sigma(x-\bar{x}) = 0$, only $n-1$ deviations need to be calculated. The final deviation must be such that the sum equals zero. One is free to calculate only $n-1$ deviations so that there are effectively $n-1$ observations in the series. A variance is therefore said to be subject to a certain number of 'degrees of freedom'. This term is important both because it will be encountered on later occasions and also because the t distribution varies according to the sample size (i.e. the number of degrees of freedom). Table 2, page 375, shows, for different degrees of freedom, the number of standard deviation units measured to the right of the mean which exclude 10, 5, $2\frac{1}{2}$, 1 and $\frac{1}{2}$ per cent of the area under the t curve (note that as with z tables only half of the curve is considered). For instance with 14 degrees of freedom and $n = 15$, $2\cdot145$ standard deviation units excludes $2\frac{1}{2}$ per cent of the area under the curve.

2.6.5   *Confidence intervals for μ*

The upper and lower confidence limits for an estimate of μ have previously been given as

$$\bar{\mu} = \bar{x} \pm z\frac{s}{\sqrt{n}}$$

The value z (the number of standard error units to be added to and subtracted from $\bar{x}$) determined the level of confidence with which the estimate was made. For small samples we shall use an appropriate value of t so that

$$\bar{\mu} = \bar{x} \pm t\frac{s}{\sqrt{n}}$$

To illustrate this, consider a power station with ten generators. In one year each is out of service for repairs and maintenance for the following number of days.

99   Testing hypotheses

Generator	Number of days out of service	$x - \bar{x}$	$(x - \bar{x})^2$
A	15	-2	4
B	16	-1	1
C	18	1	1
D	13	-4	16
E	21	4	16
F	14	-3	9
G	15	-2	4
H	17	0	0
I	23	6	36
J	18	1	1
	170	0	88

$$\bar{x} = \frac{\Sigma x}{n} = \frac{170}{10} = 17 \qquad s = \sqrt{\frac{\Sigma (x - \bar{x})^2}{n-1}} = \sqrt{\frac{88}{9}} = 3 \cdot 13$$

For a 95 per cent confidence level we look up the t value for 9 degrees of freedom, excluding $2\frac{1}{2}$ per cent of the area under the curve in each tail. The appropriate figure is 2·26 so that

$$\underline{\mu} = 17 \pm 2 \cdot 26 \frac{3 \cdot 13}{\sqrt{10}} = 17 \pm 2 \cdot 24$$

The average period per year that each generator can be expected to be out of service in the future lies between 14·76 and 19·24 days with 95 per cent confidence.

2.6.6 Test of hypotheses

2.6.6.1 Evidently, tests concerned with differences between $\bar{x}$ and μ can proceed in exactly the same manner as those discussed in 2.2.3.4 except that the critical values will now be expressed in ts and not zs and the actual difference (in standard error units) will be calculated from

$$t \text{ (calc.)} = \frac{\bar{x} - \mu}{s/\sqrt{n}}$$

Using the results from 2.6.5 ($\bar{x} = 17$ and $s = 3 \cdot 13$) we might ask whether this power station loses more production time than the national average, which is 16 days per generator. In other words

$$H_0 : \mu = 16$$

$$H_A : \mu > 16$$

$$\alpha = 0 \cdot 05$$

Notice that we are conducting a one-tail test here, so that the 5 per cent of sample means which will cause the H_0 to be rejected are concentrated in the right tail of the t distribution. Therefore the critical value in this case for 9 degrees of freedom is 1·83.

Now

$$t \text{ (calc.)} = \frac{17 - 16}{3 \cdot 13 / \sqrt{10}} = \frac{1}{0 \cdot 99} = 1 \cdot 01$$

$1 \cdot 01 < 1 \cdot 83$, so we will accept the null hypothesis and reject the inference that the difference between $\bar{x}$ and μ is significant at a 5 per cent level.

2.6.6.2   Using parallel reasoning, the alternative hypothesis that $\mu \neq 16$ or $\mu < 16$ can be tested against the null hypothesis, and we can also establish a performance or power function; many examples of these types have been provided in earlier sections, so the reader should now possess complete familiarity with these aspects of the decision problem. If at all unsure however, he can work out several β values for the test performed in 2.6.6.

Our next logical step would seem to be that of discussing t tests for differences between two sample means, $\bar{x}_1$ and $\bar{x}_2$, but for reasons which will become apparent in 2.8.2 we shall consider F tests first.

2.7   *F* tests

2.7.1   This test is concerned with sample variances. In 1.9.5 we saw that it is possible to draw up a sampling distribution of s^2. This will be normal as long as the population from which the random samples have been drawn is normal and the sample size large ($n > 100$). The mean of the sampling distribution is the same as σ^2 (demonstrated in 1.9.5) and the standard error is estimated from

$$\sigma_{s^2} = s^2 \sqrt{\frac{2}{n}}$$

By extension of previously established principles, probability estimates of a population variance may be made from

$$\bar{\sigma}^2 = s^2 \pm z s^2 \sqrt{\frac{2}{n}}$$

2.7.2   Generally, however, the social researcher is not so much concerned with estimates of σ^2 from s^2 as with testing whether two sample variances are drawn from populations with the same variance. The approach in this case is not to test the difference between s_1^2 and s_2^2, but to examine the ratio $\dfrac{s_1^2}{s_2^2}$ (where $s_1^2 > s_2^2$) and its probability of occurrence in the sampling (F) distribution for $\sigma_1^2 = \sigma_2^2$. This F distribution varies in form depending upon the degrees of freedom of the two sample estimates. It can be looked upon as built up of all the possible ratios which would result when s_1^2 and s_2^2 are based upon different sample sizes. A typical F distribution is shown in fig. 28.

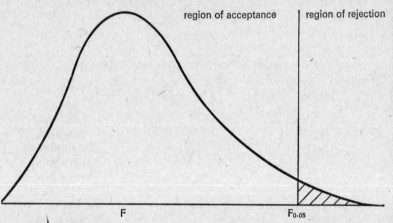

region of acceptance | region of rejection

F $F_{0.05}$

Fig. 28   The F distribution.

Generally, although not necessarily, a one-tail test is conducted. The alternative hypothesis will be that the population variance which has generated the larger sample variance is greater than that generating the smaller sample variance. The procedure adopted in the test is to enter table 3, page 376, which shows values of F significant at 5, 2·5 and 1 per cent levels for varying degrees of freedom (only these three levels are shown, otherwise a large three dimensional table would be required with the degrees of freedom occupying two axes and the F values the third). Finding the column headed by the degrees of freedom in the numerator of

$$F\,(\text{calc.}) = \frac{s_1^2}{s_2^2}$$

we read down until we arrive at the row of entries corresponding to the degrees of freedom in the denominator. If the calculated $F > F_{0.05}$, then the H_0 is rejected and the H_A accepted at a 5 per cent significance level.

2.7.3 In deciding which of two makes of electric wall clocks should be purchased for the lecture rooms on the campus of a large university, consistency must be of prime concern. A test is undertaken by the statistics
department in which ten clocks of each make, purchased from retailers
throughout a town, are checked over one week. The following are the
number of minutes lost or gained during this period:

Make A	Make B
−2	+1
0	0
+3	0
−4	+2
−2	+1
+1	+2
+1	0
+3	−1
0	0
−1	+1

The variance in the first case was $s_1^2 = 4.99$ while in the second
$s_2^2 = 0.93$. With

$$H_0 : \sigma_1^2 = \sigma_2^2$$
$$H_A : \sigma_1^2 > \sigma_2^2$$
$$\alpha = 0.05$$

and the calculated ratio given by

$$F \text{ (calc.)} = \frac{4.99}{0.93} = 5.37$$

we must decide to reject H_0 and accept H_A. The critical $F_{0.05}$ value for 9
and 9 degrees of freedom at a 5 per cent significance level (one tail) is
3.18, so that the calculated F is larger.

It would seem that make B is to be preferred, as these clocks are subject
to less variability than those of make A; although on average make B
clocks gain $\frac{6}{10}$ minute per week, there will be a smaller total spread of
gain or loss.

2.8 t Test: $\bar{x}_1 - \bar{x}_2$

2.8.1 In addition to the previously mentioned assumption about the 'normality' of the populations from which small samples are drawn, t tests

for sample means usually stipulate that the populations are homoscedastic (have the same variances). Any difference between the variance of the first sample and the variance of the second sample would, under this assumption, be caused by sampling variation alone. Consequently, as an improved estimate of the common population variance, the two sample variances should be pooled. Following the procedure adopted in 2.5.2 when π was estimated from p_1 and p_2, we take a weighted average of the sample variances s_1^2 and s_2^2,

$$\hat{\sigma}^2 = \frac{\Sigma(x_1 - \bar{x}_1)^2 + \Sigma(x_2 - \bar{x}_2)^2}{n_1 - 1 + n_2 - 1}$$

The main application of pooling s_1^2 and s_2^2 is in the formula for the standard error of the difference between sample means; as before this is defined as:

$$\sigma_{\bar{x}_1 - \bar{x}_2} = \sqrt{\left\{ \frac{\sigma_1^2}{n_1} + \frac{\sigma_2^2}{n_2} \right\}}$$

When $\sigma_1^2 = \sigma_2^2$ and the estimate of both is given by $\hat{\sigma}^2$, this becomes

$$\sigma_{\bar{x}_1 - \bar{x}_2} = \sqrt{\left\{ \frac{\Sigma(x_1 - \bar{x}_1)^2 + \Sigma(x_2 - \bar{x}_2)^2}{n_1 + n_2 - 2} \left(\frac{1}{n_1} + \frac{1}{n_2} \right) \right\}}$$

2.8.2   Any difference between $\bar{x}_1$ and $\bar{x}_2$ is converted into standard error units by dividing by $\sigma_{\bar{x}_1 - \bar{x}_2}$ and this value is then compared with the critical value of t for $n_1 + n_2 - 2$ degrees of freedom and the appropriate significance level.

For instance, a correspondence college might try to show that on average the marks of its students taking the examinations of a professional association are no different from those of students undertaking a full or part-time course in universities or colleges. Its investigation, based upon random sampling, produced the following results:

	Correspondence students	Full- or part-time students
n	12	20
$\bar{x}$	38%	45%
$\Sigma(x - \bar{x})^2$	780	1150

For the two-tail test, using a 1 per cent significance level, the critical values of t are $\pm 2 \cdot 75$ (30 degrees of freedom) and the calculated value is found from:

$$t\,(\text{calc.}) = \frac{\bar{x}_1 - \bar{x}_2}{\sigma_{\bar{x}_1 - \bar{x}_2}}$$

which gives

$$t\,(\text{calc.}) = \frac{38 - 45}{\sqrt{\left\{\dfrac{780 + 1150}{12 + 20 - 2}\left(\dfrac{1}{12} + \dfrac{1}{20}\right)\right\}}}$$

$$= \frac{-7}{\sqrt{8 \cdot 58}}$$

$$= \frac{-7}{2 \cdot 93}$$

$$= -2 \cdot 39$$

$-2 \cdot 39 > -2 \cdot 75$ so that the null hypothesis, in stating that there is no difference between the average marks obtained by the two groups, is not disproved at a 1 per cent level of significance. The correspondence college seems to have made its point. By establishing a few β values for $\mu_1 - \mu_2 \neq 0$ the reader may well care to dispute this fact.

2.8.3　Using an F test on the sample variances may in some situations dissuade the researcher from the belief that the assumption of homoscedasticity is a valid one. If the sample variances do differ significantly, then $\sigma_1{}^2 \neq \sigma_2{}^2$ and there is obviously no point in obtaining an estimate of a non-existent common population variance. Nevertheless, one is still justified in undertaking the test for means with $s_1{}^2$ and $s_2{}^2$ used as the respective estimates of the two different population parameters. The calculated value of t is found from

$$t\,(\text{calc.}) = \frac{\bar{x}_1 - \bar{x}_2}{\sqrt{\left\{\dfrac{s_1{}^2}{n_1} + \dfrac{s_2{}^2}{n_2}\right\}}}$$

Establishing the critical value of t is a rather different proposition. The problem is that of deciding how many degrees of freedom should be used, and several solutions have been put forward at different times. One approximation of the number of degrees of freedom may be found from:

$$\text{Degrees of freedom} = \frac{\left(\dfrac{s_1{}^2}{n_1} + \dfrac{s_2{}^2}{n_2}\right)^2}{\dfrac{\left(\dfrac{s_1{}^2}{n_1}\right)^2}{n_1 + 1} + \dfrac{\left(\dfrac{s_2{}^2}{n_2}\right)^2}{n_2 + 1}} - 2$$

(to the nearest whole number).

An alternative approach is to estimate the critical value of t for a 5 per cent level of significance directly from

$$t = \frac{\left(\dfrac{s_1{}^2}{n_1} \times t_1\right) + \left(\dfrac{s_2{}^2}{n_2} \times t_2\right)}{\dfrac{s_1{}^2}{n_1} + \dfrac{s_2{}^2}{n_2}}$$

where t_1 and t_2 are the 5 per cent significance values for t found from entering table 2 with n_1-1 and n_2-1 degrees of freedom.

2.8.4   To illustrate this, suppose that two groups of students are chosen such that their age, sex and general ability conform as far as possible to each other. One group attends a routine lecture course on marginal analysis in economic principles, while the other covers the same ground using a teaching machine. In a test which both groups take, the following results are obtained:

Lecture group	Teaching machine group
$n = 15$	$n = 12$
$\bar{x} = 41$	$\bar{x} = 45$
$\Sigma(x - \bar{x})^2 = 3623$	$\Sigma(x - \bar{x})^2 = 9935$
$s^2 = 258\cdot8$	$s^2 = 903\cdot2$

The calculated F value is $\dfrac{903\cdot2}{258\cdot8} = 3\cdot49$ and the 5 per cent critical value for 11 and 14 degrees of freedom is $2\cdot57$. Thus at a 5 per cent level we must conclude that the population variances are not the same. Therefore the test for the means is undertaken as follows:

$$t = \frac{41-45}{\sqrt{\left\{\dfrac{258\cdot8}{15} + \dfrac{903\cdot2}{12}\right\}}} = \frac{-4}{9\cdot62} = -0\cdot42$$

The number of degrees of freedom for the critical value of t is found from

$$\frac{\left(\dfrac{258\cdot8}{15} + \dfrac{903\cdot2}{12}\right)^2}{\dfrac{\left(\dfrac{258\cdot8}{15}\right)^2}{16} + \dfrac{\left(\dfrac{903\cdot2}{12}\right)^2}{13}} -2 \simeq 19-2 = 17$$

and the critical value itself is $t = 2 \cdot 11$ for a 5 per cent level of significance. Because $0 \cdot 42 < 2 \cdot 11$ we must conclude that the mean achievement from the two methods of teaching does not differ significantly, even though the consistency of achievement is significant.

2.9 Analysis of variance

2.9.1   The major limitation inherent in all the tests of hypotheses which we have examined is that only two means or two proportions or two variances can be considered at one time. If the businessman requires to evaluate the merits of five different manufacturing processes, he will have $^5C_2 = 10$ tests to carry out. An educationalist trying to assess the achievement of students using eight different textbooks will have to undertake $^8C_2 = 28$ tests.

Evidently a method is required for carrying out a test on several sets of observations simultaneously. The *analysis of variance* is the appropriate test where one is interested in arithmetic means. As the name suggests, the approach involves comparing (using the F test) two different estimates of the variance of the assumed common normal populations from which the samples have been drawn (the assumption of homoscedasticity can be avoided in the analysis of variance, but this development is outside the scope of the book).

2.9.2   The first estimate of the common population variance is found from pooling the sample variances, as was done in the t test discussed above. However, instead of finding the weighted average of two sample variances, we now have a number (k) of groups in the analysis of variance each possessing a certain number of observations m_j. The total number of observations in all groups together is $\sum\limits_{j=1}^{k} m_j = n$ or km_j (if $m_1' = m_2 = \ldots = m_k$). This also introduces the following notation. The samples or groups are lettered $j = 1, 2, 3, \ldots, k$, while the observations in each sample are lettered $i = 1, 2, 3, \ldots, m$. Thus x_{ij} is the ith observation in the jth sample and $\bar{x}_{ij}$ is the mean value of the n observations. A specific value in the jth sample will be shown by $x_{.j}$ and the mean value of the observations in the jth sample is therefore $\bar{x}_{.j}$. Now pooling the variances will be achieved from

$$\frac{\sum\limits_{j=1}^{k} \sum\limits_{i=1}^{mj} (x_{.j} - \bar{x}_{.j})^2}{n-k}$$

which will indicate the variability within the groups. In computing the sum of the squares of deviations round the individual sample means it is preferable to use the formula

$$\frac{\sum_{j=1}^{k}\left[\sum_{i=1}^{m_j}x_{.j}^{2}-\frac{\left(\sum_{i=1}^{m_j}x_{.j}\right)^{2}}{m_j}\right]}{n-k}$$

which requires only the sums and sums of squares of the separate series. To illustrate this, let us find the first estimate of the population variance from the following data:

Time taken (minutes) by five groups of eight experienced operators for a set of calculations using five different makes of electric calculating machines

Operator	Make of calculating machine									
	A		B		C		D		E	
	x_1	x_1^2	x_2	x_2^2	x_3	x_3^2	x_4	x_4^2	x_5	x_5^2
1	2·1	4·41	3·2	10·24	5·2	27·04	4·0	16·00	2·5	6·25
2	3·2	10·24	4·0	16·00	2·0	4·00	3·5	12·25	3·1	9·61
3	5·4	29·16	3·5	12·25	3·1	9·61	3·2	10·24	2·4	5·76
4	6·2	38·44	3·6	12·96	4·2	17·64	2·1	4·41	3·0	9·00
5	3·4	11·56	2·8	7·84	4·7	22·09	4·9	·24·01	2·5	6·25
6	2·7	7·29	3·0	9·00	5·4	29·16	3·9	15·21	3·4	11·56
7	4·2	17·64	2·4	5·76	3·2	10·24	2·8	7·84	2·8	7·84
8	2·7	7·29	2·8	7·84	3·9	15·21	4·1	16·81	2·6	6·76
	29·9	126·03	25·3	81·89	31·7	134·99	28·5	106·77	22·3	63·03

$$\sum_{i=1}^{m_j}x_{.j}^{2}-\frac{(\sum x_{.j})^{2}}{m_j}$$

| 14·28 | | 1·88 | | 9·38 | | 5·24 | | 0·87 | |

The estimate of the population variance based upon the variation within groups will be

$$\frac{14\cdot28+1\cdot88+9\cdot38+5\cdot24+0\cdot87}{40-5}=\frac{31\cdot65}{35}=0\cdot90$$

with 35 degrees of freedom. It should be remembered that even when the populations from which these samples are taken are subsequently shown to have means which differ, this estimate of the common variance of population distributions is still quite valid.

2.9.3   The second estimate of the population variance, which is independent of the first, is based upon the variation between the groups. We know from Chapter 1 that $\sigma_{\bar{x}}{}^2 = \dfrac{\sigma^2}{n}$; it then follows that $n\sigma_{\bar{x}}{}^2 = \sigma^2$. The population variance can be found by multiplying the sample size by the standard error of the mean. Now if $\mu_1 = \mu_2 = \mu_3 = \mu_4 = \mu_5$ in the example we are considering, then the five sample means are part of the full sampling distribution of $\bar{x}$. We have a sample of sample means, so that we may obtain an estimate of the sampling distribution variance from

$$\sigma_{\bar{x}}{}^2 = \frac{\displaystyle\sum_{j=1}^{k} (\bar{x}_{.j} - \bar{x}_{ij})^2}{k-1}$$

$\sigma^2 = n\sigma_{\bar{x}}{}^2$ will therefore be estimated from

$$\frac{\displaystyle\sum_{j=1}^{k} m_j (\bar{x}_{.j} - \bar{x}_{ij})^2}{k-1}$$

From a computational standpoint we shall prefer the expansion of this, equal to

$$\frac{\displaystyle\sum_{j=1}^{k} \left\{ \frac{\left(\displaystyle\sum_{i=1}^{m_j} x_{.j} \right)^2}{m_j} \right\} - \frac{\left(\displaystyle\sum_{j=1}^{k} \sum_{i=1}^{m_j} x_{ij} \right)^2}{n}}{k-1}$$

$$= \frac{\dfrac{(\Sigma x_{.1})^2}{m_1} + \dfrac{(\Sigma x_{.2})^2}{m_2} + \ldots + \dfrac{(\Sigma x_{.k})^2}{m_k} - \dfrac{(\Sigma x_{.1} + \Sigma x_{.2} + \ldots + \Sigma x_{.k})^2}{m_1 + m_2 + \ldots + m_k}}{k-1}$$

In the calculating machines example this gives

$$\frac{(29 \cdot 9)^2}{8} + \frac{(25 \cdot 3)^2}{8} + \frac{(31 \cdot 7)^2}{8} + \frac{(28 \cdot 5)^2}{8} + \frac{(22 \cdot 3)^2}{8} -$$

$$\frac{- \dfrac{(29 \cdot 9 + 25 \cdot 3 + 31 \cdot 7 + 28 \cdot 5 + 22 \cdot 3)^2}{40}}{5-1}$$

$$= \frac{7 \cdot 03}{4} = 1 \cdot 76 \text{ with 4 degrees of freedom.}$$

2.9.4   If the null hypothesis that the population means are equal is true, then the two estimates which we have obtained of σ^2 from the variation (within groups $= 0 \cdot 90$ with 35 degrees of freedom; between groups $= 1 \cdot 76$ with 4 degrees of freedom) should differ only within the limits of random sampling. But if the true group means do vary, then the mean square (the estimates of the population variance) between groups will be increased, even though the mean square within groups will be unaltered. To find the reason for this we must refer to 2.6.3, where we mentioned that the sum of the squared deviations from a mean is at a minimum. Now our estimate of

$$\sigma_{\bar{x}}^2 = \frac{\sum\limits_{j=1}^{k}(\bar{x}_{\cdot j}-\bar{x}_{ij})^2}{k-1}$$

rests upon the assumption of a common population mean. If in fact the population means differ, then this formula will give the estimated variation of the means about some average value of these different population means. The common mean in the first case will not equal the average of the means in the second, so that

$$\frac{\sum\limits_{j=1}^{k}(\bar{x}_{\cdot j}-\bar{x}_{ij})^2}{k-1} > \frac{\sigma^2}{n}$$

and

$$\frac{\sum\limits_{j=1}^{k}m_j(\bar{x}_{\cdot j}-\bar{x}_{ij})^2}{k-1} > \sigma^2$$

(where $\mu_1 \neq \mu_2 \neq \mu_3 \neq \mu_4 \neq \mu_5$).
However, the mean square within groups will not be altered because both the $x_{\cdot j}$ and $\bar{x}_{\cdot j}$ in

$$\frac{\sum\limits_{j=1}^{k}\sum\limits_{i=1}^{mj}(x_{\cdot j}-\bar{x}_{\cdot j})^2}{n-k}$$

will be affected by any differences in the population means. The net result will be nil, and we still have an estimate of σ^2; this can be shown by considering the following figures:

x	$(x-\bar{x})^2$	x	$(x-\bar{x})^2$
1	1	2	1
3	1	4	1
3	1	4	1
1	1	2	1
$\overline{8}$	$\overline{4}$	$\overline{12}$	$\overline{4}$

In the second series each value and the mean is one unit higher than in the first, yet the sum of squares in both cases is identical.

Summarizing these points, we can see that if the null hypothesis is untrue, then the mean square between groups is greater than the mean square within groups. We make use of this fact in conducting a one-tail F test on the mean squares, where

$$F \text{ (calculated)} = \frac{\text{Mean square between groups}}{\text{Mean square within groups}}$$

Only if the mean square between groups is actually greater than the mean square within groups, i.e. F (calculated) > 1, will there be any evidence against the null hypothesis and therefore any need to ascertain the critical value of $F_{0.05}$. Notice that the numerator and denominator of the variance ratio are fixed in the analysis of variance; we no longer put the larger variance estimate in the numerator and the smaller in the denominator.

2.9.5 Let us now perform the F test on the earlier data:

$$F \text{ (calculated)} = \frac{1 \cdot 76}{0 \cdot 90} = 1 \cdot 96$$

The critical value of $F_{0.05}$ (one-tail) for 4 and 35 degrees of freedom is $2 \cdot 64$, so that we accept the null hypothesis in this case. There is no evidence to suggest that calculations can be performed on some machines more quickly than on others.

2.9.6 Let us now establish a formal procedure for the analysis of variance. The results are summarized in the following form:

Analysis of variance

	Degrees of freedom d.f.	Sum of squares of deviations s.s.	Estimated variance (mean square) m.s.	Variance ratio v.r.
Variation between groups	4	7·03	1·76	1·96
Variation within groups	35	31·65	0·90	
Total variation	39	38·68		

The total variation is included because the variation within groups and the variation between groups are components of this total variation of the 40 observations round the overall mean. This is shown below:

$$\sum_{j=1}^{k} \sum_{i=1}^{m_j} (x_{ij} - \bar{x}_{ij})^2 = \sum_{j=1}^{k} \sum_{i=1}^{m_j} (x_{\cdot j} - \bar{x}_{\cdot j})^2 + \sum_{j=1}^{k} m_j (\bar{x}_{\cdot j} - \bar{x}_{ij})^2$$
$$\text{total} \qquad = \qquad \text{within} \qquad + \qquad \text{between}$$

A quicker way than the formula method for determining the variation within groups is to compute the total variations from

$$\sum_{j=1}^{k}\sum_{i=1}^{m_j} x_{ij}^2 - \frac{\left(\sum_{j=1}^{k}\sum_{i=1}^{m_j} x_{ij}\right)^2}{n}$$

giving
$$512\cdot71 - \frac{18961\cdot29}{40} = 38\cdot68$$

and then to subtract the sum of squares and degrees of freedom between groups from this value ($n-1$ degrees of freedom). Thus the analysis of variance table will be constructed as follows:

	d.f.	s.s.	m.s.	v.r.
Between groups	$k-1$	$\sum_{j=1}^{k} m_j(\bar{x}_{\cdot j} - \bar{x}_{ij})^2$	$\dfrac{s.s.}{d.f.}$	$\dfrac{\text{m.s. between groups}}{\text{m.s. within groups}}$
Within groups	$n-k$	$\sum_{j=1}^{k}\sum_{i=1}^{m_j} (x_{\cdot j} - \bar{x}_{\cdot j})^2$	$\dfrac{s.s.}{d.f.}$	
Total	$n-1$	$\sum_{j=1}^{k}\sum_{i=1}^{m_j} (x_{ij} - \bar{x}_{ij})^2$		

2.9.7 To demonstrate the method of interpretation when the null hypothesis is rejected, consider the following situation which shows the tensile strength of samples of drive shafts, made from different alloys, which were tested to destruction.

Tensile strength of drive shafts
(100 lbs. in.^{2})

Alloy A	Alloy B	Alloy C	Alloy D
5·8	8·3	4·9	8·7
6·3	6·2	5·2	6·5
5·6	7·9	4·8	9·2
7·2	8·5	5·0	7·3
5·9	7·5	5·3	6·8

	d.f.	*s.s.*	*m.s.*	*v.r.*
Between groups	3	24·98	8·33	12·43
Within groups	16	10·77	0·67	
Total	19	34·42		

The calculated F ratio of 12·43 exceeds by far the $F_{0.05}$ value for 3 and 16 degrees of freedom $= 3·24$, so one may conclude that the mean tensile strength of shafts made from different alloys does vary. We now need to know something about the tensile strength of the individual alloy shafts, so let us put the sample means in a descending order of magnitude:

	Alloy D	*Alloy B*	*Alloy A*	*Alloy C*
Mean strength	7·70	7·68	6·16	5·04

We can use the mean square within groups in estimating the standard error of the difference between these sample means, i.e.:

$$\sigma_{\bar{x}_1 - \bar{x}_2} = \sqrt{\left\{ \frac{\sigma_1^2}{n_1} + \frac{\sigma_2^2}{n_2} \right\}}$$

Because the variances of the population are assumed to be identical this reduces to

$$\sqrt{\left\{ \sigma^2 \left(\frac{1}{n_1} + \frac{1}{n_2} \right) \right\}}$$

giving

$$\sqrt{\left\{ 0·67 \left(\frac{1}{5} + \frac{1}{5} \right) \right\}} = 0·52.$$

Now referring to table 2 we find the $t_{0.05}$ value for 16 degrees of freedom to be 2·12, so a difference between two means of $\pm 2·12 \times 0·52 = \pm 1·10$ will be exceeded by chance with a probability of only 0·05. There will thus be evidence of a significant difference between adjacent means if the gap between them is greater than 1·10. Inspection of the sample means above shows there to be no significant differences between the two alloys D and B which showed the highest tensile strength, but a significant difference between these two and A and between pair A and C.

It should be noticed that we only consider adjacent pairs and not all possible pairs. If, for instance, the highest and lowest means were selected the difference may be highly significant, but we would expect this to be so, for a biased selection of observations from the universe of sample means has been made. From our knowledge of the sampling distribution it will be realized that an apparently significant difference is most likely to be produced by a selection of means from the extremes.

2.9.8   This discussion of the analysis of variance has merely been an introduction to an experimentation technique which has many uses and applications in the social, biological and physical sciences. Further detailed discussion is outside the scope of this book, but it may be worthwhile to indicate briefly the direction of these developments.

The comparison of sets of observations relating to one variable is often complicated by the inability of the experimenter to hold all other factors constant. The number of periodicals purchased by women of different marital status may vary not only as a result of this characteristic, but also because of the differences in age, family structure, and income in each of the marital categories. The effect of these factors is then said to be *orthogonal* to the effect of marital status. The reader should not conclude that the effects are necessarily independent of each other by virtue of their orthogonality.

For example, the corrosion on a metal surface may be reduced either by painting or by treating the surface with a rust killer. If, however, the reduction in the corrosion is greater, when both paint and rust killer are applied, than the sum of the individual reductions resulting from each, then the difference measures the interaction of the two effects.

The means of achieving orthogonality through randomized block analysis, the problems associated with incomplete blocks, and the study of interaction are the corner-stones of more advanced variance analysis.

2.9.9   By way of conclusion, let us briefly consider the assumptions underlying the various tests of hypotheses which have been discussed. In all the z tests for means and proportions we were forced to use large samples, for only with this assumption was the relevant sampling distribution normal. When relaxing this restriction and considering small samples in the t and F tests and the analysis of variance, the sampling distributions conformed to these theoretical forms only if the population distribution was normal. In addition to being normal, it was assumed with one exception that the populations were homoscedastic.

Now if these assumptions are valid, then it can be shown that these tests are the most powerful available. However, the assumptions are rarely tested and are usually accepted implicitly, so obviously we should test for normality and homoscedasticity. There are statistical tests to this end, just as there are tests which may be applied when the above assumptions are disputed. These are the non-parametric or distribution-free tests, which are likely to become more and more frequently used by social scientists (see Chapter 6) and require no knowledge of the parameters of the normally distributed population.

2.10 Mathematical notes

2.10.1 *The variance of the sum or difference of two independent series is equal to the sum of the variances of these series.*

Let the deviations from the means of two series be given by $(x_1-\bar{x}_1)$ and $(x_2-\bar{x}_2)$. The variance of the first series σ_1^2, will be given by the mean of the squared deviations, $(x_1-\bar{x}_1)^2$. Similarly, σ_2^2 is the mean value of $(x_2-\bar{x}_2)^2$. Now the deviation of the sum of each possible pair of x_1 and x_2 values from the mean value of the pairs is defined as $(x_{1+2}-\bar{x}_{1+2}) = (x_1-\bar{x}_1)+(x_2-\bar{x}_2)$. The variance of the sum of the pairs will therefore be found from the mean value of

$$[(x_1-\bar{x}_1)+(x_2-\bar{x}_2)]^2 = [(x_1-\bar{x}_1)^2+2(x_1-\bar{x}_1)(x_2-\bar{x}_2)+(x_2-\bar{x}_2)^2]$$

But $(x_1-\bar{x}_1)=(x_2-\bar{x}_2)=0$ on average. Thus the middle term disappears so that σ_{1+2}^2 is the mean value of

$$[(x_1-\bar{x}_1)^2+(x_2-\bar{x}_2)^2]$$

i.e.
$$\sigma_{1+2}^2 = \sigma_1^2+\sigma_2^2$$

For the difference between the pairs of x_1 and x_2 values the penultimate expression becomes

$$[(x_1-\bar{x}_1)^2-2(x_1-\bar{x}_1)(x_2-\bar{x}_2)+(x_2-\bar{x})^2]$$

The middle term still disappears so that, as before

$$\sigma_{1-2}^2 = \sigma_1^2+\sigma_2^2$$

2.10.2 *To show that* $\Sigma(x-\bar{x})^2 <\Sigma(x-a)^2 \ (a\neq\bar{x})$.

Let
$$u=(x-a) \tag{i}$$
$$d=(x-\bar{x}) . \tag{ii}$$

Subtracting (ii) from (i) gives
$$u-d=(x-a)-(x-\bar{x})=(\bar{x}-a)$$

or
$$u=(\bar{x}-a)+(x-\bar{x})$$

Squaring and summing both sides gives

$$\Sigma(x-a)^2 = \Sigma(x-\bar{x})^2 + 2(\bar{x}-a)\Sigma(x-\bar{x}) + n(\bar{x}-a)^2$$

But $\Sigma(x-\bar{x}) = 0$, so that the middle term on the right disappears.

$$\Sigma(x-a)^2 = \Sigma(x-\bar{x})^2 + n(\bar{x}-a)^2$$

$$\Sigma(x-a)^2 > \Sigma(x-\bar{x})^2 \text{ by } n(\bar{x}-a)^2$$

Only if $a = \bar{x}$ will $\Sigma(x-a)^2 = \Sigma(x-\bar{x})^2$.

2.10.3 *To justify the use of $n-1$ as the divisor of the sum of squared deviations from the sample mean in calculating the variance.*
From 2.10.2, and putting $a = \mu$, we know that

$$\Sigma(x-\bar{x})^2 > \Sigma(x-\mu)^2 \text{ by } n(\bar{x}-\mu)^2 = \frac{(\Sigma x - n\mu)^2}{n}$$

Alternatively,

$$\Sigma(x-\bar{x})^2 = \Sigma(x-\mu)^2 - \frac{(\Sigma x - n\mu)^2}{n} \tag{i}$$

Now it was stated in 2.6.5 that if μ were known, σ^2 would be estimated from $\dfrac{\Sigma(x-\mu)^2}{n}$, so that $n\sigma^2 = \Sigma(x-\mu)^2$.

In sampling theory

$$\frac{\Sigma(\bar{x}-\mu)^2}{n^2} = \frac{\sigma^2}{n}, \text{ but } \frac{\Sigma(\bar{x}-\mu)^2}{n^2} = \frac{(\Sigma x - n\mu)^2}{n^2}$$

Therefore $(\Sigma x - n\mu)^2 = n\sigma^2$
Substituting these values in (i) above gives

$$\Sigma(x-\bar{x})^2 = n\sigma^2 - \frac{n\sigma^2}{n}$$

$$= (n-1)\sigma^2$$

$$\frac{\Sigma(x-\bar{x})^2}{n-1} = \sigma^2$$

2.11 Examples

2.11.1 z tests

(a) The average age of students reading for a first degree in 1952 was established as 21·0 years. In 1967 a nation-wide sample survey revealed the following situation:

Age	Percentage of students (1967)
17	1
18	23
19	38
20–21	19
22–23	11
24–25	8
	100

Sample size: 400

By calculating the mean and standard deviation from the above distribution, suggest whether the average age of students has changed between 1952 and 1967.

(b) As a result of a disagreement between an employers' association and a trade union over the number of hours overtime worked by maintenance workers, a sample of 200 men was taken with the following results:

Number of hours overtime	Number of men
0 but under 4	27
4 but under 6	91
6 but under 8	42
8 but under 10	23
10 but under 14	10
14 but under 20	7
	200

The employers claimed that the mean number of hours of overtime was 5·5. The trade union officials, in disputing this figure, suggested that 6·5 hours was more realistic. What would you decide on the basis of the available evidence, given that the risk of either a type I or type II error should be the same?

(c) The tensile strength of drive shafts made from two different alloys was tested for two samples of 200. The results are shown below:

Tensile strength (lb. in.^{2})	Number of shafts	
	Alloy A	Alloy B
500–549	8	2
550–574	23	16
575–599	62	34
600–624	45	76
625–649	31	43
650–674	20	17
675–725	11	12
Total:	200	200

Is there a significant difference between the mean tensile strength of the shafts made from the two alloys? Comment fully on your results.

(d) The annual net rents of a sample of households in England during 1959 was as follows:

Annual net rent	Percentage of households	
	Decontrolled private tenancies	Council tenancies
£9 or less	1	1
£10–19	10	1
£20–29	12	8
£30–39	10	14
£40–49	6	17
£50–59	8	16
£60–69	8	20
£70–79	4	12
£80–99	11	9
£100 or more	30	2
	100	100
Sample size	118	283

This data is based on random samples. Test the hypothesis that there is no difference in the average annual net rent paid by the two groups of households. Interpret your results, explaining the reasoning underlying the test.

(University of London, 1963)

(e) A commercial television company informs your advertising department that 54 per cent of all viewers will see your advertisement if it is put out between 8.00 p.m. and 9.00 p.m. on Thursday evenings. To check this figure you decide to sample 200 households. If, on the basis of the sample proportion obtained, it is decided to accept that 45 per cent of viewers or less are tuned to this channel during this time you will withdraw the advertisement.

Given that you are prepared to accept a risk of 5 per cent of incorrectly rejecting that $\pi = 54$ per cent, what will be the maximum risk of accepting the television company's claim when in fact 45 per cent or less are watching the programme?

What will be your decision if the sample proportion turns out to be 50 per cent?

(f) A simple random sample of size n drawn from a large population gives a proportion p possessing a certain attribute; develop an argument whereby you would accept as reasonable the hypothesis that the population proportion possessing the attribute is π.

A sample of 100 households showed 13 per cent to be living below a defined poverty line. Does this indicate an improvement over a previously established figure of 15 per cent? If the sample size were 10,000 with the same proportion (13 per cent), explain how and why your conclusions would be altered.

(University of London, 1965)

(g) A marriage survey was undertaken in Great Britain in 1960, covering a random sample of persons age 16 to 59. The following table is based on the answers to one question, which was directed only to married respondents.

Attitude to birth control	Respondents married in 1930–39 (per cent)	Respondents married 1950–60 (per cent)
Full approval	63·5	69·0
Qualified approval	8·0	5·7
Entire disapproval	16·2	13·7
Neutral attitude	9·3	7·6
No opinion	3·0	4·0
Total	100	100
Number of respondents	635	739

Test whether these data provide evidence that a higher proportion of persons married in 1950–60 than of those married in 1930–39 express full approval of birth control. Comment in detail on the conclusions to be drawn from the data and from the results of your test, paying particular attention to any qualifications which you think should be attached to them.

(University of London, 1963)

2.11.2 *Small sample tests*

(a) A company manufacturing computers establishes an aptitude test for potential programmers. During the first three months, 50 candidates take the test. The company is interested in discovering whether candidates with a mathematical background show greater aptitude than those without this background. The results of the tests are as follows:

Marks obtained in aptitude tests	*Candidates*	
	With mathematics	*Without mathematics*
21– 40	1	2
41– 50	3	5
51– 60	9	8
61– 70	8	7
71– 80	2	3
81–100	1	0
101–140	0	1
	24	26

What conclusion should be drawn about the mean score of the two groups and about the variability of scores?

(b) The following data record the productivity of two sets of firms, one using a new and one using an old process:

Number of screws produced per day

New process	Old process
3200	2900
3100	2700
3700	3200
3900	
4000	
4200	

Find if there was any significant difference between the productivities.

(University of Birmingham, 1963)

(c) Use the variance ratio test to decide whether the variability between the tyre wear on three family saloons is significant.

	Make of car		
	A	B	C
Number of car tests	11	25	18
Sum of squares $\Sigma\,(x-\bar{x})^2$ (in millimetres of tread wear)	82	69	70

(d) Interviewers working in four towns give their assessment of the social class of the town. The results are as follows:

Index of social class

Town A	Town B	Town C	Town D
108	102	121	132
105	100	117	117
114	114	113	121
110	108	109	140

Using the analysis of variance, decide whether there are significant differences between the social class of the four towns.

Chapter 3
Statistical sampling practice

3.1 Sampling in specialized fields

3.1.1   In Chapters 1 and 2 we have tried to show the importance of the concepts and applications of statistical sampling as applied generally to the behavioural sciences, and illustrations have shown that the taking of samples is accepted practice in a wide variety of disciplines. Savings in time and money are not the only virtues of sampling: the practice has a number of other advantages. For example, although the cost per unit in a sample is greater than in a complete investigation, the total cost will be less, because the sample will be so much smaller than the statistical population from which it has been drawn. A sample survey can also be completed faster than a full investigation so that variations from sample unit to sample unit over time will largely be eliminated, whilst the results can be processed and analysed with increased speed and precision because there are fewer of them. More detailed information may be obtained from each sample unit and, after detailed checking, queries and omissions can be followed up, a procedure which might prove impossible in a complete survey. Finally, as noted in Chapter 1, sampling is the only feasible possibility where tests to destruction are undertaken or where the population is effectively infinite.

3.1.2   This chapter is devoted to the use of sampling in specific fields. We shall first consider the methods and problems associated with sampling from human populations. The reader will no doubt have been in contact, either personally or via the mass media of communication, with the work of market research agencies, opinion pollsters, radio and television audience researchers and the wide variety of social and economic investigations sponsored by government departments or private research organizations. The majority of this work is based upon sampling, where information from individual people is elicited either by interviewers or through postal questionnaires.

Secondly, we shall examine the role of sampling in statistical quality control. Not only will the construction and interpretation of traditional control charts be considered, but also developments in sequential analysis and cumulative sum techniques as applied to quality control problems.

3.2 Sampling from human populations

3.2.1 Before a sample of people is taken a number of decisions must be made. To begin with, the definition of the sampling unit must be established. The obvious choice would seem to be the natural unit, the individual person, but this is not necessarily the most convenient unit. If random sampling is to be used a sampling frame must be prepared, which includes every member of the human population under study. While electoral lists suffice for some purposes, these are often out of date, and in any case contain only the names of people over the minimum voting age. If a sample of teenagers or of school-children is required, some alternative method must be employed; we might for instance take a sample of households and interview people of the required type living in them, or a sample of schools. The original sampling unit in these examples is not fundamentally the person, but the institution for which a sampling frame exists or may be constructed.

3.2.2 The sampling procedure must also be fixed. Our discussion up to now has been based entirely on simple random sampling, where every population member has the same chance of being included in the sample. For several reasons the use of simple random sampling may be rejected in favour of some alternative sample design. The impracticability or impossibility of producing a satisfactory sampling frame is a very common reason, because a sample based upon an incomplete frame can produce the most misleading results, no matter how large a sample is selected. The investigation carried out by the *Literary Digest* in 1936, prior to the American presidential elections, bears witness to this: although the sample size was ten million individuals, the forecast of the successful candidate was completely incorrect. One of the main reasons was the use of telephone directories and *Digest* subscription lists as the sampling frame, with the result that only the intentions of the wealthier voters were canvassed, accentuated by an 80 per cent non-response rate to the postal questionnaires; it is reasonable to believe that the 20 per cent of replies came from the better educated and politically more highly motivated section of the community.

3.2.3   Even where a simple random sample is feasible, considerations of time and expense may prohibit this design. A simple random sample of the voters in the United Kingdom would possibly involve visits not only to different parts of many cities and towns, but also to outlying and remote regions away from large population centres and off the main transportation routes. The task of locating the residence of the sample units and the need for recalls when these are out would involve hundreds of interviewers in weeks of work.

3.2.4   Possibly the most important reason for a modification to simple random sampling is the lack of homogeneity in human populations. If each possible sample has the same probability of occurring, then there is always the possibility of a very unrepresentative sample being drawn; this occurrence is purely the result of chance and is in no way due to a biased selection of sample units. For example, if one took a sample of 100 students from 3500 registered at a university, it could happen that the 100 were all first year students or all male; the sample could not, in these circumstances, be thought of as representative of all students registered, even though it has been selected on a conceptually sound basis. Where there are well defined categories within the population, such as the year of the course, subject, sex and age, this possibility of an unrepresentative sample can be avoided by taking a predetermined number of sample units from each defined section or stratum. The accuracy of the result, as measured by the standard error, will then be improved. Because human populations do differ noticeably in terms of sex, age, occupation, socio-economic grouping, educational background, geographical location, etc., some degree of stratification will often be employed (more will be said about this in 3.3.2).

3.2.5   The last problem which has to be considered in advance of the survey is the description or measurement of the sample units. While it should be possible to eliminate bias in the decision about the sample unit and in the sampling procedure, it can be very difficult to remove this possibility when the 'examination' of sample units takes place.

Potentially the most dangerous form of bias in this field is interviewer variability. The optimum situation would be such that

our training, testing and briefing all aim at assuring that the overt behaviour of interviewers shall be so standardised that differences between the behaviour of different interviewers shall not lead to their obtaining responses of a different nature. We need to know

(a) that each interviewer is in fact obtaining data of a similar nature, and
(b) that the data is either

(i) of the nature we intended it to be, or at least
(ii) of a nature which we are able to describe.*

Rarely is it possible to claim this degree of perfection. Interviewers do vary considerably in terms of their general background, in their attitudes to the subject of the survey, in their personal demeanour and in their honesty. Bias can result from these and many other factors. Race, accent, mode of dress, tone of voice, self-possession or unsureness can easily cause variations in data provided by different respondents. While careful selection and rigorous training of interviewers can do much to eliminate these inherent causes of bias, and follow-ups by survey supervisors can detect substantial interviewer variability, it should be borne in mind that few research organizations have either the necessary facilities or resources at their disposal to institute appropriate selection methods and to provide adequate training.

No matter how good the interviewer, he will be powerless to prevent bias if his instructions about the conduct of each interview and the phrasing of the questions are unsatisfactory. A party worker engaged in estimating the percentage of the electorate intending to vote for his political candidate will be unlikely to achieve unbiased results if his approach is to first state his personal allegiance and interest and then to ask his question. Many of the voters will answer to his satisfaction just to get rid of him. Similarly the expressed attitude of workers in a car factory to the trade union movement will vary depending on their knowledge of the survey sponsor. They are likely to be far more critical if the union itself is carrying out the investigation than if it has been initiated by the factory management.

Another important point about a survey is that questions should always be phrased to avoid stereotyped answers. A leading question such as 'Are you racially prejudiced?' is hardly likely to produce a meaningful result: only by building up a composite picture of attitudes to such things as mixed marriages, religion, housing and education problems will the respondent's tolerance or intolerance be evaluated. Another difficulty in connexion with question design is lack of immediate understanding. The respondent may well ask for clarification or further information before answering a question, and unless the interviewers have full instructions concerning the amount and type of guidance to be given marked variations may emerge. In this connexion, a valuable aid to the elucidation of correct answers is the inclusion of 'check' questions. For example, a man

* H. D. Willcock (1952), Social Survey Papers, Methodological Series; Paper M. 48, Interviewer Research II, page 1.

asked to provide information about the length of his service with his current firm may easily be a year or more out in his estimate, but if he is also asked to state the date his employment with the firm commenced the investigator has a means of checking the answer.

3.2.6   Bias can also be caused at the 'examination' stage by unrepresentative or inappropriate survey times and the changing outlook of the respondent (or a mixture of the two). A market research investigation initiated to discover what women think of frozen meals should not be conducted at 3.00 p.m. in the afternoon, when only full time housewives will be at home; their opinions may be quite different from those of working wives. Similarly, women may give different answers to questions about the political parties or the trade union movement when asked in front of their husbands than they would if asked when alone. In this case daytime calls would be preferred to evening visits to the house. Many other illustrations of the changing disposition of the respondent are associated with the time of day or week or year, and with the passage of time. A motorist who has had difficulty starting his car on a cold morning, who has been stuck for an hour in a traffic jam, and who has sought vainly for a parking space will be likely to provide quite definite (and possibly unprintable) answers on the topic of motor taxation. Ask the same man the same questions as he drives to the beach during a glorious summer day and he will be more inclined to believe he is getting value for his money.

3.2.7   Finally the problem of late returns and non-response has to be dealt with. An interviewer may have considerable difficulty in contacting the sample units and a decision then has to be taken about how many recalls should be made. From what has already been said it will be realized that the longer the time period over which the survey is conducted, the greater will be the potential variations in attitudes and opinions of the respondents. A defined cut-off date is generally established, but even this is fraught with danger. It may be one particular section of the community which cannot be contacted, such as young married couples without children who are working and therefore away from home during the day, whilst being without the restrictions of a young family they have more freedom for recreational activities in the evenings. Similarly, it may be difficult to find men who work away from home, such as travelling salesmen, or night shift workers who are out in the evening and sleeping during the day. Bias can evidently be produced unless great care is taken and the interviewers are prepared to persevere.

Although the refusal of sample units to co-operate is encountered in interview surveys, it is far more of a problem in mail surveys. It is not uncommon to find the response rate to mail questionnaires as low as 15 or

20 per cent. The provision of information about the purpose of the survey certainly helps by stimulating interest, especially if it can be shown that the work will be to the advantage of the respondent in the long run. Similarly, the respondent will be encouraged to reply if a pre-paid and addressed envelope is sent out with the questionnaire and if some small reward is to be despatched to the respondent on receipt of a completed questionnaire form. In general, however, the response rate will be determined by the sponsor, the subject of the survey and the population to be covered. Official surveys automatically get high response even when they are not backed by the sanctions of the law, and professional bodies also tend to get speedy response from members. All in all, it does seem that the mail survey can be useful under conditions where the sample units are known to have a high motivation to participate, cheapness outweighing the slight increase in non-response. In other circumstances the sponsor should consider whether the saving in cost is worth the risk of bias through high and localized non-response.

3.3 Sample design

3.3.1 When a simple random sample is taken, either by using the lottery method or tables of random numbers, the researcher simply selects n (the sample size) sample units from the sampling frame of N (population size) units which might be included. The sampling fraction, $\dfrac{n}{N}$, gives the probability of including each sample unit in the sample and tells us the proportion of the population included in the sample. However, the numbering of each sample unit can be quite tedious in which case a modification is sometimes introduced. Supposing a sample of 200 people from a list of 5000 is required. The sampling fraction is $\dfrac{200}{5000} = \dfrac{1}{25}$.

Starting at a number, randomly selected, between 1 and 25, the inclusion of every 25th sample units will produce the desired sample size. Suppose that the random number found was 18, then the 18th, 43rd, 68th, 93rd, 118th, . . ., 4993rd names on the list would be interviewed. This systematic or quasi-random sampling is theoretically less sound than simple random sampling, but in practice it is perfectly adequate as long as the sampling list is free from any regular pattern and can be thought of as randomly arranged. This is a reasonably valid assumption for lists of names in alphabetical order or street lists or electoral registers. The major difference between systematic and simple random sampling is that in the former the selection of the first sample unit from the table of random numbers determines the selection of the rest, so that the selection of one sample member is not independent of the selection of any other. As a concomitant observation it also follows that there are only 25 different possible samples in the systematic sampling plan considered above, instead of the astronomical number, any one of which might occur, which exists under simple random sampling.

3.3.2 Stratified sampling

3.3.2.1　It has already been observed that a simple random sample can be unrepresentative. One way of reducing this possibility is to increase the sample size. The other is to stratify. Where there are distinguishable groups (in the sense that they are likely to produce information which is similar within each group but which differs from group to group) within a population to be surveyed, there will be variations in response between these groups, e.g. between the sexes, between different age groups, between different regions and so on. Within each of these categories sample units will also vary among themselves. With a simple random sample both sources of variation are allowed for in the calculated sampling error, but in a stratified plan the possibility of variations between groups has already been eliminated. Each stratum has automatically been represented in the sample in appropriate proportion to its size and homogeneity within the whole population; as a result the sampling error associated with the stratified sample will be smaller.

3.3.2.2　Let us now consider the methods employed in drawing a stratified sample. A college of education is to conduct a survey among past students who are now teaching, the subject being their attitude to current educational policy. It is felt that length of service and the type of school in which they are employed are the two main factors which will affect the attitude of practising teachers to the selection procedure for secondary schools at 11 years of age. The college records show that past students are now teaching in the following numbers in the different types of school:

Length of service (years)	Primary	Secondary modern and grammar	Comprehensive	Total
0–5	525	290	175	990
5–10	250	200	100	550
10–15	260	100	100	460
Total	1035	590	375	2000

Now if the sample required is 400 teachers it would seem logical to take the same proportion of teachers from each group, using a uniform sampling fraction for all strata. The appropriate fraction is given by:

$$\frac{\text{Total sample size}}{\text{Total population size}} = \frac{n}{N} = \frac{400}{2000} = \frac{1}{5}$$

Thus the sample size within each of the nine strata will be as follows:

Length of service (years)	Primary	Secondary modern or grammar	Comprehensive	Total
0–5	105	58	35	198
5–10	50	40	20	110
10–15	52	20	20	92
Total	207	118	75	400

These will be drawn from the respective strata sampling frames.

3.3.2.3   While the gain in precision from this type of stratification is considerable, it can be increased still further when the survey is to produce variable data. If it is known that the variability in response will be greater for some strata than for others it is common sense to realize that a larger sample will be required to achieve adequate coverage where the dispersion is great than when the dispersion is small. If the sampling fraction to be applied to each stratum is made proportionate to the standard deviation of the observations in the stratum, then these considerations will have been taken into account.

Suppose that a survey is to be conducted to establish the income and expenditure pattern of households situated in the area of a local authority.

	Number of households in local authority area	Standard deviation (weekly income in £)
Council tenants	1500	3
Private rented house	750	7
Private rented flat	900	8
Owner occupiers	1850	4
	5000	

If the above strata are distinguished, the respective sampling fractions will be found using the following reasoning. Designating the sampling fraction for the first stratum as $\frac{1}{F}$, then the sampling fractions for the second, third and fourth will be $\frac{7}{3}, \frac{8}{3}$, and $\frac{4}{3}$ larger, i.e. $\frac{7}{3F}, \frac{8}{3F}$, and $\frac{4}{3F}$. Now if the total sample size is to be 500, then

$$\frac{1}{F} \times 1500 + \frac{7}{3F} \times 750 + \frac{8}{3F} \times 900 + \frac{4}{3F} \times 1850 = 500.$$

From this

$$\frac{4500 + 5250 + 7200 + 7400}{3F} = 500$$

and

$$F = \frac{4500 + 5250 + 7200 + 7400}{1500} = 16 \cdot 23$$

The appropriate sample size for the first stratum will be $\frac{1}{16 \cdot 23} \times 1500 = 92$, for the second $\frac{7}{3 \times 16 \cdot 23} \times 750 = 108$, for the third $\frac{8}{3 \times 16 \cdot 23} \times 900 = 148$ and for the last $\frac{4}{3 \times 16 \cdot 23} \times 1850 = 152$.

Compare these with the figures which would have been obtained from the use of a uniform sampling fraction of $\frac{500}{5000} = \frac{1}{10}$.

	Number of households in survey	
	Variable sampling fraction	Uniform sampling fraction
Council tenants	92	150
Private rented houses	108	75
Private rented flats	148	90
Owner occupiers	152	185
Total sample size	500	500

It can be seen at a glance that more households will be interviewed from the strata where this is most needed; that is, those where the chances of an unrepresentative set of responses is higher because of the greater potential variability of response.

3.3.2.4   Two general points in connexion with the use of a variable sampling fraction are important. Firstly, the gain in precision (i.e. the reduction in the sampling error) will assume large proportions only if the differences between the standard deviations of the strata are themselves large. Secondly (and inter-related), there is the problem of estimating the strata standard deviations in advance. We evidently need this information before the survey is undertaken, so reliance must be placed either upon the results of earlier surveys covering the same ground or upon a pilot survey.

3.3.2.5   Although the reduction in the potential sampling error is an important justification for stratification, there are other advantages. Often one is interested in the results of the separate strata. For instance, are women's attitudes different from those of men; do people living in different parts of the country exhibit different characteristics? Administratively, stratification can be helpful because the total number of sample units to be contacted is already apportioned into well-defined groups, each of which may be given to one organizer or interviewer. Finally, many sampling frames are already in a subdivided form, so that an element of stratification is available for immediate utilization.

3.3.3   *Sampling with probability proportionate to size*

When variable sampling fractions are employed in a stratified sampling plan one is often faced with the fact that some of the strata sample sizes are very small. To overcome this it is possible to abandon stratification as such, and select the original sampling unit with probability proportionate to size. For instance, a survey of school children in a city may be undertaken using the institution (i.e. the school) as the first-stage sampling unit Recognizing that some of the schools are very much larger than others, we give a higher probability of selection to those which are large compared with those which are small, and then include the same number of children from each school selected in the final sample. By this means, each child in the city has the same chance of being selected. As a simple illustration, suppose the situation shown in the table overleaf is faced.

The probability of each child being included is 0·0125, and is the same for each school. The practical method of selecting (say) five schools to be included on this basis involves the listing of the schools, the construction of a cumulative frequency table of school children attending, and the selection of five random numbers between one and the total school

School	Size of school (number of children)	Probability of selection of school (P_I)	Size of sample in each school	Probability of child being included (P_{II})	$P_I \times P_{II}$
A	1950	$\dfrac{1950}{4000} = 0.4875$	50	50/1950	0.0125
B	950	$\dfrac{950}{4000} = 0.2375$	50	50/950	0.0125
C	800	$\dfrac{800}{4000} = 0.2000$	50	50/800	0.0125
D	300	$\dfrac{300}{4000} = 0.0750$	50	50/300	0.0125
	$\overline{4000}$				

population. The schools which correspond to these numbers in the C.F. table are then the ones from which the sample of children will be drawn.

School	Size of school	Cumulative total
A	1950	1950
B	950	2900
C	800	3700
D	300	4000
E	1011	5011
F	677	5688
G	828	6516
H	754	7270
I	450	7720
J	320	8040
K	920	8960
L	1450	10410

If the random numbers taken from the tables are 9228, 5450, 6031, 4017 and 0373 then schools L, F, G, D and A will be included.

3.3.4 Multi-stage sampling

3.3.4.1 Another modification to simple random sampling, which like stratification is introduced into most extensive sample surveys from human populations, is 'staging'. For instance, the example considered in 3.3.3

used the school as the original sampling unit; this is one stage in the sampling process. Having selected which schools were to be included in the survey a random sample of children (possibly with stratification) could then be taken from each; this is then the second stage. If a survey of this type was to be carried out on a national scale then another stage might well have been introduced. We could start with the local education authority as the first-stage unit, stratifying according to type of authority (county or county borough), size and geographical region. For each first-stage unit selected we could then stratify the schools by type (grammar, technical, comprehensive, modern), size and location within the authority, finally (as the third stage) selecting the children from within the second-stage units.

3.3.4.2   The main benefit to be derived from multi-stage sampling is that the field work will be carried out in a limited number of areas and/or institutions so that the considerable time and cost of other sampling plans is avoided. Together with this advantage is the fact that a complete sampling frame of individual persons in the population is unnecessary. In the school-children survey the list of pupils is required only for those schools which emerge from the second-stage selection process. All that is required at the first and second stages is a list of L.E.A.s and of schools within these, both of which are readily available.

In many instances, there may be no frame in existence at all. A survey of people living and working in an American city which has been planned on

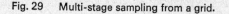

1	2	3	4	5	6	7
14	13	12	11	10	9	8
15	16	17	18	19	20	21
28	27	26	25	24	23	22
29	30	31	32	33	34	35
42	41	40	39	38	37	36

Fig. 29   Multi-stage sampling from a grid.

the rectangular grid basis can be conducted using the blocks as first stage sample units (see fig. 29).

After the first stage selection of blocks 2, 7, 8 and 23 a sampling frame may be constructed for each and a sample taken from this. Because only frames for these 4 are required, a considerable amount of work has been saved. (It should be noticed that all the inhabitants and workers in the four blocks might have been interviewed, in which case we say that a 'cluster sample' has been taken; if, at any stage, all the sample units are included the term cluster sampling may be used.)

The last advantage of multi-stage sampling is that when a first-stage natural sampling unit is absent, a quite arbitrary one may be constructed. We might, for example, superimpose a rectangular grid onto a six-inch ordnance survey map and interview those households falling into the squares selected.

3.3.4.3   The inherent disadvantage of multi-stage or cluster sampling is that the sampling error will be greater than for simple random sampling. The cause of this is not hard to find. When human beings are considered in groups, it is invariably the case that the groups will be made up of people exhibiting the same environment, background and general characteristics. If blocks of flats are used at the first stage it is fairly easy to appreciate that each block will contain a certain type of flat with regard to size, facilities and amenities. It is rare to find one building housing accommodation ranging from luxury apartments with a rent of £1000 p.a. down to bed-sitters letting at £2 10s. 0d. per week.

Because of this feature of clustering, it is quite possible that a highly unrepresentative sample may be drawn, and at any of the stages of the survey design it is therefore always preferable to have a large number of small groups or clusters rather than a small number of large clusters. It also follows that the individuals within the clusters should be as hetero-geneous as possible, which is the opposite requirement to stratified samp-ling where sampling units within strata should be as homogeneous as possible. Practical problems may, of course, prevent these ideals being achieved, in which case the precision of an estimate based upon a multi-stage or cluster sample design will be less than for a simple random sample.

3.3.5   *Multi-phase sampling*

Often it is desirable to interview all the sample units in depth, but time considerations and the burden imposed on the individual respondent prohibit this as a possibility. However, it may prove feasible to ask all the interviewees a basic set of questions, but requesting more detailed information from a subset of the sample using the basic sample as the frame for later sub-samples. Perhaps the best illustration of this method is found in the 1961 census of population in the United Kingdom. All heads of households were required to provide a list of the occupants of the house on census night, but a 10 per cent sample had to give additional information about such things as the facilities and amenities of the house. The multi-phase design is particularly useful where high precision estimates of the population's fundamental characteristics are wanted, but where there is also an interest in related features for which the same degree of precision is unnecessary.

3.3.6 *Quota sampling*

3.3.6.1 All the designs considered so far have finally rested upon random or quasi-random sampling, but in commercial surveys particularly random sampling is often rejected in favour of quota sampling. Here the selection of the sample units from the frame is no longer dictated by chance; indeed, a sampling frame is not used at all, and the choice of the actual sample units to be interviewed is left to the discretion of the interviewer. He or she is, however, restricted by 'quota controls'. An analysis of secondary data will have been conducted to determine the age, sex, marital status, occupational category, and social class composition of the population; one particular interviewer may then be told to interview five married women between thirty and forty years of age, living in town X, whose husbands are professional workers. Obviously these features may apply to many hundreds or even thousands of women, but the selection of the five sample units to be interviewed is nevertheless left to the interviewer.

3.3.6.2 The advantages of quota sampling are self-evident. There is no need to have available or to construct a frame; furthermore, because a frame is not being used it is possible to implement a greater degree of stratification in setting up the controls. When a random sample is to be taken from an electoral register, it may be possible to distinguish male and female voters from their christian names, but no information about age, marital status, etc. will be determinable. This problem can be overcome by utilizing the secondary data from the community as a whole, which contains just this very information.

If random sampling is not employed, however, it is no longer theoretically possible to evaluate a sampling error. Not only is the fundamental method deficient, but the actual practice may also be suspect, for bias may easily be introduced as a result of the unsuitable selection of sample units by the interviewer. Although he may put some qualifying questions to a potential respondent in order to determine whether he or she is of the type prescribed by the quota controls, some features must necessarily be decided arbitrarily by the interviewer, the most difficult of these being social class. If mistakes are being made it is almost impossible for the organizers to detect these, because follow-ups are not feasible unless a detailed record of the respondents name, address etc. has been kept. Falsification of returns is therefore more of a danger in quota than in random sampling.

Although there are these limitations, it has been shown* that a well organized quota survey with well trained interviewers can produce quite adequate results, and because of cost reductions the quota approach is now widely adopted in commercial surveys such as consumer market research.

3.3.6.3   It should be realized that in practice several sampling techniques are incorporated into each survey design, and only rarely will a simple random sample be used, or a multi-stage design find employment without stratification. This will be illustrated in the next section when some actual designs are outlined.

3.4   Practical illustrations of sample design

3.4.1   Let us now consider various surveys carried out to elucidate information on such topics as political opinion, audience size and reaction, educational policy and readership.

These surveys are not selected because they are necessarily any better than others which are available, but simply because they provide a cross-section of the methods and disciplines in which sampling can be an aid.

3.4.2   *Political opinion surveys*

3.4.2.1   National Opinion Polls Ltd conduct regular political surveys, the results of which are reproduced, together with a critical interpretation, in the *Daily Mail.*

Since March 1965 the sample design has been basically two stage. After the selection of the 100 constituencies which are used in every survey from the 618 in Great Britain, 30 voters chosen from the electoral register are interviewed from each one; the total feasible sample size at each survey is thus 3000.

*F. Edwards (1953), 'Aspects of random sampling for a commercial survey', *Incorporated Statistician*, vol. 4, pp. 9–27.

For the selection of a representative cross-section of constituencies the following principles were followed:

All the constituencies were listed in the order of the Registrar General's Standard Regions. Within each of the ten Standard Regions and Scotland, Borough constituencies were placed before County Constituencies. Within the resulting 22 categories, constituencies were listed according to the ratio of Conservative to Labour votes cast at the General Election of 1964.

The sample drawn (a systematic probability sample) gave each constituency a chance of selection proportionate to the number of electors it contained. This method ensures that the correct proportion of Borough and County constituencies are drawn within each region. It also ensures that, within groups of Borough or County constituencies in any one region, a wide cross-section of constituencies is selected – varying from the safely held seats to the more marginal ones.*

Although the same hundred constituencies are used in each survey, the sample of thirty electors from each is different every time. The method of selecting these from the electoral register is a modification of systematic sampling and varies between county and borough constituencies. In the county constituencies a random number between one and the total electorate is taken and the person corresponding to this number on the register together with every tenth person (up to a total of 30 in all) is included. In the borough constituencies the same procedure is followed, but only 15 sample units are selected. The second 15 are chosen by first adding to or subtracting from the random number half of the total electorate; this number determines the 16th person to be included, the remaining 14 being at ten-person intervals thereafter.

3.4.2.2   The following procedure is employed for obtaining a political opinion survey:

(a) The questionnaire contains four or five regular questions about voting intentions, attitude to the prime minister and leader of the opposition, and issues which are politically topical.

(b) Each interviewer has 4–5 days in which to contact and interview about thirty people.

(c) No substitutes are allowed when sample units are out or away from home. As a result of several recalls, an 85 per cent response rate is obtained from those people still living at the address given in the register.

(d) Twelve area supervisors are employed to check the work of the interviewers.

* 'Simple Guide to the Workings of an N.O.P. Political Survey', National Opinion Polls Ltd, 1965.

3.4.3 *Audience size and reaction*

3.4.3.1 The Audience Research Department of the British Broadcasting Corporation undertakes surveys to estimate the size of the audience attracted by every programme transmitted on sound radio and all television channels, as well as assessing the audience reaction to B.B.C. programmes. To obtain the audience size estimate a stratified quota sample of 4000 people is undertaken daily, questions being posed on the previous day's listening and viewing; as the intention is to estimate the total audience no one is excluded, even if he or she does not possess a radio or television set. The sample size is determined by the need to achieve variable strata sample sizes not only in B.B.C.'s seven regions but also amongst adults and children by sex, age, social class and occupation. The strata sample size averages out at 400 and *ad hoc* investigations (on such things as the 8.00 p.m. news bulletin) suggest that this is adequate to eradicate the majority of sampling variations.

3.4.3.2 The following procedure is employed for obtaining an audience size survey:

(a) The interviewing is spread among approximately 300 interviewers who contact a different group of 10–15 people each day; the interviewers are themselves drawn from a pool of personnel which is partly reconstituted at three-weekly intervals. Of the 300 actively engaged, 200 interview adults and 100 (all women) interview children over five.

(b) The daily interviewing takes the interviewer 2–3 hours, and the interviews may, within certain limits, be undertaken at any time; calls at houses after 9.00 p.m. are generally discouraged and children must be contacted between 4.30 p.m. and 6.30 p.m.

(c) Those engaged in the interviewing of children are not given quotas in the usual way but are given a list of houses at which to call. All the children (five to fourteen years) in each household are then interviewed, a procedure which usually produces about a dozen interviews per day.

(d) Each interviewer is provided with a 'log' of the previous day's programmes so that the respondent is aided in recalling what was heard and/or seen, using the principle of 'association of ideas'.

(e) The work of each interviewer is scrutinized by full-time supervisors before acceptance, and a random 5 per cent of adults whom interviewers claim to have seen are contacted by post to provide verification of this fact.

3.4.3.3 The audience reaction investigation is conducted on a fundamentally different basis. Instead of different people being contacted each day, a 'panel' of listeners and viewers has been established to provide continuous information on their reactions to programmes. In practice, there are several different panels. The viewing panel has 2000 members, the B.B.C.2 panel has 700 members, and the listening panel for the Home, Light and Network Three programmes is regionally organized with 600 members in each of the seven B.B.C. regions; finally, the Third Programme has a panel of 1000. Panel members (who are recruited by direct appeal or invitation) are selected on much the same lines as interviewees for the audience-size surveys, thus ensuring representation of the whole population. Each listening panel member serves for approximately fifteen months, whilst the viewer members have a fixed period of six months' service.

The following procedure is employed for obtaining an audience-reaction survey:

(a) Weekly batches of questionnaires are sent to panel members about a wide variety of programmes. It is stressed that there is no obligation for members to listen to or watch programmes which would not normally be heard or seen. Pre-panel listening or viewing habits should be maintained.

(b) The questions vary in detail, but all contain a space for comments and a 'reaction summary' in the form A+, A, B, C and C−. Strictly, B is the norm and A+ and C− should only be used to express exceptional enjoyment and extreme dislike. In practice there tends to be a distortion to the A+ end of the scale, but as the final appreciation index is purely a comparative measure it is not important.

(c) The presentation of the reaction index not only gives the 'average' reaction but also indicates the spread of reactions over the five-point scale. As we have noticed before, two distributions may give the same average while being very different in structure.

3.4.4 *Educational policy*

3.4.4.1 In the report of the Committee on Higher Education under the chairmanship of Lord Robbins several sample surveys were undertaken to provide information about the student population engaged in advanced courses, one of which was for students in institutions of further education. The table shown overleaf summarizes the sample design employed.

For this two-stage and stratified design (with variable sampling fractions) the sampling frames were, for the first stage, a list of all the colleges running advanced courses which was prepared by the Ministry of Education and the Scottish Education Office, and, for the second stage, lists of students on advanced courses within each selected college.

3.4.4.2 The following procedure was employed to obtain this educational survey:

Summary of sample design

Stage	Unit	Stratification	Number of units selected	Method of selection
I	Colleges or group of colleges	Type of college		
		Colleges of Advanced Technology	9	All
		Regional colleges and regional colleges of art	16	1 in 2
		Other colleges in England and Wales stratified into (i) Counties (ii) County Boroughs	58	Proportional to number of advanced students in 1960–1
		Central Institutions (Scotland)	6	1 in 2
		Further Education Centres (Scotland)	2	Proportional to number of advanced students in 1960–61
		Total	91	
II	Individuals	Method of study		Variable sampling fraction giving an *overall* sampling fraction of
		Continuous full time	1930	1:12
		Sandwich	1681	1:6·7
		Part-time day	1006	1:45
		Evening	1344	1:38
		Total	5961	

(Report of the Committee on Higher Education, appendix 2(B), annex GG, table GG.1)

(a) Out of the 118 colleges making up the 91 institutions, interviews were conducted in 115 (the remainder either had no advanced courses, refused to co-operate, did not reply, or were too late supplying information). The effective student response rate from these 115 was 91 per cent. Those students who had left the course and students engaged on non-advanced courses were not part of the effective sample, and the balance of 9 per cent resulted either from non-contact or (in 124 cases) from absence of the students concerned on the industrial training period of a sandwich course.

(b) Where there was distinct conflict between the type of course (full time, sandwich etc.) indicated by the college register and that reported by the student in question, the information collected was excluded from the results.

(c) The fieldwork was carried out over a period of four months from February to May 1962. Information not available on 31 May 1962 was omitted to avoid delay in collating and analysing the results.

3.4.5 *Readership*

3.4.5.1 The Institute of Practitioners in Advertising carry out annual national readership surveys based upon interviews with approximately 16,000 adults in Great Britain. The results provide readership estimates for the various periodicals covered, both in relation to the whole sample and to the various sub-groups within it.

The sample design in 1965 was stratified and multi-stage, with systematic selection of first and second stage units; probability was proportionate to size at the first stage, which was made up of 624 polling districts from the 614 parliamentary constituencies located south of the Caledonian canal. The constituencies were listed by standard region, by five types within each standard region (i.e. conurbation, mixed conurbation and other urban, other urban, mixed other urban and other rural, other rural), and in ascending order by the percentage Labour vote at the 1959 general election (for conurbation and urban constituencies) and by the percentage of the electorate living in rural administrative districts (for constituencies which were partly rural).

A cumulative sum of electorates for the constituencies within each standard region was formed, and from a random starting point a systematic selection with an appropriate constant interval produced the 624 constituencies for which polling districts were to be identified. (Some constituencies were included more than once and some not at all.)

A cumulative sum of electorates in each of the selected 575 constituencies was then prepared according to the order of polling districts on the register, and the numbers found above were used to identify the appropriate polling districts.

The second stage was the selection of individuals. From the register for each polling district, a systematic selection was used with the sampling interval determined by the required sample size. In addition to the elector, one non-elector living in the household was also interviewed (either someone between 16 and 21 years of age, or someone not on the register for some other reason).

3.4.5.2   The following procedure is employed to obtain a readership survey:

(a) Where there was more than one 'non-elector' living in the household, a procedure was evolved to make the selection of the person to be interviewed random. The results of the interviews from these non-electors was weighted according to the number of non-electors in the household divided by the number of names in the register leading to that household.

(b) A special procedure was adopted when the elector chosen to be included in the sample lived at an hotel, was in hospital or was resident at some other institution.

(c) When the chosen elector had moved, no attempt was made to follow him or her to the new address nor was any substitute taken.

(d) Up to two recalls were allowed in attempting to make the contact. If the elector or 'non-elector' still had not been interviewed, the attempt was then abandoned.

(e) The questionnaire sought to establish whether the respondent had looked at any copy of the periodical considered (i.e. he had been exposed to an advertisement appearing in the issue) during a period from the day of interview back to the interval at which the periodical appeared. As an *aide-mémoire* a booklet with reproductions of the mast heads of each periodical included was shown to the respondent.

(f) The final report was based upon the combined results of interviews carried out between 1 January and 31 December 1965.

3.5 Statistical quality control

3.5.1   In 2.1.3 we discussed in general terms the conceptual problems involved in statistical quality control. The practical procedures and methods of this industrial application of sampling theory will now be developed at greater length. Before doing so, however, we must discuss the logical foundations of the technique. Firstly, we should stress the impossibility of constructing a machine or process which is capable of producing exactly identical units of output. A multitude of independent and minor factors influence the quality of the finished product, although it should be stressed that this inherent variability in quality can be distinguished from variations caused by controllable major imperfections. For instance, little can be done about the very slight wear on the cutting edge of a machine tool which results from the production of each unit of output; the variations in quality from one unit to the next will in part be accounted for by this, but other factors include the machine temperature, the machine speed, the hardness of the metal of the component, the efficiency of lubrication, etc. On the other hand, if the cutting edge disintegrates completely this is immediately apparent from the appearance of large variations in quality.

By making spot checks on the output of any machine or process at regular intervals, and by keeping a continuous record of the results, the existence of controllable or assignable causes of variations in quality should become immediately or cumulatively apparent. If the inspection is undertaken on the factory floor during the production process, defective production will not only be detected, but avoided. It is too late to shout 'stop' when a whole day's output has to be rejected as a result of subsequent inspection.

3.5.2 *The control chart*

A spot check and inspection of one unit of output is likely to be of dubious value. For this reason, small samples of the output are taken and the quality characteristic exhibited by the sample is recorded on a control chart. These quality characteristics vary in form. They may be the result of precisely measuring sample units (producing sample means) or the outcome of an 'all or nothing' procedure, which classifies each component as either perfect or defective (thus producing a sample proportion of defective items). In either case the chart will be so constructed that only significant departures from an established norm in the sample quality characteristic will provoke a suspicion of trouble. Conventionally it is

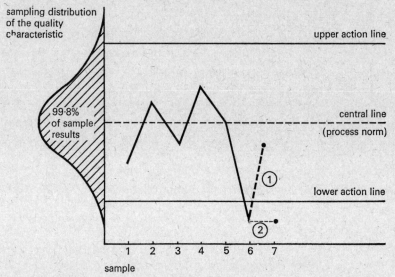

Fig. 30   The control chart.

accepted that 99·8 per cent of possible sampling variation should be expected and tolerated for individual samples; action lines will therefore be set so that the probability of a false alarm and inappropriate action is kept at a level of 0·001 for a plot on the chart at each extreme. Fig. 30 shows schematically a control chart constructed on this basis.

The plotted quality characteristics for the first five samples are quite satisfactory. The sixth point, however, lies outside the lower action line. The inspector must decide whether this is the one sample out of a thousand which he can expect to lie outside the lower action line, or whether this is a true reflection of change in the process quality norm. He cannot afford to wait until the next inspection period to answer this if the process is out of control, so he must immediately seek further evidence by examining other samples. If the additional samples indicate a return to the normal pattern of variation (① in fig. 30) then he concludes that a false alarm has occurred. If, on the other hand, he finds other delinquent sample results (② in fig. 30) then he has corroborative evidence to support his original suspicion of trouble.

3.5.2.1   In practice the inspector may not wait for a point to fall outside the action lines. A shift in the process norm may be indicated by a trend of values. In this connexion warning lines, in addition to the action lines, are frequently placed on the chart. Only one sample result in twenty should lie between both the warning and action lines if the process is in control; if more appear, as in fig. 31, then a drift in quality is occurring.

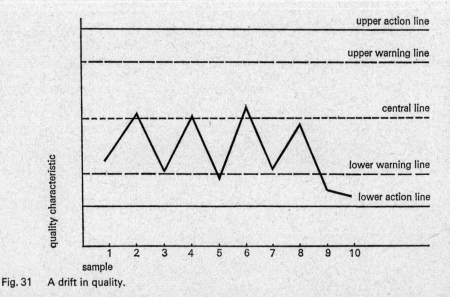

Fig. 31   A drift in quality.

3.5.2.2   Although the detection of unsatisfactory quality is the main reason for keeping continuous control charts, it is not the exclusive reason. The appearance of high quality output may provide important information to the mechanical engineer who designs the equipment, or to the person responsible for purchasing the raw materials used. As much information as possible about changes in production conditions, raw materials, personnel etc. should be included on the chart, if the full potential of the scheme is to be realized.

3.5.3   Control charts for variables

Let us now examine the procedures used in establishing the various limits on control charts where the sample quality characteristic results from precise measurement of the sample units. The main sample statistic indicating quality will be the mean value of the sample measurements, but we must not forget that very different distributions can produce the same mean. Side by side with the mean sample value we should have a measure of the dispersion within each sample, and for this the range is employed (principally because of the simplicity of its calculation, an important consideration under factory conditions). We shall therefore need to consider the construction of both mean and range charts.

3.5.4   The mean and range charts

3.5.4.1   An engineering firm wishes to establish a control scheme over its output of push-rods for motor engines. The first step should be to take 30 samples, each of say 5 rods, from the manufacturing process while it is in control (as far, that is, as control is possible in advance). Each rod, of nominal diameter $\frac{1}{4}$ in., is measured on a device which records (in thousandths of an inch) not the actual diameter but deviations from the nominal value. The results are shown below.

Sample	1	2	3	4	5	6	7	8	9	10
	2	0	2	1	2	3	-2	3	3	1
	-1	0	1	-1	2	-5	-2	2	-1	0
	-2	0	-1	-2	0	0	-1	-3	0	0
	1	1	-2	-3	0	-1	0	1	0	0
	0	1	0	3	0	-2	0	1	-1	-2
Mean $\bar{x}$	0	0.4	0	-0.4	0.8	-1.0	-1.0	0.8	0.2	-0.2
Range R	4	1	4	6	2	8	2	6	4	3

145   Statistical sampling practice

Sample	11	12	13	14	15	16	17	18	19	20
	1	0	5	-1	4	-1	1	2	1	2
	-2	0	1	-1	1	-1	1	-3	1	-1
	-3	0	2	2	2	2	-3	4	0	0
	-4	1	-2	0	0	1	0	0	0	0
	1	1	-2	-1	-1	0	1	-1	3	2
Mean $\bar{x}$	-1·4	0·4	0·8	-0·2	1·2	0·2	0	0·4	1·0	0·6
Range R	5	1	7	3	5	3	4	7	3	3

Sample	21	22	23	24	25	26	27	28	29	30
	4	2	-1	1	0	-4	2	-2	3	5
	-1	2	0	2	5	-1	1	-1	-2	2
	0	-1	0	0	-3	0	0	0	-3	-1
	0	0	0	3	1	1	1	1	1	0
	1	1	-1	-2	1	-1	1	1	1	0
Mean $\bar{x}$	0·8	0·8	-0·4	0·8	0·8	-1·0	1·0	-0·2	0	1·2
Range R	5	3	1	5	8	5	2	3	6	6

The process norms will be the mean of the sample means, $\bar{\bar{x}}$, and the mean of the sample ranges, $\bar{R}$.

$$\bar{\bar{x}} = \frac{6\cdot4}{30} = 0\cdot21 \qquad\qquad \bar{R} = \frac{125}{30} = 4\cdot2$$

The action and warning lines for both charts might be set by establishing the form of the sampling distribution of means and ranges and estimating the respective standard errors. In practice, tables of conversion factors have been compiled which enable these limits to be fixed from no more than a knowledge of $\bar{\bar{x}}$ and $\bar{R}$. These are shown on the next page.

The limits will be found as follows:

Mean chart

Upper and low action $= \bar{\bar{x}} \pm A_1\bar{R}$ $0\cdot21 \pm 0\cdot59 \times 4\cdot2 = 2\cdot69$ and $-2\cdot27$
Upper and low warning $= \bar{\bar{x}} \pm A_2\bar{R}$ $0\cdot21 \pm 0\cdot38 \times 4\cdot2 = 1\cdot81$ and $-1\cdot39$

Range chart

Upper action	$= D_1 \times \bar{R}$	$2 \cdot 34 \times 4 \cdot 2 = 9 \cdot 8$
Upper warning	$= D_2 \times \bar{R}$	$1 \cdot 81 \times 4 \cdot 2 = 7 \cdot 6$
Lower warning	$= D_3 \times \bar{R}$	$0 \cdot 37 \times 4 \cdot 2 = 1 \cdot 6$
Lower action	$= D_4 \times \bar{R}$	$0 \cdot 16 \times 4 \cdot 2 = 0 \cdot 7$

Conversion factors

Mean chart		Range chart					*d*
Sample size	Action 99·8% A_1	Warning 95% A_2	Upper action 99·8% D_1	Upper warning 95% D_2	Lower warning 95% D_3	Lower action 99·8% D_4	Mean sample range ($\bar{R}$) to population standard deviation (σ)
2	1·94	1·23	4·12	2·81	0·04	0·00	1·13
3	1·05	0·67	2·99	2·17	0·18	0·04	1·69
4	0·75	0·48	2·58	1·93	0·29	0·10	2·06
5	0·59	0·38	2·36	1·81	0·37	0·16	2·33
6	0·50	0·32	2·22	1·72	0·42	0·21	2·53
7	0·43	0·27	2·12	1·66	0·46	0·26	2·70
8	0·38	0·24	2·04	1·62	0·50	0·29	2·85
9	0·35	0·22	1·99	1·58	0·52	0·32	2·97
10	0·32	0·20	1·94	1·56	0·54	0·35	3·08

The control lines should now be put on the control charts, together with the observed sample statistics as they appear (fig. 32). The reader should not be alarmed that the control lines on the range chart are not equidistant from $\bar{R}$; the sampling distribution of sample ranges is skewed when the sample size is small and this is reflected in the position of the control lines. Nor should the reader doubt the validity of placing lower action and warning lines on the range chart. Although the appearance of sample units exhibiting little or no variability is unlikely to cause positive action, the manufacturer would nevertheless probably try to discover what is producing such a satisfactory situation (it might be someone 'rigging' the samples!).

In this instance it can be seen that the 30 samples exhibit only a controlled pattern of quality variation, so that the control limits have been based on a stable situation. It may occur in other cases that one or more of the sample means or ranges will lie outside the upper and lower action lines. When this happens, the extreme samples should be ignored and the control limits recalculated on the basis of the remaining mean or range

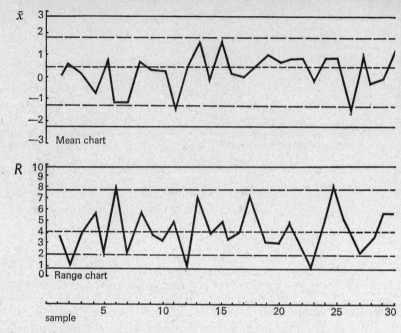

Fig. 32   The mean and range charts.

values. If they are left in, then the control lines will be too far away from $\bar{\bar{x}}$ and $\bar{R}$ so that the probability of 0·001 of a sample mean lying outside each will be reduced.

3.5.4.2   Once the chart has been established the maintenance of continuous control over quality is largely a matter of routine. There is, however, one practical problem which we have failed to discuss. The relationship between a designer's tolerance limits and the chart action limits is important, and failure to appreciate the differences between the two concepts can result in considerable confusion.

The designer of the push-rod, in our example, will undoubtedly have decided that one hundred per cent accuracy is an impossibility. He will be quite happy if each of the rods deviates around the normal value of $\frac{1}{4}$ in. by no more than 5 thousandths of an inch each way. The question to be answered is whether the evidence of the 30 samples indicates that the process is capable of producing to these limits. The reader may look at the upper and lower action limits (2·69 and −2·27 thousandths of an inch) on the mean chart and immediately conclude that these tolerance limits can be achieved. This first impression is not necessarily correct. The action lines reflect the variability in the sample means and not in the original values; if the latter is measured by the population standard deviation σ, then the former is smaller by $\frac{1}{\sqrt{n}}$, i.e. $\frac{\sigma}{\sqrt{n}}$.

It would seem that we need an estimate of the population standard deviation. Once more the conversion factors come to our aid. On page 147 the tables show a column headed 'd Mean sample range ($\bar{R}$) to population standard deviation (σ)'. For each sample size a conversion factor is given which should be divided into the mean range, i.e.

$$\sigma = \frac{\bar{R}}{d}$$

This gives $\frac{4 \cdot 2}{2 \cdot 326} = 1 \cdot 81$. On the assumption that the distribution of the individual diameters is normal we know that almost all the push-rods will fall within a range of $6\sigma = 6 \times 1 \cdot 81 = 10 \cdot 86$ thousandths of an inch. The total range allowed by the designer is ± 5 thousandths $= 10$ thousandths of an inch, so that it is inevitable that some of the output from this machine will lie outside these design limits. The firm has three choices: it can accept this

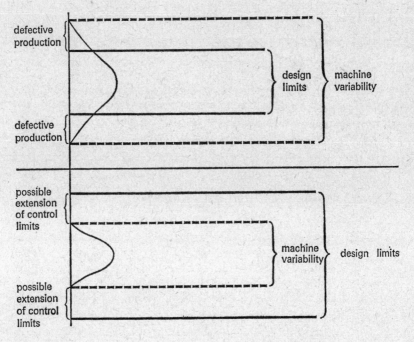

Fig. 33

situation, the designer can reduce his standards, or a more refined machine or process can be introduced. The main thing to bear in mind is that the construction of the control charts in no way improves on the inherent variability of the machine; bringing in the action lines will only produce more false alarms and thus hamper production.

3.5.4.3   If the designer's tolerance limits happen to be greater than the inherent machine variability, then obviously the action lines might be extended. Even if a drift away from the nominal value is occurring this may not have immediate consequences and may be tolerated. The two opposing situations are shown schematically in fig. 33.

3.5.5   Control chart for attributes

3.5.5.1   Where the test of quality is of the accept/reject type, the statistic measuring the sample quality will be the proportion p. A control chart showing the proportion of defective units in each sample will have to be prepared. For example, suppose that electric light bulbs are being produced in large numbers and that at hourly intervals 100 bulbs are tested, with the following results:

Sample	1	2	3	4	5	6	7	8	9	10
Number of bulbs defective	6	5	6	8	3	3	7	5	11	0
Sample proportion (p)	0·06	0·05	0·06	0·08	0·03	0·03	0·07	0·05	0·11	0

Sample	11	12	13	14	15	16	17	18	19	20
Number of bulbs defective	2	8	4	9	6	5	9	0	7	5
Sample proportion (p)	0·02	0·08	0·04	0·09	0·06	0·05	0·09	0	0·07	0·05

Sample	21	22	23	24	25	26	27	28	29	30
Number of bulbs defective	6	7	2	6	8	6	3	8	8	5
Sample proportion (p)	0·06	0·07	0·02	0·06	0·08	0·06	0·03	0·08	0·08	0·05

Sample	31	32	33	34	35	36	37	38	39	40
Number of bulbs defective	0	6	1	8	4	5	3	0	1	4
Sample proportion (p)	0	0·06	0·01	0·08	0·04	0·05	0·03	0	0·01	0·04

The total number of bulbs which failed to light up when tested was 200. The total number tested in these 40 samples was 4000. The process proportion of defective bulbs is therefore given by

$$\bar{p} = \frac{200}{4000} = 0{\cdot}05$$

Now in this case the binomial sampling distribution of proportions is approximately normal ($n\bar{p} = 5$) so that the control limits may be set as follows:

Action lines | Warning lines
99·8% | 95·0%

$$\bar{p} \pm 3 \sqrt{\left\{ \frac{\bar{p}(1-\bar{p})}{n} \right\}} \qquad \bar{p} \pm 2 \sqrt{\left\{ \frac{\bar{p}(1-\bar{p})}{n} \right\}}$$

(Note that adding to and subtracting 3 and 2 standard errors from $\bar{p}$, instead of 3·09 and 1·96, is justified because the sampling distribution is only an approximation of the normal distribution.)

This gives us:

$$\text{Upper action line} \;= 0{\cdot}05 + 3 \sqrt{\left\{ \frac{0{\cdot}05(0{\cdot}95)}{100} \right\}} = 0{\cdot}12$$

$$\text{Upper warning line} = 0{\cdot}05 + 2 \sqrt{\left\{ \frac{0{\cdot}05(0{\cdot}95)}{100} \right\}} = 0{\cdot}09$$

$$\text{Lower warning line} = 0{\cdot}05 - 2 \sqrt{\left\{ \frac{0{\cdot}05(0{\cdot}95)}{100} \right\}} = 0{\cdot}01$$

$$\text{Lower action line} \;= 0{\cdot}05 - 3 \sqrt{\left\{ \frac{0{\cdot}05(0{\cdot}95)}{100} \right\}} = 0$$

A negative sample proportion is impossible in practice so that the bottom line is zero. In any case the reader will appreciate that the lower the sample proportion the happier the inspector will be (subject to the reservations

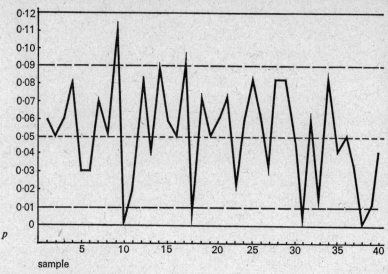

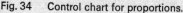

Fig. 34   Control chart for proportions.

made earlier about unexpectedly high quality). The control chart will now look like fig. 34.

3.5.5.2   The normal approximation to the binomial sampling distribution of proportions cannot invariably be applied. In quality-control situations the process norm in terms of $\bar{p}$ is very often extremely small and the sample size insufficiently large to eliminate the skewness of the sampling distribution. In this case the reader will appreciate the considerable tedium involved in working out each term in the full expansion from

$$P\left(\frac{x}{n} = p\right) = \frac{n!}{x!(n-x)!}\,\bar{p}^{x}(1-\bar{p})^{n-x}$$

in order to establish the positions of the control lines. However, in these circumstances the binomial distribution is approximated by the Poisson distribution (see 3.8), where

$$P\left(\frac{x}{n} = p\right) = \frac{a^{x}e^{-a}}{x!}$$

($a = n\bar{p}$ = mean number of defective items in each sample, and

$$e = \frac{1}{0!} + \frac{1}{1!} + \frac{1}{2!} + \frac{1}{3!} + \ldots + \frac{1}{n!} + \ldots$$

$$= 2\cdot7183 = \text{base of Napierian logarithms;}$$

these values of e^{-x} are shown in table 4, page 379).

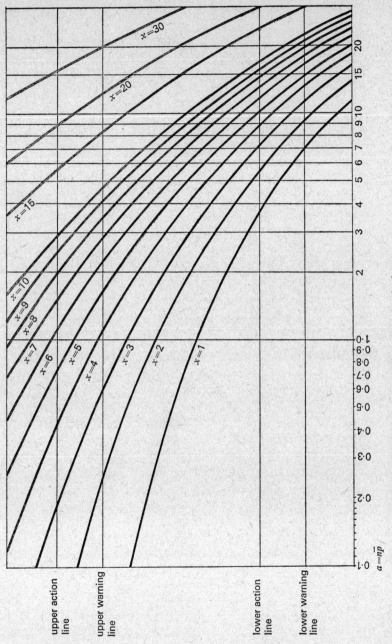

upper action line

upper warning line

lower action line

lower warning line

$a = \overline{np}$

Fig. 35   Modified Poisson probability paper (control line determination).

To illustrate the closeness of the two distributions consider a situation where the sample size is 20 and $\bar{p} = 0.05$.

	Binomial $P\left(\dfrac{x}{n}\right) = {}^{20}C_x\,0.05^x 0.95^{20-x}$	Poisson $P\left(\dfrac{x}{n}\right) = \dfrac{1.0^x . e^{-1.0}}{x!}$
0	0·3585	0·3679
1	0·3773	0·3679
2	0·1887	0·1839
3	0·0596	0·0613
4	0·0133	0·0153
5	0·0023	0·0031
6	0·0003	0·0005
7	0·0000	0·0001
	1·0000	1·0000

3.5.5.3   Although the calculation of the Poisson probabilities is very much more straightforward than in the case of the binomial expansion, this is not the main advantage of using the approximation. More important is the fact that specially prepared graph paper is available which shows the probability of occurrence of different x values for different values of $a = n\bar{p}$. Fig. 35 shows a modified version of this paper as relevant to the control chart problem. To establish the position of the control lines, follow the value of $a = n\bar{p}$ vertically until it cuts the action and warning lines probability values. Reading between the curved lines then fixes the value of x in the proportion $x/n = p$. In the example cited above $a = n\bar{p} = 1.0$ so that the upper action line lies between 5/20 and 6/20, the upper warning line between 3/20 and 4/20 and the lower control lines disappear at zero. Although a sample proportion between 5/20 and 6/20 and between 3/20 and 4/20 cannot occur it is worth placing the control lines between these limits, so that a value of six defectives or four defectives out of twenty is already indicating a potential lack of control. A chart showing these limits is given in fig. 36 together with the hypothetical sample results which generated the $\bar{p} = 0.05$.

3.5.5.4   While discussing the Poisson chart one final point should be considered. In fig. 35 values of $a = n\bar{p}$ which are greater than 5 have been included. This may seem peculiar to the reader, who will naturally conclude that for $n\bar{p} > 5$ the normal approximation to the binomial distribution will be appropriate. However, there are occasions when the Poisson distribution will be the only distribution which can be considered for the establishment of control limits. In these circumstances the Poisson is not an approximation to the binomial distribution; the binomial is irrelevant. A situation of this type will occur when an inspector is checking the number of faults in a piece of linen cloth or in the finish of a car. Here there is no sample size, n; all we can say is that there are a certain number of faults in a particular piece of cloth or on a particular car. We have the value of a immediately, so that the values of x which indicate the positions of the action and warning lines can be read off fig. 35. It seems from this consideration that the inclusion of values of $a > 5$ is justified.

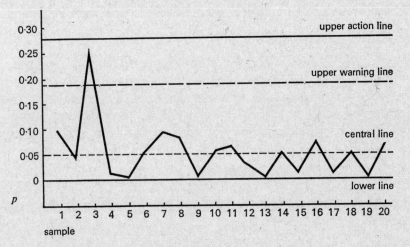

Fig. 36.   Control chart for proportions (Poisson approximation)

3.6   Cumulative sum charts

3.6.1   So far, emphasis has been given to the establishment of action lines such that inappropriate action will have been taken only once every thousand times when the plot falls outside one or the other of the control lines. Put another way, we have set the α risk of a type I error at a probability of 0·002 (taking into account the two tails). From Chapter 2 we know that the type I error in quality control constitutes the producer's risk. We have said nothing about the level of consumer's risk: the situation where defective production is being produced even though the sample quality characteristic has failed to indicate the drift out of control. Where the design limits exceed the standard control limits, it is possible to calculate both the sample size and the position of the action lines in order to achieve some desired balance between the α and β errors. However, without doing

155   Statistical sampling practice

this we were able to indicate in 3.5.2.2 that the detection of a drift in quality is made possible by studying the trends of sample results within the action lines. This is further facilitated by studying not the individual sample results in isolation but the cumulative sum of sample results.

3.6.2   As with standard control charts, the cumulative sum technique studies the data in the sequence of occurrence. From each sample result a constant (e.g. the process norm) is subtracted and the resulting answers aggregated consecutively. These cumulative sums are then plotted on a chart so that any changes in a process norm can immediately be detected and the magnitude of the change evaluated. This is best illustrated by a simple example. Suppose that a process has produced the following sample mean results:

(*Constant K = 16*)

$\bar{x}$ (millimetres)	$\bar{x} - K$	Cumulative sum
13	−3	−3
17	1	−2
14	−2	−4
19	3	−1
15	−1	−2
12	−4	−6
18	2	−4
13	−3	−7
15	−1	−8
14	−2	−10
19	3	−7
12	−4	−11
19	3	−8
16	0	−8
20	4	−4
13	−3	−7
17	1	−6
19	3	−3
14	−2	−5
21	5	0

The standard control chart for these data is shown in fig. 37 and it appears that the process is in control (in terms of the sample means). In fact, although the process norm is 16 millimetres (also revealed by these 20 samples) the mean of the first ten sample means is only 15 millimetres while the mean of the last ten is 17 millimetres. The continuous control

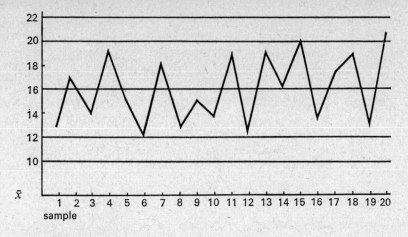

Fig. 37   The standard control chart.

chart has failed to reveal this drift, first below the process norm and then above this figure. The calculation and plotting of the cumulative sum values will, however, give an immediate impression of the changes in the process mean which has occurred. It can be seen in fig. 38 that the general slope of the first ten 'cusum' points is downwards while for the second ten

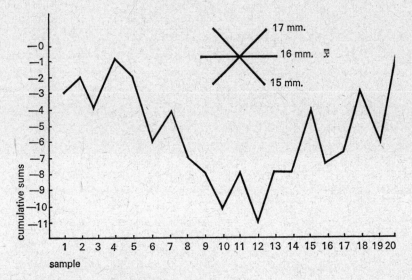

Fig. 38   The cumulative sum chart.

it is upwards. With $K = 16$ (the process norm) the cusum would be horizontal if the process stayed in control (i.e. if we had only sampling variability round 16 millimetres); the fall of 10 millimetres for the first ten points shows that over this range the process mean is $16 - \dfrac{10}{10} = 15$ millimetres, while the increase of 10 millimetres for the second ten indicates a process mean of $16 + \dfrac{10}{10} = 17$ millimetres. As an aid in evaluating the actual process mean over any range it is useful to insert a gradient scale as in fig. 38.

3.6.3   Although we were able to decide after these 20 samples had been taken that the process mean had changed twice, we cannot afford in practice to wait for this amount of evidence. A procedure for coming to a decision speedily has to be devised. The method is to construct a 'V mask' which is superimposed over the cusum chart with the vertex of the V a predetermined distance horizontally in advance of the last plot. As long

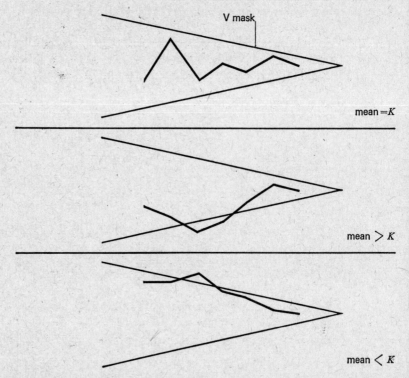

Fig. 39   The V mask.

as all the previous points lie inside the V then the process is assumed to be operating in control, but if any part of the cusum path is outside the V shape it indicates either an increase or decrease in the process mean (fig. 39).

Evidently the appearance of cusum points outside the V mask will depend upon the distance that the vertex of the V is ahead of the last point, and also upon the angle between the arms of the V. In practice these two parameters may be set to achieve any acceptable probability of real changes going undetected and/or false alarms occurring; the method of fixing them is, however, beyond the scope of this text (see Suggestions for further reading, page 372).

3.7 Sequential analysis

3.7.1 We have hitherto concentrated on quality-control inspection on the shop floor. Preventing unsatisfactory quality is obviously better than detecting it after a batch of items has been produced. Nevertheless the consumer will frequently require to make his own check on quality as goods are received, and just as the manufacturer has to rely upon sample evidence, so the consumer will also utilize this method of economizing on inspection effort. We shall look in outline at one method used in acceptance sampling that, like the cumulative sum technique, relies upon an aggregative impression of quality. This procedure is based on the inspection of one

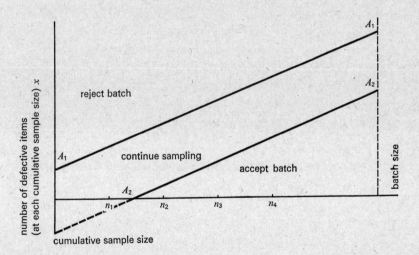

Fig. 40 The sequential chart.

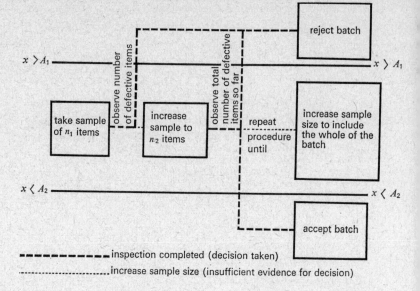

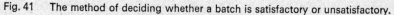

- - - - - - - - - - inspection completed (decision taken)
.... increase sample size (insufficient evidence for decision)

Fig. 41   The method of deciding whether a batch is satisfactory or unsatisfactory.

item at a time from a batch and is known as sequential analysis; it can best be discussed by using the schematic representation illustrated in figs. 40 and 41.

3.7.2   A sequential chart is divided into three parts by two lines, A_1 and A_2. After the first sample of n_1 items has been taken the number of defectives is observed, and if this figure is higher than the position of the A_1 line then the whole batch is rejected as possessing a higher percentage of defective items than is tolerable. If the number of defectives is less than A_1, then a larger sample is needed before a conclusive decision can be taken (notice that no decision to accept the batch can be made until the A_2 line crosses the horizontal axis). In the latter case additional sample units will be taken and the procedure repeated. The sample size is increased progressively until the number of defectives is such that a decision is made, or alternatively until the whole batch is inspected in which case the true percentage defective will have been established and a completely accurate conclusion about the batch quality drawn. At worst, in other words, a 100 per cent inspection of each batch will be required, but at best a small sample may suffice to provide the necessary evidence for a decision.

3.7.3   The establishment of the A_1 and A_2 lines is outside the present field (see Suggestions for further reading, page 372), so it will suffice to say that the method enables the probability of incorrectly accepting or rejecting a batch to be fixed and be balanced against the probability of continuing the procedure when a decision should already have been made.

3.8 Mathematical note

The Poisson distribution approximates the binomial distribution when n is large and π ($\bar{p}$ in quality control) is small.

$$\text{Let} \quad P\left(\frac{x}{n}\right) = \frac{n!}{x!(n-x)!}\, \pi^x\,(1-\pi)^{n-x} \qquad \text{Binomial}$$

$$= \frac{n(n-1)(n-2)\ldots(n-x+1)}{x!}\, \pi^x\, \frac{(1-\pi)^n}{(1-\pi)^x}$$

$$= \frac{n\pi(n\pi-\pi)(n\pi-2\pi)\ldots(n\pi-x\pi+\pi)(1-\pi)^n}{x!(1-\pi)^x}$$

Now we have defined $a = n\pi$. Thus the last expression becomes

$$\frac{a(a-\pi)(a-2\pi)\ldots(a-x\pi+\pi)(1-a/n)^n}{x!(1-\pi)^x}$$

Since π is small $(1-\pi)^x \doteqdot 1$ and $a(a-\pi)(a-2\pi)\ldots(a-x\pi+\pi) \doteqdot a^x$. The expression now becomes

$$\frac{a^x(1-a/n)^n}{x!}$$

But when n is large

$$(1-a/n)^n \doteqdot 1-a+\frac{a^2}{2!}-\frac{a^3}{3!}+\ldots+\frac{a^n}{n!} = e^{-a}$$

$$\text{Thus} \quad P\left(\frac{x}{n}\right) = \frac{a^x e^{-a}}{x!} \qquad \text{Poisson}$$

3.9 Examples

3.9.1 *Sample design*

(a) Design a questionnaire for sending to a random sample of manufacturing firms in an industrial city in order to elucidate information on their utilization of published statistics in planning for the future. Assuming this to be a postal questionnaire, what would you do in attempting to assure a high response rate?

(b) A survey of dwellings is to be undertaken in a suburb made up almost exclusively of council houses and flats built in the middle 1920s. The object of the survey is to evaluate occupancy (particularly under-occupancy) and attitudes to rehousing. The electoral registers for the forty polling districts are available. Suggest ways in which a sample might be taken bearing in mind that the number of interviewers is limited.

(c) The following information is to be used in defining the quota controls for a survey of the inhabitants of a town. If the sampling fraction is to be 1/10, set out the different strata and calculate the strata sample sizes.

Size of town: 20,000 inhabitants; 50 per cent male, 50 per cent female; 70 per cent working class, 30 per cent white-collar workers.

Age distribution: 25 per cent under 16 years, 60 per cent between 16 and 65 years, 15 per cent over 65 years.

(d) A survey of schools is to be conducted in order to discover the staff–pupil ratio. The area to be covered contains 2500 schools. They are broken down in the following way:

	Number of schools	Estimated standard deviation (number of pupils per class)
Urban areas		
Primary	850	2
Secondary		
Non-selective	580	4
Selective	300	5
Rural areas		
Primary	480	9
Secondary		
Non-selective	210	5
Selective	80	6

Twenty per cent of the schools will be interviewed. How many schools of each type would be interviewed if (a) a constant sampling fraction is employed and (b) a variable sampling fraction is employed?

(e) Carry out a survey of the results of political opinion polls over the last few years. How far have they correctly reflected the intentions of voters as shown by the results of elections?

3.9.2 Control charts

(a) An engineering company produces six-inch high-tensile bolts. Samples of 4 are taken at 30 minute intervals and are tested to destruction. The following are the mean and range breaking strengths of the first 30 samples (in lb./in.²).

Sample	Mean	Range	Sample	Mean	Range
1	2002	32	16	2008	30
2	1993	25	17	1983	10
3	2010	10	18	1989	10
4	2001	28	19	1992	15
5	1983	27	20	2008	23
6	2015	13	21	2010	30
7	2012	14	22	1990	26
8	1996	30	23	2014	15
9	1999	22	24	1988	23
10	2005	20	25	1992	34
11	2001	31	26	2010	25
12	1988	27	27	2013	26
13	1989	8	28	1987	31
14	2015	11	29	1990	28
15	2000	22	30	2017	14

Construct mean and range charts for this process and plot the sample results on these. The bolts are intended to have a tensile strength of 2000 ± 50 lb./in.². Is the process capable of producing to these specifications?

(b) Samples of 200 ball bearings are tested periodically to determine whether they are spherical. After 20 samples the number of unsatisfactory ball bearings in each sample was found to be:

Sample	1	2	3	4	5	6	7	8	9	10
Number of defective ball bearings	18	21	10	35	30	27	14	16	8	21

Sample	11	12	13	14	15	16	17	18	19	20
Number of defective ball bearings	23	14	18	21	32	15	20	25	13	19

Construct a control chart for the proportion (or number) of defective ball bearings, remembering that any sample falling outside the action lines should be eliminated and the control lines recomputed.

(c) Samples of 20 precision pressure gauges are thoroughly tested at hourly intervals. The number of gauges not up to specification are as follows for the first 25 samples.

Sample	1	2	3	4	5	6	7	8	9	10	11	12	13
Number of gauges rejected at each sample	0	1	0	0	2	1	0	0	1	2	0	1	1

Sample	14	15	16	17	18	19	20	21	22	23	24	25
Number of gauges rejected at each sample	0	0	0	1	0	0	2	0	3	0	1	0

Using the Poisson approximation to the binomial distribution, calculate the action and warning lines for a control chart of the proportion (or number) of gauges rejected.

(d) The manageress of a large typing pool decides to institute quality checks on the work of the copy typists. Each girl has 5 pages of typing checked for mistakes every day. If it is accepted that 2 mistakes per page constitutes satisfactory quality, what would you do about a girl whose work over a five day week exhibited the following number of mistakes:

3, 2, 0, 0, 1, 2, 3, 2, 5, 0, 0, 0, 1, 1, 4, 5, 1, 2, 0, 0, 0, 1, 4, 5, 0.

(The reader is recommended to construct an outline control chart for this situation.)

(e) In an activity study of the working of a packing department, 5 men are observed for 5 minute periods randomly selected every hour. The observation periods over a working week show the average number of cartons packed per man to be as follows:

Observation period	1	2	3	4	5	6	7	8	9	10
	17	12	8	10	14	3	13	3	11	5

Observation period	11	12	13	14	15	16	17	18	19	20
	15	9	14	8	12	16	7	13	20	9

Observation period	21	22	23	24	25	26	27	28	29	30
	14	15	8	14	9	18	14	7	11	19

Observation period	31	32	33	34	35	36	37	38	39	40
	13	9	4	13	11	8	13	3	7	11

Construct a cumulative sum chart for this data and suggest what the cusum path conveys to you about the work of this department over one week.

Chapter 4
Non-linear and multiple regression and correlation

4.1 Limitations of the two-variable linear model

4.1.1 The many reservations and limitations to be borne in mind when considering the two-variable linear model of regression and correlation were outlined in *Statistics for the Social Scientist: 1 Introducing Statistics*. These reservations fall into three broad categories. Firstly, the relationship between two variables is not necessarily linear. Although this is the most common form, it is always unwise to conclude out of hand that there is little or no association when the coefficient of linear correlation is low, as it may well be that some non-linear relationship provides a better fit of the data being considered. Consequently, as a first step, one should always plot a scatter diagram to ascertain whether the data is more likely to conform to the linear than to some non-linear pattern.

Secondly, it is assumed in the two-variable model that the dependent variable can be explained mainly in terms of one 'independent' variable. On the basis of this assumption it is accepted that the multitude of other factors which may influence the dependent variable are individually of only minor importance and collectively sum to zero. In the social sciences this will rarely be a valid assumption. Human behaviour is a complex phenomenon and it is not likely to be determined predominantly in terms of one single variable factor. A family's level of expenditure will largely depend upon its income, but it will also be influenced by the size of the family, its age distribution, and its social class. Similarly, a man's performance at his job may be determined in part by his experience of the job, but his natural aptitude and intelligence and the amount of training he has received are also important and must be taken into account: they cannot be relegated to the place of minor self-cancelling effects without the loss of considerable definition in the regression equation. As a general rule it should always be realized that a low coefficient of correlation may be attributed not only to the existence of little association between variables but also to the incorrect specification of the regression model, since important variables may have been omitted or insignificant variables included.

The third and final reservation concerns the problems associated with sampling. In many situations the estimated regression equation and coefficient of correlation will have been obtained from sample data. Before statistically acceptable conclusions can be drawn from the calculations we need to know whether the relationships discovered could have occurred by chance as a result of the random sampling procedure, even though there is no real association between the variables being studied. We will also need to calculate confidence limits for the regression equation and correlation coefficient so that we are aware of the degree of error associated with estimates and predictions based upon the sample statistics obtained.

4.1.2 In this chapter we shall extend the regression and correlation theory to answer in part these three difficulties. We shall examine in detail some of the more important non-linear relationships which will be encountered in the social sciences and indicate in outline those which may be met with less frequently. The extension of the two-variable linear model to a consideration of multiple (and, in passing, partial) linear regression and correlation will be achieved by the development of the three-variable case. This restriction on the number of variables is necessitated partly by the magnitude of the computational task which will face the student lacking a knowledge of linear algebra.

However, a discussion of the three-variable model and an indication of the extensions involved in including more variables will provide the necessary principles on the basis of which the interested student can extend his knowledge to a more general level. Mention will be made of multiple non-linear regression and correlation, and coverage of the inference problems will include the form of significance tests for the regression coefficient b, and the correlation coefficient r, together with the establishment of confidence limits for (i) the parameters α and β in the regression models, (ii) predicted y values, and (iii) the population coefficient of correlation ρ.

4.2 Non-linear regression: the linear transformations

4.2.1 It was shown in *Statistics for the Social Scientist: 1 Introducing Statistics* that time series data showing a constant proportionate rate of change can be graphed in the form of a straight line if the logarithms of the variable values rather than the absolute values are plotted against the time periods. This semi-logarithmic presentation is equally valid in the construction of a scatter diagram. The regression model then assumes that a unit increase in the x variable will be accompanied by a fixed proportional increase in the y variable; the regression equation when plotted on this basis will be linear even though the natural scale presentation is non-linear. The great advantage of this and other linear transformations is that the least squares method, as developed for the two-variable linear model, and the product moment coefficient of correlation can be applied without elaboration or modification.

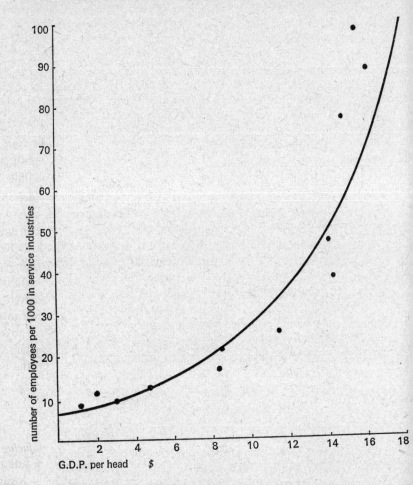

Fig. 42

4.2.2   Consider the following hypothetical data (which is graphed in fig. 42) showing the proportion of the working population in the service industries and the gross domestic product per head in twelve countries.

Gross domestic product per head (hundreds of dollars)	Number of employees per 1000 in service industries
2·0	12·0
1·2	8·0
14·8	76·4
8·3	17·0
8·4	21·3
3·0	10·0
4·8	12·5
15·6	97·3
16·1	88·0
11·5	25·0
14·2	38·6
14·0	47·3

It is immediately evident that the pattern of points on this scatter diagram is non-linear. However, if we plot the points on semi-log scale as in fig. 43 we find that the basic curvature has been drastically eliminated. We have our first justification for believing that the proportion of workers occupied in the service industries may rise at a constant percentage with increases in the level of wealth as measured by gross domestic product per head.

Reasoning on an *a priori* basis may also suggest that this is a reasonable assumption. As a nation develops economically and socially from one of self-supporting family or village groups to a highly specialized industrial community, it is inevitable that many service industries must grow. The division of labour, necessitating the exchange of goods, will generate a whole host of specialist buyers, hauliers, wholesalers and distributors. The basic transactions will need to be financed, and this will result in the establishment of banks, discount houses, insurance companies, hire purchase companies and so on. It seems that in the process of economic development, which produces an increase in real wealth, the number of workers gainfully employed in providing services to the community will rise. What is more, the rise in the numbers is unlikely to be linear; a snow-ball effect may produce the constant proportionate rate of increase which we find in this situation.

4.2.3   Now the only difference between the simple linear model and the

169   Non-linear and multiple regression and correlation

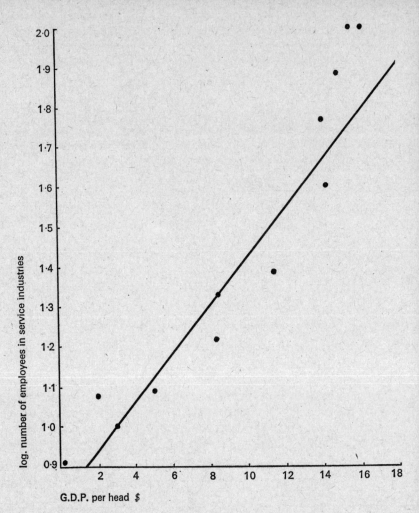

Fig. 43

semi-logarithmic model is that in our calculations the y values will be replaced by the logarithms of those values, so that

$$\log y = \log a + x \log b$$

Taking the antilogs of both sides of this expression will then enable the general form of the non-linear regression equation to be stated as

$$y = ab^x$$

In the example cited the tabulated calculations are as follows:

x	y	$\log y$	x^2	$(\log y)^2$	$x\log y$
2·0	12·0	1·0792	4·00	1·1647	2·1584
1·2	8·0	0·9031	1·44	0·8156	1·0837
14·8	76·4	1·8831	219·04	3·5461	27·8699
8·3	17·0	1·2304	68·89	1·5139	10·2123
8·4	21·3	1·3284	70·56	1·7646	11·1586
3·0	10·0	1·0000	9·00	1·0000	3·0000
4·8	12·5	1·0969	23·04	1·2032	5·2651
15·6	97·3	1·9881	243·36	3·9525	31·0144
16·1	88·0	1·9445	259·21	3·7811	31·3065
11·5	25·0	1·3979	132·25	1·9541	16·0759
14·2	38·6	1·5866	201·64	2·5173	22·5297
14·0	47·3	1·6749	196·00	2·8053	23·4486
113·9		17·1131	1428·43	26·0184	185·1231

As a first step, we calculate the coefficient of linear correlation between x and $\log y$ from

$$r_{\log y . x} = \frac{n\Sigma x\log y - \Sigma x \Sigma \log y}{\sqrt{[\{n\Sigma x^2 - (\Sigma x)^2\}\{n\Sigma(\log y)^2 - (\Sigma\log y)^2\}]}}$$

$$= \frac{(12)(185\cdot1231) - (113\cdot9)(17\cdot1131)}{\sqrt{[\{(12)(1428\cdot43) - 113\cdot9^2\}\{(12)(26\cdot0184) - 17\cdot1131^2\}]}}$$

$$= \frac{272\cdot2951}{\sqrt{\{(4167\cdot95)(19\cdot3626)\}}} = \frac{272\cdot2951}{284\cdot0816} = 0\cdot959$$

This provides us with ample evidence to support our belief that such a relationship between y and x is acceptable (notice that the coefficient of determination is 0·920); the reader may care to compute the coefficient of linear correlation between y and x to check that it is lower. We can now calculate the constants in the regression equation from

$$\log b = \frac{n\Sigma x\log y - \Sigma x\Sigma\log y}{n\Sigma x^2 - (\Sigma x)^2}$$

and

$$\log a = \frac{\Sigma\log y - \log b\Sigma x}{n}$$

giving

$$\log b = \frac{272\cdot2951}{4167\cdot95} = 0\cdot0653$$

and

$$\log a = \frac{17\cdot1131 - (0\cdot0653)(113\cdot9)}{12} = 0\cdot8063$$

The regression equation is therefore
$$\log y = 0 \cdot 8063 + 0 \cdot 0653x$$
which is shown on fig. 43. Taking the antilogs gives
$$y = (6 \cdot 401)(1 \cdot 162)^x$$
which is shown on fig. 42 (note that if $\log b$ or $\log a$ equals $-2 \cdot 3410$ we are faced with a problem because the decimal part (mantissa) of a logarithm is always positive. The characteristic may be negative (i.e. $\bar{2}$ or $\bar{3}$) so that instead of moving negatively from $\bar{2}$ (i.e. $\bar{2} - 0 \cdot 3410$) we move positively from $\bar{3}$ (i.e. $\bar{3} + [1 \cdot 0000 - 0 \cdot 3410] = \bar{3} \cdot 6590$). The same point is reached and we have conformed with the rules of logarithms. Now the anti-log of $\bar{3} \cdot 6590$ is $0 \cdot 004560$.

The value of b indicates that a unit increase in gross domestic product per head will be accompanied by a $16 \cdot 2$ per cent increase in the number of men per thousand working in the service industries.

4.2.4 *The double-log transformation*

4.2.4.1 Instead of transforming only the y variable to a log form, it is sometimes found that a scatter diagram on a double log scale more exactly eradicates the curvature found in the natural scale presentation. This is the case for the following data:

Year	Number of employees in manufacturing industry (millions)	Production in manufacturing industry in U.K. (1958 = 100)
1934	5·8	48·8
1936	6·3	58·2
1938	6·5	59·9
1946	6·8	62·7
1948	7·6	72·3
1950	8·0	82·1
1952	8·0	82·5
1954	8·5	93·5
1956	8·7	99·1
1958	8·6	100·0
1960	9·0	114·6
1962	9·1	115·2

Key Statistics of the British Economy 1900–1962; produced by London and Cambridge Economic service for *The Times Review of Industry and Technology*, 1963

Now the regression model on the assumption of the double-log transformation is

$$\log y = \log a + b \log x$$

which gives

$$y = ax^b$$

as the non-linear equation. The calculation of $r_{\log y . \log x}$, $\log a$ and b involves the use of $\log x$ and $\log y$ instead of the original x and y values.

x	y	$\log x$	$\log y$	$(\log x)^2$	$(\log y)^2$	$(\log x)(\log y)$
5·8	48·8	0·7634	1·6884	0·5828	2·8507	1·2889
6·3	58·2	0·7993	1·7649	0·6389	3·1149	1·4107
6·5	59·9	0·8129	1·7774	0·6608	3·1592	1·4448
6·8	62·7	0·8325	1·7973	0·6931	3·2303	1·4963
7·6	72·3	0·8808	1·8591	0·7758	3·4563	1·6375
8·0	82·1	0·9031	1·9143	0·8156	3·6645	1·7288
8·0	82·5	0·9031	1·9165	0·8156	3·6730	1·7308
8·5	93·5	0·9294	1·9708	0·8638	3·8841	1·8317
8·7	99·1	0·9395	1·9961	0·8827	3·9844	1·8753
8·6	100·0	0·9345	2·0000	0·8733	4·0000	1·8690
9·0	114·6	0·9542	2·0591	0·9105	4·2399	1·9648
9·1	115·2	0·9590	2·0614	0·9197	4·2494	1·9769
		10·6117	22·8053	9·4326	43·5067	20·2555

$$r_{\log y . \log x} = \frac{n\Sigma \log x \log y - \Sigma \log x \Sigma \log y}{\sqrt{[\{n\Sigma(\log x)^2 - (\Sigma \log x)^2\}\{n\Sigma(\log y)^2 - (\Sigma \log y)^2\}]}}$$

$$= \frac{(12)(20 \cdot 2555) - (10 \cdot 6117)(22 \cdot 8053)}{\sqrt{[\{(12)(9 \cdot 4326) - (10 \cdot 6117)^2\}\{(12)(43 \cdot 5067) - (22 \cdot 8053)^2\}]}}$$

$$= \frac{1 \cdot 0630}{\sqrt{(0 \cdot 5830 \times 1 \cdot 9987)}}$$

$$= 0 \cdot 985$$

$$b = \frac{n\Sigma \log x \log y - \Sigma \log x \Sigma \log y}{n\Sigma(\log x)^2 - (\Sigma \log x)^2}$$

$$= \frac{1 \cdot 0630}{0 \cdot 5830} = 1 \cdot 8233$$

$$\log a = \frac{\Sigma \log y - b \Sigma \log x}{n}$$

$$= \frac{22 \cdot 8053 - (1 \cdot 8233)(10 \cdot 6117)}{12} = 0 \cdot 2881$$

The regression equation is given by

$$\log y = 0.2881 + 1.8233 \log x$$

or $\quad y = 1.941 x^{1.823}$

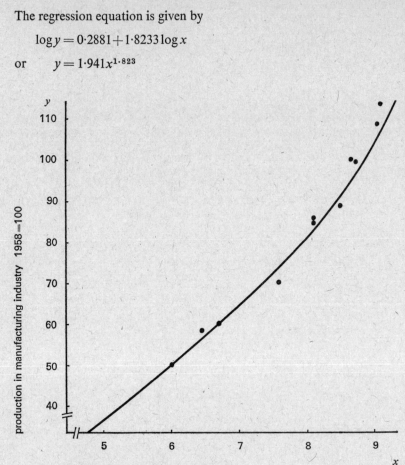

Fig. 44

These are the equations plotted in figs. 45 and 44 respectively. It would appear that over the years 1934 to 1962 a 1 per cent increase in the labour force employed by manufacturing industry has resulted in a 1·823 per cent increase in production. In other words, labour productivity has been increasing as a result of the more efficient labour utilization associated with the use of automated and mass production techniques. This in its turn has only been achieved by the gradual conversion of manufacturing industry from a labour-intensive to a capital-intensive basis.

4.2.4.2   At this point, let us make some general observations about the semi-log

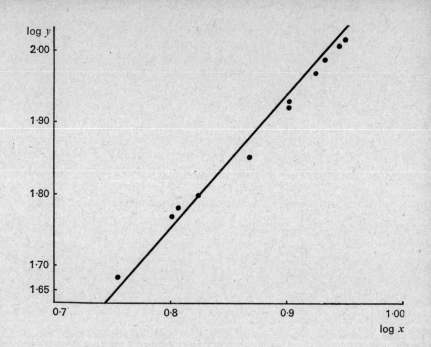

Fig. 45

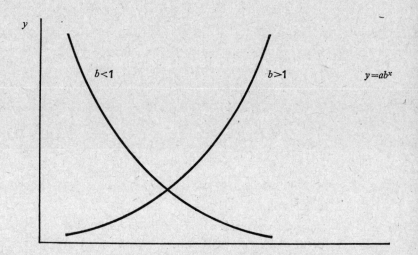

Fig. 46   The forms of $y = ab^x$.

175   Non-linear and multiple regression and correlation

and double log transformations. First we should notice that the slope of a curve in the form $y = ab^x$ must be continually decreasing when $b < 1$ (i.e. when the curve is downwards from left to right) and continually increasing when $b > 1.0$ (i.e. when the curve is upwards from left to right). This is shown in fig. 46.

It is not possible for the equation $y = ab^x$ to generate a curve which is sloping upward from left to right, yet continually decreasing in slope (or vice versa, although this is not true of the less common semi-log transformation in x, i.e. $y = a + b \log x$) nor can it generate a curve which has a negative slope at one point and a positive slope at another (this second observation is equally true for all the linear transformations considered in the present section). Fig. 47 illustrates these situations.

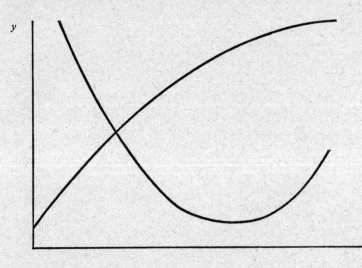

Fig. 47   Forms not generated by $y = ab^x$.

The double log transformation of $y = ax^b$ can, on the other hand, exhibit slopes that are either continually increasing or decreasing when b is positive, although only continually decreasing slopes occur when b is negative (figs. 48 and 49).

For $y = ax^{-b}$ and $b = 1$ it should be noticed that we have a rectangular hyperbola, i.e. a situation where the product of the co-ordinates of each point on the curve is constant. The student of economics will readily recognize this as the necessary condition of a demand curve possessing unit elasticity throughout its length. It is also true that any demand curve

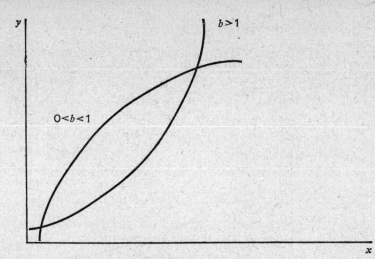

Fig. 48　$y = ax^b$.

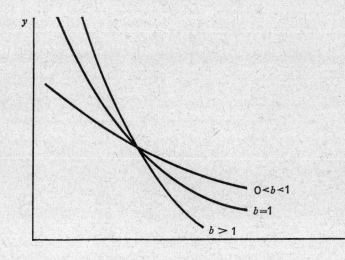

Fig. 49　$y = ax^{-b}$.

depicted by $y = ax^{-b}$ will exhibit constant, although not unitary, elasticity. It is for this reason that econometricians frequently utilize the double-log transformation in their models.

177　Non-linear and multiple regression and correlation

4.2.5 Other linear transformations

4.2.5.1 It would merely be repetitive to work through specific examples of the other linear transformations, so we will indicate only the general principles involved in the *reciprocal* and *root transformations*, and the evaluation of their regression equations.

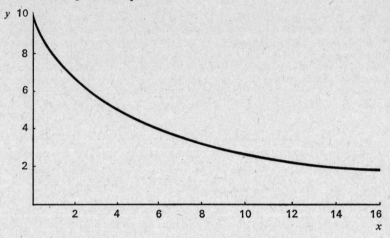

Fig. 50

Consider the following series, which has been plotted in fig. 50.

y	10	8	5	4	2·5	2	1/y	1/10	1/8	1/5	1/4	10/25	1/2
x	0	1	4	6	12	16	x	0	1	4	6	12	16

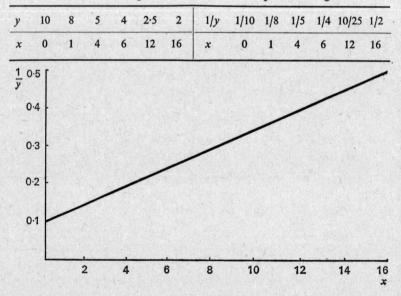

Fig. 51

If instead of the actual values of y we plot their reciprocals we achieve the perfectly straight line shown in fig. 51. This transformation of the y variable enables us to use as our regression model

$$\frac{1}{y} = a + bx$$

which is linear. The product moment coefficient of correlation will be given by

$$r_{1/y.x} = \frac{n \Sigma x \frac{1}{y} - \Sigma x \Sigma \frac{1}{y}}{\sqrt{\left\{ n \Sigma x^2 - (\Sigma x)^2 \right\} \left\{ n \Sigma \left(\frac{1}{y} \right)^2 - \left(\Sigma \frac{1}{y} \right)^2 \right\}}}$$

and the values of b and a by

$$b = \frac{n \Sigma x \frac{1}{y} - \Sigma x \Sigma \left(\frac{1}{y} \right)}{n \Sigma x^2 - (\Sigma x)^2}$$

$$a = \frac{\Sigma \left(\frac{1}{y} \right) - b \Sigma x}{n}$$

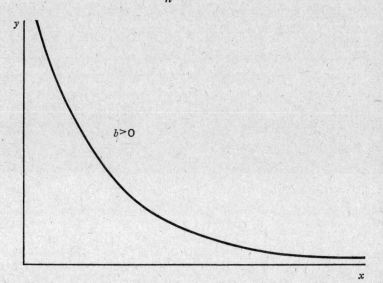

Fig. 52 $\dfrac{1}{y} = a + bx.$

179 Non-linear and multiple regression and correlation

Some important aspects of this transformation may indicate whether it can be used as a realistic representation of the situation being considered. We should notice that when b is positive (as in fig. 52) the curve gets closer and closer to the horizontal axis without ever touching it. In other words, as x approaches infinity y approaches 0. We say that zero is the *asymptotic level* to which the curve tends. If b is negative, however, then as x approaches $\dfrac{a}{b}$, y tends to infinity. (For $x > \dfrac{a}{b}$, $\dfrac{1}{y} < 0$ and y is negative.) This is shown in fig. 53.

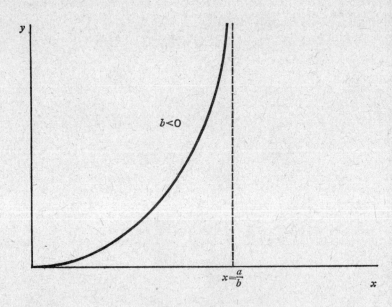

Fig. 53 $\dfrac{1}{y} = a - bx.$

If reasoning suggests that an asymptotic level other than zero exists for the circumstances under review, one can often usually employ the reciprocal transformation in x, namely

$$y = a + \frac{b}{x}$$

The reader can convert the earlier formulae for r, b and a to achieve this regression model. It will be found that as x approaches infinity, when b is positive, y will approach a. When b is negative the curve, running upwards from left to right, has a progressively decreasing slope with y

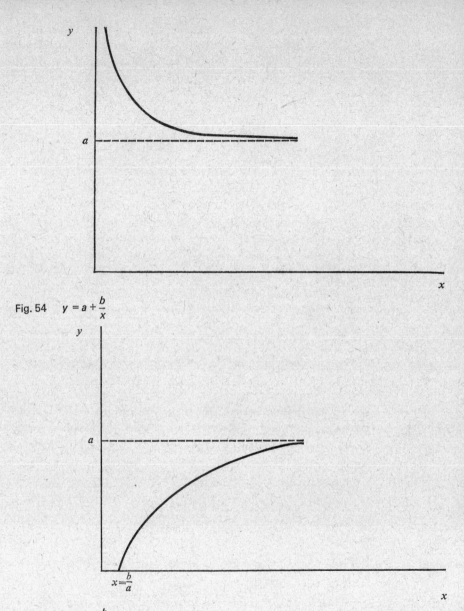

Fig. 54 $y = a + \dfrac{b}{x}$

Fig. 55 $y = a - \dfrac{b}{x}$

again approaching a as x approaches infinity. These two cases where a is the asymptote are shown in figs. 54 and 55.

4.2.5.2   The final transformation which may sometimes be employed is that involving the use of $\sqrt{y}$ rather than y, or $\sqrt{x}$ instead of x. In the former case the three formulae will be given by

$$r_{y.x} = \frac{n\Sigma(x\sqrt{y}) - \Sigma x \Sigma(\sqrt{y})}{\sqrt{\{n\Sigma x^2 - (\Sigma x)^2\}\{n\Sigma(\sqrt{y})^2 - (\Sigma\sqrt{y})^2\}}}$$

$$b = \frac{n\Sigma x(\sqrt{y}) - \Sigma x \Sigma(\sqrt{y})}{n\Sigma x^2 - (\Sigma x)^2}$$

$$a = \frac{\Sigma\sqrt{y} - b\Sigma x}{n}$$

One may again be justified in using this particular transformation on *a priori* grounds. Croxton and Cowden (see Suggestions for further reading, page 372), in trying to find the most satisfactory non-linear relationship to fit to a set of data showing the diameter and volume (in board feet) of twenty pine trees, recognize that a tree is similar to a cylinder and that

the volume of a cylinder is directly related to its length and to the square of the radius (or diameter) of its circular cross section.

They therefore found the linear regression of the square root of the volume of timber on the diameter of the trees, which yields a very high coefficient of correlation.

It should be stressed continually that in all circumstances one should look for some theoretical basis for narrowing down the possible range of non-linear regression equations which may be fitted to the data under review.

4.3   *Non-linear regression: polynomials*

4.3.1   The alternative to seeking some transformation of the original data so that the linear model may be utilized is to fit an appropriate non-linear relationship. In many cases the least squares method yields complex (and often insoluble) estimating equations, but there is one category of non-linear relationship which does not produce insuperable difficulties. This is the family of polynomials, which we have already encountered in the form of the linear equation

$$y = a + bx.$$

This is a polynomial of the first degree. Polynomials of the second degree (parabola) and third degree (cubic) are as follows:

$$y = a + bx + cx^2$$
$$y = a + bx + cx^2 + dx^3$$

It was observed in *Statistics for the Social Scientist: 1 Introducing Statistics* that a polynomial of the second degree has one bend in it, a third-degree polynomial has two bends and so on. It is because the higher-order polynomials can exhibit a positive slope at one point and a negative slope at another that they are complementary to the linear transformations, none of which possesses this important property.

4.3.2 Consider the following hypothetical data, which show the amount of electricity generated by the national electricity authority and the air temperature on 20 days randomly selected throughout the year.

Temperature (°F.)	Kilowatt-hours of electricity generated (tens of millions)
28	62
34	60
35	58
37	55
40	52
40	51
43	47
45	45
47	42
50	40
53	41
54	39
56	36
59	34
63	37
66	38
67	37
71	40
74	41
77	43

From the scatter diagram shown in fig. 56 it is evident that by and large the colder the day the greater the demand for electricity (mainly for heating purposes) and the larger the amount generated. However, we notice that there is a tendency for electricity generation to increase on particularly hot days. Presumably this is caused by the increasing use at

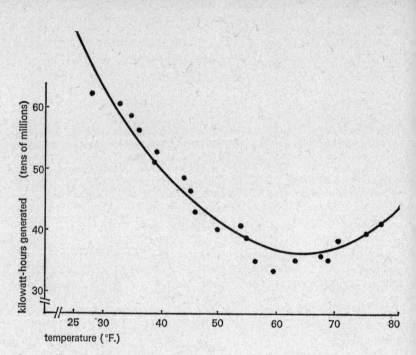

Fig. 56.   Scatter diagram of temperature and electricity generated on twenty days.

these times of cooling equipment such as refrigeration plants in factories and shops, domestic refrigerators, fans, etc. Because of this noticeable upturn in the scatter diagram it will be necessary to use at least a second-degree polynomial.

4.3.3   Utilizing the least-squares method for

$$y = a + bx + cx^2$$

involves the minimization of $\Sigma(y-a-bx-cx^2)^2$. Applying an extension of the procedure for minimizing the sum of squares (*Statistics for the Social Scientist: 1*) gives the following three normal equations:

$$\Sigma y = na + b\Sigma x + c\Sigma x^2 \qquad \text{(i)}$$
$$\Sigma xy = a\Sigma x + b\Sigma x^2 + c\Sigma x^3 \qquad \text{(ii)}$$
$$\Sigma x^2 y = a\Sigma x^2 + b\Sigma x^3 + c\Sigma x^4 \qquad \text{(iii)}$$

We will require to calculate Σx, Σy, Σx^2 and Σxy as usual. In addition Σx^3, Σx^4 and $\Sigma x^2 y$ will be needed in order to estimate a, b and c. Finally Σy^2 must be computed for use in the calculation of the coefficient of non-linear correlation. It is important to remember that this measure of association cannot be obtained by the product moment approach; only when the regression coefficients have been calculated can we evaluate the coefficient of determination from the ratio, Explained variation÷Total variation, and thus the coefficient of non-linear correlation.

It is not directly possible to produce simple formulae for a, b and c from the three normal equations, so we must solve the three equations simultaneously. We shall eliminate a (by multiplication and subtraction) from (i) and (ii) and similarly from (i) and (iii). The resulting equations in b and c, which we shall number (iv) and (v) will be solved by the simple method for two unknowns. The values of b and c will then be replaced in (i) to determine a.

x	y	x^2	x^3	x^4	xy	x^2y	y^2
28	62	784	21952	614656	1736	48608	3844
34	60	1156	39304	1336336	2040	69360	3600
35	58	1225	42875	1500625	2030	71050	3364
37	55	1369	50653	1874161	2035	75295	3025
40	52	1600	64000	2560000	2080	83200	2704
40	51	1600	64000	2560000	2040	81600	2601
43	47	1849	79507	3418801	2021	86903	2209
45	45	2025	91125	4100625	2025	91125	2025
47	42	2209	103823	4879681	1974	92778	1764
50	40	2500	125000	6250000	2000	100000	1600
53	41	2809	148877	7890481	2173	115169	1681
54	39	2916	157464	8503056	2106	113724	1521
56	36	3136	175616	9834496	2016	112896	1296
59	34	3481	205379	12117361	2006	118354	1156
63	37	3969	250047	15752961	2331	146853	1369
66	38	4356	287496	18974736	2508	165528	1444
67	37	4489	300763	20151121	2479	166093	1369
71	40	5041	357911	25411681	2840	201640	1600
74	41	5476	405224	29986576	3034	224516	1681
77	43	5929	456533	35153041	3311	254947	1849
1039	898	57919	3427549	212870395	44785	2419639	41702

The normal equations are:

$$898 = 20a + 1039b + 57919c \qquad \text{(i)}$$

$$44785 = 1039a + 57919b + 3427549c \qquad \text{(ii)}$$

$$2419639 = 57919a + 3427549b + 212870395c \qquad \text{(iii)}$$

Multiply (i) by $\dfrac{\Sigma x}{n} = 51{\cdot}95$

giving $\qquad\qquad 46651{\cdot}10 = 1039a + 53976{\cdot}05b + 3008892{\cdot}05c$

Subtracting modified (i) from (ii) gives

$$-1866{\cdot}10 = 3942{\cdot}95b + 418656{\cdot}95c \qquad\qquad \text{(iv)}$$

Multiply (i) by $\dfrac{\Sigma x^2}{n} = 2895{\cdot}95$

giving $\qquad 2600563{\cdot}10 = 57919a + 3008892{\cdot}05c + 167730528{\cdot}05$

Subtracting modified (i) from (iii) gives

$$-180924{\cdot}10 = 418656{\cdot}95b + 45139866{\cdot}95c \qquad\qquad \text{(v)}$$

To solve (iv) and (v) simultaneously for b and c

multiply (iv) by $\dfrac{418656{\cdot}95}{3942{\cdot}95} = 106{\cdot}1786099$

giving $\quad -198139{\cdot}903934 = 418656{\cdot}95b + 44452412{\cdot}975974c$

Subtracting modified (iv) from (v) gives

$$17215{\cdot}803934 = 687453{\cdot}974026c$$

$$c = \frac{17215{\cdot}803934}{687453{\cdot}974026} = 0{\cdot}025043$$

Replacing this value of c in (iv) gives

$$b = \frac{-1866{\cdot}10 - 418656{\cdot}95 \times 0{\cdot}025043}{3942{\cdot}95}$$

$$= -\frac{123505{\cdot}259989}{3942{\cdot}95} = -3{\cdot}132306$$

Replacing these values of b and c in (i) gives

$$a = \frac{898 - (-3{\cdot}132306 \times 1039) - (0{\cdot}025043 \times 57919)}{20}$$

$$= \frac{2702{\cdot}000417}{20} = 135{\cdot}100021$$

The regression equation is

$$y = 135{\cdot}1 - 3{\cdot}132 + 0{\cdot}02504x^2$$

which can be checked by substituting in normal equation (ii) the values of a, b and c giving

$$1039 \times 135 \cdot 100021 - 3 \cdot 132306 \times 57919 + 0 \cdot 025043 \times 3427549 = 44785$$

which is correct.

This is the regression line plotted on fig. 56.

4.3.4   The coefficient of determination (see *Statistics for the Social Scientist: 1 Introducing Statistics*) is now found from

$$r_{y.x.x^2}^2 = \frac{\text{Explained variation}}{\text{Total variation}} = \frac{\Sigma(y'-\bar{y})^2}{\Sigma(y-\bar{y})^2}$$

where explained variation is given by

$$\Sigma(y'-\bar{y})^2 = a\Sigma y + b\Sigma xy + c\Sigma x^2 y - \frac{(\Sigma y)^2}{n}$$

$$= (135 \cdot 100021 \times 898) + (-3 \cdot 132306 \times 44785) +$$

$$+ (0 \cdot 025043 \times 2419639) - \left(\frac{898}{20} \times 898\right)$$

$$= 1314 \cdot 314125$$

and total variation can be calculated from

$$\Sigma(y-\bar{y})^2 = \Sigma y^2 - \frac{(\Sigma y)^2}{n}$$

$$= 41702 - \frac{898}{20} \times 898$$

$$= 1381 \cdot 8$$

$$r_{y.x.x^2}^2 = \frac{1314 \cdot 314}{1381 \cdot 8} = 0 \cdot 951$$

$$r_{y.x.x^2} = \sqrt{0 \cdot 951} = 0 \cdot 975$$

The coefficient of non-linear correlation in this case (and indeed for all polynomials) has no sign because the slope of the regression line is positive at one point but negative at another.

4.3.5   It may have been noticed from the scatter diagram that although there is a tendency for the generation of electricity to increase when the temperature drops below 35° F. it does so at a decreasing rate. The opposite situation occurs in the range of temperatures from 60° F. to 35° F. If this is a true tendency then we may find that a third-degree polynomial

187   **Non-linear and multiple regression and correlation**

provides a slightly better fit of the data. Once again there are reasons for exploring this possibility. As the demand for electricity reaches its peak during cold winter days, generating plant will be working towards its full capacity output. As this level is approached it will become progressively more difficult for output to be increased, with the possible result of cuts in supply or reductions in voltage.

4.3.6   In the third degree equation

$$y = a+bx+cx^2+dx^3$$

we are faced with four normal equations,

$$\Sigma y = na+b\Sigma x+c\Sigma x^2+d\Sigma x^3 \tag{i}$$

$$\Sigma xy = a\Sigma x+b\Sigma x^2+c\Sigma x^3+d\Sigma x^4 \tag{ii}$$

$$\Sigma x^2 y = a\Sigma x^2+b\Sigma x^3+c\Sigma x^4+d\Sigma x^5 \tag{iii}$$

$$\Sigma x^3 y = a\Sigma x^3+b\Sigma x^4+c\Sigma x^5+d\Sigma x^6 \tag{iv}$$

In addition to the calculations already undertaken, Σx^5, Σx^6 and $\Sigma x^3 y$ will now be required. These are shown below:

x^5	x^6	$x^3 y$
17210368	481890304	1361024
45435424	1544804416	2358240
52521875	1838265625	2486750
69343957	2565726409	2785915
102400000	4096000000	3328000
102400000	4096000000	3264000
147008443	6321363049	3736829
184528125	8303765625	4100625
229345007	10779215329	4360566
312500000	15625000000	5000000
418195493	22164361129	6103957
459165024	24794911296	6141096
550731776	30840979456	6322176
714924299	42180533641	6982886
992436543	62523502209	9251739
1252332576	82653950016	10924848
1350125107	90458382169	11128231
1804229351	128100283921	14316440
2219006624	164206490176	16614184
2706784157	208422380089	19630919
13730624149	911997804859	140198425

Substituting in the normal equations gives

$$898 = 20a + 1039b + 57919c + 3427549d \qquad \text{(i)}$$

$$44785 = 1039a + 57919b + 3427549c + 212870395d \qquad \text{(ii)}$$

$$2419639 = 57919a + 3427549b + 212870395c + 13730624149d \qquad \text{(iii)}$$

$$140198425 = 3427549a + 212870395b + 13730624149c + 911997804859d \qquad \text{(iv)}$$

We proceed in the same way as before, solving equations (i) and (ii), (i) and (iii), and (i) and (iv), in each case eliminating a. This gives equations (v), (vi) and (vii) as follows:

$$-1866 \cdot 10 = 3942 \cdot 95b + 418656 \cdot 95c + 34809224 \cdot 45d \qquad \text{(v)}$$

$$-180924 \cdot 10 = 418656 \cdot 95b + 45139866 \cdot 95c + 3804613622 \cdot 45d \qquad \text{(vi)}$$

$$-13698525 \cdot 10 = 34809224 \cdot 45b + 3804613622 \cdot 45c +$$

$$324593197488 \cdot 95d \qquad \text{(vii)}$$

We now eliminate b by solving (v) and (vi) and (v) and (vii) giving

$$17215 \cdot 803934 = 687453 \cdot 974026c + 108618558 \cdot 651908d \qquad \text{(viii)}$$

and

$$2775813 \cdot 592138 = 108618557 \cdot 813870c + 17289755444 \cdot 069719d \qquad \text{(ix)}$$

Solving (viii) and (ix) for the two unknowns gives

$$d = 0 \cdot 000435$$

$$c = -0 \cdot 043689$$

Substituting these values in (v), (vi) or (vii) gives

$$b = 0 \cdot 325291$$

Now substituting b, c and d in (i), (ii), (iii) or (iv) enables the remaining unknown to be found as

$$a = 79 \cdot 973102$$

The third degree polynomial regression equation is therefore

$$y = 80 \cdot 0 + 0 \cdot 325x - 0 \cdot 0437x^2 + 0 \cdot 000435x^3$$

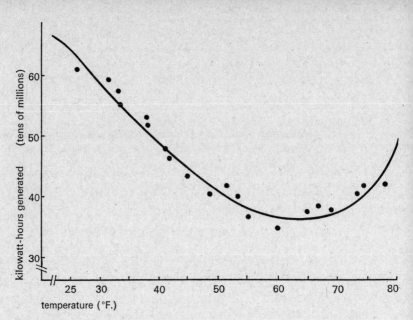

Fig. 57 Third degree polynomial fitted to data for temperature and electricity generated on twenty days.

which is shown in fig. 57. This again can be checked by substitution in one of the three normal equations not used to estimate a. In the case of normal equation (ii):

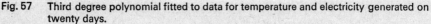

$$(1039 \times 79 \cdot 973102) + (57919 \times 0 \cdot 325291) + (3427549 \times -0 \cdot 043689) +$$

$$(212870395 \times 0 \cdot 000435) = 44785,$$

which is correct.

4.3.7   Lastly, the coefficient of determination is found by calculating

$$\Sigma(y' - \bar{y})^2 = a\Sigma y + b\Sigma xy + c\Sigma x^2 y + d\Sigma x^3 y - \frac{(\Sigma y)^2}{n}$$

$$= (79 \cdot 973102 \times 898) + (0 \cdot 325291 \times 44785) + (-0 \cdot 043689 \times 2419639) +$$

$$(0 \cdot 000435 \times 140198425) - \frac{(898)^2}{20}$$

$$= 1338 \cdot 509635$$

and dividing by the total variation, which is the same as for the second degree polynomial (1381·8):

$$r_{y.x.x^2.x^3}^2 = \frac{1338 \cdot 510}{1381 \cdot 8} = 0 \cdot 969$$

Therefore the coefficient of correlation is given by

$$r_{y.x.x^2.x^3} = \sqrt{0 \cdot 969} = 0 \cdot 984$$

4.3.8   The use of the third degree polynomial has indeed been vindicated. The coefficient of determination has increased from $0 \cdot 951$ to $0 \cdot 969$ as a result of the modification of the regression model. However, the increased amount of computation involved in achieving this result is considerable and from the standpoint of time may be deemed impractical. Even with a calculating machine the student might have difficulty in producing the results found here quickly and correctly and, what is more, the computational problem mushrooms exponentially as polynomials of each higher degree are tackled. Thus although the flexibility of the family of polynomials makes them attractive in the formulation of regression models, the reader will be well advised to utilize the linear transformation wherever appropriate.

4.4   Multiple linear regression and correlation

4.4.1   The introduction of additional independent variables into a regression model requires the use of a number of new concepts and techniques, but it should be realized that fundamentally the approach adopted and the principles involved are exactly the same as for two-variable regression and correlation. Now the dependent variable will be estimated not from one but from two, three or more independent variables, the main justification (as in the case of non-linear models) being the appearance of higher coefficients of determination and correlation. The greater the variation of the dependent variable which the regression equation can explain, the more reliable will be the predictions and estimates based upon this model. It is possible to imagine in theory the inclusion of every variable factor which influences the dependent variable; in these circumstances, the explained variation would be equal to the total variation and the perfect estimating equation would have been achieved. In practice only the most important and quantifiable influences on the dependent variable can be included so that there will always be some unexplained variation.

4.4.2   The multiple regression model for three variables can be stated in the following form:

$$y_1 = a_{1.23} + b_{12.3}x_2 + b_{13.2}x_3$$

A number of points need clarification in this equation. Firstly, we see that the variables are numbered 1, 2 and 3 by the use of subscripts. The first variable is the dependent variable and is lettered y_1 (we maintain the letter y for the sake of consistency with the earlier discussions). The second and third variables (the independents) are lettered respectively x_2 and x_3. We might of course utilize different letters for the three variables, but this could produce confusion when more than three letters are employed: the use of numerical subscripts, which immediately indicate the number of variables involved, produces greater clarity, particularly in connexion with the rest of the subscript notation which must now be discussed.

The equation which is shown above represents the regression of y_1 on x_2 and x_3. In a diagrammatic form it indicates a plane in three-dimensional space (fig. 58; four or more variables involve multidimensional geometry which cannot be depicted diagrammatically).

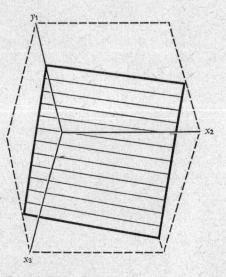

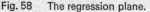

Fig. 58　The regression plane.

The intercept made by the plane on the y axis is $a_{1.23}$ (the hypothetical value of y_1 when x_2 and x_3 are both equal to zero); $b_{12.3}$ denotes the amount by which a unit change in x_2 is expected to affect y_1, when x_3 is kept constant; $b_{13.2}$ is interpreted analogously. It can be seen that the figures preceding the point indicate to which variables the b coefficient relates, while the figures after the point indicate which other variables have been included in the estimating equation, and which are given specific consideration within each coefficient.

4.4.3 Applying the least-squares criteria to the multiple-regression equation produces three normal equations. These are

$$\Sigma y_1 = na_{1.23} + b_{12.3}\Sigma x_2 + b_{13.2}\Sigma x_3 \quad \text{(i)}$$

$$\Sigma x_2 y_1 = a_{1.23}\Sigma x_2 + b_{12.3}\Sigma x_2{}^2 + b_{13.2}\Sigma x_2 x_3 \quad \text{(ii)}$$

$$\Sigma x_3 y_1 = a_{1.23}\Sigma x_3 + b_{12.3}\Sigma x_2 x_3 + b_{13.2}\Sigma x_3{}^2 \quad \text{(iii)}$$

Solving these in a parallel fashion to that outlined in 4.3.3 enables $a_{1.23}$, $b_{12.3}$ and $b_{13.2}$ to be found. Having obtained these we can compute the coefficient of multiple determination (using a simple extension of the method developed in *Statistics for the Social Scientist: 1 Introducing Statistics*) from

$$R_{1.23}{}^2 = \frac{\Sigma(y_1' - \bar{y}_1)^2}{\Sigma(y_1 - \bar{y}_1)^2}$$

where $\Sigma(y_1' - \bar{y}_1) = a_{12.3}\Sigma y_1 + b_{12.3}\Sigma y_1 x_2 + b_{13.2}\Sigma y_1 x_3 - \dfrac{(\Sigma y_1)^2}{n}$

The coefficient of multiple correlation $R_{1.23}$ is then obtained by taking the square root of the coefficient of multiple determination. $R_{1.23}$, as with the polynomial correlation coefficients, has no sign as one of the regression coefficients may be positive when the other is negative

4.4.4 To illustrate these techniques, let us consider the hypothetical data on page 194. For twenty borough wards of equal size, randomly selected throughout the country, it shows the number of convictions for drunkenness, the occupancy rate (number of people per room), and the level of unemployment during one month. We shall seek to discover the regression of convictions for drunkenness (y_1) on occupancy rate (x_2) and unemployment (x_3).

Substituting the computed sums into the normal equations leaves us with

$$710 = 20a_{1.23} + 12 \cdot 77 b_{12.3} + 45 \cdot 0 b_{13.2} \quad \text{(i)}$$

$$467 \cdot 70 = 12 \cdot 77 a_{1.23} + 8 \cdot 3773 b_{12.3} + 29 \cdot 192 b_{13.2} \quad \text{(ii)}$$

$$1766 \cdot 6 = 45 \cdot 0 a_{1.23} + 29 \cdot 192 b_{12.3} + 136 \cdot 82 b_{13.2} \quad \text{(iii)}$$

Proceeding as before we solve (i) and (ii) and (i) and (iii) together, eliminating $a_{1.23}$ in each case, which gives

$$14 \cdot 365000 = 0 \cdot 223655 b_{12.3} + 0 \cdot 459500 b_{13.2} \quad \text{(iv)}$$

$$169 \cdot 100000 = 0 \cdot 4595 b_{12.3} + 35 \cdot 57 b_{13.2} \quad \text{(v)}$$

193 Non-linear and multiple regression and correlation

Solving (iv) and (v) simultaneously for $b_{13.2}$ and $b_{12.3}$ gives

$$b_{13.2} = 4 \cdot 03$$

$$b_{12.3} = 55 \cdot 9$$

Borough ward	Number of convictions during month y_1	Occupancy (number of people per room) x_2	Unemployment (per cent) x_3	$y_1{}^2$	$x_2{}^2$	$x_3{}^2$	$y_1 x_2$	$y_1 x_3$	$x_2 x_3$
1	45	0·80	2·1	2025	0·6400	4·41	36·00	94·5	1·680
2	38	0·59	1·9	1444	0·3481	3·61	22·42	72·2	1·121
3	50	0·72	3·4	2500	0·5184	11·56	36·00	170·0	2·448
4	50	0·64	4·5	2500	0·4096	20·25	32·00	225·0	2·880
5	35	0·59	1·2	1225	0·3481	1·44	20·65	42·0	0·708
6	32	0·42	5·0	1024	0·1764	25·00	13·44	160·0	2·100
7	43	0·60	3·8	1849	0·3600	14·44	25·80	163·4	2·280
8	34	0·61	2·0	1156	0·3721	4·00	20·74	68·0	1·220
9	27	0·52	1·5	729	0·2704	2·25	14·04	40·5	0·780
10	30	0·60	1·0	900	0·3600	1·00	18·00	30·0	0·600
11	47	0·73	2·9	2209	0·5329	8·41	34·31	136·3	2·117
12	20	0·59	2·3	400	0·3481	5·29	11·80	46·0	1·357
13	20	0·61	0·1	400	0·3721	0·01	12·20	2·0	0·061
14	32	0·72	3·2	1024	0·5184	10·24	23·04	102·4	2·304
15	17	0·51	0·6	289	0·2601	0·36	8·67	10·2	0·306
16	35	0·60	0·3	1225	0·3600	0·09	21·00	10·5	0·180
17	45	0·75	3·0	2025	0·5625	9·00	33·75	135·0	2·250
18	41	0·82	2·1	1681	0·6724	4·41	33·62	86·1	1·722
19	21	0·54	0·9	441	0·2916	0·81	11·34	18·9	0·486
20	48	0·81	3·2	2304	0·6561	10·24	38·88	153·6	2·592
	710	12·77	45·0	27350	8·3773	136·82	467·70	1766·6	29·192

The substitution of these answers in (i), (ii) or (iii) enables the regression constant, $a_{1.23}$, to be found as

$$a_{1.23} = -9 \cdot 29$$

which can be checked in the usual manner. The regression equation is therefore

$$y_1 = -9 \cdot 29 + 55 \cdot 95 \, x_2 + 4 \cdot 03 \, x_3$$

4.4.5   Explained variation is calculated from

$$\Sigma(y_1' - \bar{y}_1)^2 = (710 \times -9 \cdot 291974) + (467 \cdot 7 \times 55 \cdot 946100) +$$

$$+ (1766 \cdot 6 \times 4 \cdot 031284) - \frac{(710)^2}{20}$$

$$= 1485 \cdot 3557$$

Total variation, as always, is given by

$$\Sigma y_1{}^2 - \frac{(\Sigma y_1)^2}{n} = 27350 - \frac{(710)^2}{20}$$

$$= 2145 \cdot 0$$

Therefore

$$R_{1.23}{}^2 = \frac{1485\cdot3557}{2145} = 0\cdot692473$$

and the coefficient of multiple correlation is

$$R_{1.23} = \sqrt{0\cdot692473} = 0\cdot832$$

It is worth noticing at this point that $R_{1.23}$ is greater than both the simple correlations. The correlation between convictions (y_1) and occupancy (x_2) is $r_{12} = 0\cdot656$, while between convictions (y_1) and unemployment (x_3) it is $r_{13} = 0\cdot612$. It seems that the three-variable model is much superior as an estimating equation.

4.4.6 *An alternative approach*

4.4.6.1   As an alternative to solving the normal equations for three unknowns directly, we may express the sets of variable values in terms of deviations from their means. Instead of Σy_1 we shall write $\Sigma(y_1 - \bar{y}_1)$, instead of $\Sigma x_2{}^2$ we shall write $\Sigma(x_2 - \bar{x}_2)^2$ and so on. The advantage of this manipulation is that the sum of the deviations of a series round its mean is zero. Thus $\Sigma(y_1 - \bar{y}_1) = \Sigma(x_2 - \bar{x}_2) = \Sigma(x_3 - \bar{x}_3) = 0$ and the first of the three normal equations disappears. We are left with

$$\Sigma(y_1 - \bar{y}_1)(x_2 - \bar{x}_2) = b_{12.3}\Sigma(x_2 - \bar{x}_2)^2 + b_{13.2}\Sigma(x_2 - \bar{x}_2)(x_3 - \bar{x}_3) \quad \text{(ii)}$$

$$\Sigma(y_1 - \bar{y}_1)(x_3 - \bar{x}_3) = b_{12.3}\Sigma(x_2 - \bar{x}_2)(x_3 - \bar{x}_3) + b_{13.2}\Sigma(x_3 - \bar{x}_3)^2 \quad \text{(iii)}$$

These may either by solved simultaneously, or we derive formulae for $b_{12.3}$ and $b_{13.2}$ as follows:

$$b_{12.3} =$$

$$\frac{\Sigma(y_1 - \bar{y}_1)(x_2 - \bar{x}_2)\Sigma(x_3 - \bar{x}_3)^2 - \Sigma(y_1 - \bar{y}_1)(x_3 - \bar{x}_3)\Sigma(x_2 - \bar{x}_2)(x_3 - \bar{x}_3)}{\Sigma(x_2 - \bar{x}_2)^2\Sigma(x_3 - \bar{x}_3)^2 - [\Sigma(x_2 - \bar{x}_2)(x_3 - \bar{x}_3)]^2}$$

and

$$b_{13.2} =$$

$$\frac{\Sigma(y_1 - \bar{y}_1)(x_3 - \bar{x}_3)\Sigma(x_2 - \bar{x}_2)^2 - \Sigma(y_1 - \bar{y}_1)(x_2 - \bar{x}_2)\Sigma(x_2 - \bar{x}_2)(x_3 - \bar{x}_3)}{\Sigma(x_2 - \bar{x}_2)^2\Sigma(x_3 - \bar{x}_3)^2 - [\Sigma(x_2 - \bar{x}_2)(x_3 - \bar{x}_3)]^2}$$

We can then find $a_{1.23}$ either by the technique described in 4.4.4 or by using the fact that the regression plane passes through the point of means, i.e. $\bar{y}_1, \bar{x}_2, \bar{x}_3$. In the latter case

$$\bar{y}_1 = a_{1.23} + b_{12.3}\bar{x}_2 + b_{13.2}\bar{x}_3$$

195   Non-linear and multiple regression and correlation

so that $a_{1.23} = \bar{y}_1 - b_{12.3}\bar{x}_2 - b_{13.2}\bar{x}_3$.

Explained variation can be found from data in deviation form from

$$\Sigma(y_1' - \bar{y}_1)^2 = b_{12.3}\Sigma(y_1 - \bar{y}_1)(x_2 - \bar{x}_2) + b_{12.3}\Sigma(y_1 - \bar{y}_1)(x_3 - \bar{x}_3)$$

enabling the coefficients of multiple determination and correlation to be quickly calculated.

4.4.6.2   The reader may blanch at the prospect of calculating the sums of squared deviations and the sums of cross products of deviations round their means, but the computation is not unduly difficult if the relationships below are utilized.

Deviation form	Original form	Example
$\Sigma(y_1 - \bar{y}_1)^2$	$\Sigma y_1^2 - \dfrac{(\Sigma y_1)^2}{n}$	$27350 - \dfrac{(710)^2}{20} = 2145$
$\Sigma(x_2 - \bar{x}_2)^2$	$\Sigma x_2^2 - \dfrac{(\Sigma x_2)^2}{n}$	$8 \cdot 3773 - \dfrac{(12 \cdot 77)^2}{20} = 0 \cdot 223655$
$\Sigma(x_3 - \bar{x}_3)^2$	$\Sigma x_3^2 - \dfrac{(\Sigma x_2)^2}{n}$	$136 \cdot 82 - \dfrac{(45 \cdot 0)^2}{20} = 35 \cdot 570$
$\Sigma(y_1 - \bar{y}_1)(x_2 - \bar{x}_2)$	$\Sigma y_1 x_2 - \dfrac{\Sigma y_1 \Sigma x_2}{n}$	$467 \cdot 70 - \dfrac{(710)(12 \cdot 77)}{20} = 14 \cdot 3650$
$\Sigma(y_1 - \bar{y}_1)(x_3 - \bar{x}_3)$	$\Sigma y_1 x_3 - \dfrac{\Sigma y_1 \Sigma x_3}{n}$	$1766 \cdot 6 = \dfrac{(710)(45 \cdot 0)}{20} = 169 \cdot 1$
$\Sigma(x_2 - \bar{x}_2)(x_3 - \bar{x}_3)$	$\Sigma x_2 x_3 - \dfrac{\Sigma x_2 \Sigma x_3}{n}$	$29 \cdot 192 - \dfrac{(45 \cdot 0)(12 \cdot 77)}{20} = 0 \cdot 4595$

We now find the regression coefficients and constant to be as follows:

$$b_{12.3} = \frac{(14 \cdot 365)(35 \cdot 570) - (169 \cdot 1)(0 \cdot 4595)}{(0 \cdot 223655)(35 \cdot 570) - (0 \cdot 4595)^2}$$

$$= \frac{433 \cdot 2616}{7 \cdot 7442681} = 55 \cdot 946100$$

$$b_{13.2} = \frac{(169 \cdot 1)(0 \cdot 223655) - (14 \cdot 365)(0 \cdot 4595)}{(0 \cdot 223655)(35 \cdot 570) - (0 \cdot 4595)^2}$$

$$= 4 \cdot 031284$$

$$a_{1.23} = \frac{710}{20} - 55 \cdot 946100 \times \frac{12 \cdot 77}{20} - 4 \cdot 031284 \times \frac{45 \cdot 0}{20}$$

$$= -9 \cdot 291974$$

We have exactly the same results as previously.

4.4.6.3 Explained variation follows from

$$\Sigma(y_1' - \bar{y}_1)^2 = (55 \cdot 946100)(14 \cdot 365) + (4 \cdot 031284 \times 169 \cdot 1)$$

$$= 1485 \cdot 3558$$

We already have total variation calculated as $\Sigma(y_1 - \bar{y}_1)^2 = 2145$, so that the coefficients of multiple determination and correlation are as before.

4.5 Partial correlation

4.5.1 In 4.4.2 we mentioned that $b_{12.3}$ indicates the effect on y_1 of a unit change in x_2 when x_3 is kept constant. In our example (4.4.4), unemployment is thought of as being held equal at the mean level for all twenty borough wards. It is as though we are measuring the regression of drunkenness convictions on occupancy for twenty wards having the same unemployment rate. Because the x_3 variable is being held statistically constant in this way, these regression coefficients are sometimes referred to as net or partial coefficients of estimation. In the social sciences, where observational rather than experimental research is undertaken, this statistical means of realizing the claim of 'other things being equal' is important and we shall therefore extend the discussion from a consideration of the partial coefficients of estimation to the study of coefficients of partial correlation. By this means we shall throw light onto the importance of the separate parts of the regression equation in the over-all estimation.

4.5.2 At the end of 4.4.5 it was observed that the simple correlation between drunkenness convictions and occupancy was $r_{12} = 0 \cdot 656$. Put another way, we can say that 43 per cent ($r_{12}^2 \times 100$) of the variation in drunkenness convictions is explained by the regression of drunkenness convictions on occupancy rate alone, while 57·0 per cent was unexplained by this regression model. When unemployment was taken into consideration the coefficient of multiple determination was observed to be 0·692, indicating that the regression of drunkenness convictions on both occupancy rate and percentage unemployment explains 69·2 per cent of the variation in the dependent variable. Through the introduction of this second independent variable an additional 69·2 − 43·0 = 26·2 per cent of the total variation has been explained. This increase in the proportion of the explained variation resulting from the introduction of an additional variable divided by the proportion of the total variation which was not explained by the two-variable regression is called the coefficient of partial determination, $r_{13.2}^2$. Its square root is the coefficient of partial correlation, $r_{13.2}$.

$$r_{13.2}^2 = \frac{R_{1.23}^2 - r_{12}^2}{1 - r_{12}^2} \quad \text{and} \quad r_{13.2} = \sqrt{\left(\frac{R_{1.23}^2 - r_{12}^2}{1 - r_{12}^2}\right)}$$

(Unexplained variation as a proportion of total variation is one minus the proportion of explained variation, i.e. $1 - r_{12}^2$ as in the denominator.)

In the example cited

$$r_{13.2}^2 = \frac{0.692473 - 0.430135}{1 - 0.430135} = \frac{0.262338}{0.569865} = 0.460351$$

and $\quad r_{13.2} = \sqrt{0.460351} = +0.678492$.

In this case $r_{13.2}$ is positive because the sign of $b_{13.2}$ in the regression equation was positive. The interpretation of $r_{13.2}$ is analogous to that for $b_{13.2}$; it is the value of the simple correlation between drunkenness convictions y_1 and unemployment x_3 which would result if we were to take our observations in twenty borough wards where occupancy x_2 is identical (specifically twenty wards where occupancy equals $\bar{x}_2$).

In just the same way as we calculated $r_{13.2}$ we also need $r_{12.3}$ for a complete evaluation of the importance of the independent variables in the regression equation.

$$r_{12.3}^2 = \frac{R_{1.23}^2 - r_{13}^2}{1 - r_{13}^2} = \frac{0.692473 - 0.374780}{1 - 0.374780} = 0.508130$$

and $\quad r_{12.3} = \sqrt{0.508130} = +0.712832$

4.5.3   Let us now make a number of observations about these partial correlation coefficients. It is usual to describe $r_{12.3}$ and $r_{13.2}$ as first-order coefficients. They are built up largely on the basis of simple or zero-order coefficients such as r_{12} and r_{13} (see 4.6.2 where they are calculated exclusively from zero-order coefficients). As more than two independent variables are introduced, so the order of the partial correlation coefficients is increased, e.g. for three independent variables one would deal with second-order coefficients: $r_{12.34}$, $r_{13.24}$, $r_{14.23}$.

Just as the coefficient of multiple correlation was greater than the zero-order coefficients r_{12} and r_{13}, so we notice that $r_{13.2}$ is greater than r_{13} (0.678 compared to 0.612) and $r_{12.3}$ is greater than r_{12} (0.713 compared to 0.656). Removing the effect of ward-to-ward variations in occupancy (in the first case) and unemployment (in the second) has produced this increase in the association between the variables. We are able to say that there is an association between both y_1 and x_2 and y_1 and x_3 over and above the association due to the influence of x_3 in the first case and x_2 in the second. It will not invariably be the case that the partial coefficients of the first order are higher than the zero-order coefficients, even when the multiple coefficient is greater. There are times when one of the independent variables may influence the dependent variable indirectly through its interaction with a second independent variable. Holding constant this second variable must then have the effect of reducing the partial coefficient. The key is the simple correlation between x_2 and x_3, namely r_{23}. For positive r_{12} and r_{13}, the lower this is positively or the higher it is negatively, the greater will be the effect of introducing the additional variable and the greater will be $R_{1.23}$, $r_{12.3}$ and $r_{13.2}$. In our example $r_{23} = 0.163$, which produces the results observed.

4.5.4   β coefficient analysis

4.5.4.1   While we are considering the interpretation of our results it will be opportune to ask ourselves whether we have ascertained the relative importance of the independent variables in the regression equation. In fact, we have not. All we know so far is that a one unit increase in occupancy will result in a 55·946 unit increase in drunkenness convictions, whilst a one unit increase in unemployment will be accompanied by a 4·031 unit increase in the dependent variable. These are absolute measures and reflect the magnitude and the spread of the series involved. What is required, and what the β coefficients provide, is a relative measure of the importance of x_2 and x_3 in their effect on y_1.

β coefficients are obtained by multiplying the absolute values of the net coefficients of estimation by the ratio of the standard deviation of their attached variable to the standard deviation of the dependent variable, thus converting these absolute values into a relative form:

$$\beta_{12.3} = b_{12.3}\frac{s_2}{s_1}$$

$$\beta_{13.2} = b_{13.2}\frac{s_3}{s_1}$$

In our example $s_1 = 10.356157$, $s_2 = 0.105749$ and $s_3 = 1.333604$ so that

$$\beta_{12.3} = \frac{(55.946100)(0.105749)}{(10.356157)}$$

$$= 0.571278$$

and
$$\beta_{13.2} = \frac{(4 \cdot 031284)(1 \cdot 333604)}{(10 \cdot 356157)}$$

$$= 0 \cdot 519125$$

Because of the nature of their calculation, it seems that $\beta_{12.3}$ and $\beta_{13.2}$ indicate how many standard deviations of movement in the y_1 variable will be occasioned by an increase of one standard deviation in x_2 or x_3. Occupancy and unemployment appear to be of approximately equal importance in our example: an increase of one standard deviation in occupancy produces an increase of $0 \cdot 571$ standard deviation in drunkenness convictions, while for unemployment the increase is $0 \cdot 519$ standard deviation.

4.5.4.2 β coefficients are also useful in showing how much of the influence of x_2 on y_1 is direct and how much of it is indirect through x_3. As was mentioned in 4.5.3, these two parts of the influence of x_2 are important. The direct effect cannot be negative so that the addition of a variable to the regression model will never produce a reduction of the correlation from this source, but the indirect influence of the additional variable may be either negative or positive so that the net effect of the two influences could be to leave the correlation unaltered.

The direct influence of any variable is the square of its β coefficient. In our example the direct effect of x_2 is $(0 \cdot 571)^2 = 0 \cdot 326359$ and of x_3 is $(0 \cdot 519)^2 = 0 \cdot 269491$. The indirect effect of x_2 through x_3 can be found from $(\beta_{12.3})(\beta_{13.2})(r_{23})$, and the indirect effect of x_3 through x_2 from $(\beta_{13.2})(\beta_{12.3})(r_{32})$ which is the same thing. In the example cited the indirect effect of x_2 through x_3 and vice versa is $(0 \cdot 571278)(0 \cdot 519125)$ $(0 \cdot 162912) = 0 \cdot 048314$. The results may now be summarized as follows:

Direct and indirect effects of the independent variables

	x_2	x_3	Total
Direct	0·326359	0·269491	0·595850
Indirect	0·048314	0·048314	0·096628
Net effect	0·374673	0·317805	0·692478

The reader will see that the sum of the direct and indirect effects is the same as $R_{1.23}^2$ (computed earlier); it should always be checked that this is the case. The direct effects constitute approximately 86 per cent of the total net effect, and again result from the low correlation between the independent variables. The indirect effects of x_2 and x_3, although low, are positive, thus enhancing the increase in the correlation which must result from the introduction of the third variable into the model.

4.6 Multiple regression and correlation: a second alternative

4.6.1 We are often confronted with the summarized results of a piece of research giving only zero-order correlation coefficients together with the means and the standard deviations of the original series. How can we calculate the regression coefficients and constant, together with the coefficients of partial and multiple correlation? Fortunately, a number of relationships exist which take some of the tedium from the methods suggested in 4.4.4 and 4.4.6. We will illustrate these by using the earlier example, setting out the data as follows:

$$\bar{y}_1 = 35 \cdot 5 \qquad \bar{x}_2 = 0 \cdot 6385 \qquad \bar{x}_3 = 2 \cdot 25$$
$$s_1 = 10 \cdot 356157 \qquad s_2 = 0 \cdot 105749 \qquad s_3 = 1 \cdot 333604$$
$$r_{12} = 0 \cdot 655847 \qquad r_{13} = 0 \cdot 612193 \qquad r_{23} = 0 \cdot 162912$$

4.6.2 The initial step in this alternative development is to calculate the first order partial correlation coefficients. By a manipulation of the basic expressions it is possible to do this directly from no more than a knowledge of the zero-order correlation coefficients (see 4.15.1):

$$r_{12.3} = \frac{r_{12} - r_{13} r_{23}}{\sqrt{(1 - r_{13}^2)} \sqrt{(1 - r_{23}^2)}}$$

$$r_{13.2} = \frac{r_{13} - r_{12} r_{23}}{\sqrt{(1 - r_{12}^2)} \sqrt{(1 - r_{23}^2)}}$$

In the example cited

$$r_{12.3} = \frac{0 \cdot 655847 - (0 \cdot 612193)(0 \cdot 162912)}{\sqrt{\{1 - (0 \cdot 612193)^2\}} \sqrt{\{1 - (0 \cdot 162912)^2\}}}$$

$$= 0 \cdot 712832$$

$$r_{13.2} = \frac{0 \cdot 612193 - (0 \cdot 655847)(0 \cdot 162912)}{\sqrt{\{1 - (0 \cdot 655847)^2\}} \sqrt{\{1 - (0 \cdot 162912)^2\}}}$$

$$= 0 \cdot 678492$$

4.6.3 Now we may proceed to the computation of the regression coefficients of estimation. Before so doing, however, let us observe that in the two-variable linear model we might have calculated b (b_{12} in the notation of multiple regression) from

$$b_{12} = r_{12}\frac{s_1}{s_2}$$

because

$$r_{12}\frac{s_1}{s_2} = \frac{\Sigma(x_2-\bar{x}_2)(y_1-\bar{y}_1)}{ns_1s_2}\frac{s_1}{s_2}$$

$$= \frac{\Sigma(x_2-\bar{x}_2)(y_1-\bar{y}_1)}{ns_2{}^2}$$

$$= \frac{\Sigma(x_2-\bar{x}_2)(y_1-\bar{y}_1)}{\Sigma(x_2-\bar{x}_2)^2}$$

$$= \frac{n\Sigma x_2 y_1-\Sigma x_2\Sigma y_1}{n\Sigma x_2{}^2-(\Sigma x_2)^2} = b_{12}$$

Similarly, the first order regression coefficients may be calculated from

$$b_{12.3} = r_{12.3}\frac{s_{1.3}}{s_{2.3}}$$

and

$$b_{13.2} = r_{13.2}\frac{s_{1.2}}{s_{3.2}}$$

Here $s_{1.2}, s_{1.3}, s_{2.3}$ and $s_{3.2}$ are first order standard deviations. Specifically $s_{1.2}$ is the standard deviation of y_1 values measured round the regression line of y_1 on x_2. Put another way, $s_{1.2}$ is the square root of the mean unexplained variation resulting from the regression model:

$$s_{1.2} = \sqrt{\left\{\frac{\Sigma(y_1-a_{12}-b_{12}x_2)^2}{n}\right\}} \quad \text{or} \quad \sqrt{\left\{\frac{\Sigma(y_1-y_1')^2}{n}\right\}}$$

The remaining first order standard deviations are interpreted analogously. Fortunately it is possible to calculate their value (see 4.15.2) from

$$s_{1.2} = s_1\sqrt{(1-r_{12}{}^2)} = 10{\cdot}356157\sqrt{\{1-(0{\cdot}655847)^2\}}$$
$$= 7{\cdot}817801$$

$$s_{1.3} = s_1\sqrt{(1-r_{13}{}^2)} = 10{\cdot}356157\sqrt{\{1-(0{\cdot}612193)^2\}}$$
$$= 8.188696$$

$$s_{2.3} = s_2\sqrt{(1-r_{23}{}^2)} = 0{\cdot}105749\sqrt{\{1-(0{\cdot}162912)^2\}}$$
$$= 0{\cdot}104336$$

$$s_{3.2} = s_3\sqrt{(1-r_{23}{}^2)} = 1{\cdot}333604\sqrt{\{1-(0{\cdot}162912)^2\}}$$
$$= 1{\cdot}315788$$

Therefore

$$b_{12.3} = \frac{(0.712832)(8.188696)}{0.104336} = \frac{5.837165}{0.104336}$$

$$= 55.945838$$

$$b_{13.2} = \frac{(0.678492)(7.817801)}{1.315788} = \frac{5.304315}{1.315788}$$

$$= 4.031284$$

4.6.4   While the principles established here provide the basis for calculating the regression coefficients in models involving more than three variables it is also worth noting that in the three-variable model the formulae given in 4.4.6.1 may be re-arranged and condensed (see 4.15.3) to yield

$$b_{12.3} = \frac{r_{12} - r_{13}r_{23}}{1 - r_{23}^2} \cdot \frac{s_1}{s_2}$$

and

$$b_{13.2} = \frac{r_{13} - r_{12}r_{23}}{1 - r_{23}^2} \cdot \frac{s_1}{s_3}$$

which do not require either the coefficients of partial correlation or the first order standard deviations.

Placing the given values in these formulae produces the previously established results

$$b_{12.3} = \frac{0.655847 - (0.612193)(0.162912)}{1 - (0.162912)^2} \cdot \frac{10.356157}{0.105749}$$

$$= \frac{(0.556113)(10.356157)}{(0.973460)(0.105749)} = \frac{5.759194}{0.102942}$$

$$= 55.946008$$

and

$$b_{13.2} = \frac{0.612193 - (0.655847)(0.162912)}{1 - (0.162912)^2} \cdot \frac{10.356157}{1.333604}$$

$$= \frac{(0.505348)(10.356157)}{(0.973460)(1.333604)} = \frac{5.233463}{1.298210}$$

$$= 4.031292$$

Using the relationship $a_{12.3} = \bar{y}_1 - b_{12.3}\bar{x}_2 - b_{13.2}\bar{x}_3$ gives

$$a_{12.3} = 35.5 - (55.946008)(0.6385) - (4.031292)(2.25)$$

$$= -9.291933$$

The slightly different answers obtained are due to the different effect of rounding in the various methods.

4.6.5   The coefficient of multiple determination may finally be obtained by the re-arrangement of the formula for $r_{13.2}{}^2$ given in 4.5.2, namely

$$r_{13.2}{}^2 = \frac{R_{1.23}{}^2 - r_{12}{}^2}{1 - r_{12}{}^2}$$

to give

$$R_{1.23}{}^2 = r_{12}{}^2 + r_{13.2}{}^2(1 - r_{12}{}^2)$$
$$= (0 \cdot 655847)^2 + (0 \cdot 678492)^2 \{1 - (0 \cdot 655847)^2\}$$
$$= 0 \cdot 692473$$

Once again it is possible, for the three-variable case alone, to derive an expression for $R_{1.23}{}^2$ in terms of zero-order correlation coefficients (see 4.15.4):

$$R_{1.23}{}^2 = \frac{r_{12}{}^2 + r_{13}{}^2 - 2r_{12}r_{13}r_{23}}{1 - r_{23}{}^2}$$

$$= \frac{(0 \cdot 655847)^2 + (0 \cdot 612193)^2 - (2)(0 \cdot 655847)(0 \cdot 612193)(0 \cdot 162912)}{1 - (0 \cdot 162912)^2}$$

$$= 0 \cdot 692473 \text{ as before.}$$

Whichever method is actually employed, the coefficient of multiple correlation may be found from

$$\sqrt{R_{1.23}{}^2} = \sqrt{0 \cdot 692473} = 0 \cdot 832$$

4.7   Multiple linear regression and correlation extended

4.7.1   Having mastered the three-variable model, the reader should have little difficulty in applying the broad principles to four or more variables, but he will find the amount of arithmetic and the complexity of the subscripts mushrooming alarmingly. For this reason he would be well advised to restrict his interest to no more than four variables until he has acquired some skill with matrix algebra. Even then the arithmetic burden is onerous, and access to a computer becomes first desirable and then essential. Most computer manufacturers carry a standard programme for multiple regression analysis which is readily available to the researcher, but for interested students we shall now nevertheless investigate the formulae applicable to both the four-variable model and to the general case of n variables. The approach involving the proliferation of normal equations will be dropped at this point, and we shall concentrate this development on an extension of the methods illustrated in section 4.6.1.

4.7.2   In setting out the second-order partial coefficients we shall see that all higher-order coefficients merely involve a knowledge of the next lower-order coefficients and so on down to the zero-order coefficients:

Four-variable case

$$r_{12.34} = \frac{r_{12.3} - r_{14.3}\,r_{24.3}}{\sqrt{(1 - r_{14.3}{}^2)}\,\sqrt{(1 - r_{24.3})^2}}$$

$$r_{13.24} = \frac{r_{13.2} - r_{14.2}\,r_{34.2}}{\sqrt{(1 - r_{14.2}{}^2)}\,\sqrt{(1 - r_{34.2})^2}}$$

$$r_{14.23} = \frac{r_{14.2} - r_{13.2}\,r_{34.2}}{\sqrt{(1 - r_{13.2}{}^2)}\,\sqrt{(1 - r_{34.2})^2}}$$

n-variable case

$$r_{12.34\cdots n} = \frac{r_{12.34\cdots(n-1)} - r_{1n.34\cdots(n-1)}\,r_{2n.34\cdots(n-1)}}{\sqrt{(1 - r_{1n.34\cdots(n-1)}{}^2)}\,\sqrt{(1 - r_{n.34\cdots(n-1)}{}^2)}}$$

etc.

Similarly for the second-order regression coefficients:

Four-variable case

$$b_{12.34} = r_{12.34} \cdot \frac{s_{1.34}}{s_{2.34}}$$

$$b_{13.24} = r_{13.24} \cdot \frac{s_{1.24}}{s_{3.24}}$$

$$b_{14.23} = r_{14.23} \cdot \frac{s_{1.23}}{s_{4.23}}$$

where

$$s_{1.23} = s_1\,\sqrt{(1 - r_{12}{}^2)}\,(\sqrt{1 - r_{13.2}{}^2})$$
$$s_{1.24} = s_1\,\sqrt{(1 - r_{12}{}^2)}\,(\sqrt{1 - r_{14.2}{}^2})$$
$$s_{1.34} = s_1\,\sqrt{(1 - r_{13}{}^2)}\,(\sqrt{1 - r_{14.3}{}^2})$$
$$s_{2.34} = s_2\,\sqrt{(1 - r_{23}{}^2)}\,(\sqrt{1 - r_{24.3}{}^2})$$
$$s_{3.24} = s_3\,\sqrt{(1 - r_{23}{}^2)}\,(\sqrt{1 - r_{34.2}{}^2})$$
$$s_{4.23} = s_4\,\sqrt{(1 - r_{24}{}^2)}\,(\sqrt{1 - r_{34.2}{}^2})$$

n-variable case

$$b_{12.34\ldots n} = r_{12.34\ldots n} \cdot \frac{s_{1.34\ldots n}}{s_{2.34\ldots n}}$$

etc.

$$s_{1.23\cdots n} = s\sqrt{(1 - r_{12}{}^2)}\,\sqrt{(1 - r_{13.2}{}^2)}\,\sqrt{(1 - r^2{}_{14.23})}\cdots$$
$$\sqrt{(1 - r_{1n.23\cdots(n-1)}{}^2)}$$

etc.

The regression constant can, as usual, be calculated from the fact that the multi-dimensional regression plane passes through the point of means:

Four-variable case

$$a_{1.234} = \bar{y}_1 - b_{12.34}\bar{x}_2 - b_{13.24}\bar{x}_3 - b_{14.23}\bar{x}_4$$

n-variable case

$$a_{1.234\cdots n} = \bar{y}_1 - b_{12.34\cdots n}\,\bar{x}_2 - b_{13.24\cdots n}\,\bar{x}_3 - b_{14.23\cdots n}\,\bar{x}_4 - \ldots - b_{1n.23\cdots(n-1)}\,\bar{x}_n$$

Finally, the coefficient of multiple determination is calculated from:

Four-variable case

$$R_{1.234}{}^2 = R_{1.23}{}^2 + r_{14.23}{}^2\,(1 - R_{1.23}{}^2)$$

or

$$R_{1.234}{}^2 = r_{12}{}^2 + r_{13.2}{}^2\,(1 - r_{12}{}^2) + r_{14.23}{}^2\,(1 - R_{1.23}{}^2)$$

n-variable case

$$R_{1.234\cdots n}{}^2 = R_{1.234\cdots(n-1)}{}^2 + r_{1n.23\cdots(n-1)}{}^2\,(1 - R_{1.234\cdots(n-1)}{}^2)$$

or

$$R_{1.234\cdots n}{}^2 = r_{12}{}^2 + r_{13.2}{}^2\,(1 - r_{12}{}^2) + r_{14.23}{}^2\,(1 - R_{1.23}{}^2) + \ldots$$
$$\ldots + r_{1n.23\cdots(n-1)}{}^2\,(1 - R_{1.234\cdots(n-1)}{}^2)$$

4.7.3   It will have become obvious that the full analysis of an original set of data becomes a most burdensome task for four variables. Even when the preliminary work of calculating means, zero-order standard deviations and correlation coefficients has been carried out, the remaining computation is still tedious and slow; although we can build up to the n-variable case, with each order of coefficient expressed in terms of the next lower order coefficients, it ceases to be a realistic or practical proposition without the aid of more advanced mathematical techniques and ultimately of electronic computational facilities.

4.8   Multiple non-linear regression and correlation

4.8.1   In the same way that relationships between two variables are sometimes more adequately described by a non-linear regression model, so multiple non-linear regression is sometimes more appropriate (although more complex) than an assumption of linearity. When this occurs we have the same choice that was faced earlier. Either we may transform one or more of the variables so that the transformation is linear, or we may utilize a polynomial equation.

4.8.2   In the former case, the estimating equation may take the form

$$\log y_1 = a_{1.23} + b_{12.3}x_2 + b_{13.2}x_3$$

or

$$y_1 = a_{1.23} + b_{12.3}\sqrt{x_2} + b_{13.2}\sqrt{x_3}$$

or

$$y_1 = a_{1.23} + \frac{b_{12.3}}{x_2} + \frac{b_{13.2}}{x_3}$$

or indeed any one of several combinations which can be conceived.

In the latter case, the basic expression may be

$$y_1 = a_{1.23} + b_{12.3}x_2 + b_{13.2}x_3^2$$

or

$$y_1 = a_{1.23} + b_{12.3}x_2^3 + b_{13.2}x_3^2$$

It should be appreciated here that the relationship between y_1 and each independent variable is not necessarily non-linear. In the examples cited above, the relationship between y_1 and x_2 in the first equation is linear, whilst between y_1 and x_3 it is quadratic (second degree polynomial). In the second equation, however, the relationship between y_1 and x_2 is cubic (third degree polynomial) whilst that between y_1 and x_3 is quadratic.

4.9 Regression and correlation analysis and the theory of sampling

4.9.1 Many of the illustrations thus far considered have involved sample data. The time has now come to look at the statistical inference problems associated with regression and correlation analysis. As before, we shall approach this topic by considering first of all the two-variable linear model, and then go on to consider the broader developments for multiple and non-linear forms of relationship.

4.9.2 The sampling theory connected with the estimation and testing of hypotheses about means and proportions rested upon a number of fundamental assumptions concerning the sample size and the distribution of the parent population from which the samples had been drawn. There are likewise crucial assumptions underlying the sampling theory of regression and correlation which must be fully understood. The first of these, portrayed in fig. 59, is that the values of the population dependent variable y are normally distributed about the population least-squares line $y = \alpha + \beta x$ with the mean of the distributions being $\alpha + \beta x$.

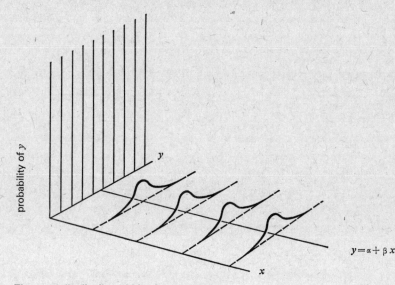

Fig. 59   The normally distributed bivariate population.

Secondly, the standard deviation of these normal population distributions is assumed constant over the whole of the least-squares line. Although this assumption is valid in many circumstances and will be held to in this discussion, we should observe that it may be invalid in certain

207   Non-linear and multiple regression and correlation

contexts. For instance, it is hardly likely that the spread in saving habits will be the same for families in higher income brackets as for those with small incomes. The very fact that the second group has less money from which savings may be made will restrict the possible magnitude of the standard deviation level of savings. The previously encountered problem of heteroscedasticity is present (see 2.8.1 and 2.9.1).

The standard deviation of these normal distributions has been encountered in a different guise in 4.6.3 as the first-order standard deviation $s_{1.2}$, where dropping the notation of multiple regression and substituting α and β for a and b gives:

$$\sigma_{yx} = \sqrt{\left(\frac{\Sigma(y-\alpha-\beta x)^2}{n}\right)}$$

In sampling theory σ_{yx} is usually called the standard error of estimate. This is perhaps something of a misnomer, so we shall refer to it as the standard deviation of regression instead. We should also realize that the formula given above assumes α and β to be known. Because they are not, and because a and b, the sample statistics, are only unbiased estimates of the population parameters, we lose two degrees of freedom. Exactly the same principle is involved here as in 2.6.3, where we showed that σ^2 should be estimated from

$$s^2 = \frac{\Sigma(x-\bar{x})^2}{n-1} \quad \text{rather than} \quad \frac{\Sigma(x-\bar{x})^2}{n}$$

This was because we were using the sample statistic $\bar{x}$ instead of μ (the population parameter). We shall therefore estimate σ_{yx} from

$$s_{yx} = \sqrt{\left(\frac{\Sigma(y-a-bx)^2}{n-2}\right)}$$

The third and final assumption requires that successive observations in the series and their deviations from the regression line are independent of each other. If they are interdependent, then one is faced with the problems of serial correlation and autocorrelation.

4.9.3   Within the framework of these assumptions we should now consider the meaning and reliability of (a) sample regression coefficients and constants and (b) coefficients of correlation. After the calculation of r, the coefficient of correlation, we should immediately test whether it is significantly different from zero. If it is not, then there is little point in carrying on, for no evidence exists of any association between the variables. If, however,

r is significantly different from zero then we can test whether it could have been generated by a population coefficient, ρ (rho), other than zero, or whether it is significantly different from a previously calculated value of r, also obtained from sample data. Whichever of these secondary alternatives is adopted, we will be interested finally in calculating confidence intervals for the coefficient of correlation. Having obtained the regression equation, the significance of the regression coefficient should be tested to see whether it is significantly different from zero and from some other non-zero value; in the two-variable model the first of these steps is an alternative to testing $\rho \neq 0$, but this is not the case for multiple estimation equations. After this preliminary test, we may carry out tests on a and construct confidence interval estimates for α and β. Alternatively (and more probably) we shall require a confidence interval estimate of the predicted value of y obtained from the sample regression equation. This of course must include a consideration of the sampling error in both a and b.

4.10 Tests for hypotheses for r

4.10.1 The main objective of these tests is to discover whether a non-zero value of r could have occurred by chance even though there is no association between the variables in the population, i.e. $\rho = 0$. As usual, we first establish null and alternative hypotheses and acceptable significance levels. For instance, we may state

$$H_0 : \rho = 0$$

$$H_A : \rho \neq 0 \quad \text{or} \quad \rho < 0 \quad \text{or} \quad \rho > 0$$

$$\alpha = 0.05$$

The appropriate alternative hypothesis will depend upon the nature of the data and the objective of the test. If there are grounds for believing the relationship to be either positive or negative, then a one-tail test should be employed, but if there is no advanced knowledge about the relationship we should utilize the two-tail test.

Before any test can be carried out we must know something about the sampling distribution of the statistic involved and its standard error. The sampling distribution of r (with $\bar{r} = \rho = 0$) is symmetrical round zero, which is to be expected because the limits of r are fixed at -1 and $+1$. As with the sampling distribution of means, the specific form of this symmetrical distribution will depend upon the sample size; when n is large the distribution tends to be normal, while for small sample sizes it will conform to the Student t distribution. It is convenient to mention at this point that the sampling distribution of r with $\rho \neq 0$ is very definitely skewed and an alternative treatment will therefore be required to deal with this problem. The two opposing situations are shown in fig. 60.

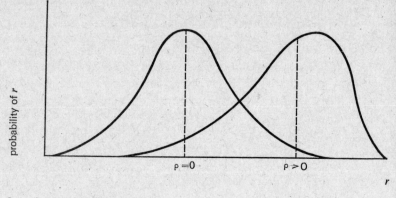

Fig. 60. Sampling distributions of r.

4.10.2   The standard error of the normal sampling distribution provides little difficulty and is given by

$$\sigma_r = \frac{1}{\sqrt{(n-1)}}$$

For small samples the standard error of the t distribution is a little more complicated, i.e.

$$\sigma_r = \sqrt{\left(\frac{1-r^2}{n-2}\right)}$$

and involves the use of $n-2$ degrees of freedom on entering the t-table.
Let us illustrate the techniques of employing these formulae by considering the average number of cars per hour passing a census check point on ten Sundays correlated with the mean temperature (see *Statistics for the Social Scientist: 1 Introducing Statistics*, page 196).

Average number of cars passing check point per hour (thousands)	Mean temperature (degrees Fahrenheit)
18	56
20	62
9	49
21	65
25	74
13	51
14	50
31	82
24	59
26	67

The regression of number of cars on temperature is given by

$$y = -15 \cdot 20 \times 0 \cdot 574x$$

and the mean of the y distribution is $20 \cdot 1$. From these two facts we can find the following:

x	y'	$(y' - \bar{y})^2$	y	$(y - \bar{y})^2$
56	16·944	9·960336	18	4·41
62	20·388	0·082944	20	0·01
49	12·926	51·466276	9	123·21
65	22·110	4·040100	21	0·81
74	27·276	51·494976	25	24·01
51	14·074	36·312676	13	50·41
50	13·500	43·560000	14	37·21
82	31·868	138·485824	31	118·81
59	18·666	2·056356	24	15·21
67	23·258	9·972964	26	34·81
		347·432452		408·90

The coefficient of determination is

$$\frac{347 \cdot 43}{408 \cdot 90} = 0 \cdot 85$$

from which we can determine the coefficient of correlation ($+0 \cdot 922$).

For the purpose of this demonstration we will assume that there were

100 observations instead of 10, and we shall use the one-tail test because there is supporting evidence that people tend to drive to the beach or countryside on warm sunny days rather than in cool cloudy weather, so that:

$$H_0 : \rho = 0$$

$$H_A : \rho > 0$$

$$\alpha = 0.05$$

Now

$$z(\text{calc.}) = \frac{r - \rho}{1/\sqrt{(n-1)}} = \frac{0.922 - 0}{1/\sqrt{(100-1)}} = \frac{0.922}{0.1005}$$

$$= 9.174$$

But $z_{0.05}$ we already know to be 1·64 for the one-tail test, so $r = +0.922$ is highly significant. We therefore reject the null hypothesis and accept that $\rho > 0$.

Returning to the correct sample size of 10 the calculations are as follows:

$$t(\text{calc.}) = \frac{r - \rho}{\sqrt{\left(\frac{1-r^2}{n-2}\right)}} = \frac{0.922 - 0}{\sqrt{\left(\frac{1-0.922^2}{10-2}\right)}} = \frac{0.922}{0.1369}$$

$$= 6.735$$

The critical value of $t_{0.05}$ for $10-2 = 8$ degrees of freedom is found from table 2 to be 1·860. Thus $t(\text{calc.}) > t_{0.05}$ and we again emphatically reject the null hypothesis at a 5 per cent level.

4.10.3   Having obtained positive results from our first test, we may also be interested to know whether $r = +0.922$ is significantly greater than some non-zero value such as 0·750. As mentioned in 4.10.1 this necessitates considering the skewed distribution of sample coefficients of correlation. Fortunately there is a logarithmic function of r which is approximately normal even though the sample may be small and the population value close to -1 or $+1$; this was evolved by Professor Sir Ronald Fisher and is known as Fisher's Z-transformation:

$$Z = \tfrac{1}{2} \log_e \left(\frac{1+r}{1-r}\right)$$

where $\log_e$ indicates that the logs are taken to the base $e = 2.71828$ instead of to the more conventional base of 10. For greater simplicity it is possible to convert this expression to logarithms to the base 10 in which case

$$Z = 1 \cdot 1513 \log_{10} \left(\frac{1+r}{1-r} \right)$$

The sampling distribution of Z is normal even though the distribution of r, on which it is based, is not. However, before we can use this information we must know something about the mean, μ_z, and standard error, σ_z, of this normal distribution.

$$\mu_z = 1 \cdot 1513 \log_{10} \left(\frac{1+\rho}{1-\rho} \right)$$

and

$$\sigma_z = \frac{1}{\sqrt{(n-3)}}$$

Formulating this, we may now state

$$H_0 : \rho = 0 \cdot 75$$

$$H_A : \rho > 0 \cdot 75$$

$$\alpha = 0 \cdot 05$$

Where

$$Z = 1 \cdot 1513 \log_{10} \left(\frac{1+0 \cdot 922}{1-0 \cdot 922} \right)$$

$$= 1 \cdot 6021$$

$$\mu_z = 1 \cdot 1513 \log_{10} \left(\frac{1+0 \cdot 750}{1-0 \cdot 750} \right)$$

$$= 0 \cdot 9730$$

and

$$\sigma_z = \frac{1}{\sqrt{(10-3)}} = 0 \cdot 3779$$

Therefore

$$z(\text{calc.}) = \frac{Z - \mu_z}{\sigma_z} = \frac{1 \cdot 6021 - 0 \cdot 9730}{0 \cdot 3779}$$

$$= 1 \cdot 665$$

In this instance $z(\text{calc.}) > z_{0.05}$, so there is just sufficient evidence for rejecting the null hypothesis and we can conclude that the population coefficient is greater than $+0 \cdot 75$. The student may care to check whether r is significantly greater than values in excess of $+0 \cdot 75$.

4.10.4   The final test which may be carried out asks whether the difference between one sample result and another is significant; it therefore parallel the tests for $\bar{x}_1 - \bar{x}_2$ and $p_1 - p_2$ discussed in Chapter 2. The Z-transformation is invoked once more because the sampling distribution of $r_1 - r$ is skewed and non-normal, while that of $Z_1 - Z_2$ is approximately normal. As in these earlier tests the hypotheses are stated as

$$H_0 : \mu_{z_1} = \mu_{z_2}$$
$$H_A : \mu_{z_1} \neq \mu_{z_2}$$
$$\alpha = 0.05$$

so that $\mu_{z_1 - z_2} = \mu_{z_1} - \mu_{z_2} = 0$.

The mean of the sampling distribution of the differences $Z_1 - Z_2$ is zero because under the null hypothesis μ_{z_1} is equal to μ_{z_2}. The standard error of the difference is derived by the same reasoning employed to find $\sigma_{\bar{x}_1 - \bar{x}_2}$, i.e

$$\sigma_{z_1 - z_2} = \sqrt{(\sigma_{z_1}{}^2 + \sigma_{z_2}{}^2)} = \sqrt{\left(\frac{1}{n_1 - 3} + \frac{1}{n_2 - 3}\right)}$$

Supposing we wished to test whether the result of $r = +0.922$ is significantly different from the result of a similar inquiry held a number of years earlier in which, from observations on fifteen days, $r = 0.833$. First we would calculate Z_1 and Z_2. We know Z_1 to be 1.6021, Z_2 we calculate from:

$$Z_2 = 1.1513 \log_{10} \left(\frac{1 + 0.833}{1 - 0.833}\right) = 1.1980$$

Therefore

$$z(\text{calc.}) = \frac{Z_1 - Z_2}{\sqrt{\left(\frac{1}{n_1 - 3} + \frac{1}{n_2 - 3}\right)}} = \frac{1.6021 - 1.1980}{\sqrt{\left(\frac{1}{10 - 3} + \frac{1}{15 - 3}\right)}}$$
$$= \frac{0.4041}{0.4756} = 0.850$$

and the difference is not significant.

4.11 Confidence intervals for ρ

After discovering that r is significantly different from zero, our final interest will be in making a probability estimate of the population coefficient of correlation. To do this we use the results of 4.10.3, which showed that for $r = +0.922$, $Z = 1.6021$ and $\sigma_z = 0.3779$. Therefore 95 per cent confidence limits for Z extend from

$$[1.6021 - (1.96)(0.3779)] \text{ to } [1.6021 + (1.96)(0.3779)] = 0.8614 \text{ to } 2.3428$$

These confidence limits for Z must now be transformed back to r by substituting each in turn in

$$Z = 1 \cdot 1513 \log_{10} \left(\frac{1+r}{1-r} \right)$$

Taking the lower limit gives

$$0 \cdot 8614 = 1 \cdot 1513 \log_{10} \left(\frac{1+r}{1-r} \right)$$

and

$$\frac{0 \cdot 8614}{1 \cdot 1513} = \log_{10} \left(\frac{1+r}{1-r} \right)$$

Taking antilogs of both sides leaves

$$5 \cdot 601 = \frac{1+r}{1-r}$$

so that

$$5 \cdot 601 - 5 \cdot 601 r = 1 + r$$

and

$$4 \cdot 601 = 5 \cdot 601 r + r$$

Thus

$$4 \cdot 601 = 6 \cdot 601 r$$

and

$$r = \frac{4 \cdot 601}{6 \cdot 601} = +0 \cdot 697$$

Using the same steps, the transformed upper limit is calculated to be $+0 \cdot 982$ so that we can claim with 95 per cent certainty that ρ lies between $+0 \cdot 697$ and $+0 \cdot 982$. It is important to remember that the sampling distribution of r is skewed, so that the confidence limits of ρ are not equidistant from r, even though those for μ_z were from Z. Each limit of r must therefore be calculated separately.

4.12 Tests of hypotheses for *b* and *a*

4.12.1 There are two ways in which a test of significance for the regression coefficient may be undertaken. The standard approach involves a knowledge of the sampling distribution of this particular sample statistic and its standard error. The alternative is to use the analysis of variance technique as developed in 2.9.1 to compare explained with unexplained variation.

If we were to compute every possible value of b which might result when samples of observations are taken from a bivariate population we would find the distribution of their values conforming to the t distribution where the mean value of b equals β (the population regression coefficient). The standard error of this sampling distribution would then be given by

$$\sigma_b = \frac{S_{yx}}{\sqrt{\{\Sigma(x-\bar{x})^2\}}}$$

4.12.2   Using the example of the car census (4.10.2) will again enable us to illustrate the application of these principles. We calculated the regression coefficient $(+0\cdot574)$ and the unexplained variation is given by $(408\cdot90-347\cdot43=61\cdot47)$; therefore s_{yx} is found from

$$S_{yx} = \sqrt{\frac{61\cdot47}{10-2}} = 2\cdot772$$

$\Sigma(x-\bar{x})^2$, although not specifically calculated at the time, is obtained from

$\Sigma x^2 - \dfrac{(\Sigma x)^2}{n}$. $\Sigma x = 615$ and $\Sigma x^2 = 38877$ so that

$$\Sigma(x-\bar{x})^2 = 38877 - \frac{615^2}{10}$$

$$= 1054\cdot5$$

The first test we shall undertake is the equivalent in the two-variable model to the initial test on r. We will seek to establish that $0\cdot574$ is significantly greater than zero. To do this, we set up the following hypotheses:

$$H_0 : \beta = 0$$

$$H_A : \beta > 0$$

$$\alpha = 0\cdot05$$

Then

$$t\text{(calc.)} = \frac{b-\beta}{s_{yx}/\sqrt{\{\Sigma(x-\bar{x})^2\}}} = \frac{0\cdot574-0}{2\cdot772/\sqrt{1054\cdot5}}$$

$$= 6\cdot722$$

Entering table 2 with $10-2=8$ degrees of freedom we find the value of $t_{0\cdot05}$ to be $1\cdot860$ so that we must reject the null hypothesis and accept the alternative that β is greater than zero. Of more importance, however, is the fact that the calculated t value is very close to that obtained in 4.10.2. In fact the difference in the second decimal place between the answers is due only to the effect of rounding. The two methods and the two formulae are actually identical, with

$$\frac{b-\beta}{s_{yx}/\sqrt{\{\Sigma(x-\bar{x})^2\}}} \equiv \frac{r-\rho}{\sqrt{\dfrac{1-r^2}{n-2}}}$$

Because of this identity the reader may well ask what point there is in considering this particular significance test. There are three reasons: firstly we may be interested to carry out tests for b when the null hypothesis is that it possesses some non-zero value; secondly it will not be true that tests for $R_{1.23}$ and for the coefficients of estimation in multiple regression analysis will be equivalent; and thirdly we must have a knowledge of the sampling distribution of b if confidence interval estimates are to be made for β.

4.12.3 *The analysis of variance*

4.12.3.1 In 2.9.6 it was observed that the variation between group means plus the variation within the groups was equal to total variation. An analogous situation exists in regression analysis, for we know that explained variation plus unexplained variation is equal to total variation. There seems to be an intuitively logical justification for using the analysis of variance approach in this situation.

There is also a more rigorous reason. If we square both sides of

$$t = \frac{b-\beta}{s_{yx}/\sqrt{\{\Sigma(x-\bar{x})^2\}}}$$

where $\beta = 0$ we get

$$t^2 = \frac{b^2\Sigma(x-\bar{x})^2}{s_{yx}^2}$$

We can show that $b^2\Sigma(x-\bar{x})^2$ equals $\Sigma(y'-\bar{y})^2$ which is the explained variation, and s_{yx}^2 we know to be the unexplained variation $\Sigma(y-y')^2$ divided by $n-2$ degrees of freedom; total variation $\Sigma(y-\bar{y})^2$ has $n-1$ degrees of freedom so that $\Sigma(y'-\bar{y})^2$ must have $(n-1)-(n-2)=1$ degree of freedom. To tidy up the picture it can be stated that the square of a t variable with $n-2$ degrees of freedom is identical to an F variable with 1 and $n-2$ degrees of freedom. Thus if we test the F ratio

$$F = \frac{\Sigma(y'-\bar{y})^2}{\Sigma(y-y')^2}$$

with 1 and $n-2$ degrees of freedom we have a third alternative to the earlier tests aimed at ascertaining whether there is any relationship between the variables being studied. It is this version which we shall employ later when dealing with multiple regression.

As usual this F test is formalized into the analysis of variance table shown below.

Source of variation	Degrees of freedom	Sum of squares	Mean square	Variance ratio
Regression of y on x	1	$\Sigma(y'-\bar{y})^2$	$\Sigma(y'-\bar{y})^2$	$\dfrac{\Sigma(y'-\bar{y})^2(n-2)}{\Sigma(y-y')^2}$
Unexplained	$n-2$	$\Sigma(y-y')^2$	$\dfrac{\Sigma(y-y')^2}{n-2}$	
Total	$n-1$	$\Sigma(y-\bar{y})^2$		

Substituting the figures from 4.10.2 gives

Source of variation	Degrees of freedom	Sum of squares	Mean square	Variance ratio
Regression of y on x	1	347·43	347·43	45·215
Unexplained	8	61·47	7·684	
Total	9	408·90		

Entering table 3 in the appendix we find that $F_{0.05}$ for 1 and 8 degrees of freedom is 5·32 and $F_{0.01}$ is only 11·26. Again we may decisively reject the hypothesis of no relationship between the two variables, but note in passing that the variance ratio is equal to t^2 in

$$t = \frac{b-\beta}{s_{yx}/\sqrt{\{\Sigma(x-\bar{x})^2\}}}$$

4.12.3.2   Having disposed of the various tests for b we may now turn briefly to tests for a. The sampling distribution of a is also a t distribution with $\bar{a} = \alpha$ and σ_a given by

$$\sigma_a = s_{yx}\sqrt{\left\{\frac{\Sigma x^2}{n\Sigma(x-\bar{x})^2}\right\}}$$

Tests to determine whether a is significantly different from any hypothetical value of α are carried out in the conventional manner, i.e.

$$t(\text{calc.}) = \frac{a - \alpha}{s_{yx} \sqrt{\left\{\dfrac{\Sigma x^2}{n \Sigma (x - \bar{x})^2}\right\}}}$$

where $t_{0.05}$ is looked up for $n - 2$ degrees of freedom.

4.13 Confidence intervals for α, β and Υ

4.13.1 The reader will realize that there is little difficulty in obtaining probability estimates of β and α. We have already pointed out that b and a have t sampling distributions and that their standard errors are known. From this information we can construct confidence intervals for the population parameters from

$$\underline{\beta} = b \pm \frac{t\, s_{yx}}{\sqrt{\{\Sigma (x - \bar{x})^2\}}}$$

and

$$\underline{\alpha} = a \pm t s_{yx} \sqrt{\left\{\dfrac{\Sigma x^2}{n \Sigma (x - \bar{x})^2}\right\}}$$

where t reflects the level of confidence for $n - 2$ degrees of freedom. The confidence interval estimates for the example in 4.10.2 are as follows:

$$\underline{\beta} = 0 \cdot 574 \pm \frac{(2 \cdot 306)(2 \cdot 772)}{\sqrt{1054 \cdot 5}}$$

$$= 0 \cdot 377 \text{ to } 0 \cdot 771$$

and

$$\underline{\alpha} = -15 \cdot 20 \pm (2 \cdot 306)(2 \cdot 772) \sqrt{\left\{\dfrac{38877}{10(1054 \cdot 5)}\right\}}$$

$$= -27 \cdot 473 \text{ to } -2 \cdot 927$$

4.13.2 In many circumstances the calculation of a probability estimate for the predicted value, Υ (upsilon), based upon the sample regression equation will be of far greater importance than the individual confidence intervals for the population regression parameters. To achieve such an estimate we must obviously take into account simultaneously the sampling error in a and in b. Notice that the variance of the sampling distribution of a is calculated by taking the mean of the squared deviations of the sample regression constants round the population regression constant, i.e. the mean value of $(a - \alpha)^2$; the variance of b is found in the same way from the

219 Non-linear and multiple regression and correlation

mean value of $(b-\beta)^2$. Now the variance of the sampling distribution of predicted values, y', must include a consideration of both sets of deviations $(a-\alpha)$ and $(b-\beta)$. It does this by substituting these deviations in the original regression equation $y = a+bx$. The variance of the sampling distribution of y' is then the mean value of

$$(y'-Y)^2 = [(a-\alpha)+(b-\beta)x]^2$$

where Y indicates the population predicted value and x is the value of the independent variable in terms of which the prediction is to be made. Expanding the right-hand side of this expression gives

$$(y'-Y)^2 = (a-\alpha)^2+(b-\beta)^2x^2+2x(a-\alpha)(b-\beta)$$

and taking the mean value term by term gives

$$\text{Variance } (y') = \text{Variance } (a)+\text{Variance } (b)x^2+2x \text{ Co-variance } (a,b)$$

NOTE. The mean value of $(a-\alpha)(b-\beta)$ is the co-variance of a, b just as $\dfrac{\Sigma(x-\bar{x})(y-\bar{y})}{n}$ is the co-variance of x, y (see *Statistics for the Social Scientist: 1 Introducing Statistics*).
The co-variance of a and b is defined as

$$\frac{s_{yx}^{2}-\bar{x}}{\Sigma(x-\bar{x})^2}$$

so that squaring σ_a and σ_b to convert standard errors to variances we can state that

$$\text{Variance}(y') = \frac{s_{yx}^{2}\Sigma x^2}{n\Sigma(x-\bar{x})^2} + \frac{s_{yx}^{2}x^2}{\Sigma(x-\bar{x})^2} + \frac{s_{yx}^{2}(-\bar{x})2x}{\Sigma(x-\bar{x})^2}$$

Simplifying (see 4.15.5) gives

$$\text{Variance}(y') = s_{yx}^{2}\left(\frac{1}{n}+\frac{(x-\bar{x})^2}{\Sigma(x-\bar{x})^2}\right)$$

and the standard error of the predicted value is found by taking the square root of both sides

$$\sigma_{y'} = s_{yx}\sqrt{\left(\frac{1}{n}+\frac{(x-\bar{x})^2}{\Sigma(x-\bar{x})^2}\right)}$$

The last piece of information required is the knowledge that the sampling distribution of y' is a t distribution. Thus confidence intervals may be calculated for any value of x from

$$\bar{Y} = (a+bx) \mp t \, s_{y.x} \sqrt{\left(\frac{1}{n} + \frac{(x-\bar{x})^2}{\Sigma(x-\bar{x})^2}\right)}$$

Confidence limits of 95 per cent can be calculated for all the values of x shown in the car census data (4.10.2) and confidence bands have been plotted round the regression line in fig. 61.

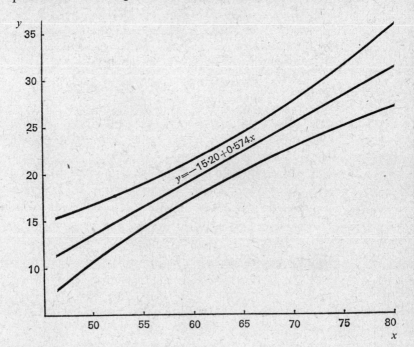

Fig. 61.   Confidence band for $y = -15.20 + 0.574x$.

x	$\underline{Y}$	$\overline{Y}$
49	9·741	16·111
50	10·466	16·534
51	11·180	16·968
56	14·650	19·238
59	16·587	20·745
62	18·362	22·414
65	19·974	24·246
67	20·964	25·552
74	24·091	30·461
82	27·354	36·382

221   Non-linear and multiple regression and correlation

4.13.3   It is apparent that the confidence bands are divergent from the point of means on the regression line. This is not unexpected as emphasis has been given to this point in the analysis, and the further we move away from $\bar{x}, \bar{y}$ the more likely does an error in the prediction become; once outside the range of the data involved in the least-square estimate we may not even be involved with the same regression structure (the extrapolation trap).

In discussing the method of calculating a confidence interval for the predicted value of y we have so far omitted to consider one important aspect which involves the assumptions made about the nature of the values of x. Our estimate has rested on the assumption that $x_1, x_2, \ldots, x_n$ are constants and the implication is that in repeated samples, although the y values may change, they are y values associated with the same set of x values. The confidence intervals we have calculated above are therefore probability estimates of the mean of these varying ys associated with each fixed x. If the assumption of constant xs is relaxed, then the additional variability entering the situation causes the confidence bands to be located further away from the regression line. The modified standard error is:

$$\sigma_{y'} = s_{yx} \sqrt{\left\{1 + \frac{1}{n} + \frac{(x - \bar{x})^2}{\Sigma(x - \bar{x})^2}\right\}}$$

This is obviously greater than the earlier version so that for a specific estimate of predicted value we must compute

$$\overline{Y} = (a + bx) \pm t s_{yx} \sqrt{\left\{1 + \frac{1}{n} + \frac{(x - \bar{x})^2}{\Sigma(x - \bar{x})^2}\right\}}$$

4.14   The analysis of variance in non-linear and multiple regression models

4.14.1   The various tests and estimation techniques which we have described in the preceding sections may also be applied to the linear transformations mentioned in 4.2.1. Although there are certain reservations about the applicability to these cases of the assumptions underlying the linear model we are largely justified in using the inference developments without modification. Notice we have not stated that the same techniques may be applied to the polynomials, however, for in this category of non-linear equations the general inference problem is more complex. Two fundamental questions nevertheless can be explored using a slight modification to the analysis of variance approach of 4.12.3. We shall test whether the relationship between y and x, x^2 or y and x, x^2, x^3 is significantly different from zero; we shall also try to find out if the refinements of a higher-degree polynomial produce a significant improvement in the explained variation as compared with the next lower polynomial. For instance, is the second-degree polynomial significantly better than the straight line? Put another way, we are asking whether c in $y = a + bx + cx^2$ is significantly different from zero. If it is not we may as well ignore the influence of x^2 and use the straight-line regression equation.

4.14.2   In testing for an over all significant relationship, the only alteration to the analysis of variance discussed in 4.12.3 will be that the number of degrees of freedom for the sum of squares (both explained and residual) will change. Specifically, unexplained variation will have $n - m$ degrees of freedom because there are m parameters in the regression equation instead of two. Total variation as usual is subject to $n - 1$ degrees of freedom so that explained variation will be subject to $(n-1) - (n-m) = m - 1$ degrees of freedom. In the case of the second-degree polynomial having three parameters the analysis of variance table will look as follows:

Source of variation	Degrees of freedom	Sum of squares	Mean square	Variance ratio
y on x, x^2	2	$\Sigma(y'-\bar{y})^2$	$\Sigma(y'-\bar{y})^2/2$	$\dfrac{\Sigma(y'-\bar{y})^2/2}{\Sigma(y-y')^2/(n-3)}$
Unexplained	$n-3$	$\Sigma(y-y')^2$	$\Sigma(y-y')^2/(n-3)$	
Total	$n-1$	$\Sigma(y-\bar{y})^2$		

Using the example in 4.3.2 and the answers obtained in 4.3.4:

Source of variation	Degrees of freedom	Sum of squares	Mean square	Variance ratio
y on x, x^2	2	1314·314	657·157	$\dfrac{657 \cdot 157}{3 \cdot 970} = 165 \cdot 531$
Unexplained	17	67·486	3·970	
Total	19	1381·800		

The calculated F value is very much higher than $F_{0\cdot05}$ or $F_{0\cdot01}$ for 2 and 17 degrees of freedom (i.e. 3·59 and 6·11) so that we reject the null hypothesis; there is a highly significant relationship between y and x, x^2. Because explained variation is still higher for the third-degree equation fitted to this data, and because the amendment to the degrees of freedom is small, it will be found that the relationship between y and x, x^2, x^3 is also highly significant.

$$F(\text{calc.}) = \frac{1338 \cdot 510/3}{43 \cdot 290/16} = 153 \cdot 795$$

while $F_{0.05}$ and $F_{0.01}$ for 3 and 16 degrees of freedom are $3 \cdot 24$ and $5 \cdot 29$.

4.14.3   The F-tests to determine (a) whether the second degree model is significantly better than the straight line, and (b) if the third degree is significantly better than the second degree (i.e. are c and d significantly different from zero) proceeds in a step-wise fashion. First we have to calculate the variation explained by the regression of y on x. The additional amount of total variation explained as a result of introducing the x^2 component is then found from

$$\text{Explained variation}_{y \text{ on } x,x^2} - \text{Explained variation}_{y \text{ on } x}$$

In a like manner the addition to explained variation resulting from the introduction of x^3 is obtained from

$$\text{Explained variation}_{y \text{ on } x,x^2,x^3} - \text{Explained variation}_{y \text{ on } x,x^2}$$

From the following results

$$\text{Explained variation}_{y \text{ on } x} = 883 \cdot 178$$

(using the data of 4.3.2 we calculated b and a and found explained variation from $\Sigma(y'-\bar{y})^2 = a\Sigma y + b\Sigma xy - \dfrac{(\Sigma y)^2}{n}$)

$$\text{Explained variation}_{y \text{ on } x,x^2} = 1314 \cdot 314$$

$$\text{Explained variation}_{y \text{ on } x,x^2,x^3} = 1338 \cdot 510$$

We set out the analysis of variance table in the following way:

Source of variation	Degrees of freedom	Sum of squares	Mean square	Variance ratio
y on x	1	883·178		
Addition of x^2	1	431·136	431·136	
y on x, x^2	2	1314·314		$\dfrac{431 \cdot 136}{3 \cdot 970} = 108 \cdot 598$
Unexplained by y on x, x^2	17	67·486	3·970	
Total	19	1381·800		

Analysis of variance table continued

y on x,x^2	2	1314·314		
Addition of x^3	1	24·196	24·196	$\dfrac{24·196}{2·707}=8·938$
y on x,x^2,x^3	3	1338·510		
Unexplained by y on x,x^2,x^3	16	43·290	2·707	
Total	19	1381·800		

We discover from the calculated F values that c is highly significant (F(calc.) = 108·598; $F_{0.01}$ for 1 and 17 degrees of freedom = 8·40), while d is also significant at the 1 per cent level, (F(calc.) = 8·938; $F_{0.01}$ for 2 and 16 degrees of freedom = 6·23). This is the final justification for the employment of the third degree polynomial on this data.

4.14.4 The tests set out above can now be used for the multiple regression model. In the example relating to drunkenness convictions, occupancy and unemployment (4.4.4) the tables are:

Source of variation	Degrees of freedom	Sum of squares	Mean square	Variance ratio
y_1 on x_2,x_3	2	1485·356	742·678	$\dfrac{742·678}{38·803}=19·140$
Unexplained	17	659·644	38·803	
Total	19	2145·000		

There is a significant association between the three variables because F(calc.) = 19·140 is greater than $F_{0.01}$ for 2 and 17 degrees of freedom (which is 6·11).

Source of variation	Degrees of freedom	Sum of squares	Mean square	Variance ratio
y_1 on x_2	1	922·641		
Addition of x_3	1	562·715	562·715	
y_1 on x_2,x_3	2	1485·356		$\dfrac{562·715}{38·803}=14·502$
Unexplained by y_1 on x_2,x_3	17	659·644	38·803	
Total	19	2145·000		

F(calc.) $= 14 \cdot 502 > F_{0 \cdot 01} = 8 \cdot 40$ for 1 and 17 degrees of freedom, so that $b_{13 \cdot 2}$ is significant and the inclusion of x_3 significantly increases the explained variation. We also need to know whether $b_{12 \cdot 3}$ is significant. This may be ascertained either by a straightforward test on the two-variable model y_1 on x_2 or by reversing the dependent variable subscripts above. In the first case:

Source of variation	Degrees of freedom	Sum of squares	Mean square	Variance ratio
y_1 on x_2	1	922·641	922·641	$\dfrac{922 \cdot 641}{67 \cdot 909} = 13 \cdot 586$
Unexplained	18	1222·359	67·909	
Total	19	2145·000		

and x_2 is significant. In the second case:

Source of variation	Degrees of freedom	Sum of squares	Mean square	Variance ratio
y_1 on x_3	1	803·903		
Addition of x_2	1	681·453	681·453	
				$\dfrac{681 \cdot 453}{38 \cdot 803} = 17 \cdot 562$
y_1 on x_3, x_2	2	1485·356		
Unexplained by y_1 on x_3, x_2	17	659·644	38·803	
Total	19	2145·000		

and once more the additional effect of x_2 over y_1 on x_3 is significant so that $b_{12 \cdot 3}$ is significantly greater than zero and should be kept in the equation.

4.15 Mathematical notes

4.15.1 *To prove that*

$$\frac{R_{1 \cdot 23}{}^2 - r_{13}{}^2}{1 - r_{13}{}^2} = \left\{ \frac{r_{12} - r_{13} r_{23}}{\sqrt{(1 - r_{13}{}^2)} \sqrt{(1 - r_{23}{}^2)}} \right\}^2 = r_{12 \cdot 3}{}^2$$

Now $$r_{12.3}^2 = \frac{\text{Explained}_{(1.23)} - \text{Explained}_{(1.3)}}{\text{Total} - \text{Explained}_{(1.3)}}$$

Using the formula from 4.4.6 gives

$$r_{12.3}^2 = \frac{b_{12.3}\Sigma(y_1-\bar{y}_1)(x_2-\bar{x}_2) + b_{13.2}\Sigma(y_1-\bar{y}_1)(x_3-\bar{x}_3) - b_{13}\Sigma(y_1-\bar{y}_1)(x_3-\bar{x}_3)}{\Sigma(y_1-\bar{y}_1)^2 - b_{13}\Sigma\{(y_1-\bar{y}_1)(x_3-\bar{x}_3)\}}$$

In 4.15.3 we shall show that

$$b_{12.3} = \frac{r_{12}-r_{13}r_{23}}{1-r_{23}^2}\cdot\frac{s_1}{s_2}$$

$$b_{13.2} = \frac{r_{13}-r_{12}r_{23}}{1-r_{23}^2}\cdot\frac{s_1}{s_3}$$

Thus by re-arrangement and cancelling

$$r_{12.3}^2 = \frac{\dfrac{\Sigma(y_1-\bar{y}_1)(x_2-\bar{x}_2)}{\sqrt{\{\Sigma(x_2-\bar{x}_2)^2\}}}\cdot\dfrac{r_{12}-r_{13}r_{23}}{1-r_{23}^2} + \dfrac{\Sigma(y_1-\bar{y}_1)(x_3-\bar{x}_3)}{\sqrt{\{\Sigma(x_3-\bar{x}_3)^2\}}}\cdot\dfrac{r_{13}-r_{12}r_{23}}{1-r_{23}^2} - \dfrac{\Sigma(y_1-\bar{y}_1)(x_3-\bar{x}_3)}{\sqrt{\{\Sigma(x_3-\bar{x}_3)^2\}}}\cdot r_{13}}{\sqrt{\{\Sigma(y_1-\bar{y}_1)^2\}} - \dfrac{\Sigma(y_1-\bar{y}_1)(x_3-\bar{x}_3)}{\sqrt{\{\Sigma(x_3-\bar{x}_3)^2\}}}\cdot r_{13}}$$

Dividing numerator and denominator by $\sqrt{\{\Sigma(y_1-\bar{y}_1)^2\}}$ gives

$$= \frac{r_{12}\dfrac{r_{12}-r_{13}r_{23}}{1-r_{23}^2} + r_{13}\cdot\dfrac{r_{13}-r_{12}r_{23}}{1-r_{23}^2} - r_{13}\cdot r_{13}}{1-r_{13}^2}$$

$$= \frac{r_{12}^2 + r_{23}^2 r_{13}^2 - 2r_{13}r_{12}r_{23}}{(1-r_{13}^2)(1-r_{23}^2)}$$

$$= \left\{\frac{r_{12}-r_{13}r_{23}}{\sqrt{(1-r_{13}^2)}\,\sqrt{(1-r_{23}^2)}}\right\}^2$$

4.15.2 *To prove that*

$$s_{1.2} = s_1\sqrt{(1-r_{12}^2)} = \sqrt{\left\{\frac{\Sigma(y_1-a_{12}-b_{12}x_2)^2}{n}\right\}}$$

Expanding

$$s_1 \sqrt{(1-r_{12}{}^2)} = \sqrt{\left\{\frac{\Sigma(y-\bar{y})^2}{n} - \frac{\Sigma(y-\bar{y})^2}{n} \cdot \frac{\Sigma(y'-\bar{y})^2}{\Sigma(y-\bar{y})^2}\right\}}$$

$$= \sqrt{\left\{\frac{\Sigma(y-\bar{y})^2}{n} - \frac{\Sigma(y'-\bar{y})^2}{n}\right\}}$$

$$= \sqrt{\left(\frac{\text{Total variation} - \text{Explained variation}}{n}\right)}$$

$$= \sqrt{\frac{\text{Unexplained variation}}{n}}$$

$$= \sqrt{\left\{\frac{\Sigma(y_1 - a_{12} - b_{12}x_2)^2}{n}\right\}}$$

4.15.3 *To prove that*

$$b_{12.3} =$$
$$\frac{\Sigma(y_1-\bar{y}_1)(x_2-\bar{x}_2)\Sigma(x_3-\bar{x}_3)^2 - \Sigma(y_1-\bar{y}_1)(x_3-\bar{x}_3)\Sigma(x_2-\bar{x}_2)(x_3-\bar{x}_3)}{\Sigma(x_2-\bar{x}_2)^2\Sigma(x_3-\bar{x}_3)^2 - \{\Sigma(x_2-\bar{x}_2)(x_3-\bar{x}_3)\}^2}$$

$$= \frac{r_{12} - r_{13}r_{23}}{1 - r_{23}{}^2} \cdot \frac{s_1}{s_2}$$

Re-arrangement gives

$$\frac{\Sigma(x_3-\bar{x}_3)^2 \left[\Sigma(y_1-\bar{y}_1)(x_2-\bar{x}_2) - \dfrac{\Sigma(y_1-\bar{y}_1)(x_3-\bar{x}_3)\Sigma(x_2-\bar{x}_2)(x_3-\bar{x}_3)}{\sqrt{\{\Sigma(x_3-\bar{x}_3)^2\}}\sqrt{\{\Sigma(x_3-\bar{x}_3)^2}}\right]}{\Sigma(x_2-\bar{x}_2)^2\Sigma(x_3-\bar{x}_3)^2 \left[1 - \dfrac{\{\Sigma(x_2-\bar{x}_2)(x_3-\bar{x}_3)\}^2}{\Sigma(x_2-\bar{x}_2)^2\Sigma(x_3-\bar{x}_3)^2}\right]}$$

$$= \frac{\dfrac{\Sigma(y_1-\bar{y}_1)(x_2-\bar{x}_2)}{\Sigma(x_2-\bar{x}_2)^2} - \dfrac{\Sigma(y_1-\bar{y}_1)(x_3-\bar{x}_3)\Sigma(x_2-\bar{x}_2)(x_3-\bar{x}_3)}{\sqrt{\{\Sigma(x_2-\bar{x}_2)^2\}}\sqrt{\{\Sigma(x_2-\bar{x}_2)^2\}}\sqrt{\{\Sigma(x_3-\bar{x}_3)^2\}}\sqrt{\{\Sigma(x_3-\bar{x}_3)^2\}}}}{1 - \dfrac{\{\Sigma(x_2-\bar{x}_2)(x_3-\bar{x}_3)\}^2}{\Sigma(x_2-\bar{x}_2)^2\Sigma(x_3-\bar{x}_3)^2}}$$

Multiplying top and bottom by $\sqrt{\{\Sigma(y_1-\bar{y}_1)^2\}}\sqrt{\{\Sigma(x_2-\bar{x}_2)^2\}}$ gives

$$\sqrt{\{\Sigma(y_1-\bar{y}_1)^2\}}\left[\frac{\Sigma(y_1-\bar{y}_1)(x_2-\bar{x}_2)}{\sqrt{\{\Sigma(y_1-\bar{y}_1)^2\}}\sqrt{\{\Sigma(x_2-\bar{x}_2)^2\}}}-\right.$$

$$\left.\frac{\Sigma(y_1-\bar{y}_1)(x_3-\bar{x}_3)\,\Sigma(x_2-\bar{x}_2)(x_3-\bar{x}_3)}{\sqrt{\{\Sigma(y_1-\bar{y}_1)^2\}}\sqrt{\{\Sigma(x_3-\bar{x}_3)^2\}}\sqrt{\{\Sigma(x_2-\bar{x}_2)^2\}}\sqrt{\{\Sigma(x_3-\bar{x}_3)^2\}}}\right]$$

$$\sqrt{\{\Sigma(x_2-\bar{x}_2)^2\}}\left[1-\frac{\{\Sigma(x_2-\bar{x}_2)(x_3-\bar{x}_3)\}^2}{\Sigma(x_2-\bar{x}_2)^2\,\Sigma(x_3-\bar{x}_3)^2}\right]$$

$$=\frac{r_{12}-r_{13}r_{23}}{1-r_{23}^2}\cdot\frac{s_1}{s_2}$$

4.15.4 *To prove that*

$$R_{1.23}^2=r_{12}^2+r_{13.2}^2(1-r_{12}^2)=\frac{r_{12}^2+r_{13}^2-2r_{12}r_{13}r_{23}}{1-r_{23}^2}.$$

It has been determined that

$$r_{13.2}^2=\frac{(r_{13}-r_{12}r_{23})^2}{(1-r_{12}^2)(1-r_{23}^2)}$$

Substituting above gives

$$R_{1.23}^2=r_{12}^2+\frac{(r_{13}-r_{12}r_{23})^2(1-r_{12}^2)}{(1-r_{12}^2)(1-r_{23}^2)}$$

$$=\frac{(1-r_{23}^2)(r_{12}^2)+r_{13}^2+r_{12}^2r_{23}^2-2r_{12}r_{13}r_{23}}{1-r_{23}^2}$$

$$=\frac{r_{12}^2+r_{13}^2-2r_{12}r_{13}r_{23}}{1-r_{23}^2}$$

4.15.5 *To prove that*

$$\text{Variance}(y')=\frac{s_{yx}^2\Sigma x^2}{n\Sigma(x-\bar{x})^2}+\frac{s_{yx}^2x^2}{\Sigma(x-\bar{x})^2}+\frac{s_{yx}^2(-\bar{x}2x)}{\Sigma(x-\bar{x})^2}$$

$$=s_{yx}^2\left\{\frac{1}{n}+\frac{(x-\bar{x})^2}{\Sigma(x-\bar{x})^2}\right\}$$

Re-arrangement gives

$$s_{yx}^2\left\{\frac{\dfrac{\Sigma x^2}{n}+x^2-2\bar{x}x}{\Sigma(x-\bar{x})^2}\right\}=s_{yx}^2\left\{\frac{\dfrac{\Sigma(x-\bar{x})^2}{n}+\dfrac{\Sigma x^2}{n}+x^2-2\bar{x}x}{\Sigma(x-\bar{x})^2}\right\}$$

$$= s_{yx}^2 \left\{ \frac{\frac{\Sigma(x-\bar{x})^2}{n} + (x-\bar{x})^2}{\Sigma(x-\bar{x})^2} \right\}$$

$$= s_{yx}^2 \left\{ \frac{1}{n} + \frac{(x-\bar{x})^2}{\Sigma(x-\bar{x})^2} \right\}$$

4.16 Examples

4.16.1 Non-linear regression

(a) A sample of areas in a large city shows that there is a negative relationship between the density of the resident population in thousands per square mile and distance from the city centre in miles. From the following data calculate an appropriate regression line and superimpose it over the scatter diagram. Calculate the coefficient of non-linear correlation.

Miles from city centre x	Density of residential population in thousands per square mile y
0·3	58·1
0·7	54·9
1·2	53·7
2·0	39·8
2·3	40·9
3·0	28·2
2·9	17·8
4·1	15·8
4·6	9·1
5·2	6·0
6·0	4·5
6·1	2·8
7·1	2·5
6·8	3·1
7·4	1·9

(b) In a period of relative stability the following real* prices and consumption of butter per head per annum were observed. Plot the scatter diagram of these data on double-log scale. Calculate the regression of consumption on price and state the elasticity of demand for this product.

Consumption of butter per person per annum (lb.)	*Price of butter ÷ retail price index (shillings)
45·7	3·1
40·7	3·2
39·6	3·4
37·1	3·3
33·1	3·4
33·2	3·5
30·2	3·7
31·3	3·9
28·2	4·0
25·1	4·1
25·3	4·3
22·4	4·8

(c) A medium-sized engineering firm carries out an analysis of production costs associated with different levels of capacity working. From past experience the following results are discovered:

Unit cost of production (shillings)	Capacity working (per cent)
116·7	40
115·4	38
114·9	44
113·8	47
113·0	46
111·5	51
111·2	61
110·4	67
109·5	72
110·2	75
109·1	82
110·0	89
110·6	95
110·6	99
111·0	100

Fit a suitable polynomial regression line to these data and ascertain the coefficient of determination. Explain the use of the polynomial in this case.

(d) A number of employees throughout the career structure of an organization compare notes about their monthly gross and net pay. The answers came out as follows:

Gross pay (£ per month)	Net pay (£ per month)
53	50
89	76
120	100
137	123
165	147
210	168
225	170
252	185
280	179
310	206
325	210
350	220

Using the reciprocal transformation find the regression of net income on gross income and say whether you think this curve is a reasonable representation of the situation shown.

4.16.2 Multiple regression and correlation

(a) Monthly data over the three-year period 1962–4 for the chemical and allied industries yield the following results for output prices, y_1 (1954 = 100); materials and fuel prices, x_2 (1954 = 100); and weekly wage rates, x_3 (all workers January 1956 = 100).

$$\bar{y}_1 = 105 \cdot 3 \qquad \bar{x}_2 = 107 \cdot 5 \qquad \bar{x}_3 = 131 \cdot 1$$

Sum of squares and cross products about means

	y_1	x_2	x_3
y_1	55·67	115·69	241·11
x_2		272·69	589·31
x_3			1639·89

Estimate the relationship $y_1 = a_{1.23} + b_{12.3}x_2 + b_{13.2}x_3$. Comment on the use of your results in explaining movements in output prices. (Note that both x_2 and x_3 have been lagged one month.)

(University of London, 1966)

(b) Let y_1 be net investment, x_2 and x_3 the previous period's output and capital stock respectively. All variables are measured in £millions at 1954 prices. From the hypothetical time series of 12 observations on each variable the following have been computed.

$$\bar{y}_1 = 5 \qquad \bar{x}_2 = 37 \qquad \bar{x}_3 = 102$$
$$s_1 = 5 \cdot 3 \qquad s_2 = 4 \cdot 2 \qquad s_3 = 12 \cdot 9$$
$$r_{12} = 0 \cdot 38 \qquad r_{13} = -0 \cdot 49 \qquad r_{23} = 0 \cdot 60$$

Carry out the calculations to obtain (i) the partial correlation coefficients, (ii) the regression coefficients of the multiple linear regression of y_1 on x_2 and x_3, and (iii) the multiple correlation coefficient. Discuss the economic meaning of your results.

(University of Bristol, 1963)

(c) Given that the sums of squares and cross products about the means for 50 observations are as follows:

	y_1	x_2	x_3	x_4
y_1	200	90	45	96
x_2		50	21	42
x_3			18	30
x_4				72

calculate the regression coefficients $b_{12.34}$, $b_{13.24}$, $b_{14.23}$ and carry out an analysis of direct and indirect effects using the β coefficient method.

4.16.3 The sampling theory of regression and correlation

(a) In a survey of 20 fish-and-chip shops in a large town the correlation between the weight of fish per portion and its price was $r = +0 \cdot 372$. Test whether r is significantly greater than zero and significantly different from the correlation between the weight and price of a portion of chips in the same 20 shops, namely $r = +0 \cdot 295$.

(b) The table on the next page shows the number of crimes committed in a sample of local authorities during a certain period.

Local authority	Population (10,000s)	Number of crimes committed
A	5	12
B	7	9
C	8	14
D	11	20
E	13	13
F	15	14
G	16	22
H	19	21
I	22	29
J	23	28

(i) Given the following information, calculate the linear regression equation of crimes committed on population.

$$\Sigma x = 139 \qquad \Sigma y = 182$$
$$\Sigma x^2 = 2283 \qquad \Sigma y^2 = 3736$$
$$\Sigma xy = 2867$$

(ii) Test whether b is significantly different from zero.

(iii) Test whether b is significantly different from one.

(iv) Produce a 95 per cent confidence-interval estimate for the mean predicted value of y associated with $x = 15$. Also make a 95 per cent confidence estimate of the predicted value for the same value of x.

(v) Make a confidence-interval estimate of the population product moment coefficient of correlation.

(c) Using the data in 4.16.1(c), test whether the use of a parabolic regression equation is significantly better than the linear model.

(d) Are $b_{12.3}$ and $b_{13.2}$ significantly greater than zero in the multiple-regression equation calculated in 4.16.2(a)? Comment fully on the meaning of your results.

Chapter 5
Mathematical trend curves and exponential smoothing

5.1 Applications of trend curves and exponential smoothing

5.1.1 Earlier considerations of time series analysis (see *Statistics for the Social Scientist: 1 Introducing Statistics*) show that simple moving averages do not entirely satisfy the requirements implied in the definition of a trend. The very slight and unpredictable oscillations which occur even when a 9-, 11-, or 13-year moving average is used are contrary to the assumed steady progress or decline of the secular trend, and where monthly or quarterly data are concerned the moving-average approach will certainly indicate not only the trend but in addition any cyclical component present in the series. An additional drawback is that a centred moving average terminates before the most recently available data, making projections for forecasting purposes on this basis at best highly subjective, if not impossible.

5.1.2 For long-term forecasting (up to a maximum of ten years ahead) the establishment of mathematical trend curves is a much more fruitful approach. This type of analysis will now be extended to cover non-linear trends, and we will be investigating those which experience has shown are the most likely to occur in economic and business series. For short-term forecasting, a modification to the moving average approach, known as exponential smoothing, may profitably be used in conjunction with adjustments both for changes in the trend and for the seasonal component. Finally, we shall need to mention the possibility of fitting confidence limits to the forecasts obtained from either of these methods of analysis.

5.1.3 Having stated the ground which is to be covered in this chapter, it is worthwhile making a number of comments about the use to which the techniques may be put. We must bear in mind that statistical forecasting in industry will only be used where firms are producing a large number of products which are sold to a large number of customers. If only a few products are involved, with a restricted market, adequate forecasts may be built up from the reports of salesmen who can readily evaluate at least the short-term requirements of customers.

In any case, the statistical technique alone should never be trusted. It should constantly be remembered that human judgement and experience can often prevent serious forecasting errors: knowledge of a competitor's sales promotion campaign or of an important new customer may cause the forecast to be adjusted upwards or downwards. As a result production may be increased so that delivery times are cut to a minimum and a potential loss in sales revenue avoided. Alternatively an inventory saving may be achieved if an optimistic and inaccurate forecast, suggesting the need to increase production, has been ignored. In many cases, forecasting will have been undertaken so that production scheduling and planning may be successfully implemented and stocks held at an optimum level, whilst long-term investment plans may be based largely upon the reports of forecasters.

The efficiency of any forecasting scheme should consequently be judged against this background and in the light of its effectiveness for the integrated business unit. A combination of objective analysis (which can often be undertaken by relatively inexperienced and unskilled personnel) and subjective commercial knowledge is more likely to predict the future with acceptable margins of error than either approach used in isolation.

5.1.4   It must be stressed that the analysis and extrapolation of single time series is not the sole method of forecasting: it may be the simplest but it is not necessarily the most successful approach. We have already seen that regression analysis provides an alternative method of predicting the outcome of events which have yet to occur. The correlation of time series where one variable is lagged may enable the most recent value of the unlagged series to be used to predict the value of the lagged series in six months, a year or two years time.

Multiple regression analysis can be employed with time as one of several independent variables. This type of analysis should be considered more appropriate where one is trying to forecast comprehensive economic series such as national product or the level of imports and exports since by their very nature these are the result of a complex of forces which may in part be analysed and stated separately.

Once the general economic and social environment has been brought into perspective, the simple extrapolation of the individual components within the economy may proceed against a known background and with some hope of success. For instance, the sales of consumer durable goods are likely to increase in a predictable fashion with the lapse of time. The reason is the increasing real wealth of the community and the increasing proportion of this wealth which can be devoted to non-essentials. One cannot, however, state that the prosperity of the nation depends simply on the passage of time: it is the way in which this time is used to devise and perfect new techniques of production (both for capital and labour), to plan transportation and to educate new generations which is important. The growth of the economy is the result of all these various forces, which should each be given separate consideration (more will be said about the problems of forecasting and planning for the economy at large in Chapter 7). None of these factors, of course, invalidates the use of the techniques suggested in this chapter for analysing the historical progress of the economy in the past.

5.2 Mathematical trend curves: linear transformations and polynomials

5.2.1   Many, though not all, of the equation forms utilized in Chapter 4 to describe non-linear relationships between two variables can also be employed for trend estimation purposes. Additional trend equations must also be considered, together with the methods available for deciding which is the most appropriate in the specific circumstances faced.

In most cases it will be necessary to plot the original data on natural and semi-log scale, and to make a rough graphical estimate of the trend. It may seem that one trend form is appropriate over one range of years, while a second more accurately fits the data over some other range. Each ought to be specified separately and in forecasting use should be made of the most recent estimating equation. Lumping two different trend situations together and making a compromise estimate is unlikely to produce useful forecasts, although it may be acceptable in a simple analysis of the past.

5.2.2   *The exponential or semi-log trend*

5.2.2.1   We have already considered the method of fitting a linear trend to a time series; this trend form should be used if the approximate trend values produce a straight line when plotted on arithmetic or natural-scale graph paper. Put another way, we may say that if the first differences between successive trend values are approximately equal, the linear trend will be employed. Examine, for instance, the following hypothetical data, which has been roughly smoothed:

The first differences are calculated as follows:

Year	Estimated trend	First differences
1950	11·5	
		1·3
1951	12·8	
		1·2
1952	14·0	
		1·2
1953	15·1	
		1·1
1954	16·3	
		1·1
1955	17·4	
		1·3
1956	18·7	
		1·2
1957	19·9	
		1·2
1958	21·2	
		1·1
1959	22·2	
		1·2
1960	24·4	
		1·2
1961	23·6	
		1·2
1962	25·9	
		1·3
1963	27·1	
		1·2
1964	28·3	

From these figures it seems reasonable to use the straight line. Although it will rarely be necessary to use this approach in the case of linear trends,

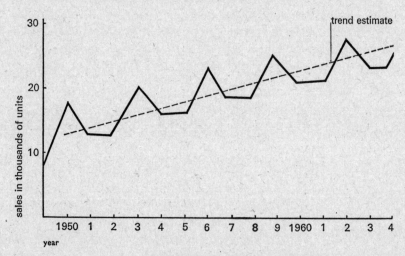

Fig. 62

it does establish a method which will produce valuable results in other circumstances.

5.2.2.2   If the rough trend appears non-linear on arithmetic scale graph paper, the first step should be to plot it on semi-log scale. If the curvature has been eliminated, then the exponential trend form

$$y_t = ab^{x_t},$$

should be utilized. This may be transformed to the linear form by taking logarithms of both sides to yield

$$\log y_t = \log a + x_t \log b$$

in which case the first differences of the logarithms should be constant. Consider the following data showing indices of the gross domestic product of the U.K. at market prices. From fig. 63 a free-hand trend form has

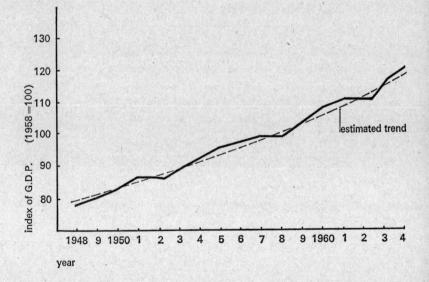

Fig. 63   G.D.P. (1958 = 100) and estimated trend.

been drawn; logarithms of the estimated trend have then been tabulated and first differences obtained:

Year	Index numbers of gross domestic product at market prices (1958 = 100)	Logs of estimated trend	First differences
1948	78·0	1·89	0·02
1949	80·5	1·91	0·01
1950	83·0	1·92	0·01
1951	85·9	1·93	0·01
1952	85·9	1·94	0·01
1953	89·9	1·95	0·01
1954	93·3	1·96	0·02
1955	96·3	1·98	0·01
1956	98·1	1·99	0·01
1957	100·0	2·00	0·01
1958	100·0	2·01	0·01
1959	104·1	2·02	0·01
1960	109·4	2·03	0·02
1961	113·0	2·05	0·01
1962	113·8	2·06	0·01
1963	118·9	2·07	0·01
1964	125·3	2·08	

(*National income and expenditure*, 1965)

There seems reasonable evidence that this linear transformation may be used. The logs of the indices are used in calculating the trend and the time units are centred, so that $\Sigma x = 0$ (see *Statistics for the Social Scientist: 1 Introducing Statistics*).

Thus
$$\log a = \frac{\Sigma \log y}{n}$$

and
$$\log b = \frac{\Sigma x \log y}{\Sigma x^2}$$

The calculations are as follows:

Year	Gross domestic product at market prices (1958=100) y	$\log y$	Time units round 1956 x	x^2	$x \log y$	Log trend $\log y_t$	Trend y_t
1948	78·0	1·8921	−8	64	−15·1368	1·8928	78·12
1949	80·5	1·9058	−7	49	−13·3406	1·9049	80·34
1950	83·0	1·9191	−6	36	−11·5146	1·9170	82·60
1951	85·9	1·9340	−5	25	−9·6700	1·9291	84·94
1952	85·9	1·9340	−4	16	−7·7360	1·9412	87·34
1953	89·9	1·9538	−3	9	−5·8614	1·9533	89·80
1954	93·3	1·9699	−2	4	−3·9398	1·9654	92·34
1955	96·3	1·9836	−1	1	−1·9836	1·9775	94·95
1956	98·1	1·9917	0	0	0	1·9896	97·63
1957	100·0	2·0000	1	1	2·0000	2·0017	100·4
1958	100·0	2·0000	2	4	4·0000	2·0138	103·2
1959	104·1	2·0175	3	9	6·0525	2·0259	106·1
1960	109·4	2·0390	4	16	8·1560	2·0380	109·1
1961	113·0	2·0531	5	25	10·2655	2·0501	112·2
1962	113·8	2·0562	6	36	12·3372	2·0622	115·4
1963	118·9	2·0752	7	49	14·5264	2·0743	118·7
1964	125·3	2·0979	8	64	16·7832	2·0864	122·0
		33·8229	0	408	4·9380		

$$a = \frac{33 \cdot 8229}{17} = 1 \cdot 9896$$

$$b = \frac{4 \cdot 9380}{408} = 0 \cdot 0121$$

The trend in log form is that

$$\log y_t = 1 \cdot 9896 + 0 \cdot 0121 x_t$$

or, taking antilogs of both sides

$$y_t = (97 \cdot 63)(1 \cdot 028)^{x_t},$$

In both cases the origin is 1956 and the unit of measurement one year. Although the second version is useful in that it shows us that the gross domestic product of the U.K. economy has been growing at an average rate of 2·8 per cent per annum, its log form is better for ascertaining the individual trend values. By adding or subtracting log b to or from log a

and then continuing the procedure with each successive log trend value, the whole series may be obtained. Antilogging these is then a simple matter and the absolute trend figures may be obtained.

5.2.2.3   Data may occasionally be encountered where some of the other linear transformations discussed in Chapter 4 are appropriate, but this will be the exception rather than the rule. The double log transformation has no real application, as the conversion of time units to a log form would seem unrealistic and is very difficult to interpret. Similarly, the reciprocal transformation with its asymptotic characteristic will generally be abandoned in favour of the various modified exponentials discussed in 5.3.6.

5.2.3 Polynomials

5.2.3.1   There is no simple graphical method of deciding whether a second- or third-degree polynomial will fit a set of data. However, by calculating second and subsequent differences of the approximate trend values, and observing whether they tend to be constant, we may determine whether the data are polynomials and if so of which degree. For instance, look at the following hypothetical trend values:

Year	Trend	First differences	Second differences
1950	20		
		19	
1951	49		2
		17	
1952	56		2
		15	
1953	71		2
		13	
1954	84		2
		11	
1955	95		2
		9	
1956	104		2
		7	
1957	111		2
		5	
1958	116		2
		3	
1959	119		2
		1	
1960	120		

The second differences are equal, so this is a second-degree parabola. In fact, the trend values have been generated from

$$y_t = 20 + 20x_t - x_t^2$$

In the same way, the trend values below are calculated from a third degree equation, $y = 12x_t + 8x_t^2 + x_t^3$, so that the third differences are equal.

Year	Trend	First differences	Second differences	Third differences
1950	21			
1951	64	43	28	
1952	135	71	34	6
1953	240	105	40	6
1954	385	145	46	6
1955	576	191	52	6
1956	819	243	58	6
1957	1120	301	64	6
1958	1485	365	70	6
1959	1920	435	76	6
1960	2431	511		

5.2.3.2   Let us consider the United Kingdom terms of trade (the ratio of export prices to import prices). Rough freehand estimation of the trend and calculation of second differences for the indices indicates that a second degree polynomial provides an adequate fit of these data.

Calculation of the second degree trend involves the three normal equations given in 4.3.3., but if the origin is centred the sums of the odd powers of the time units equal zero (i.e. $\Sigma x = \Sigma x^3 = \Sigma x^5 = 0$), and the normal equations reduce to

$$\Sigma y = na + c\Sigma x^2 \qquad \text{(i)}$$

$$\Sigma xy = b\Sigma x^2 \qquad \text{(ii)}$$

$$\Sigma x^2 y = a\Sigma x^2 + c\Sigma x^4 \qquad \text{(iii)}$$

From these

$$b = \frac{\Sigma xy}{\Sigma x^2}$$

and a and c may either be solved simultaneously from (i) and (iii) or deduced from the following formulae:

$$c = \frac{n\Sigma x^2 y - \Sigma x^2 \Sigma y}{n\Sigma x^4 - (\Sigma x^2)^2}$$

$$a = \frac{\Sigma y - c\Sigma x^2}{n}$$

United Kingdom terms of trade, 1933–1962

Year	Terms of trade (1958=100) y	Time-units round 1947–8 x	x^2	x^4	xy	x^2y	Trend y_t
1933	111	−29	841	707281	−3219	93351	112·12€
1934	108	−27	729	531441	−2916	78732	109·60
1935	106	−25	625	390625	−2650	66250	107·23€
1936	103	−23	529	279841	−2369	54487	105·02
1937	97	−21	441	194481	−2037	42777	102·98
1938	106	−19	361	130321	−2014	38266	101·08
1939	104	−17	289	83521	−1768	30056	99·35
1940	91	−15	225	50625	−1365	20475	97·78
1941	95	−13	169	28561	−1235	16055	96·36
1942	102	−11	121	14641	−1122	12342	95·112
1943	94	−9	81	6561	−846	7614	94·014
1944	102	−7	49	2401	−714	4998	93·074
1945	99	−5	25	625	−495	2475	92·293
1946	99	−3	9	81	−297	891	91·66
1947	92	−1	1	1	−92	92	91·20
1948	89	1	1	1	89	89	90·89
1949	91	3	9	81	273	819	90·75
1950	90	5	25	625	450	2250	90·76
1951	80	7	49	2401	560	3920	90·931
1952	85	9	81	6561	765	6885	91·25
1953	90	11	121	14641	990	10890	91·74
1954	90	13	169	28561	1170	15210	92·38
1955	89	15	225	50625	1335	20025	93·192
1956	91	17	289	83521	1547	26299	94·15
1957	94	19	761	130321	1786	33934	95·273
1958	100	21	441	194481	2100	44100	96·551
1959	100	23	529	279841	2300	52900	97·988
1960	101	25	625	390625	2525	63125	99·583
1961	104	27	729	531441	2808	75816	101·337
1962	106	29	841	707281	3074	89146	103·24
	2909	0	8990	4842014	−1367	914269	

(*Key Statistics of the British Economy 1900–1962*, produced by London an€ Cambridge Economic Service for *The Times Review of Industry and Technology*, 1963.

Using the tabulated calculations, we may substitute in these expressions to give

$$b = \frac{-1376}{8990} = -0·153059$$

$$c = \frac{(30)(914269) - (8990)(2909)}{(30)(4842014) - (8990)^2} = 0·019804$$

and
$$a = \frac{2909 - (0 \cdot 019804)(8990)}{30} = 91 \cdot 032068$$

so that
$$y_t = 91 \cdot 032068 - 0 \cdot 153059 x_t + 0 \cdot 019804 x_t{}^2$$

(Origin halfway between 1947 and 1948, unit $\frac{1}{2}$ year or 6 months.)
The trend values are then calculated from this equation by substituting each of the time unit values in turn and we see from fig. 64 the characteristic shape of the parabola. For forecasting purposes this particular

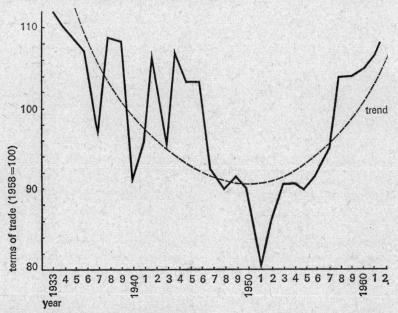

Fig. 64   Terms of trade and second-degree trend.

trend equation is of dubious value, although for an analysis of the period 1933 to 1962 it is quite useful. It seems that the war and post-war situation in Britain, coupled with the general world trading position in the 1940s, turned the terms of trade against the United Kingdom. It is quite feasible that this could happen again, and if the country lost its competitive position because of rapid domestic inflation and/or rising commodity prices associated with shortages of industrial raw materials another decline could take place. In fact if the series had been started in the 1920s we would have observed a second period when the terms of trade were unfavourable to the United Kingdom: this was associated with the worldwide devaluation of currencies when Britain was still on the gold standard, and a general loss of markets to the industrializing nations of Europe, North America and Asia.

5.2.3.3 The analyst should always be wary about the use of polynomials for long term prediction purposes. According to the portion of the curve upon which the series falls, it can go on either rising or falling continually; alternatively it may change its slope, possibly more than once. Common sense may suggest that the future trend pattern indicated is unrealistic, with the result that only short term forecasts can be made. As and when marked changes in the series occur, a new trend form will have to be fitted to the most recent data if the efficiency of the forecasting is to be maintained.

5.2.3.4 For this reason separate examples will be omitted for the higher degree polynomials, and we will simply state the equations and formulae which will be used in fitting the third degree polynomial. The normal equations given in 4.3.6 will reduce, on centring the time units, to

$$\Sigma y = na + c\Sigma x^2 \qquad \text{(i)}$$
$$\Sigma xy = b\Sigma x^2 + d\Sigma x^4 \qquad \text{(ii)}$$
$$\Sigma x^2 y = a\Sigma x^2 + c\Sigma x^4 \qquad \text{(iii)}$$
$$\Sigma x^3 y = b\Sigma x^4 + d\Sigma x^6 \qquad \text{(iv)}$$

It is apparent that equations (i) and (iii) are identical to those for the second degree trend, so that a and c may be calculated from the formulae given in 5.2.3.2. Equations (ii) and (iv) may be solved simultaneously for b and d, or we may derive the following algebraic formulae:

$$d = \frac{\Sigma x^2 \Sigma x^3 y - \Sigma xy \Sigma x^4}{\Sigma x^2 \Sigma x^6 - (\Sigma x^4)^2}$$

$$b = \frac{\Sigma xy - d\Sigma x^4}{\Sigma x^2}$$

5.2.3.5 For forecasting it is particularly desirable to have the simplest possible trend form, and as business and economic time series are generally held to exhibit smooth rates of growth exponential trends are preferred. One such trend form is the log parabola

$$y_t = ab^{x_t}c^{(x_t)^2}$$

which in log form is

$$\log y_t = \log a + x_t \log b + x_t^2 \log c$$

This should be used if the second differences of the logarithms of the approximate trend values tend to be constant. In these circumstances, the plotting of the trend in semi-log scale will fail to remove the trend curvature; the proportionate rate of change, instead of being constant, will either increase or decrease as the trend rises or falls. The trend equation may be established from

$$b = \frac{\Sigma x \log y}{\Sigma x^2}$$

$$c = \frac{n \Sigma x^2 \log y - \Sigma x^2 \Sigma \log y}{n \Sigma x^4 - (\Sigma x^2)^2}$$

$$a = \frac{\Sigma \log y - c \Sigma x^2}{n}$$

5.3 Mathematical trend curves: modified exponentials

5.3.1 It has been observed that some series show a tendency to increase in absolute terms, but with a declining amount or proportion of increase in each successive year, whilst other series have a decreasing trend with the amount or proportion of the decrease becoming progressively smaller from year to year. We already know that the simple parabola or log parabola may be fitted to these series, but we have also noticed that because polynomial trends will change their slope at some stage they are not attractive for long term forecasting. What is needed is a family of trends which possess the characteristics mentioned above throughout their whole length. The implication of such a trend, which continually increases in magnitude but has a smaller absolute or proportionate amount of growth in each year, is that it possesses an upper ceiling (or asymptotic level). Let us consider three such growth curves:

A. The simple modified exponential

$$y_t = k + ab^{x_t}$$

B. The Gompertz curve

$$y_t = ka^{b^{x_t}} \quad \text{or} \quad \log y_t = \log k + (\log a) b^{x_t}$$

C. The logistic curve

$$\frac{1}{y_t} = k + ab^{x_t}$$

Apparently B and C are respectively semi-log and reciprocal transformations of A. Therefore if we can establish a means of fitting the simple modified exponential it will be a straightforward task to convert the basic expressions for use with the Gompertz and logistic trends.

5.3.2 Unfortunately the normal equations which are generated by the simple modified exponential are very complicated and difficult to solve, i.e.

$$\Sigma y = nk + a \Sigma b^x \qquad \text{(i)}$$

$$\Sigma b^x y = k \Sigma b^x + a \Sigma b^{2x} \qquad \text{(ii)}$$

$$\Sigma xy b^{x-1} = k \Sigma x b^{x-1} + a \Sigma x b^{2x-1} \qquad \text{(iii)}$$

In consequence we shall abandon the least squares approach in this one instance and use the three point method. This involves splitting the data into three equal sections, abandoning one or two years at the beginning of the series when necessary. In terms of the trend equation the first, second and third five-year periods in a fifteen year series would be:

First period	Time units	Second period	Time units	Third period	Time units
$k+ab^0$	0	$k+ab^5$	5	$k+ab^{10}$	10
$k+ab^1$	1	$k+ab^6$	6	$k+ab^{11}$	11
$k+ab^2$	2	$k+ab^7$	7	$k+ab^{13}$	12
$k+ab^3$	3	$k+ab^8$	8	$k+ab^{13}$	13
$k+ab^4$	4	$k+ab^9$	9	$k+ab^{14}$	14
Σy_1		Σy_2		Σy_3	

Taking the mean values of the three periods, we get

$$\bar{y}_1 = k + a \left(\frac{b^0 + b^1 + b^2 + b^3 + b^4}{n} \right) \qquad \text{(i)}$$

$$\bar{y}_2 = k + a \left(\frac{b^5 + b^6 + b^7 + b^8 + b^9}{n} \right) \qquad \text{(ii)}$$

$$\bar{y}_3 = k + a \left(\frac{b^{10} + b^{11} + b^{12} + b^{13} + b^{14}}{n} \right) \qquad \text{(iii)}$$

Subtracting (i) from (ii) and (ii) from (iii) gives

$$\bar{y}_2 - \bar{y}_1 = a \frac{(b^5 + b^6 + b^7 + b^8 + b^9) - (b^0 + b^1 + b^2 + b^3 + b^4)}{n} \qquad \text{(iv)}$$

and

$$\bar{y}_3 - \bar{y}_2 = a \frac{(b^{10} + b^{11} + b^{12} + b^{13} + b^{14}) - (b^5 + b^6 + b^7 + b^8 + b^9)}{n} \qquad \text{(v)}$$

Dividing (v) by (iv) gives

$$\frac{\bar{y}_3 - \bar{y}_2}{\bar{y}_2 - \bar{y}_1} = \frac{(b^{10} + b^{11} + b^{12} + b^{13} + b^{14}) - (b^5 + b^6 + b^7 + b^8 + b^9)}{(b^5 + b^6 + b^7 + b^8 + b^9) - (b^0 + b^1 + b^2 + b^3 + b^4)} = b^5$$

Therefore

$$b = \sqrt[5]{\left(\frac{\bar{y}_3 - \bar{y}_2}{\bar{y}_2 - \bar{y}_1}\right)}$$

Substituting in (iv) or (v) enables a to be found from

$$a = \frac{n(\bar{y}_2 - \bar{y}_1)}{(b^5 + b^6 + b^7 + b^8 + b^9) - (b^0 + b^1 + b^2 + b^3 + b^4)}$$

Finally a and b may be placed in (i), (ii) or (iii) to give

$$k = \bar{y}_1 - a\left(\frac{b^0 + b^1 + b^2 + b^3 + b^4}{n}\right)$$

More generally, if the number of periods in the series is n (where $n/3$ is an integer) and $\overline{b^{x_1}}$, $\overline{b^{x_2}}$, and $\overline{b^{x_3}}$, are the mean values of the powers of b in each section:

$$b = \sqrt[n/3]{\left(\frac{\bar{y}_3 - \bar{y}_2}{\bar{y}_2 - \bar{y}_1}\right)}$$

$$a = \frac{\bar{y}_2 - \bar{y}_1}{\overline{b^{x_2}} - \overline{b^{x_1}}}$$

$$k = \bar{y}_1 - a\overline{b^{x_1}},$$

5.3.3   The characteristics of the simple modified exponential can be demonstrated by considering the trend,

$$y_t = 20 - (10)(0.7^{x_t})$$

which produces the following data:

Year	Trend	First difference	Percentage of preceding first difference
1950	10·0		
1951	13·0	3·0	
1952	15·1	2·1	70
1953	16·57	1·47	70
1954	17·599	1·029	70
1955	18·3193	0·7203	70
1956	18·82351	0·50421	70
1957	19·176457	0·352947	70
1958	19·4235199	0·2470629	70
1959	19·59646393	0·17294403	70

Evidently k (in this example 20) is the asymptotic level towards which the trend moves. We also see that each first difference is a constant percentage of the preceding first difference; wherever this occurs the simple modified exponential should be fitted. Lastly we notice that this particular trend rises from left to right to an upper asymptote. This type of trend, having a value of a which is negative and a value of b which is less than one, is the most common situation that the reader is likely to encounter. Less frequently we may find a series falling from left to right with a lower asymptote in which case a will be positive and b less than one. The other possibilities (b greater than one or less than zero) have limited relevance to the social sciences.

5.3.4   The fitting of the simple modified exponential will be illustrated by looking at hypothetical sales data for a highly competitive office duplication machine from shortly after its promotion to a point where market saturation is nearly complete:

Year	Sales (numbers)	Section total	Section mean	Time units	Trend
1948	1452			0	1159·054
1949	2986			1	2858·815
1950	4542			2	4275·110
1951	5010		5054·8571	3	5455·085
1952	6507			4	6438·380
1953	7355			5	7257·504
1954	7532	35384		6	7940·073
1955	8473			7	8508·812
1956	9276			8	8982·677
1957	8910			9	9377·463
1958	9973		9594·8571	10	9706·315
1959	10021			11	9980·545
1960	10032			12	10208·917
1961	10479	67164		13	10399·177
1962	10523			14	10557·743
1963	10714			15	10689·814
1964	10759			16	10799·873
1965	10862		10858·7143	17	10891·589
1966	10950			18	10968·018
1967	11082			19	11031·608
1968	11121	76011		20	11084·701

Now

$$b = \sqrt[7]{\left(\frac{10858 \cdot 7143 - 9594 \cdot 8571}{9594 \cdot 8571 - 5054 \cdot 8571}\right)} = \sqrt[7]{0 \cdot 2784}$$

Dividing the log of 0·2784 by 7 and antilogging gives

$$b = 0 \cdot 8332$$

Using this value we find

$$a = \frac{7(9594 \cdot 8571 - 5054 \cdot 8571)}{1 \cdot 2053775 - 4 \cdot 3239254} = -10190 \cdot 643$$

$$k = 5054 \cdot 8571 + 10190 \cdot 643 (0 \cdot 617704)$$

$$= 11349 \cdot 658$$

The trend equation given by

$$y_t = 11349 \cdot 658 - (10190 \cdot 643)(0 \cdot 8332^{x_t})$$

(Origin 1948, unit 1 year)

has been used to determine each trend value by successively substituting $x_t = 0, 1, 2 \ldots 20$ (b^{x_t} is calculated to begin with so that $\overline{b^{x_1}}$ and $\overline{b^{x_2}}$ can be worked out, after which these values are first multiplied by a and then

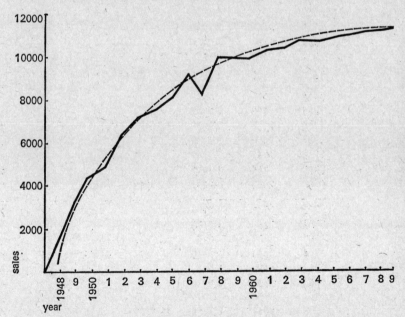

Fig. 65   Sales of office duplicating equipment and simple modified exponential trend.

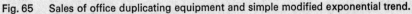

251   Mathematical trend curves and exponential smoothing

added to k). The trend and the original series are shown in fig. 65 from which we see the characteristic shape of the simple modified exponential.

5.3.5 The growth of many business, economic and social institutions differs in one important respect from that suggested by the simple modified exponential trend: instead of a sudden upsurge in the variable involved, followed by a relative decline as the asymptotic level is neared, there are often three stages. The growth of a new industry may be relatively slow at

Sales of men's cosmetics (Gompertz trend)

Year	Value of sales (£000's at) 1960 constant prices y	log y	Section totals	Section means	Time units	Trend
1945	12	1·0792			0	14·64
1946	23	1·3617			1	28·03
1947	45	1·6532			2	50·30
1948	85	1·9294		1·978287	3	85·15
1949	251	2·3997			4	136·7
1950	200	2·3010			5	209·5
1951	263	2·4200			6	307·3
1952	481	2·6821	15·8263		7	433·9
1953	508	2·7059			8	592·0
1954	1004	3·0017			9	783·0
1955	998	2·9991			10	1007
1956	1153	3·0618		3·123150	11	1263
1957	1490	3·1732			12	1549
1958	2062	3·3143			13	1861
1959	2185	3·3395			14	2195
1960	2453	3·3897	24·9852		15	2547
1961	3092	3·4903			16	2911
1962	3258	3·5130			17	3283
1963	3782	3·5777			18	3658
1964	3854	3·5860		3·615987	19	4146
1965	4490	3·6522			20	4403
1966	4706	3·6726			21	4765
1967	5100	3·7076			22	5116
1968	5351	3·7285	28·9279		23	5454

first while manufacturing techniques are developed and consumer acceptance of the product achieved. After the initial stage, investment may be stepped up and large-scale marketing arrangements established with the result that output and sales rise quickly. Finally, as saturation of the market occurs the surge in sales diminishes and the existing level of production is maintained but not radically increased.

Both the Gompertz curve and the logistic curve may be fitted to data of this type, i.e. with a zero asymptotic level at one extreme, an upper asymptotic level at the other and a point of inflection in the middle where the slope changes from being > 1 to being < 1.

5.3.6   Once again, general guidance is available for a decision as to which is the most appropriate curve. If the freehand estimate of the trend is plotted on semi-log scale graph paper and resembles the simple modified exponential, then the Gompertz curve should be fitted. On the other hand, if the plotting of the reciprocals of the trend values on arithmetic graph paper produces a curve resembling the simple modified exponential, then the logistic curve should be employed. Alternatively, if the first differences of either the logarithms or the reciprocals are changing by a constant percentage then the Gompertz or logistic trend should respectively be used. For illustrative purposes, we shall now compute a Gompertz trend for the sales of men's cosmetics by a large manufacturing company, and a logistic trend for the number of television receivers operated in a country from the time that a national broadcasting service was inaugurated. Both series are entirely fictitious, although based on logical premises.

For the Gompertz trend

$$\log y_t = \log k + (\log a)(b^{x_t})$$

$$b = \sqrt[n/3]{\left(\frac{\overline{\log y_3} - \overline{\log y_2}}{\overline{\log y_2} - \overline{\log y_1}}\right)} = \sqrt[8]{\left(\frac{3\cdot615987 - 3\cdot123150}{3\cdot123150 - 1\cdot978287}\right)} = 0\cdot9000$$

$$\log a = \frac{\overline{\log y_2} - \overline{\log y_1}}{\overline{b^{x_2}} - \overline{b^{x_1}}} = \frac{8(3\cdot123156 - 1\cdot978287)}{2\cdot451654 - 5\cdot695328}$$

$$= -\frac{9\cdot158904}{3\cdot246374}$$

$$= -2\cdot821272$$

$$\log k = \overline{\log y_1} - (\log a)(\overline{b^{x_1}})$$

$$= 1\cdot978287 + (2\cdot821272)(0\cdot711916)$$

$$= 3\cdot986796$$

Therefore the trend is

$$\log y_t = 3{\cdot}986796 - (2{\cdot}821272)(0{\cdot}9^{xt})$$

or in natural scale

$$y_t = (9701)(0{\cdot}001509)^{0{\cdot}9^{xt}}$$
(Origin 1945, unit 1 year)

As with the simple exponential trend it is preferable to calculate the logs of the trend values from the first of these expressions and antilog. This has been done above. The trend together with the original series is shown in fig. 66.

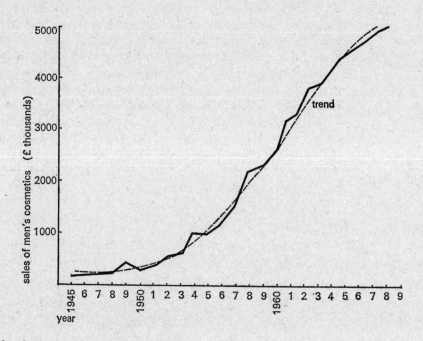

Fig. 66   Sales of men's cosmetics and Gompertz trend.

5.3.7   The calculation of the logistic trend differs from the Gompertz computation in only one respect. Instead of working with the logarithms of the original series we shall use the reciprocal transformation of these values.

Number of television receivers in use (logistic trend)

Year	Number of television receivers in use (thousand)	$1/y$	Section totals	Section means	Time units	Trend
1952	25	0·04			0	25·054
1953	54	0·0185185			1	50·046
1954	100	0·010000		0·0154971	2	99·841
1955	190	0·00526316			3	198·693
1956	270	0·00370370	0·07748536		4	393·469
1957	770	0·00129870			5	771·746
1958	1480	0·000675676			6	1486·109
1959	2850	0·000350877		0·000532797	7	2766·365
1960	4750	0·000210526			8	4860·529
1961	7800	0·000128205	0·002663984		9	7819·483
1962	11205	0·0000892459			10	11238·618
1963	14380	0·0000695410			11	14391·421
1964	16950	0·0000589971		0·0000651666	12	16733·834
1965	18000	0·0000555556			13	18216·318
1966	19050	0·0000524934	0·000325833		14	19060·629

$$b = \sqrt[n/3]{\left(\frac{\overline{1/y_3} - \overline{1/y_2}}{\overline{1/y_2} - \overline{1/y_1}}\right)} = \sqrt[5]{\left(\frac{0·0000651666 - 0·000532797}{0·000532797 - 0·0154971}\right)}$$

$$= \sqrt[5]{0·03125}$$

$$= 0·5$$

$$a = \frac{\overline{1/y_2} - \overline{1/y_1}}{\overline{b^{x_2}} - \overline{b^{x_1}}} = \frac{5(0·014964303)}{0·0605467625 - 1·9375}$$

$$= \frac{0·074821515}{1·87695324}$$

$$= +0·0398634$$

$$k = \overline{1/y_1} - a\overline{b^{x_1}} = 0·01549717 - (0·0398634)(0·3875)$$

$$= 0·0000500325$$

The logistic trend is therefore

$$\frac{1}{y_t} = 0·0000500325 + (0·0398634)(0·5^{x_t})$$

(Origin 1952, unit 1 year)

The reciprocals of the trend values are calculated from this equation and converted to produce the series given above. The trend and the original data are shown in fig. 67.

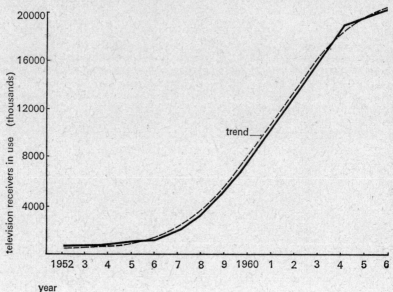

Fig. 67   Television receivers in use and logistics trend.

5.4   Trend curve selection: the Gregg, Hossell and Richardson technique

5.4.1   We have suggested a number of ways to ascertain the most appropriate non-linear trend for a given time series. In essence all these rest upon the subjective fitting of a freehand trend to the original series, but it is unfortunately possible for the analyst's hand to be guided by a preconceived notion of the correct curve rather than by objective draughtsmanship. As a final resort, several trends may be calculated and the sum of the squared deviations of the actual variable values round each obtained; the trend form producing the lowest sum of squared deviations will then be selected for further analysis of the data and/or projection.

5.4.2   An alternative solution to these difficulties has been suggested by Gregg, Hossell and Richardson (see Bibliography, page 370). The method rests upon an ability to judge whether or not some transformation of the original series conforms to a straight line; this is a very much simpler task than making a selection from a number of non-linear curves.

Each trend equation has some function which is linear. For instance, by taking the first derivative of the second degree parabola

$$y = a + bx + cx^2$$

we obtain

$$\frac{dy}{dx} = b + 2cx$$

which is linear. Since the first derivative indicates the curve's rate of change at any point, we need some means of estimating the slope of the series at each time period. Because we expect there to be irregular fluctuations in the series, it would be dangerous simply to calculate the first differences between successive observations and use these to estimate the slope.

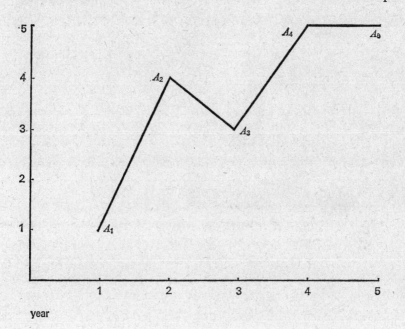

year

Fig. 68

What we must do is establish the average slope over 5, 7 or 9 years, and then use this average value to estimate the slope at the middle year. For example, fig. 68 shows five points in a time series, which are lettered chronologically $A_1 A_2 A_3 A_4 A_5$. Now the slope of the line between A_1 and A_2 is $\dfrac{A_2 - A_1}{2 - 1}$ (giving the slope of the hypotenuse) $= \dfrac{4-1}{1} = 3$; between

257 Mathematical trend curves and exponential smoothing

A_1 and A_3 it is $\dfrac{3-1}{2}=1$; between A_1 and A_4 it is $\dfrac{5-1}{3}=\dfrac{4}{3}$ and between A_1 and A_5 it is $\dfrac{5-1}{4}=1$. Similarly for the remaining lines which join all possible pairs of observations, i.e.:

$$A_2 \text{ and } A_3 = \frac{3-4}{1} = -1$$

$$A_2 \text{ and } A_4 = \frac{5-4}{2} = \frac{1}{2}$$

$$A_2 \text{ and } A_5 = \frac{5-4}{3} = \frac{1}{3}$$

$$A_3 \text{ and } A_4 = \frac{5-3}{1} = 2$$

$$A_3 \text{ and } A_5 = \frac{5-3}{2} = 1$$

$$A_4 \text{ and } A_5 = \frac{5-5}{1} = 0$$

We might simply take the arithmetic mean of these values, but we are far more likely to trust an estimate of the gradient which is based on the difference between series values three or four years apart than one based on adjacent series values that will be subject to short term irregularities. It is preferable to calculate a weighted average of the individual slopes, using the intervals between the pairs of values as weights.

$$\frac{\begin{aligned}A_2-A_1+A_3-A_1+A_4-A_1+A_5-A_1+A_3-A_2+\\ A_4-A_2+A_5-A_2+A_4-A_3+A_5-A_3+A_5-A_4\end{aligned}}{1+2+3+4+1+2+3+1+2+1}$$

$$=\frac{3+2+4+4-1+1+1+2+2+0}{20}$$

$$=\frac{18}{20}=0\cdot90$$

Alternatively, we may simplify the above expression to

$$\frac{-4A_1-2A_2+2A_4+4A_5}{20}.$$

$$= \frac{-2A_1 - A_2 + A_4 + 2A_5}{10}$$

$$= \frac{-2 - 4 + 5 + 10}{10}$$

$$= \frac{9}{10} = 0 \cdot 9$$

In either case the slope calculated relates to period A_3. More generally the slope for period t, where m years in the series are taken into account, will be:

slope at $t =$

$$\frac{-\frac{m-1}{2}A_{t-\frac{m-1}{2}} - \ldots - A_{t-1} + A_{t+1} + \ldots + \frac{m-1}{2}A_{t+\frac{m-1}{2}}}{\left(\frac{m}{3}\right)\left(\frac{m-1}{2}\right)\left(\frac{m+1}{2}\right)}$$

so that for 5, 7 and 9 years the slope at t will be:

Five years...

$$\frac{-2A_{t-2} - A_{t-1} + A_{t+1} + 2A_{t+2}}{10}$$

Seven years...

$$\frac{-3A_{t-3} - 2A_{t-2} - A_{t-1} + A_{t+1} + 2A_{t+2} + 3A_{t+3}}{28}$$

Nine years...

$$\frac{-4A_{t-4} - 3A_{t-3} - 2A_{t-2} - A_{t-1} + A_{t+1} + 2A_{t+2} + 3A_{t+3} + 4A_{t+4}}{60}$$

5.4.3   While the plotting of the slopes will indicate whether the appropriate trend is linear or a second degree parabola, the majority of the remaining transformations require in addition an estimate of the trend. For instance, the function of

$$\log y_t = \log a + x_t \log b$$

which is linear, is $\dfrac{\log b}{y_t}$. If the trend value y_t is estimated by a 5-year moving average, the transformed series which should be calculated and plotted is

$$\frac{\text{Slope}}{\text{Moving average}} = \frac{5(-2A_{t-2}-A_{t-1}+A_t+2A_{t+2})}{10(A_{t-2}+A_{t-1}+A_t+A_{t+1}+A_{t+2})}$$

If this appears to be linear (specifically horizontal) the simple exponential should be fitted. These and the other transformations are summarized below.

Calculate and plot transformation	Position of straight line which may be fitted to transformed data	Trend suggested
Slope	Horizontal	Linear
Slope	Diagonal (positive or negative slope)	Second degree polynomial
Slope/moving average	Horizontal	Simple exponential
Slope/moving average	Diagonal (positive or negative slope)	Log parabola
Log slope	Diagonal (negative slope)	Simple modified exponential
Log (slope/moving average)	Diagonal (negative slope)	Gompertz
Log (slope/moving average²)	Diagonal (negative slope)	Logistic

5.4.4   An example of the application of these principles will indicate the general methodology involved. Taking the following data, we will firstly calculate the moving averages in the usual manner and then the slopes. The various ratios and log ratio will finally be computed and plotted.

Year	Series	Sum of five years	Moving average	$-2A_{t-2}-A_{t-1}+A_{t+1}+2A_{t+2}$	Slope	Slope/ moving average	Log slope	Log slope/ moving average	Log slope/ moving average²
1	23								
2	38								
3	33		39·0	$-46-38+50+102$	6·8	0·1744	0·8325	$\bar{1}$·2415	3·6505
4	50		45·8	$-76-33+51+114$	5·6	0·1223	0·7482	$\bar{1}$·0874	3·4425
5	51	195	55·2	$-66-50+57+170$	11·1	0·2011	1·0453	$\bar{1}$·3034	3·5615
6	57	229	66·2	$-100-51+85+176$	11·0	0·1662	1·0414	$\bar{1}$·2206	3·3999
7	85	276	77·4	$-102-57+88+212$	14·1	0·1822	1·1492	$\bar{1}$·2606	3·3701
8	88	331	95·2	$-114-85+106+280$	18·7	0·1964	1·2718	$\bar{1}$·2932	3·3145
9	106	387	114·2	$-170-88+140+304$	18·6	0·1629	1·2695	$\bar{1}$·2116	3·1541
10	140	476	137·2	$-176-106+152+400$	27·0	0·1968	1·4314	$\bar{1}$·2941	3·1565
11	152	571	164·6	$-212-140+200+450$	29·8	0·1810	1·4742	$\bar{1}$·2577	3·0414
12	200	688							
13	225	823							

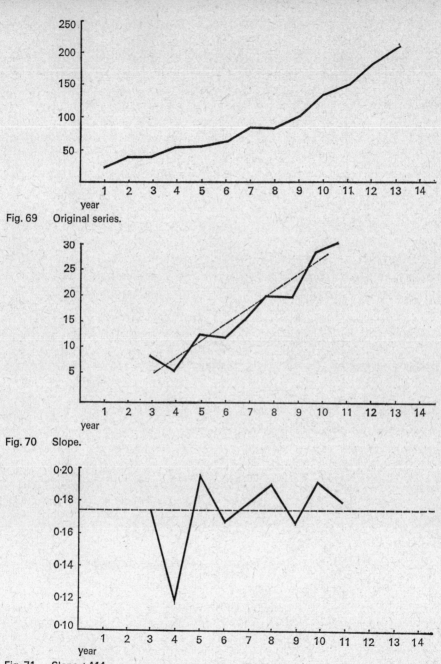

Fig. 69   Original series.

Fig. 70   Slope.

Fig. 71   Slope ÷ *MA*.

261   Mathematical trend curves and exponential smoothing

Fig. 69 shows the original series. From fig. 70, which shows the graph of the slope, we can be certain that a linear trend would be inappropriate, but it seems that a second degree polynomial is quite likely. The approximately horizontal arrangement of the graph of slope/moving average values (fig. 71) indicates a second possibility, the simple exponential trend, and eliminates the log parabola. The simple modified exponential and the Gompertz trends can also be excluded because of the positive slope of the series (log slope and log slope/moving average) plotted in figs. 72 and 73. However, the logistic curve is suggested as the third and final trend which

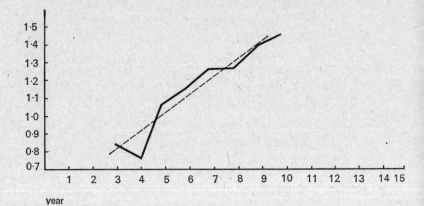

Fig. 72   Log. slope.

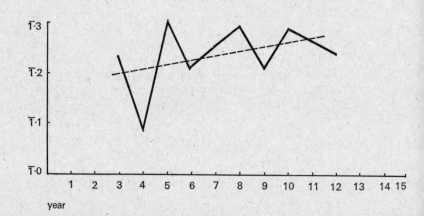

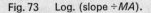

Fig. 73   Log. (slope ÷ *MA*).

may be fitted by the negative slope of the series slope/moving average^2 shown in fig. 74.

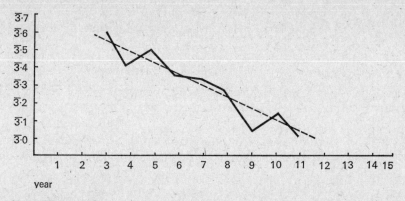

Fig. 74   Log. (slope $\div MA^2$).

Having restricted the choice to three trend forms the final selection may be dictated by *a priori* reasoning. If it seems that the series is likely to level off to an upper asymptote, then the logistic curve will be fitted at the expense of the parabola and simple exponential, but if this does not seem to be the case, then both second-degree polynomial and simple exponential trends should be calculated. The trend which yields the lower sum of squared deviations will be selected.

5.5   Exponentially weighted moving averages

5.5.1   It has already been seen that the calculation of a simple moving average achieves the smoothing of the short term fluctuations in a series. In addition, we have indicated that the simple moving average provides no basis on which a forecast may be made, because each moving average is centred and there is thus inevitably a gap at the end of the series.

The exponentially weighted moving average, on the other hand, achieves an equally efficient measure of smoothing while giving values over the whole period of the series and hence providing a basis on which forecasts may be made. The exponential smoothing process is based on the belief that the most recent value in the series should be given more importance than earlier values, which should be taken into account but with progressively less weight attached to each preceding one. Specifically, the data for the most recent time period, A_t, is given a weight w. The weight given to the data from the previous period, A_{t-1}, is a fraction, k, of w, so that

$$w(at.t-1) = wk$$

Similarly the weight given to A_{t-2} is the same fraction of the weight given to A_{t-1}, i.e.:

$$w(at.t-2) = w(at.t-1)k = wk^2$$

and the weight for A_{t-n} is wk^n. In other words the series of weights

$$w, wk, wk^2, \ldots wk^n$$

constitutes a geometric progression. For convenience, the values of w and k in this geometric progression are established such that

$$\sum wk^x = 1$$

or

$$\frac{w}{1-k} = 1$$

$\left(\dfrac{w}{1-k}\right.$ is the sum to infinity of a convergent geometric progression$\left.\right)$. Thus the exponentially weighted moving average for t is

$$\exp MA_t = wA_t + wkA_{t-1} + wk^2 A_{t-2} + \ldots wk^n A_{t-n}$$

$$= w(A_t + kA_{t-1} + k^2 A_{t-2} + \ldots k^n A_{t-n})$$

and for $t-1$ is

$$\exp MA_{t-1} = w(A_{t-1} + kA_{t-2} + k^2 A_{t-3} \ldots k^n A_{t-n})$$

But

$$k \exp MA_{t-1} = \exp MA_t - wA_t$$

or

$$\exp MA_t = wA_t + k \exp MA_{t-1}$$

$$= \exp MA_{t-1} + w(A_t - \exp MA_{t-1})$$

It seems that the appearance of the latest value of the series enables the new average to be calculated using no more than a knowledge of the old. Either the new value A_t can be multiplied by w and added to k times the earlier exponential weight average, $\exp MA_{t-1}$, or this old average may be added to w times the difference between the latest series value and the old average. The smoothing procedure is illustrated by reference to the following data, showing the sales of footwear by manufacturers. This is taken from various issues of the *Monthly Digest of Statistics*. The original series and the exponentially weighted moving averages are plotted in fig. 75.

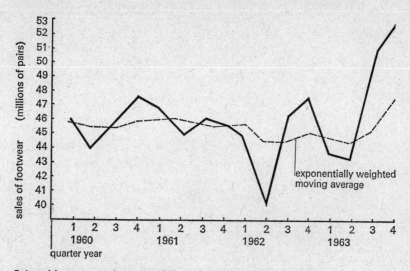

Fig. 75.   Sales of footwear and exponentially weighted moving average.

Manufacturers' footwear sales (millions of pairs)

Year	Quarter	Actual data	Exponential moving average
1960	1	45·8	45·60
	2	43·6	$45·60 + 0·2(43·6 - 45·60) = 45·20$
	3	45·5	$45·20 + 0·2(45·5 - 45·20) = 45·26$
	4	47·5	$45·26 + 0·2(47·5 - 45·26) = 45·71$
1961	1	47·2	$45·71 + 0·2(47·2 - 45·71) = 46·01$
	2	44·6	$46·01 + 0·2(44·6 - 46·01) = 45·73$
	3	46·3	$45·73 + 0·2(46·3 - 45·73) = 45·84$
	4	46·0	$45·84 + 0·2(46·0 - 45·84) = 45·87$
1962	1	45·4	$45·87 + 0·2(45·4 - 45·87) = 45·78$
	2	40·4	$45·78 + 0·2(40·4 - 45·78) = 44·70$
	3	46·1	$44·70 + 0·2(46·1 - 44·70) = 44·98$
	4	47·5	$44·98 + 0·2(47·5 - 44·98) = 45·48$
1963	1	43·9	$45·48 + 0·2(43·9 - 45·48) = 45·16$
	2	43·4	$45·16 + 0·2(43·4 - 45·16) = 44·81$
	3	50·1	$44·81 + 0·2(50·1 - 44·81) = 45·87$
	4	53·0	$45·87 + 0·2(53·0 - 45·87) = 47·30$

5.5.2   The reader will wonder how the value of $w = 0.2$ and the first moving average value of 45·60 were determined. It is apparent that w might be fixed anywhere between 0 and 1. The lower it is, the greater will be the smoothing of the series, but if the series is smoothing too much, real changes in the sales of the footwear will be slow to show themselves. If w is close to 1 the moving average series will include a substantial portion of the random and irregular fluctuations and the real increases in sales performance will have been masked. A compromise has to be made, and this may be facilitated by trying in turn several different values of w; Coutie *et al*. (see Bibliography, page 370) have suggested that in most series w is appropriately fixed between 0·1 and 0·3.

The starting value may either be established by taking the mean of the first year's quarterly sales or by calculating a series of simple moving averages and extrapolating this back by freehand to the first period.

5.5.3   In the absence of any other information, the last exponentially weighted moving average figure of 47·3 provides a forecast not only for the first quarter of 1964 but also for each subsequent quarter. It is apparent, however, that in two circumstances this will probably produce misleading and inaccurate forecasts: if the trend of the series is rising then this should be taken into account, and if a marked seasonal pattern occurs it must be included.

The trend may be calculated and revised at regular intervals by a very simple device. If the mean quarterly value of sales for the most recent year is found and the mean quarterly sales in the previous year subtracted from this, the resulting answer, on dividing by 4, will show the growth of the trend per quarter. Thus we would estimate the trend increases from the data given as

$$\frac{(53\cdot0 + 50\cdot1 + 43\cdot4 + 43\cdot9)/4 - (47\cdot5 + 46\cdot1 + 40\cdot4 + 45\cdot4)/4}{4}$$

$$= \frac{2\cdot75}{4} = 0\cdot69 \text{ (millions of pairs) per quarter.}$$

The seasonal component should be calculated by using either the additive or the multiplicative model as appropriate (see *Statistics for the Social Scientist: 1 Introducing Statistics*); in this case it will be estimated from the data given above, although in general as many years as possible should be included. To obtain the following results a moving average was calculated and extended at each end so that all time periods are considered.

Detrended series

Year	First quarter	Second quarter	Third quarter	Fourth quarter
1960	−0·80	−1·90	−0·28	1·42
1961	0·90	−1·61	0·50	0·95
1962	0·90	−4·26	1·44	2·65
1963	−1·83	−3·51	2·10	4·00
Total	−0·83	−11·28	3·76	9·02
Corrected −0·17	−1·00	−11·45	3·59	8·85
Average 4	−0·25	−2·86	0·90	2·21

5.5.4

With this information we can now make forecasts for two years ahead based upon knowledge available at the fourth quarter of 1963.

Components of forecast

Year	Quarter	Exp. M.A. at third quarter of 1963	Trend increase	Seasonal component	Forecast
1964	1	47·30	0·69	−0·25	47·74
	2	47·30	1·38	−2·86	45·82
	3	47·30	2·07	0·90	50·27
	4	47·30	2·76	2·21	52·27
1965	1	47·30	3·45	−0·25	50·50
	2	47·30	4·14	−2·86	48·58
	3	47·30	4·83	0·90	53·03
	4	47·30	5·52	2·21	55·03

These figures will continually be revised as new data become available, the same principles being involved at each forecasting stage.

		Forecast at:		Forecast for 1964				Forecast for 1965			
Year	Quarter	Actual data	Exp. M.A.	First quarter	Second quarter	Third quarter	Fourth quarter	First quarter	Second quarter	Third quarter	Fourth quarter
1963	4		47·30	47·74	45·82	50·27	52·27	50·50	48·58	53·03	55·03
1964	1	50·4	47·92		45·75	50·20	52·20	50·43	48·51	52·96	54·96
	2	49·2	48·18			49·77	51·77	50·00	48·08	52·53	54·53
	3	52·4	49·02				51·92	50·15	48·23	52·68	54·68
	4	50·0	49·22					49·66	47·74	52·19	54·19
1965	1	47·7	48·92						46·79	51·28	53·32
	2	47·2	48·58							50·21	52·25
	3	50·6	48·98								51·92
	4	52·2	49·62								

Notice that the estimate of the trend increase was revised at the end of 1964. The updating produced the quarterly trend increase of 0·73 which was applied to the forecast at and after the fourth quarter of 1964. Additionally the seasonal pattern might have been re-explored, although this step will usually be required at less frequent intervals.

5.6 Confidence limits for the forecast

5.6.1 Confidence limits may be assessed for forecasts based upon mathematical trend curves by an extension of the principles established for linear regression analysis, as Gregg, Hossell and Richardson have shown (see Bibliography, page 370), but of greater importance is the fixing of probability limits for short-term planning purposes. For instance, if a manufacturer knows the upper limit of a 95 per cent confidence interval for a sales forecast three or six months ahead, buffer stocks may be set aside to minimize at 2·5 per cent the probability of running out.

5.6.2   If the differences between the actual sales and forecasts made one month or one quarter previously are obtained from past data, it will often be found that the resulting distribution is approximately normal or conforms to some other theoretical distribution (at least fifty differences or forecasting errors should be used, which may involve a considerable amount of previous data). If in fact the distribution is normal, the calculation of the standard deviation (or standard error of the sampling distribution of forecast errors) enables the 95 per cent confidence interval to be found lying two standard errors above and below the forecast. It is important to realize that these limits relate only to predictions one month or one quarter ahead of the last available sales data. Forecasts three or four months ahead are likely to be less accurate, so that the standard error of forecast will be larger and should be calculated separately. The divergent confidence limits for the forecasts conform with the analysis developed in Chapter 4 in connexion with the linear regression model.

The final decision about the form of the distribution of forecasting errors may be made using the principles to be discussed in the next chapter, where we shall introduce a test of significance which indicates whether a sample distribution has been drawn from a specified theoretical population distribution.

5.7 Examples

5.7.1 Non-linear trends

(a) Fit an exponential trend to the following data. Using the trend equation, forecast the number of cars and commercial vehicles likely to be produced in 1964 and 1965.

Year	Cars and commercial vehicles produced (thousands)
1945	139
1946	365
1947	442
1948	498
1949	629
1950	784
1951	734
1952	690
1953	834
1954	1038
1955	1237
1956	1005
1957	1149
1958	1364
1959	1560
1960	1811
1961	1464
1962	1675

(b) Fit a second degree polynomial trend to the following data and suggest why it may appropriately be used.

Mining and quarrying: gross fixed capital formation
(£million at 1958 prices)

1954	1955	1956	1957	1958	1959	1960	1961	1962	1963	1964
96	99	99	106	105	117	95	103	94	98	94

(National Income and Expenditure 1965)

(c) From the data of the volume of production in United States agriculture between 1921 and 1945 fit a polynomial trend of suitable degree. Comment on the use of the trend form selected.

Year	Index of volume of production (1935-9 = 100)
1921	91
1922	97
1923	98
1924	97
1925	99
1926	101
1927	100
1928	102
1929	101
1930	98
1931	105
1932	102
1933	95
1934	82
1935	97
1936	87
1937	107
1938	104
1939	105
1940	108
1941	111
1942	123
1943	120
1944	124
1945	123

Project your trend to 1950, making a forecast for that year. Plot the original data and the trend.

(d) Fit asymptotic growth curves to the following series. Choose the ones which you consider most suitable, using any criteria of choice. Graph the original series and your trends.

(i)

Year	Number of cars per mile of first class roads
1910	3·2
1915	5·6
1920	8·6
1925	12·2
1930	16·2
1935	20·3
1940	24·4
1945	25·4
1950	31·7
1955	35·2
1960	37·3
1965	39·7

(ii)

Year	United States petroleum production (millions of barrels)
1876	9·13
1881	27·66
1886	28·07
1891	54·29
1896	60·69
1901	69·39
1906	126·49
1911	220·45
1916	300·77
1921	472·18
1926	770·87
1931	851·08
1936	1099·69
1941	1402·28

271 Mathematical trend curves and exponential smoothing

(iii)

Year	Output of man-made fibre (millions of pounds weight)
1949	60
1950	310
1951	430
1952	725
1953	868
1954	1096
1955	1150
1956	1210
1957	1268
1958	1305
1959	1339
1960	1328
1961	1406
1962	1425
1963	1496
1964	1472

(iv)

Week from original promotion	Sales of a new brand of cigarettes (millions)
1	3·8
2	21·6
3	38·3
4	49·2
5	58·7
6	70·5
7	69·2
8	74·3
9	78·6
10	81·3
11	82·1
12	85·5
13	83·5
14	87·2
15	90·1
16	92·3
17	93·1
18	93·8

(e) By calculating the slope and other functions of the original data, suggest which trend form should be employed with the following series.

Year	Sales
1	22
2	34
3	35
4	37
5	57
6	68
7	83
8	90
9	112
10	125
11	138
12	179

5.7.2 Exponentially weighted moving averages

(a) Using the data below and employing an exponentially weighted moving average, smooth the figures of passenger miles flown by domestic services of United Kingdom airlines for the quarters of 1959 to 1961 inclusive. Using the seasonal indices given below, make projections for all quarters two years ahead, revising your forecasts as new data become available. Compare your various forecasts with the actual data shown for 1962, 1963 and 1964.

Passenger-miles flown by domestic services of United Kingdom airlines (millions of passenger-miles)

Year	1st	2nd	3rd	4th
1959	81·31	88·37	95·43	102·49
1960	109·55	116·61	123·67	130·73
1961	137·79	144·85	151·91	158·97
1962	166·03	173·09	180·15	187·21
1963	194·27	201·33	208·39	215·45
1964	222·35	229·57	236·63	243·69

| Seasonal indices: | 0·586 | 1·124 | 1·167 | 0·673 |

Chapter 6
Non-parametric methods

6.1 **Applications of non-parametric methods**

6.1.1 There are non-parametric equivalents of most of the methods and tests which have been discussed both in the earlier part of this book and in *Statistics for the Social Scientists: 1 Introducing Statistics*. To have mentioned each in the appropriate place would have produced a certain amount of discontinuity and in all probability a confusion and lack of awareness of the distinction between the parametric and non-parametric methods. By bringing all these techniques together for discussion in one chapter we shall underline the increasing importance of this relatively new area of the statistical method, demonstrate the fundamental differences in the assumptions made, and illustrate the broad methodology.

6.1.2 The limiting nature of the requirements of the parametric models was discussed fully at the end of Chapter 2, and the same limitations were seen in Chapter 4 to apply to the sampling theory connected with regression and correlation analysis. Let us nevertheless briefly restate these assumptions and add a new one which has so far been omitted.

In all but the tests based on large samples, the population or populations from which the samples were drawn were assumed normal, and the variances of the normal populations were (with one exception) held to be equal. In all the tests, and with equal applicability for non-parametric methods, it was assumed that the samples were randomly selected. While it is rare for these assumptions to be tested, it is even rarer for us to stop and ask whether the basic computation of means and standard deviations is justified.

6.1.3 When measurements are undertaken in statistics they may be of three types. *Classificatory* measurements have already been encountered when looking at the estimation and general inference problem associated with proportions. For example, a person may agree with, disagree with or be indifferent to a government policy decision: there is no implication that one attitude is better than any other or by how much, and we simply observe that there are three distinct attitudes.

As soon as an order is implied we move up the scale of measurement to *ordinal* or *ranked* measurements. A coal merchant who grades fuel as A1, A2, B1, B2 and C is indicating that A1 is of superior quality to A2, B1, B2 and C and that A2 is superior to B1, B2 and C. He does not attempt to say by how much A1 is superior to A2, even if this is suggested by his pricing policy. Whenever one category of observation is preferable, better or higher than another, and where the other categories can similarly be ranked, this scale of measurement is implied.

Once we are able to say by how much one observation is higher than another, we have achieved an *interval* scale of measurement. If three lorries have an unladen weight of 25 cwt, 42 cwt and 100 cwt we need not only say that the second is heavier than the first and the third is heavier than the second, for we also get an impression of the absolute increase in size. Addition and subtraction may be undertaken to ascertain the differences in weights, and multiplication and division can be used to find that the heaviest is $\dfrac{100}{25} = 4$ times as large as the smallest. These are the very arithmetic manipulations which are required for determining means and standard deviations. Thus only if data are of interval scale should these calculations be undertaken; if ordinal scale data are involved the appropriate measure of central tendency is the median, whilst for classificatory data the only possibility is the mode.

6.1.4　It may be thought that most of the series likely to be encountered will be of interval scale. While this is largely true it is better to question the validity of an assumption than to leave it untried. For instance, we may glibly calculate the mean and standard deviation of a set of I.Q.s obtained at an entrance examination for a college or school, but is it valid to assume that the difference in potential between two students with scores of 70 and 80 is the same as the difference in potential between two students with scores of 130 and 140? If there is any doubt about this, then one is dealing at best with ordinal rather than interval scale measurements. The appropriate average is the median and not the mean in these circumstances.

To sum up, it would seem necessary to provide not only tests which are free from the normality and homescedasticity assumptions, but also tests which are suitable for ordinal and classificatory data. Although it will be impossible to give adequate coverage here to all the non-parametric methods, we shall attempt to provide an example of the main alternatives to the parametric procedures.

6.1.5   Before discussing separate topics, the reader should clearly understand that the methodology involved in non-parametric tests of hypotheses is identical to that for z, t and F tests. First a sampling distribution of some sample characteristic is derived on the basis of a null hypothesis. Having prescribed an acceptable level for the type I error, a decision criterion is then fixed and if the sample characteristic falls into the region of rejection under the sampling distribution, then it is deemed significant at the 5 per cent level. If on the other hand, the sample characteristic is not critical, the null hypothesis is accepted subject to the reservation that a type II error may have been committed.

For samples of the same size non-parametric tests are always subject to a higher level of β compared with their parametric counterparts, but this deficiency can always be remedied by taking a larger sample size and in any case the non-parametric methods make up in generality what they lack in power. The conclusions reached have universal application since they do not depend upon assumptions which may only apply in the situation under study and possibly not even then.

6.2 χ^2 Tests

6.2.1   The χ^2 (chi-square) test ably illustrates the similarity of approach between parametric and non-parametric methods. We may use it, in testing to see if a sample distribution sufficiently conforms to some theoretical distribution, to decide whether or not the sample has been drawn from a population having the specified distribution; the χ^2 test can be employed to check the normality assumption implicit in t and F tests.

A second application is in testing to see if there is a significant difference in the frequency with which several categories of observation in two or more samples occur. This is therefore an extension of the tests of proportions where only two categories of observation could be dealt with. Instead of merely recording 'yes' or 'no' to a question directed at a sample of men and a sample of women, classified answers such as 'fully approve', 'indifferent' and 'completely disapprove' may be accepted and analysed using the χ^2 test.

6.2.2   The rationale of the test is the same in both contexts: the sample frequencies are compared with the frequencies which would be expected if the null hypothesis is true. The comparison is achieved by calculating the χ^2 statistic.

$$\chi^2 = \sum \frac{(O-E)^2}{E}$$

where O = the observed frequency and E = the corresponding expected frequency. If this calculated χ^2 value is large in comparison with what might be expected under the null hypothesis assumption, it is held to be significant and the H_0 is rejected. Put another way, we may reject the null hypothesis if χ^2 (calculated) falls into the rejection region of the χ^2 sampling distribution (see fig. 76).

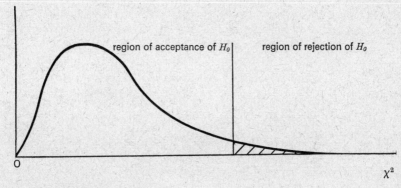

region of acceptance of H_0 region of rejection of H_0

Fig. 76   The χ^2 sampling distribution.

6.2.3   Although the χ^2 sampling distribution, like the normal distribution, is continuous and in practice will be derived mathematically, it is possible to conceive of its construction in less rigorous terms. Suppose that an unbiased die were thrown thirty-six times and the results achieved were recorded. It is possible that six 1s, six 2s, six 3s, etc. would appear (the probability of this happening is only 0·0002579). In this case, what the laws of probability tell us will happen in the long run has occurred in a relatively small sample. Thus $\chi_{\text{(calc.)}}^2 = 0$, as we show below.

Value on die	Observed frequency (O)	Expected frequency (E)	$O - E$	$(O-E)^2$	$(O-E)^2/E$
1	6	6	0	0	0
2	6	6	0	0	0
3	6	6	0	0	0
4	6	6	0	0	0
5	6	6	0	0	0
6	6	6	0	0	0
				$\chi_{\text{(calc.)}}^2 = 0$	

This provides the justification for the zero origin of the horizontal axis in fig. 76. However, if this experiment with the unbiased die were repeated thousands of times it is likely that a large proportion of samples would exhibit not equal frequencies but frequencies which only slightly diverge from those expected. We would therefore expect a large number of samples to generate relatively low $\chi_{(\text{calc.})}^2$ values. A few samples will, of course, produce by chance an observed distribution which is markedly different from that expected, so that a few χ^2 values will be large. It seems that the skewness in the sampling distribution is explained by this type of reasoning.

6.2.4   Although the basic form of the χ^2 distribution has been justified we have not exhausted all the possibilities. Carrying out a similar set of experi-

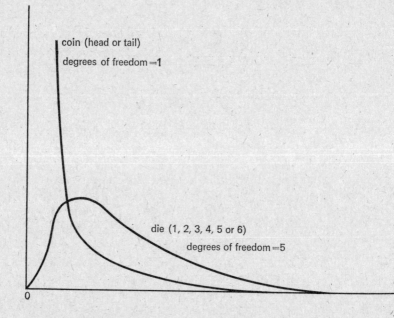

coin (head or tail)

degrees of freedom =1

die (1, 2, 3, 4, 5 or 6)

degrees of freedom =5

0

χ^2

Fig. 77   Differing χ^2 distributions.

ments with a coin would also yield a χ^2 distribution, but one which is very much more skewed than was found above (fig. 77).

The reason for the increasing skewness as the number of possible categories of result is reduced from six to two (heads or tails) is not difficult to find. If the coin was tossed 36 times the probability of exactly 18 heads and

18 tails occurring would be 0·1324; this is therefore the probability of $\chi^2 = 0$. But it was observed earlier that $P(\chi^2 = 0) = 0·0002579$ for the dice example, so the two distribution curves commence at noticeably different heights. What is more, the range of possible χ^2 values is lower for the coin tossing example than for the die equivalent, as is shown below by considering the results which would yield the maximum values:

Value of die	Observed frequency (O)	Expected frequency (E)	(O − E)	(O − E)²	(O − E)²/E
1	36	6	30	900	150
2	0	6	− 6	36	6
3	0	6	− 6	36	6
4	0	6	− 6	36	6
5	0	6	− 6	36	6
6	0	6	− 6	36	6

$$\chi_{(calc.)}^2 = 180$$

Outcome from coin	Observed frequency (O)	Expected frequency (E)	(O − E)	(O − E)²	(O − E)²/E
Heads	36	18	18	324	18
Tails	0	18	− 18	324	18

$$\chi_{(calc.)}^2 = 36$$

The range of χ^2 values in the first case is 0–180 and in the second 0–36. This, taken together with the different probabilities of $\chi^2 = 0$, provides an intuitively plausible explanation for the differing shape of the sampling distributions.

6.2.5   The reader will have noticed that the curves in fig. 77 have been marked respectively 'degrees of freedom = 1' and 'degrees of freedom = 5'. Although the number of categories of observation does influence the shape of the sampling distribution, it is more correct to say that the amount of skewness depends upon the number of degrees of freedom present in the problem faced. The magnitude of the degrees of freedom is calculated in a similar (though not identical) manner to that used in

279   Non-parametric methods

Chapter 2. We have to ask ourselves how many features of the sample must be ascertained before the expected frequencies may be calculated. This number, subtracted from the number of categories present, gives the number of degrees of freedom, i.e.

Degrees of freedom $(d.f.) =$ Number of categories —

$\qquad$ —Number of sample characteristics needed to obtain E's

In the examples above the only feature of the samples which is needed is the sample size, n. The probability of a 1, 2, 3, 4, 5 or 6 appearing from the throw of a die is $1/6$; $P(1) \times$ Sample size $=$ 1st expected frequency and so on. An identical approach applies to the coin tossing situation, and the degrees of freedom are therefore $6-1 = 5$ and $2-1 = 1$ respectively.

As an alternative approach to the degrees of freedom problem the reader may ask himself how many of the expected frequencies could be separately calculated without restriction and how many would have to be given by the necessary condition that the expected frequencies must sum to the same total as the observed frequencies. We might apply simple probability theory to calculate the expected frequencies of the first $k-1$ categories, but the kth expected frequency has to be given by addition and subtraction so that $\Sigma E = \Sigma O$.

6.2.6   Before proceeding to specific uses of the test, table 5 (page 380) must be explained. We mentioned earlier that the precise form of the χ^2 distribution is derived mathematically. Using this method it is equally possible to calculate and tabulate for different degrees of freedom the proportion of the area of the χ^2 sampling distribution lying to the right of any given value. Thus for five degrees of freedom we find that 5 per cent of the area under the curve lies to the right of $\chi^2 = 11 \cdot 070$, 1 per cent of the area to the right of $\chi^2 = 15 \cdot 086$, etc. For any particular test we can look up the value of χ^2 which separates the region of acceptance from the region of rejection, so that if $d.f. = 10$ and $\alpha = 0 \cdot 05$ the decision criterion is $\chi_{0 \cdot 05}{}^2 = 18 \cdot 307$. $\chi_{(calc.)}{}^2 > \chi_{0 \cdot 05}{}^2$ causes the null hypothesis to be rejected while $\chi_{(calc.)}{}^2 < \chi_{0 \cdot 05}{}^2$ fails to disprove H_0. This follows exactly the procedure implemented in the one-tail t test.

6.2.7   *Testing for goodness of fit*

6.2.7.1   A wholesale chemist wishes to establish buffer stocks of an important drug to minimize the probability of running out. To determine the size of these stocks the firm requires some knowledge of the distribution of delay between placing an order with manufacturers and receiving the merchandise. In 100 orders placed with the manufacturers over two years, the following delivery times were observed:

Time before orders filled	Number of occasions
24 but less than 48 hours	5
48 but less than 60 hours	13
60 but less than 72 hours	13
72 but less than 78 hours	14
78 but less than 84 hours	17
84 but less than 90 hours	12
90 but less than 102 hours	15
102 but less than 114 hours	7
114 but less than 138 hours	4
	100

This distribution constitutes a sample drawn from some population. Could it be drawn from a normally distributed population of delivery times? If so, then the known probability features of the normal distribution may be used in determining optimum buffer stocks. To test whether this distribution may be considered normal we must first calculate the expected frequencies, using the mean and standard deviation and the sample size ($\bar{x} = 79 \cdot 19$, $s = 20 \cdot 112$ and $n = 100$). With these figures the following method of establishing the expected frequencies can be used:

Values in series up to w	$z = \dfrac{w - \bar{x}}{s}$	Proportion of area under normal curve for $x < w$	Proportion of area in class interval	Expected frequency
48	$-1 \cdot 55$	0·0606	0·0606	6·06
60	$-0 \cdot 95$	0·1711	0·1105	11·05
72	$-0 \cdot 36$	0·3594	0·1883	18·83
78	$-0 \cdot 06$	0·4761	0·1167	11·67
84	$0 \cdot 24$	0·5948	0·1187	11·87
90	$0 \cdot 54$	0·7054	0·1106	11·06
102	$1 \cdot 13$	0·8718	0·1664	16·64
114	$1 \cdot 73$	0·9582	0·0864	8·64
138 and over		1·0000	0·0418	4·18

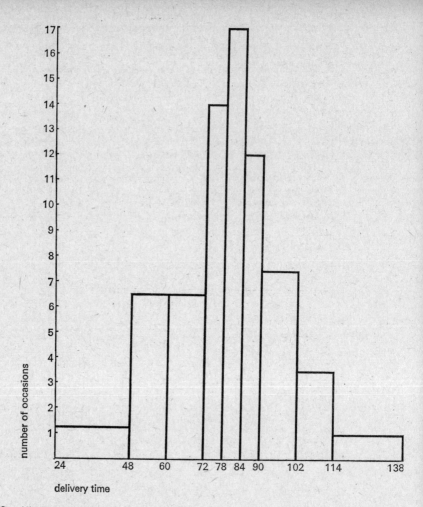

Fig. 78   Histogram of delivery time distribution.

The w figures shown in the first column are the upper boundaries of the class intervals; from these, z values have been calculated in the usual way and are converted into cumulative proportions of the area under the normal curve by referring to table 1, page 374. Thus $z = -1.55$ shows that the relative frequency of all values up to 48 hours is 0·0606; $z = -0.95$ shows that for all values up to 60 hours the relative frequency is 0·1711 and so on. By finding the first differences of the cumulative proportions the relative frequency of each class interval is obtained, and conversion to the expected frequencies is finally achieved on multiplication by $n = 100$. At this stage the calculation of χ^2 follows the earlier procedure exactly.

Observed frequencies O	Expected frequencies E	$O - E$	$(O - E)^2$	$\dfrac{(O - E)^2}{E}$
5	6·06	−1·06	1·1236	0·1854
13	11·05	1·95	3·8025	0·3441
13	18·83	−5·83	33·9889	1·8050
14	11·67	2·33	5·4289	0·4652
17	11·87	5·13	26·3169	2·2171
12	11·06	0·94	0·8836	0·0799
15	16·64	−1·64	2·6896	0·1616
7	8·64	−1·64	2·6896	0·3113
4	4·18	−0·18	0·0324	0·0078

$$\chi_{(\text{calc.})}^2 = 5\cdot5774$$

If the hypotheses are established as

H_0 : Sample drawn from a normal population
H_A : Sample not drawn from a normal population
$\alpha = 0\cdot05$

we have no evidence for rejecting the null hypothesis. Three of the sample characteristics were involved in finding the expected frequencies, while there were nine class intervals in all, so that the number of degrees of freedom is 6 ($d.f. = 9 - 3 = 6$) and the decision criterion for a 5 per cent significance level is found from table 5 to be 12·592. $\chi_{(\text{calc.})}^2 = 5\cdot577$ is much less than $\chi_{0\cdot05}^2 = 12\cdot592$, so we must accept that this sample distribution could have been drawn from a population having a normal distribution.

6.2.7.2   The same approach may be adopted in testing whether any sample distribution conforms to some specified law of distribution. Suppose that an inquiry into domestic accidents was undertaken by asking in a sample of 5000 households in how many years out of the last five had members of the household received injuries needing medical treatment. The following replies might be received.

Number of years in which there were injuries x	Number of households f	fx
0	3096	0
1	1500	1500
2	325	650
3	69	207
4	7	28
5	3	15
	5000	2400

Perhaps we feel that the regularity of homes having accidents would tend to be constant, in which case a binomial distribution may fit this data. To calculate the expected frequencies we must estimate π by p, and know the sample size N. In this sample the total number of injuries sustained in the 5000 homes was $\Sigma fx = 2400$ so that the average number was $\frac{2400}{5000} = 0.48$ per year. Now the mean of a binomial distribution has been defined as np, where in this case $n = 5$. Therefore

$$p = \frac{np}{n} = \frac{0.48}{5} = 0.096$$

Using the general expression of the binomial expansion we may calculate the probability of 0, 1, 2, 3, 4 and 5 injuries from

$$^nC_x p^x (1-p)^{n-x}$$

x	$P(x) = {}^5C_x (0.096)^x (0.904)^{x-5}$	$P(x) \times N = Expected frequency$
0	0.603729	3018.65
1	0.320564	1602.82
2	0.068185*	340.42
3	0.007230	36.15
4	0.000384	1.92
5	0.000008	0.04
	1.000000	5000.00

*The sixth decimal place was 4, giving the sum of the probabilities as 0.999999; as the seventh decimal place for this probability was closest to 5, the sixth has therefore been raised.

The expected frequencies are obtained on multiplication of $P(x)$ by N:

x	Observed frequency O	Expected frequency E	$O-E$	$(O-E)^2$	$\dfrac{(O-E)^2}{E}$
0	3096	3018·65	77·35	5983·0225	1·9820
1	1500	1602·82	−102·82	10571·9524	6·5958
2	325	304·42	−15·42	237·7764	0·6985
3	69	36·15	32·85	1079·1225	29·8512
4 and over	10	1·96	8·04	64·6416	32·9804

$$\chi_{(calc.)}^2 = 72\cdot1079$$

In conducting this χ^2 test notice that the final two observed and expected frequencies have been pooled. This is necessary if the basically discrete situation faced is to be sufficiently approximated by the continuous and theoretical values of χ^2 given in table 5. As a working rule, the χ^2 test should not be used if any expected frequency is less than one, or if more than 20 per cent of expected frequencies are less than five. A difficulty of this kind may be overcome if adjacent categories of observation are combined. In this example the expected frequencies of four and five injuries together are greater than one, and we are left with one out of five categories with an expected frequency of less than five. This is just acceptable.

6.2.7.3   The degrees of freedom for the test of the goodness of fit of the binomial distribution are found from

$$d.f. = \text{Number of categories} - 2$$

because the arithmetic mean and sample size are required from the sample. For $5-2=3$ degrees of freedom the decision criterion is $\chi_{0.05}^2 = 7\cdot815$ so that $\chi_{(calc.)}^2 = 72\cdot1079$ is highly significant and we may be almost certain that the binomial distribution is inappropriate in this case.

6.2.7.4   As the binomial distribution does not fit this data, it is worthwhile trying the Poisson distribution (see 3.5.5.2) where

$$P(x) = \frac{e^{-a}\, a^x}{x!}$$

Remembering that $a=np$ we may calculate the expected frequencies as follows (as e^{-a} is given to only four decimal places in table 4 the probabilities are also only given to four places):

x	$P(x) = e^{-0.48}\dfrac{0.48^x}{x!}$	$P(x) \times N$
0	0·6188	3094·0
1	0·2970	1485·0
2	0·0713	356·5
3	0·0114	57·0
4	0·0014	7·0
5	0·0001	0·5

$\chi_{(calc.)}^2$ is now found using the same rule of pooling as before.

x	Observed frequency O	Expected frequency E	$O - E$	$(O-E)^2$	$\dfrac{(O-E)^2}{E}$
0	3096	3094·0	2·0	4·00	0·0013
1	1500	1485·0	15·0	225·00	0·1515
2	325	356·5	−31·5	992·25	2·7833
3	69	57·0	12·0	144·00	2·5263
4	10	7·5	2·5	6·25	0·8333

$$\chi_{(calc.)}^2 = 6\cdot2957$$

In this case $\chi_{(calc.)}^2 = 6\cdot296 < \chi_{0.05}^2 = 7\cdot815$ (the degrees of freedom are as before) so we may accept that this data is adequately fitted by the Poisson distribution.

6.2.8 Contingency tables

6.2.8.1 The second type of problem for which the χ^2 test is of use involves testing the difference between the observed frequencies of several classifications of two or more samples. In this context the use of either classificatory or ordinal scale is permissible. For instance, we may ask whether the social origin of students in autonomous university institutions is the same as that of students studying at colleges in the public sector.

Socio-economic class of father	Students at universities	Students at colleges in the public sector	Totals
Professional, administrative	53	29	82
Shopkeepers, shop assistants and clerical workers	71	42	113
Foremen	60	96	156
Skilled workers	105	82	187
Semi-skilled workers	80	109	189
Unskilled workers	23	49	72
Other categories	20	60	80
Total	412	467	879

From these two samples set out in a contingency table, we are able to provide an answer to this question. The calculation of expected frequencies again follows the laws of probability, and an empirical approach being adopted. The probability of one of the 879 students in the two samples attending a university is $\frac{412}{879} = 0.4687$. Using the row totals we can also state that the probability of an individual student having a father who is an administrator or in the professions is $\frac{82}{879} = 0.0933$, or who is a shopkeeper, shop assistant or clerical worker is $\frac{113}{879} = 0.1286$, and so on.

Now if the socio-economic grouping of the student's father is independent of the type of institution attended, the multiplication law of independent events may be invoked to ascertain the probability of a student both coming from a professional-administrative background and studying at a university. In this instance, the probability is

$$\frac{412}{879} \times \frac{82}{879} = 0.4687 \times 0.0933 = 0.0437.$$

To find the expected frequency of occurrence of the group (as opposed to the individual student) under the null hypothesis of no association between social class and institution attended, we must multiply by the total number of students in the two samples, i.e. 879:

$$\text{Expected frequency} = \frac{412}{879} \times \frac{82}{879} \times 879 = 0.0437 \times 879 = 38.41$$

In general the expected frequency of any cell is obtained by calculating

$$\text{Expected frequency} = \frac{\text{Column total}}{\text{Grand total}} \times \frac{\text{Row total}}{\text{Grand total}} \times \text{Grand total}$$

$$= \frac{\text{Column total} \times \text{Row total}}{\text{Grand total}}$$

6.2.8.2   The table of expected frequencies is set out in the following manner:

Socio-economic class of father	Students studying at universities	Students studying at colleges in the public sector	Total
Professional, administrative	$\frac{412 \times 82}{879} = 38\cdot41$	$82 - 38\cdot41 = 43\cdot59$	82
Shopkeepers, shop assistants and clerical workers	$\frac{412 \times 113}{879} = 52\cdot96$	$113 - 52\cdot96 = 60\cdot04$	113
Foremen	$\frac{412 \times 156}{879} = 73\cdot12$	$156 - 73\cdot12 = 82\cdot88$	156
Skilled workers	$\frac{412 \times 187}{879} = 87\cdot65$	$187 - 87\cdot65 = 99\cdot35$	187
Semi-skilled workers	$\frac{412 \times 189}{879} = 88\cdot59$	$189 - 88\cdot59 = 100\cdot41$	189
Unskilled workers	$\frac{412 \times 72}{879} = 33\cdot75$	$72 - 33\cdot75 = 38\cdot25$	72
Other categories	$412 - 374\cdot48 = 37\cdot52$	$80 - 37\cdot52 = 42\cdot48$	80
Total	412	467	879

The expected frequencies for those cells enclosed within the double lines have been calculated using the method outlined above; the remaining values have been obtained by addition and/or subtraction. The expected frequency of occurrence of students at universities with fathers in 'other categories' of work was obtained by adding the first six expected frequencies in the column and subtracting this sum from the column total. All the values in the column headed 'Students studying at colleges in the public sector' are found by subtracting the first expected frequency from the row total, e.g. $82 - 38\cdot41 = 43\cdot59$.

It seems that out of the 14 cells only 6 expected frequencies are obtained from first principles; the remainder derive from the requirement that row and column totals of expected frequencies must equal observed row and column totals. In other words there are 6 degrees of freedom in this example. If the reader has any difficulty in finding the number of degrees of freedom, a simple method is available as follows:

Degrees of freedom = (Number of rows − 1) × (Number of columns − 1)

In this case there are two columns and seven rows so that

$$d.f. = (7-1)\times(2-1) = 6$$

6.2.8.3　The testing procedure will now be defined as it should be used in practice.

Socio-economic class of father	Students studying at universities	Students studying at colleges in the public sector	Total
Professional, administrative	53 (38·41)	29　(43·59)	82
Shopkeepers, shop assistants and clerical workers	71 (52·96)	42　(60·04)	113
Foremen	60 (73·12)	96　(82·88)	156
Skilled workers	105 (87·65)	82　(99·35)	187
Semi-skilled workers	80 (88·59)	109 (100·41)	189
Unskilled workers	23 (33·75)	49　(38·25)	72
Other categories	20 (37·52)	60　(42·48)	80
Total	412	467	879

H_0:　Socio-economic class of father independent of type of institution attended

H_A:　Socio-economic class of father associated with type of institution attended

$$\alpha = 0\cdot05$$
$$d.f. = 6$$

Decision criterion $\chi_{0.05}^2 = 12\cdot592$

From table over page $\chi_{(\text{calc.})}^2 = 56\cdot3060 > \chi_{0.05}^2 = 12\cdot592$. Therefore we reject the null hypothesis and conclude that there is an association between the background of the student and the type of institution attended (calculations of the first two values in the final column would have led to the same decision).

6.2.8.4　Before providing an illustration of the χ^2 test as applied to more than two samples let us mention the simplest form of contingency table, in which two samples (each having only a dichotomous division) are given. Although the simple approach may be used, there is an alternative one which has the great advantage of enabling a correction for continuity to be incorporated. The reader will remember that in theory the χ^2 distribution is continuous, but in practical calculations it is discrete. The

Observed frequency O	Expected frequency E	$O - E$	$(O - E)^2$	$\dfrac{(O - E)^2}{E}$
53	38·41	14·59	212·8681	5·5420
71	52·96	18·04	325·4416	6·1450
60	73·12	− 13·12	172·1344	2·3541
105	87·65	17·35	301·0225	3·4344
80	88·59	− 8·59	73·7881	0·8329
23	33·75	− 10·75	115·5625	3·4241
20	37·52	− 17·52	306·9504	8·1810
29	43·59	− 14·59	212·8681	4·8834
42	60·04	− 18·04	325·4416	5·4204
96	82·88	13·12	172·1344	2·0769
82	99·35	− 17·35	301·0225	3·0299
109	100·41	8·59	73·7881	0·7349
49	38·25	10·75	115·5625	3·0212
60	42·48	17·52	306·9504	7·2258

$$\chi_{(calc.)}^2 = 56{\cdot}3060$$

approximation of the computed χ^2 value to the continuous distribution is much improved by the following device. Let us letter a 2×2 table:

Category	Sample 1	Sample 2	Total
X	A	B	A+B
Y	C	D	C+D
Total	A+C	B+D	A+B+C+D

Then

$$\chi_{(calc.)}^2 = \frac{\left(AD - BC - \dfrac{A+B+C+D}{2}\right)^2 (A+B+C+D)}{(A+B)(C+D)(A+C)(B+D)}$$

Two groups of randomly selected motorists were asked to use a nameless brand of petrol for one month and report on overall performance; unknown to them, half were driving on the existing retailed mixture while the remainder had a new 'improved' brand containing additives. The following answers were received:

Car performance report	Motorists using existing brand	Motorists using 'new improved' brand	Total
No improvement	47	35	82
Improvement	53	65	118
Total	100	100	200

If there is no significant difference between the replies of the two groups it may be deemed inappropriate to introduce the new brand.

$$\chi_{(calc.)}{}^2 = \frac{\left[(47 \times 65) - (53 \times 35) - \dfrac{200}{2}\right]^2 \times 200}{(100)(100)(82)(118)}$$

$$= \frac{242000000}{96760000}$$

$$= 2 \cdot 501$$

In this case

$$d.f. = (2-1)(2-1) = 1$$

and the decision criterion at a 5 per cent level is $\chi_{0 \cdot 05}{}^2 = 3 \cdot 841$. The calculated χ^2 is not significant, so we may conclude that motorists' impressions of their cars' performances are the same regardless of the brand of petrol used.

6.2.8.5   The expansion of the contingency table from a 2×2 or 2×7 to a 4×4 or 10×8 introduces no new principles of calculation. The expected frequencies, degrees of freedom and χ^2 value will be obtained in exactly the same way, but it is worth noticing that in looking at the manifold classification of several samples we are conducting a test which corresponds to the analysis of variance. Admittedly the scale of measurement is lower, as is the power of the test, but the conclusions drawn are parallel to those in the analysis of variance, i.e. we shall conclude that there is an over-all association if the test proves significant. We will not, however, be able to point to specific samples as the delinquents and say that these are raising the significance of the result (without applying further statistical tests).

As the last illustration of the χ^2 test let us analyse data showing the attitude of housewives in various parts of the country to product X.

Attitude to product	North	Midlands	South	Total
Like	51 (30·56)	23 (40·64)	35 (37·80)	109
Indifferent	28 (37·01)	65 (49·21)	39 (45·78)	132
Dislike	18 (29·43)	41 (39·15)	46 (36·42)	105
	97	129	120	346

Observed frequency O	Expected frequency E	$O - E$	$(O - E)^2$	$\dfrac{(O - E)^2}{E}$
51	30·56	20·44	417·7936	13·6713
28	37·01	−9·01	81·1801	2·1935
18	29·43	−11·43	130·6449	4·4392
23	40·64	−17·64	311·1696	7·6567
65	49·21	15·79	249·3241	5·0665
41	39·15	1·85	3·4225	0·0874
35	37·80	−2·80	7·8400	0·2074
39	45·78	−6·78	45·9684	1·0041
46	36·42	9·58	91·7764	2·5199

$$\chi_{(calc.)}^2 = 36\cdot8460$$

The probability of $\chi^2 = 36\cdot8460$ occurring by chance when there is no association between geographical area of residence and attitude to product X is something less than 0·001. We can therefore state that $\chi_{(calc.)}^2 = 36\cdot8460$ is significant at 0·1 per cent level, with $\chi_{0\cdot001}^2 = 18\cdot465$ for $(3-1)(3-1) = 4$ degrees of freedom.

6.3 The contingency coefficient

6.3.1 Directly connected with the χ^2 test is the contingency coefficient C, which measures the degree of association between two sets of attributes. Fundamentally C is the same as the coefficient of correlation, but it may be applied to classificatory or ordinal-scale data in addition to interval scale measurements. Its calculation assumes a knowledge of the value of χ^2 obtained from the sample, but thereafter it is very simple:

$$C = \sqrt{\left(\frac{\chi^2}{N + \chi^2}\right)}$$

where $N =$ grand total of observations.

For instance, the example used in 6.2.8.2 produced a value of 56·306 from 879 observations. Therefore

$$C = \sqrt{\left(\frac{56 \cdot 306}{879 + 56 \cdot 306}\right)} = \sqrt{0 \cdot 0602}$$

$$= 0 \cdot 245$$

Similarly the example in 6.2.8.5 yields

$$C = \sqrt{\left(\frac{36 \cdot 846}{346 + 36 \cdot 846}\right)} = \sqrt{0 \cdot 0962}$$

$$= 0 \cdot 310$$

6.3.2   Unlike the product moment coefficient of correlation, values of C can only be compared directly under certain circumstances. When there is no association C will always equal zero, whilst at the other extreme C will never attain a unitary value. What is more, its maximum value will vary with the number of categories of observation studied: for a 2×2 table the maximum value of C is 0·707, for a 3×3 table it is 0·816 and so on.

Contingency table	2×2	3×3	4×4	5×5	6×6	7×7	8×8	9×9	10×10
Maximum C	0·707	0·816	0·866	0·894	0·913	0·926	0·935	0·943	0·949

The maximum values associated with rectangular tables such as 2×7 or 3×4 are as yet unknown. The general conclusion must be that only C values resulting from similar contingency tables may be compared, but notwithstanding this criticism the contingency coefficient is extremely useful because of its generality. There is no assumption about the populations from which the samples are taken, nor about the continuity of the variables involved: this is not the case with the product moment coefficient of correlation or with any of the other methods which will be discussed in 6.7.1 and 6.8.1.

293   Non-parametric methods

6.4 The median test

6.4.1 The median test is the first of the two methods which will be described for determining whether two or more samples differ in respect of their average values. Like the z and t tests for means, two- or one-tailed versions may be employed, i.e.

$$H_0 : M_1 = M_2$$

$$H_A : M_1 > M_2 \text{ or } M_2 > M_1 \text{ or } M_1 \neq M_2$$

The test depends upon knowing the probability of occurrence of the number of observations in each sample with values or ranks above the collective median when the population medians are equal. Thus in the case of two samples the probability sampling distribution is defined by

$$P(AB) = \frac{(A+C)!(B+D)!(A+B)!(C+D)!}{A!\,C!\,B!\,D!\,(A+B+C+D)!}$$

where A is the number of observations above the combined median in the first sample, B is the number of observations above the combined median in the second sample, and C and D are respectively the numbers of observations in the first and in the second samples which are below the combined median.

Setting out this situation gives

	Sample 1	Sample 2	Total
Observations above combined median	A	B	$A+B$
Observations below combined median	C	D	$C+D$
Total	$A+C$	$B+D$	$A+B+C+D$

which is identical to the 2×2 table in the χ^2 test. In fact the coincidence goes further. As long as $A+B+C+D \geqslant 20$ and no expected frequency is less than 5, the sampling distribution of AB is approximated by the χ^2 distribution and the test procedure given in 6.2.8.4 may be used.

6.4.2 Suppose that a panel of twenty men and twenty women are asked to watch a television comedy series and indicate their appreciation of the programme on a tenpoint scale. The following results might be obtained.

| Men | 7 | 6 | 8 | 7 | 6 | 3 | 7 | 4 | 8 | 9 | 6 | 4 | 6 | 5 | 3 | 8 | 7 | 6 | 9 | 7 |
| Women | 6 | 5 | 3 | 1 | 8 | 9 | 4 | 6 | 3 | 4 | 5 | 4 | 2 | 8 | 4 | 4 | 4 | 7 | 5 | 6 |

The median rating of all forty panel members is found to be 5·5, and the following results are therefore quickly obtainable:

	Men	Women	Total
Appreciation rating above combined median of 5·5	15	7	22
Appreciation rating below combined median of 5·5	5	13	18
Total	20	20	40

If we test a null hypothesis that the median appreciation rating of all men and all women is the same against an alternative hypothesis that the population medians are different, the two-tail test will be employed and the decision criterion is $\chi_{0.05}^2 = 3.841$ at a 5 per cent level (one degree of freedom). However, if we specify in advance that men's ratings will be higher than women's, then the one-tail test should be used in which case the decision criterion for a 5 per cent level will be found from $\chi_{0.10}^2 = 2.706$.

$\chi_{(calc.)}^2$ is found in the prescribed manner from

$$\chi_{(calc.)}^2 = \frac{\left[AD - BC - \dfrac{A+B+C+D}{2}\right]^2 (A+B+C+D)}{(A+B)(C+D)(A+C)(B+D)}$$

$$= \frac{\left[(15 \times 13) - (5 \times 7) - \left(\dfrac{40}{2}\right)\right]^2 \times 40}{20 \times 20 \times 22 \times 18}$$

$$= 4.949$$

Whichever alternative hypothesis is invoked in this case, the difference between sample medians is found to be significant and we conclude that men and women have different tastes in humour.*

6.4.3   By using this hypothetical example it has been demonstrated that the median test requires the use of no more than ordinal-scale measurements, such as the ratings given by viewers to programmes. Of course, interval-

* This finding is confirmed by:

$$P(15,7) = \frac{22!20!20!18!}{15!7!5!13!40!} = 0.0106$$

scale data may also be involved, as is shown by looking at the following application of the median test when used with several samples instead of two.

6.4.4   A city councillor has received a number of complaints about defects in newly-built houses. He undertakes a survey of 80 householders occupying property less than two years old who are asked to indicate which of the faults specified on a prepared list they have noticed. The results, analysed on the basis of builders, are as follows:

Builder A	Builder B	Builder C	Builder D	Builder E
4 –	8 +	4 –	17 +	10 +
8 +	7 –	7 –	4 –	7 –
23 +	6 –	3 –	9 +	12 +
6 –	9 +	8 +	8 +	13 +
10 +	5 –	2 –	7 –	7 –
5 –	14 +	6 –	14 +	3 –
7 –	3 –	12 +	3 –	1 –
3 –	7 –	9 +	7 –	0 –
2 –	3 –	3 –	4 –	0 –
8 +	8 +	5 –	9 +	8 +
9 +	4 –	13 –	6 –	9 +
16 +	2 –	4 –	10 +	2 –
3 –	7 –	8 +	6 –	1 –
0 –	6 –	8 +	7 –	8 +
1 –	5 –	7 –		8 +
5 –	16 +	13 +		4 –
6 –	10 +			

The common combined median is 7, which is one of the values in the series occurring several times. Thus the + and − signs above indicate respectively the observation in excess of the median and the observations not exceeding the median (i.e. including the median value). The results may be summarized in the following manner:

	Builder A	Builder B	Builder C	Builder D	Builder E	Total
Observation exceeding median of 7	6 (6·8)	6 (6·8)	7 (6·4)	6 (5·6)	7 (6·4)	32
Observations not exceeding median of 7	11 (10·2)	11 (10·2)	9 (9·6)	8 (8·4)	9 (9·6)	48
Total	17	17	16	14	16	80

The expected frequencies in this case are found in the usual way, but if the median had exactly split the observations the expected frequencies would be given by dividing the column totals by 2.

Observed frequency O	Expected frequency E	$O - E$	$(O - E)^2$	$\dfrac{(O - E)^2}{E}$
6	6·8	− 0·8	0·64	0·0941
6	6·8	− 0·8	0·64	0·0941
7	6·4	0·6	0·36	0·0562
6	5·6	0·4	0·16	0·0286
7	6·4	0·6	0·36	0·0562
11	10·2	0·8	0·64	0·0627
11	10·2	0·8	0·64	0·0627
9	9·6	−0·6	0·36	0·0375
8	8·4	−0·4	0·16	0·0190
9	9·6	−0·6	0·36	0·0375

$$\chi_{(\text{calc.})}^2 = 0.05486$$

$$H_0 : M_1 = M_2 = M_3 = M_4 = M_5$$

$$H_A : M_1 \neq M_2 \neq M_3 \neq M_4 \neq M_5$$

$$\alpha = 0.01$$

Decision criterion $= \chi_{0.01}^2 = 13.28$ (4 degrees of freedom).

We accept the null hypothesis: there is insufficient evidence to support a belief that the median number of defects in houses varies with the building contractor.

6.5 The randomization test

6.5.1 The non-parametric test directly equivalent to the small sample t test for means is the randomization test. Its principles are very simple. If two samples involving interval scale measurements are assumed to be drawn from populations with the same means, i.e.:

$$H_0 : \mu_1 = \mu_2$$

$$H_A : \mu_1 \neq \mu_2$$

then we would expect the variable values in each to be randomly distributed. It is not to be expected that all the highest figures will fall into one sample while the lowest values fall into the second. The probability of this situation being encountered is easily calculated: the number of ways of arranging fifteen values into two samples of seven and eight is given by $^{15}C_7 = \dfrac{15!}{7!8!} = 6435$, so that the probability of finding the following arrangement is $\dfrac{1}{6435} = 0.0001554$:

First sample	Second sample
x_1	x_2
23	8
17	10
12	11
15	9
18	8
27	6
19	10
12	—
—	62
143	

This probability is so small that if a difference between Σx_1 and Σx_2 of $143 - 62 = 81$ occurred in practice we would undoubtedly reject out of hand any hypotheses that the two samples were drawn from the same population of variable values. Indeed, using the conventional inductive reasoning we would say that any difference, $\Sigma x_1 - \Sigma x_2$, which had a probability of occurrence under the null-hypothesis assumption of less than 0.05 (or 0.01) would lead us to reject H_0. Thus the $\frac{1}{2} \alpha \; {}^{(n_1+n_2)}C_{n_1}$ highest positive differences and the lowest $\frac{1}{2} \alpha \; {}^{(n_1+n_2)}C_{n_1}$ negative differences would constitute the region of rejection for the two-tail test; in a one-tail test the $\alpha \; {}^{(n_1+n_2)}C_{n_1}$ highest positive or lowest negative differences would be considered significant. In the example cited the $\dfrac{0.05}{2}(6435) = 161$ arrangements which yield the highest differences and the 161 arrangements producing the lowest differences would be the region of rejection for the two-tail test when $\alpha = 0.05$.

6.5.2   The application of these principles is conveniently illustrated from the following data. Ten fifteen-year-old boys of approximately equal ability are selected from a school and five (randomly assigned) take the mathematics examination of board A while the other five take the examination of board B, which is based upon exactly the same syllabus. All ten boys receive identical tuition from the same teacher. The marks obtained are as follows:

Board A	Board B
49	42
59	58
75	70
62	51
48	36
293	257

To test the hypothesis that board A gives higher marks than board B, i.e.

$$H_0 : \mu_A = \mu_B$$

$$H_A : \mu_A > \mu_B$$

$$\alpha = 0 \cdot 05$$

we must find a value of $\Sigma x_1 - \Sigma x_2$ which excludes the highest 5 per cent of such differences in this particular sampling distribution: we therefore require to know the $0 \cdot 05 \dfrac{10!}{5!5!} \doteqdot 13$ differences which are as high as possible. The relevant figures are obtained successively by interchanging one, two or three figures at a time between samples, such that each difference is as close to the last one as possible:

Board A	Σx_1	Board B	Σx_2	$\Sigma x_1 - \Sigma x_2$
75, 70, 62, 59, 58	324	51, 49, 48, 42, 36	226	98
75, 70, 62, 59, 51	317	58, 49, 48, 42, 36	233	84
75, 70, 62, 58, 51	316	59, 49, 48, 42, 36	234	82
75, 70, 62, 59, 49	315	58, 51, 48, 42, 36	235	80
75, 70, 62, 58, 49	314	59, 51, 48, 42, 36	236	78
75, 70, 62, 59, 48	314	58, 51, 48, 42, 36	236	78
75, 70, 62, 58, 48	313	59, 51, 49, 42, 36	237	76
75, 70, 59, 58, 51	313	62, 49, 48, 42, 36	237	76
75, 70, 59, 58, 49	311	62, 51, 48, 42, 36	239	72
75, 70, 59, 58, 48	310	62, 51, 49, 42, 36	240	70
75, 70, 62, 59, 42	308	58, 51, 49, 48, 36	242	66
75, 70, 62, 58, 42	307	59, 51, 49, 48, 36	243	64
75, 70, 62, 51, 49	307	59, 58, 48, 42, 36	243	64

The difference between the samples obtained in practice was $293 - 257 = 36$ which does not fall into the region of rejection of the null hypothesis as defined above. There is no significant difference between the marks given by the two boards.

6.5.3   It is apparent that the calculation of the values making up the region of rejection will become laborious as the sample sizes increase. In these circumstances, however, the randomization sampling distribution is closely approximated by the t distribution; the t test utilized in 2.8.1 may then be employed but without the demand on assumptions implicit in the parametric technique.

6.6   The binomial test

Before moving on to methods and tests which can be used when the assumptions involved in the parametric correlation and regression analysis fail to be met, it is worthwhile mentioning the test which should be employed when the binomial sampling distribution of proportions is not sufficiently approximated by the normal distribution (i.e. when the sample size is small). All that is involved here is the binomial expansion, i.e.

$$P\left(\frac{x}{n}=p\right) = {}^nC_x p^x (1-p)^{n-x}$$

For instance, a firm may claim in advertisements that only 5 per cent of its packets will contain broken biscuits. To test this claim, a consumer research agency visits twenty retailers and purchases a packet of biscuits at each. Sixteen out of the twenty packets are found to be perfect. Establishing the hypotheses as

$$H_0 : \pi = 0\cdot05 \text{ or less}$$

$$H_A : \pi > 0\cdot05$$

$$\alpha = 0\cdot05$$

what decision should be taken? Following normal procedure we shall ask what is the probability of a sample proportion of $p = \dfrac{4}{20}$ or higher occurring when $\pi = 0\cdot05$. It is quicker to calculate the first four probabilities and subtract from one than to calculate the remaining sixteen probabilities, so this is given by:

$$\sum_{i=4}^{20} P\left(\frac{x_i}{20}\right) = 1 - \sum_{i=0}^{3} P\left(\frac{x_i}{20}\right)$$

where

$$P\left(\frac{0}{20}\right) = 0.95^{20} = 0.3581$$

$$P\left(\frac{1}{20}\right) = \frac{20!}{1!\,19!}\,0.05^{1}0.95^{19} = 0.3770$$

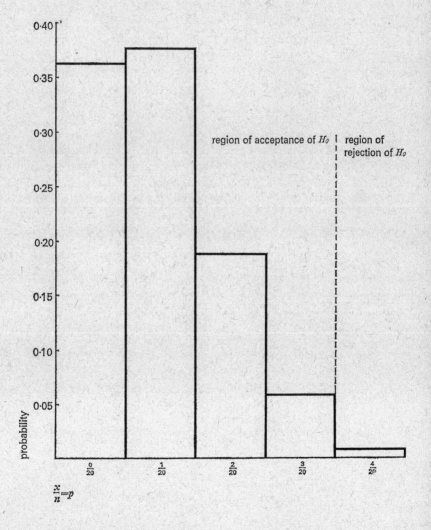

Fig. 79   The sampling distribution of p (n small).

$$P\left(\frac{2}{20}\right) = \frac{20!}{2!\,18!}\,0.05^2 0.95^{18} = 0.1886$$

$$P\left(\frac{3}{20}\right) = \frac{20!}{3!\,17!}\,0.05^3 0.95^{17} = 0.0595$$

$$\sum_{i=0}^{3} P\left(\frac{x_i}{20}\right) = 0.9832$$

and
$$\sum_{i=4}^{16} P\left(\frac{x_i}{20}\right) = 1 - 0.9832 = 0.0168$$

Diagrammatically we see in fig. 79 that $p = \dfrac{4}{20}$ lies in the region of rejection of the test. This fact has already been indicated from

$$\sum_{i=4}^{20} P\left(\frac{x_i}{20}\right) = 0.0168,$$

which is rather less than $\alpha = 0.05$. The consumer research agency has evidence either for a further investigation or to place before the manufacturers which indicates that the advertising claim is inaccurate.

6.7 Spearman's coefficient of rank correlation

6.7.1 There are many occasions when it is desirable to measure the association between two sets of observations which are expressed in an ordinal rather than an interval scale of measurement. For instance, in a school the pupils' preferences for eight different subjects may or may not differ between male and female students; in another example the order of merit awarded in a competition may or may not vary from judge to judge. It is the degree of agreement or disagreement which interests us in both cases and Spearman's coefficient of rank correlation, r_s, provides the means of measuring the association between two sets of ranked data. We derive r_s from the Pearson product moment formula

$$r = \frac{\Sigma(x - \bar{x})(y - \bar{y})}{n\sigma_x \sigma_y}$$

which reduces to

$$r_s = 1 - \frac{6\Sigma d^2}{n(n^2 - 1)}$$

(where $d = x - y$; see 6.10) when the variable values are simply the first n integers.

6.7.2   A paint manufacturer trying to produce a laboratory technique for measuring the durability of new types of paint compares the results of tests carried out under natural as opposed to artificial weathering conditions. Seven types of paint had been applied to similar surfaces. After inspection the paints were classified as follows:

	Durability rank	
Type of paint	Natural weathering (after 3 years) x	Artificial weathering in laboratory (after 14 days) y
A	3	4
B	5	5
C	1	3
D	4	1
E	6	7
F	7	6
G	2	2

$(x - y) = d$	d^2
$3 - 4 = -1$	1
$5 - 5 = \ \ 0$	0
$1 - 3 = -2$	4
$4 - 1 = \ \ 3$	9
$6 - 7 = -1$	1
$7 - 6 = \ \ 1$	1
$2 - 2 = \ \ 0$	0
	$\overline{16}$

$$r_s = 1 - \frac{(6)(16)}{7(49 - 1)} = 1 - \frac{96}{336}$$

$$= +0 \cdot 714$$

The agreement between the two sets of results is reasonably good. The laboratory technique, possibly after some refinement, should provide a quick and accurate assessment of the weathering qualities of new paints.

6.7.3   Two aspects of Spearman's coefficient should be mentioned. Firstly, r_s (like r) can take any value between -1 and $+1$. When $r_s > 0$ there is an agreement between the rankings in the same direction, i.e. high ranks in one series tend to go with high ranks in the second. If $r_s < 0$, however, the ranking in the two series is diametrically opposed, as follows:

Rank			
x	y	d	d^2
1	5	-4	16
2	4	-2	4
3	3	0	0
4	2	2	4
5	1	4	16
			40

$$r_s = 1 - \frac{6 \times 40}{5(25-1)} = 1 - \frac{240}{120}$$

$$= -1$$

Secondly, we should notice that the procedure varies if ties occur in one or both of the series. The tied observations are given the mean value of the ranks which they cover and a correction is introduced to avoid the increase in r_s which would otherwise occur. The correction for each tie is to add $\dfrac{t^3 - t}{12}$ to Σd^2 where t is the number of tied observations. For instance, if

Rank			
x	y	d	d^2
1	2	-1	1
5	4	1	1
2·5	2	0·5	0·25
2·5	2	0·5	0·25
4	6	-2	4
7	8	-1	1
6	5	1	1
8	7	1	1
			9·5

$$r_s = 1 - \frac{6\left(9 \cdot 5 + \frac{2^3 - 2}{12} + \frac{3^3 - 3}{12}\right)}{8(8^2 - 1)}$$

$$= 1 - \frac{(6)(12)}{(8)(63)}$$

$$= +0 \cdot 857$$

There was a tie in the first series between two observations at rank 2 and 3, so that the value used is $2 \cdot 5$ and the correction is $\frac{2^3 - 2}{12} = 0 \cdot 5$. In the second series the first three observations tied so that the 2 replaces each of the first three ranks and the correction is $\frac{3^3 - 3}{12} = 2$.

6.7.4   Just as we were interested in knowing whether a sample value of r was significantly greater or less than zero (i.e. if there is an association between the variable in the population from which the sample was drawn) so we will require to test

$$H_0 : \rho_s = 0$$
$$H_A : \rho_s > \text{ or } < 0$$
$$\alpha = 0 \cdot 05$$

The sampling distribution of r_s under the null hypothesis is again defined by simple probability theory. For every ranking of the x variable any conceivable ranking of the y variable may occur if there is no association between the two, as the following table demonstrates:

| Rank | Possible rank y | | | | | |
x	y_1	y_2	y_3	y_4	y_5	y_6
1	1	1	2	2	3	3
2	2	3	1	3	1	2
3	3	2	3	1	2	1

There are $n!$ orders of the y variable which may accompany a given order of the x variable. In the above example $n = 3$ so that there are $3! = 3 \times 2 \times 1 = 6$ possible rankings of y. From each let us calculate r_s:

$$x \text{ and } y_1 \quad 1 - \frac{(6)(0)}{(3)(8)} = 1 = r_s$$

$$x \text{ and } y_2 \quad 1 - \frac{(6)(2)}{(3)(8)} = 0 \cdot 5 = r_s$$

$$x \text{ and } y_3 \quad 1 - \frac{(6)(2)}{(3)(8)} = 0 \cdot 5 = r_s$$

$$x \text{ and } y_4 \quad 1 - \frac{(6)(6)}{(3)(8)} = -0 \cdot 5 = r_s$$

$$x \text{ and } y_5 \quad 1 - \frac{(6)(6)}{(3)(8)} = -0 \cdot 5 = r_s$$

$$x \text{ and } y_6 \quad 1 - \frac{(6)(8)}{(3)(8)} = -1 = r_s$$

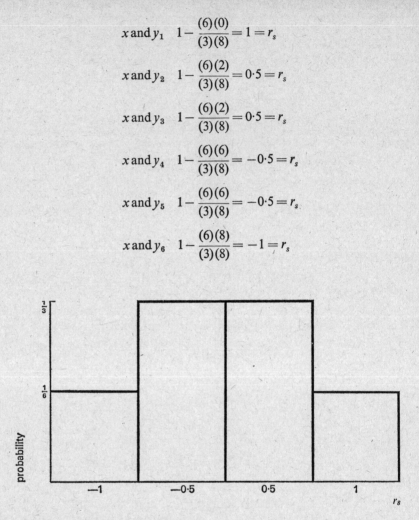

Fig. 80. Sampling distribution of r_s (when $n = 3$).

Grouping enables the sampling distribution in fig. 80 to be produced.

The values in table 6, page 381 have been produced by the same reasoning except that they relate to samples from 4 to 30 in size, and only one-tail 5 per cent and 1 per cent significance levels are shown.

6.7.5　Using the data in 6.7.2 which gave $r_s = 0 \cdot 714$ from seven observations, we may conclude that r_s is just significantly greater than zero at a 5 per cent level ($r_{s \, 0 \cdot 05} = 0 \cdot 714$ for $n = 70$), although it is not significant at the

1 per cent level ($r_{s0.01} = 0.893$). If $r_s = 0.714$ had been generated from a series comprising twenty ranks instead of only seven observations, what would be concluded? We could obviously use the tabled value for $n = 20$ to infer that r_s is significant at less than a 1 per cent level. We might also utilize the fact that the sampling distribution or r_s is closely approximated by the t distribution when $n > 10$. Thus the test introduced in 4.10.2 for the product-moment coefficient can be used, but without the assumptions underlying the parametric method:

$$t_{(\text{calc.})} = \frac{r_s - \rho_s}{\sqrt{\left(\dfrac{1 - r_s^2}{n - 2}\right)}}$$

($t_{0.01}$ found for $n - 2$ degrees of freedom)

In the situation described

$$t_{(\text{calc.})} = \frac{0.714 - 0}{\sqrt{\left(\dfrac{1 - 0.714}{20 - 2}\right)}} = 5.662$$

For eighteen degrees of freedom $t_{0.01} = 2.552$, so r_s is significantly greater than zero at a level of 1 per cent.

6.8 Kendall's coefficient of concordance

6.8.1 When more than two sets of ranks are involved in an experiment or survey there are two alternative courses open to the statistician who requires an estimate of the over-all association between the several series. He might calculate r_s for all possible pairs of series and average the coefficients. This procedure produces quite acceptable and meaningful results, but is not to be recommended if there are a large number of series because the number of r_s coefficients to be calculated will be $^kC_2$; this means that for seven series $^7C_2 = 21$ individual ranking measures would be involved.

The alternative is to use Kendall's coefficient of concordance, W, which although differing from $\dfrac{\Sigma r_s}{k}$ is nevertheless linearly related to it. W is defined as follows:

$$W = \frac{12 \Sigma \left(\Sigma r_a - \dfrac{\Sigma \Sigma r_a}{n} \right)^2}{k^2 n(n^2 - 1)}$$

Let us illustrate the use of this formula by considering the order of preference housewives in four different age groups show for eight brands of soap powder:

	Under 25 years	25–35 years	36–45 years	Over 45 years	Σr_a
Brand A	6	3	1	1	11
Brand B	7	5	3	2	17
Brand C	8	6	2	3	19
Brand D	2	1	5	6	14
Brand E	5	8	8	4	25
Brand F	3	4	7	5	19
Brand G	1	2	6	7	16
Brand H	4	7	4	8	23
				$\Sigma\,\Sigma r_a = 144$	

Σr_a is the sum of the ranks given by the four groups of housewives to each brand, while $\Sigma\Sigma r_a$ is the sum of these sums; k is the number of sets of ranks and n is the number of ranks in each set.

Thus $\dfrac{\Sigma\Sigma r_a}{n} = \dfrac{144}{8} = 18$ so that the sum of the square deviations of the Σr_as from their mean value is found as follows:

$\Sigma r_a - \overline{\Sigma r_a}$	$(\Sigma r_a - \overline{\Sigma r_a})^2$
$11 - 18 = -7$	49
$17 - 18 = -1$	1
$19 - 18 = 1$	1
$14 - 18 = -4$	16
$25 - 18 = 7$	49
$19 - 18 = 1$	1
$16 - 18 = -2$	4
$23 - 18 = 5$	25
	146

Therefore

$$W = \frac{(12)(146)}{(4)^2(8)(64-1)} = \frac{1752}{8064}$$

$$= 0{\cdot}217$$

which suggests relatively weak association between the preferences shown by the four groups of housewives. This may well be a reflection of the fact that brands A to D were well-established and found more favour with the older housewives, while the younger users were impressed by the claims made for the new detergent and optical brightener brands, namely E to H. In any case notice that W, like the coefficient of multiple correlation to which it corresponds, cannot be negative.

6.8.2   In the eventuality of ties the same correction $\dfrac{t^3-t}{12}$ used for r_s is applied.

In this case, however, the effect of ties is to depress W so that $\dfrac{t^3-t}{12}$ for each tie must be subtracted from the denominator of the expression given above. Thus for a tie in one group:

$$W = \frac{12\Sigma\left(\Sigma r_a - \dfrac{\Sigma\Sigma r_a}{n}\right)^2}{k^2 n(n^2-1)-\dfrac{t^3-t}{12}}$$

6.8.3   The test of significance for W is based upon the sampling distribution of the sum of squared deviations of the Σr_as round $\overline{\Sigma r_a}$. This in turn is developed by reasoning analogous to that used in defining the sampling distribution of r_s. Decision criteria for the one-tail test at 5 per cent and 1 per cent significance levels are tabulated (for k from 3 to 20 and for n from 3 to 7) in table 7, page 381. For $n > 7$ the sampling distribution is approximated by the χ^2 distribution with $n-1$ degrees of freedom, in which case

$$\chi_{(\text{calc.})}^2 = \frac{12\Sigma\left(\Sigma r_a - \dfrac{\Sigma\Sigma r_a}{n}\right)^2}{kn(n+1)}$$

In the example cited above $n=8$ so that

$$\chi_{(\text{calc.})}^2 = \frac{(12)(146)}{(4)(8)(9)} = \frac{1752}{288} = 6\cdot083$$

But $\chi_{(\text{calc.})}^2 = 6\cdot083 < \chi_{0\cdot05}^2\,(8-1=7 \text{ degrees of freedom}) = 14\cdot07$; we have no evidence for rejecting a null hypothesis that there is no association between the groups in the parent population.

6.9 The runs test

6.9.1 When a sample is drawn from a population at a moment in time, the use of lottery methods or tables of random numbers as discussed in Chapter 1 will provide an adequate guarantee of the randomness of the sample (assuming that the sampling frame is complete). It has been shown in Chapter 3, however, that in conducting surveys of human populations the sample units will rarely be interviewed on the same day and that indeed several months may elapse between the commencement and termination of the investigation. In these circumstances it is quite possible for the characteristics of the population to change and in consequence the sample taken will tend to produce non-random results over time. As a result the use of tests based upon the random-sampling assumption would be invalid.

A situation of this type might occur if we sampled the work of a punch-card operator throughout one day. Supposing that five cards are selected at intervals of thirty numbers and verified, the number of misplaced holes being counted and recorded in chronological order. At the end of the day the median number of incorrectly punched holes is found and individual observations in excess of this median value given the symbol +, while those below the median are given a − sign. The following series may result (median = 3·5):

Order of sample	Number of punching errors x	Median > or < x	
1	3	−	} 1
2	2	−	
3	8	+	2
4	0	−	
5	1	−	} 3
6	3	−	
7	6	+	} 4
8	4	+	
9	1	−	} 5
10	0	−	
11	4	+	
12	5	+	} 6
13	8	+	
14	7	+	
15	2	−	7
16	6	+	8

The number of positive or negative sign runs is found to be 8 (we are not interested in the length of runs). What does this mean? Let us first consider what interpretation would be given to the following possible results:

Order of sample	Number of punching errors x	Median > or < x	
1	1	−	⎫
2	3	−	
3	0	−	
4	1	−	⎬ 1
5	0	−	
6	2	−	
7	2	−	
8	3	−	⎭
9	4	+	⎫
10	6	+	
11	7	+	
12	8	+	⎬ 2
13	5	+	
14	6	+	
15	7	+	
16	6	+	⎭

Order of sample	Number of punching errors x	Median > or < x
1	6	+ 1
2	1	− 2
3	4	+ 3
4	0	− 4
5	8	+ 5
6	2	− 6
7	5	+ 7
8	3	− 8
9	9	+ 9
10	0	− 10
11	4	+11
12	1	− 12
13	8	+13
14	3	− 14
15	5	+15
16	2	− 16

In the first case there are only two runs, suggesting that the operator is working efficiently in the mornings but inefficiently in the afternoons. This may be attributed to fatigue or boredom or both, but whatever the reason it is evident that this sample does not constitute a random sample from a stable population. Instead of the sample units being independent of each other there is a noticeable time dependence. In the second case there are more runs than would be expected in a random sample. Just as we would doubt the fairness of a coin which came down alternately heads and tails in twenty tosses, so we have to reject the randomness of this sample and a lack of independence is again indicated.

6.9.2   The sampling distribution of all the possible values of v (the number of runs observed) which could occur from a random sample has been found. It depends upon the length of the sequence and the numbers of $+$ and $-$ signs, n_+ and n_- in the sequence. Admittedly, when the median is used to distinguish 'high' and 'low' values, $n_+ = n_-$; we will encounter other situations, however, where some criterion other than the median is introduced and where $n_+ \neq n_-$. Thus table 8, page 382 shows the values of v for n_+ and n_- which are significant at the 5 per cent level ($\alpha = 0.05$). They indicate when the null hypothesis of randomness should be rejected. In the example cited above $n_+ = n_- = 8$; table 8 shows us that $v \leqslant 4$ or $v \geqslant 14$ would occur only once in twenty times from a random sample of 16 observations, so our result of $v = 8$ is therefore not significant and the sample may be considered random. Notice that the critical values of v are tabulated for values of n_+ and n_- up to 20; thereafter the sampling distribution becomes normal with

$$\mu_v = \frac{2n_+ n_-}{n_+ + n_-} + 1$$

$$\sigma_v = \sqrt{\frac{2n_+ n_- (2n_+ n_- - n_+ - n_-)}{(n_+ + n_-)^2 . (n_+ + n_- - 1)}}$$

A z-test may therefore be carried out in the usual manner with

$$z_{(\text{calc.})} = \frac{v - \mu_v}{\sigma_v}$$

6.9.3   To illustrate the use of these formulae, consider the following data collected very simply by the author. It was observed that when a class of students were put into a room having more seats than required there was firstly a general tendency for the first few rows of seats to be unoccupied, and secondly a tendency for bunching to occur in the remaining seats.

Starting with the left-hand side of the front row, and giving a $+$ sign to an occupied seat and a $-$ sign to an empty seat, the following sequence was observed in a fifty-seat room accommodating only thirty students.

Front

			1			2	3				
$-$	$-$	$-$	$-$	$-$	$+$	$-$	$-$	$-$	$+$		1st row

4   5

| $+$ | $+$ | $-$ | $-$ | $-$ | $-$ | $-$ | $-$ | $-$ | $+$ | 2nd row |

6   7   8

| $+$ | $+$ | $+$ | $-$ | $-$ | $+$ | $+$ | $+$ | $+$ | $+$ | 3rd row |

9

| $+$ | $+$ | $+$ | $-$ | $-$ | $+$ | $+$ | $+$ | $+$ | $+$ | 4th row |

10

| $+$ | $+$ | $+$ | $+$ | $+$ | $+$ | $+$ | $+$ | $+$ | $+$ | 5th row |

The number of runs, v, is 10 (or 11 if we start at the right-hand side of the first row), $n_+ = 30$ and $n_- = 20$. Thus

$$\mu_r = \frac{(2)(30)(20)}{(30+20)} + 1 = \frac{1200}{50} + 1 = 25$$

$$\sigma_r = \sqrt{\left[\frac{(1200)(1200-30-20)}{(30+20)^2(30+20-1)}\right]} = \sqrt{11 \cdot 265} = 3 \cdot 357$$

and

$$z_{(calc.)} = \frac{10-25}{3 \cdot 357} = -4 \cdot 47$$

$$(\text{or } \frac{11-25}{3 \cdot 357} = -4 \cdot 17)$$

In this case the null hypothesis will be directional because we assumed in the earlier discussion that too few runs were likely to occur because of bunching. For a one-tail test we know $z_{0.05}$ to be $-1 \cdot 64$; $z_{(calc.)}$ is much smaller than this so we may conclude that the way in which students arrange themselves in the classroom is non-random.

6.9.4   The runs test may be used in a third capacity. A series which at first sight appears to be a time series, with the implication of time dependence, may turn out to be random on using the runs test. To accept that time dependence exists we will expect the calculated v to fall in the rejection region of the sampling distribution of runs. For example, the following series might be explored for time dependence:

Year	x	Median $>$ or $<x$	
1	8	−	
2	6	−	
3	9	−	
4	6	−	
5	10	−	1
6	12	−	
7	11	−	
8	15	−	
9	11	−	
10	15	−	
11	18	+	2
12	14	−	3
13	21	+	
14	17	+	
15	16	+	
16	20	+	
17	25	+	4
18	23	+	
19	20	+	
20	27	+	
21	28	+	
22	28	+	

Here $v = 4$, $n_+ = 11$ and $n_- = 11$, Table 8 shows that $v = 7$ is significant at a 5 per cent level, so this series is non-random. Fig. 81 indicates that there is in fact a noticeable trend present and the use of time series analysis would therefore be justified.

6.10 Mathematical notes

To prove that

$$\frac{\Sigma(x-\bar{x})(y-\bar{y})}{n\sigma_x\sigma_y} = 1 - \frac{6\Sigma d^2}{n(n^2-1)}$$

when the variable values are the first n natural numbers.

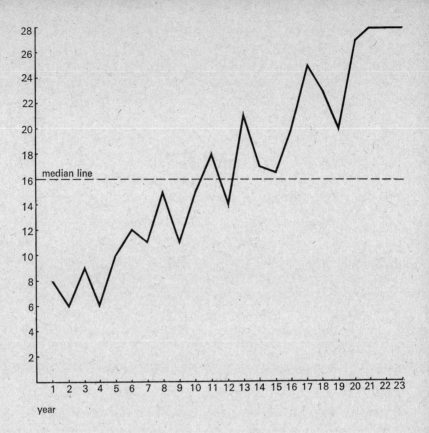

Fig. 81

$$\sigma_x^{\,2} = \frac{\Sigma x^2}{n} - \left(\frac{\Sigma x}{n}\right)^2 = \frac{\Sigma x^2}{n} - \bar{x}^2 \text{ and } \sigma_y^{\,2} = \frac{\Sigma y^2}{n} - \bar{y}^2$$

But the sum of the first n natural numbers is given by

$$\tfrac{1}{2}n(n+1)$$

and the sum of the squares of the first n natural numbers by

$$\tfrac{1}{6}n(n+1)(2n+1)$$

Therefore $\qquad \bar{x} = \bar{y} = \dfrac{\tfrac{1}{2}n(n+1)}{n} = \dfrac{n+1}{2}$

and
$$\sigma_x{}^2 = \sigma_y{}^2 = \frac{\frac{1}{6}n(n+1)(2n+1)}{n} - \left(\frac{n+1}{2}\right)^2$$

$$= \frac{2(n+1)(2n+1) - 3(n+1)^2}{12}$$

$$= \frac{n^2-1}{12}$$

Hence
$$\sigma_x \sigma_y = \frac{n^2-1}{12}$$

Now defining
$$d = x - y = (x - \bar{x}) - (y - \bar{y})$$
we have

$$\Sigma d^2 = \Sigma[(x-\bar{x}) - (y-\bar{y})]^2$$
$$= \Sigma[(x-\bar{x})^2 - 2(x-\bar{x})(y-\bar{y}) + (y-\bar{y})^2]$$
$$= \Sigma(x-\bar{x})^2 - 2\Sigma(x-\bar{x})(y-\bar{y}) + \Sigma(y-\bar{y})^2$$

But
$$\frac{\Sigma(x-\bar{x})^2}{n} = \frac{\Sigma(y-\bar{y})^2}{n} = \sigma_x{}^2 = \sigma_y{}^2 = \frac{n^2-1}{12}$$

Therefore
$$\Sigma(x-\bar{x})^2 = \Sigma(y-\bar{y})^2 = \frac{n(n^2-1)}{12}$$

and
$$\Sigma d^2 = \frac{2n(n^2-1)}{12} - 2\Sigma(x-\bar{x})(y-\bar{y})$$

so that
$$\Sigma(x-\bar{x})(y-\bar{y}) = \frac{n(n^2-1)}{12} - \frac{6\Sigma d^2}{12}$$

and
$$r = \frac{\Sigma(x-\bar{x})(y-\bar{y})}{n\sigma_x\sigma_y} = \frac{[n(n^2-1) - 6\Sigma d^2]/12}{n(n^2-1)/12}$$

$$= 1 - \frac{6\Sigma d^2}{n(n^2-1)}$$

$$= r_s$$

6.11 Examples

6.11.1 χ^2 tests

(a) A new drug is used as an aid in anaesthetizing patients. The degree of consciousness 10 minutes after an operation is observed for a sample of patients and compared with the results already obtained for patients having only the standard drugs and gases. The two sets of results are as follows:

Degree of consciousness 10 minutes after the operation

	Unconscious	Semi-conscious	Conscious	Total
New drug used	25	15	10	50
New drug not used	25	45	15	85
	50	60	25	135

Apply the χ^2 test to determine whether the figures above support the view that the new drug has some real effect on the degree of consciousness. State your conclusions carefully.

(University of Birmingham, 1962)

(b) Fit a normal distribution to the following data and test the goodness of fit.

Yield of grain in lb. Midpoint of range	Frequency
2·9	19
3·3	67
3·7	141
4·1	157
4·5	94
4·9	22
	500

(University of London, 1966)

(c) The following data gives the number of connections to wrong telephone numbers in a given period.

					Number of wrong connections								
0–3	4	5	6	7	8	9	10	11	12	13	14	15 and over	Total
6	11	14	22	43	31	40	35	20	18	12	7	8	267

Calculate the average number of wrong connections and use this value to fit a Poisson distribution to the data. Test the goodness of fit of a Poisson distribution to these data.

(d) An inspection of 500 packets of razor blades (5 blades to a packet) shows the number of defectives in each to be:

Defective blades	No. of packets
0	390
1	89
2	11
3	7
4	2
5	1
	500

Test whether the binomial distribution fits this distribution.

(e) Patients in hospital were asked questions on smoking habits with the following results:

Patients with	Cigarettes smoked		Total
	0 and under 5	5 and over	
Lung cancer	52	48	100
Other diseases	78	22	100
	130	70	200

On this evidence, what would you say about the association between smoking and lung cancer?

(University of London, 1963)

(f) Calculate the contingency coefficient, C, for the data in (a) and (e) above. What may be concluded from these two measures of association?

6.11.2 Tests for averages and proportions

(a) From a list of colleges in two cities undertaking the same type of work, two are randomly selected and their staffs graded according to salary. The following situation was observed.

Rank of salary	
College A	College B
1	3
2	5
4	6
7	8
9	10
11	14
12	16
13	18
15	21
17	22
19	23
20	25
24	27
26	28

Is there any significant difference in the median salary paid by these two colleges?

(b) Use the randomization test on the following data to decide whether the mean number of screws produced per day by firms using the two processes (old and new) is significantly different.

Firm	Screws produced by old process	Firm	Screws produced by new process
A	5329	A	2730
B	2583	B	3562
C	4740	C	4859
D	4900	D	2610

(c) A claim that at least 90 per cent of families on a large housing development own cars is checked by questioning twenty families; fifteen are found to be car owners. Using the binomial test decide whether the claim is justified.

6.11.3 *Ranking tests*

(a) Two motoring magazines carry out independent surveys of the new models introduced at a motor show. Each ranks the new models according to their estimation of the improvements incorporated in the new designs. The following results were published:

Model	Magazine X	Magazine Y
A	2	1
B	3 =	2 =
C	6	4
D	1	2 =
E	3 =	5
F	3 =	6
G	9	7 =
H	7	7 =
I	10	10
J	8	7 =

Calculate Spearman's coefficient of rank correlation and test whether it is significantly different from zero.

(b) Eight companies are classified in size according to different criteria, e.g. men employed, turnover, capital/labour ratio, etc. With the following results calculate Kendall's coefficient of concordance and interpret its meaning.

Firm	Labour-force	Turnover	Fixed investment	Capital/labour ratio
A	6	6	7	5
B	1	1	2	3
C	2	4	4	4
D	3	2	3	1
E	4	3	1	2
F	7	8	5 =	6
G	5	5	5 =	8
H	8	7	8	7

6.11.4 The Runs Test

(a) A sociologist suggests that manual and non-manual workers tend to select houses next to those occupied by the same type of worker. To test this, a long street made up of identical houses is visited. The arrangement of manual (M) and non-manual (N) workers was as follows:

N N M M N M M N N N M M M M N N M M M N M N N M

Using the runs test, indicate if the suggestion is statistically valid.

(b) Test whether the series shown in 5.7.1(e) is really a time series.

Chapter 7
Econometrics and operational research

7.1 Further developments of statistics

7.1.1 Because of the wide-spread use of statistics in many fields, specialists have developed the subject to meet their own particular needs. This evolutionary process has generated new disciplines: subjects in their own right, but drawing extensively on the foundation of general statistics.

We now find books on such topics as biometrics, psychometrics, sociometrics, econometrics, or operational research. As most of these names suggest, the subjects are concerned with measurement (Greek metron, a measure). They rely upon the observation, recording and analysis of actual situations in the real world, sometimes with the object of testing general 'laws' which have been propounded on an *a priori* basis, sometimes for the purpose of establishing these general propositions from empirical evidence. Whatever the primary objective, the final result leads to a method of taking decisions and planning future policy that enables the situation to be evaluated more definitely, both from the quantitative and the qualitative points of view.

7.1.2 This chapter will deal with two specialized extensions of statistics that are of particular interest to the social scientist: econometrics and operational research. The former plays an important part in many government policy matters and is one of the key concepts in a planned growth programme for the economy at large; operational research techniques also make a contribution to the achievement of growth targets, as they can be employed in many forms of private and public organization seeking to rationalize their operations and improve their efficiency.

7.2 The basis of econometrics

7.2.1   The name 'econometrics' was first used in 1926 by a Norwegian economist and statistician, Ragnar Frisch, although as a separate subject it had already developed before the First World War. By the early 1930s it had a recognized place in the field of economics and in 1933 the first econometrical journal appeared.

7.2.2   Econometrics is closely related to economic theory and to economic statistics. Economic theory sets out certain laws concerning the behaviour of individuals, institutions and the state according to their economic capacity. Insofar as these general laws can be put into a mathematical form, econometrics seeks to provide some empirical validity by using the techniques of statistical analysis. The raw material of the statistical analysis is regularly-collected economic data in many forms which is arranged and presented by the economic statistician.

The data used will generally be in the form of statistical series giving measurements of variables; these series may either be of a variable over a period of time (such as gross national product between 1948 and 1965), or of a variable at a moment in time when a cross-section of observations is taken (as in the case of the family expenditure surveys).

7.2.3   These series are treated as samples, and one of the main tasks is therefore to estimate the parameters of the population from which the samples are taken. Many readers may find the idea that these are sample series quite difficult to appreciate: figures for gross national product appear at first sight to be absolute (population results). Think of them, however, as the end product of a set of decisions which could have been taken in an infinite variety of ways; the universe or statistical population becomes all the possible sets of decisions which could lead to a figure for gross national product (G.N.P.), the actual figure being one of these and therefore a sample. The same rationalization applies to cross-sectional series. If a random sample of the balance sheets of firms in an industry is taken, there seems to be no problem: this is obviously a sample. If all the balance sheets are considered, however, we once more see the results as the end product of decisions which could have been taken in many different ways.

It is evident from what has been said that econometrics cannot be conducted on the basis of controlled experiments. One can only use the actual outcomes of the economic process; it is not possible to set up a situation and observe what happens. For example, it would be of little use to give a group of people different incomes in different weeks and then observe their expenditure behaviour, because this type of abstraction from reality would necessarily be reflected in the results. The problem is, of course, that external conditions cannot be held constant.

A further problem is that in relying on published data the essence of random sampling may be missing. Very often the econometrician has to make use of what is available rather than what he would like to have, but the departures from random sampling are generally well defined and can be taken into account (see Chapter 3).

7.2.4 The three main fields in which econometrics has developed are the trade cycle, market demand and supply, and national economic planning. The first of these was the subject of considerable attention during the inter-war years when oscillations in the national and world economy were both puzzling and apparently unavoidable. Market demand and supply was the principal aspect of the subject in the 1940s and is still important today in evaluating the consequences of changes in indirect taxes, or a devaluation of the currency (in the U.S.A. agricultural price supports to achieve stability of farm incomes are based upon econometric methods of demand analysis). National economic planning has been of prime concern since 1945, with the universal desire of nations to improve their over-all economic well-being; many advances in this area have only been made possible by the advent of computers and the development of mathematical methods suitable for computer solution.

The problems and methods of market demand and supply, and national economic planning will be considered in this chapter.

7.3 Market demand

7.3.1 Economic theory postulates a relationship between the price of a product and the quantity of the product demanded. This relationship in the market situation is based upon the concept of consumer behaviour (utility) and is generally considered to be inverse, so that price and quantity demanded move in opposite directions (the demand curve has a negative slope). More than one form of the relationship has been put forward, followers of A. A. Cournot and L. Walras postulating the functional dependence of demand on price:

$$d = f(p)$$

The opposite approach was taken by A. Marshall, who assumes that price depends upon quantity sold:

$$p = f'(d)$$

This form of the relationship is a sales function, since it gives a means of determining the price at which a specified quantity can be sold on the market.

To the econometrician it is immaterial which relationship is used, but for convenience the European convention (that demand varies with price) will be followed here.

7.3.2   The econometrician's task is to employ economic data to determine the precise form of the market demand relationship for different products. To ascertain the relationship between price and demand, the classical approach using time series data (i.e. price and quantity at different times) is used. The family budget approach can be incorporated in this technique, but by itself it provides only information about the effect of income changes on the demand for different produces.

7.3.3   The essence of the technique is to plot the data for price and quantity sold on a scatter diagram, and find the line of best fit using appropriate regression methods.

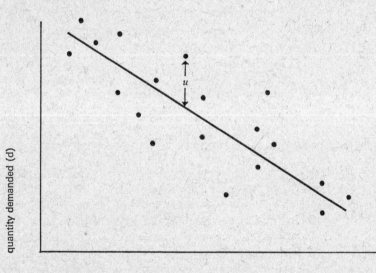

Fig. 82

In fig. 82 the demand relationship is shown in the simplest form

$$d = \alpha + \beta p$$

the random disturbances u having been eliminated by the method of least squares.

Given that non-linear estimating equations may be employed it may appear to the reader that there is nothing more to be said, but only rarely can a picture of demand be ascertained as easily as H. Wold showed in the case of butter (see Bibliography, page 370). In the majority of cases there are many difficulties which need to be ironed out.

7.3.4 *Mongrel relationships*

When one observes the price of a commodity and the quantity of it sold at different times, all that is actually shown is a set of market equilibrium positions, i.e. the price and quantity at which demand and supply are equal. If both demand and supply conditions are changing over time we get the result shown in fig. 83.

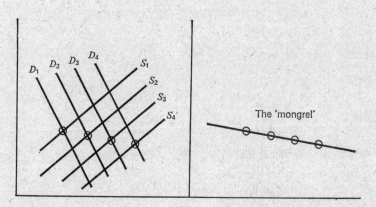

price

Fig. 83 The mongrel curve.

The curve fitted to these market equilibrium points is obviously neither a demand curve nor a supply curve; it is simply a mixture of the two and as such has little meaning or value. We will return to this particular problem later.

Some result can be achieved, however, if it is possible to show evidence in support of the belief that either demand or supply has been reasonably constant over the period in which the market data have been collected. If demand has been constant but supply has varied, then the market equilibrium points do indeed identify the demand curve (fig. 84).

Similarly, if demand has changed but the supply position has remained unaltered, the supply curve can be identified (fig. 85).

Only rarely, of course, will either one or the other stand still in practice.

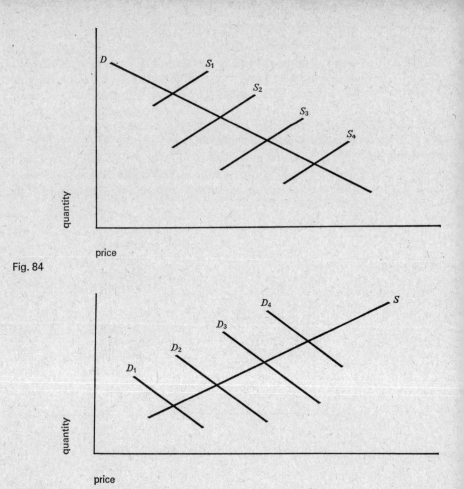

Fig. 84

Fig. 85

However, if there is greater variability in one than in the other, then an approximation of the second relationship will be provided. In any case, we have indicated an important aspect of econometrics: statistical techniques alone will not provide answers to the problems, because additional evidence is required from the economic and social statistician before meaningful conclusions can be drawn from the results.

7.3.5 *Other things being equal*

7.3.5.1 The *ceteris paribus* condition plays a crucial part in the economic theory of the market. Changes in price and quantity are considered in isolation, with the assumption that tastes, incomes, prices of other products and the general environment are fixed.

In the real world this will not often be the case. As the evidence for a study of demand is collected over a period of time, it is inevitable that circumstances will alter, and in the identification problem it is only the fact that supply (demand) has changed that enables us to find the demand (supply) relationship. Now if other factors do not remain constant, they must as far as possible be taken into account. Demand will no longer have a simple functional dependence on price: it will be influenced by many variables so that the equation will take the following form:

$$d = \alpha_1 + \alpha_2 p_1 + \alpha_3 p_2 + \alpha_4 I + \alpha_5 z + \ldots$$

The earliest approach to the problem of additional variables was to attempt to isolate and then eliminate them from the series; this was thought in particular to overcome the difficulty of the mongrel relationship (fig. 83). Henry Schultz, an American pioneer in econometrics (see Bibliography, page 370), saw that, as well as being a function of price, demand was also dependent on time. In the time span from which the data for an econometric study are taken there will inevitably be changes in the circumstances surrounding the market; both supply and demand may shift, giving the mongrel trend line of market equilibrium points.

Therefore we now have

$$d = f(p) + l(t) \ .$$

The logic underlying the statistical procedure is quite simple. The demand curves have shifted in parallel over a period of time because of such things as an increase in national income; this is the $l(t)$ component above. If the trend of this demand shift can be isolated (i.e. by finding the least squares line) and the trend figures are eliminated from the original time series (by subtraction), then a picture of a stable curve will emerge with demand dependent on price alone. In the context of fig. 83 we will establish the D_1 demand curve.

The key assumption underlying this approach is that the effect of time is merely to cause a parallel shift in the demand curve. Its shape remains the same. If national income is increasing this may be reasonable and it is possible to consider $f(p)$ and $l(t)$ as independent and therefore additive. If, however, tastes change as the community's wealth increases, then the two functions are no longer independent. Not only will the demand curves shift in parallel, they will also vary in shape over time. Schultz's method will no longer have applicability, for now the two components $f(p)$ and $l(t)$ are related and cannot simply be added together.

In this case the $l(t)$ must be broken down into more detail and the parameters of the constituents found. This is the approach which is now used and which Schultz suggested was preferable.

7.3.5.2   Let us now consider which variables should be and have been taken into account. Some index of the increasing real wealth of the nation is obviously crucial: this may be G.N.P., national income or personal disposable income. The prices of other commodities and services will also be important in certain circumstances. We may simply be interested in the general level of prices, in which case the index of retail prices or the index of wholesale prices could be used, or we might be interested specifically in the price of products which are either close substitutes or complementary. For instance, it is fairly obvious that the demand for margarine not only depends on its price but also on the price of butter; these are substitutes. Again, the demand for petrol will certainly depend not only on its price but also on the price of cars; these are complements.

For semi-luxuries or luxuries we may take into account the surplus of income after the basic necessities of life have been satisfied, or the availability of credit from the banks or finance companies; improvements in the general quality of products should also be allowed for where applicable.

In many situations there will be a time-lag before a change in price affects demand. If the price of cars in the export market is reduced at time t the demand will not increase till $t+1$, because the orders for period t will have been placed at the price ruling at $t-1$. There may also be an apparently similar lag caused by the 'speculative motive'. If a producer finds that the price of his raw material falls, he may defer buying an increased amount in expectation of the price falling further, but if the price increases he may drastically enlarge his order and stockpile as a safeguard against further increases. Consequently, a speculative component will be found in the demand equation.

7.3.5.3   Some of the explaining variables have been mentioned here, but the list is by no means exhaustive. What will be included and what left out very much depends upon the situation. It is this decision which is the very essence of the art of the econometrician. He cannot include every factor or his equations would be far too complex, so he must try to establish which are of fundamental importance. If he succeeds, then the error term in the equation can be thought of as the sum of a large number of minor factors causing the deviations from the mathematical curve of demand.

7.3.6   *The shape of the demand curve*

7.3.6.1   For simplicity we have considered demand curves in a two dimensional form. Once the demand equations take a multi-variable form we are unable to visualize them in a concrete state, but it is nevertheless worthwhile to maintain the simplified assumption for a little longer. Even with a complex equation it is possible to draw a two-dimensional demand curve. To achieve this form the variables, apart from price, are held constant (if they are in index form, as will often be the case, the variables will be set at base equal to 100) and the equation is then rationalized by multiplying the parameters by the constant variables, leaving

$$d = \alpha + \beta p$$

We have utilized explicitly assumed linear demand functions up to this point, but it is evident that they need not necessarily be linear. Indeed, it is far more likely that the functions will be non-linear in some way. The choice of form is very largely subjective and arbitrary, so we often choose a non-linear form that can easily be transformed into a linear form by taking logarithms, i.e. exponential or double logarithmic. The more popular is the double logarithmic, in which the elasticity of demand is equal to the parameter β in

$$\log d = \log \alpha + \beta \log p \qquad \text{(see 4.2.4)}$$

and is constant throughout the curve. Fitting any curve to a set of data is an approximation, and the use of the most convenient form is justified because many different forms may be found to fit the data equally well.

7.3.6.2   The magnitude of errors in the calculated parameters should be assessed according to the method outlined in Chapter 4, bearing in mind that in econometrics there is the possibility of equation error in addition to measurement errors through inaccurate or biased collection of data. Equation errors occur if the demand equation has not been specified correctly, the omission of an important variable being one of the most frequent causes of inaccuracies.

7.3.7   *The cross-section approach*

7.3.7.1   We have already found that one of the more important factors which influence demand, apart from price, is income. The dependence of demand on income can be evaluated if a number of families are studied simultaneously and their expenditure on different categories of goods is recorded together with the family income. Prices are held constant by this method as the same market price structure faces all the families at the time of the survey.

This approach was first suggested by Ernst Engel, a German statistician, who in the nineteenth century observed that as income grows so the proportion of it spent on food decreases; 'Engel's law' has been fully tested and conclusively proved by the results of empirical evidence.

The two methods of finding Engel's curves are closely associated. Fig. 86 illustrates the first method, in which income is measured horizontally and expenditure on food vertically; points mark the situation of each family and the regression line of expenditure on income can be determined.

Alternatively we can divide the families into specific income groups and plot the average family income of each group against the average expenditure of the group (shown by circles in fig. 86). The least squares line fitted to these group averages is almost identical with that found from the simple scatter diagram.

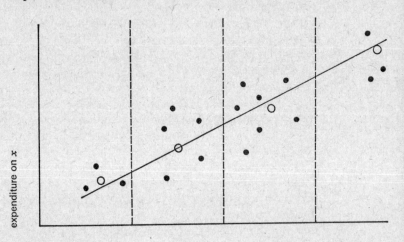

Fig. 86   Engel's curve.

This is a simplified model and account should really be taken of other variables besides price: family size, social status, occupation, length of time in receipt of present income, geographical location and family age must all play a part. Many of these lead the econometrician into the realms of sociology and he must accept this fact as a part of his subject.

7.3.7.2   The establishment of the relationship between income and demand is obviously useful in itself because planning of future output requirements can be facilitated if some estimate of the increase in real income is obtainable. Consumption of what Engel called superior goods will need to increase, whereas there may be a contraction in demand for staple goods as the nation and its individual members become wealthier. There is, however, a second use for the results of the cross-sectional approach. They can be combined with those from the time series method to establish more accurate equations of demand. Time series studies alone are often subject to the phenomenon known as *multicollinearity*. This is an expression of the fact that many economic series move together over a period of time because they are all affected by a common cause, such as the trend of the trade cycle or the overall pattern of business activity.

Where multicollinearity is present, it is impossible to separate from a time study the effect in the demand equation of income on the one hand and price on the other. In these circumstances the difficulty can be overcome if the effect of price is estimated from a time series study and the effect of income from a cross-sectional study. The results of the two can then be pooled.

7.3.7.3 In concluding this section, we should notice that demand studies are not only the domain of the economist or statistician as such. They are also of increasing importance in the business world as a means of sales forecasting and many large firms make use of these econometric tools. For this reason, and in view of the fact that the majority of econometricians stress this aspect of market analysis, we have concentrated on the question of demand rather than on the equally important consideration of supply.

7.4 National economic planning

7.4.1 Estimating the precise mathematical forms of demand is part of what can broadly be described as micro-economics (the study of individual components in the economy). Demand equations are based on the theory of the consumer and his behaviour. Similarly, supply equations depend for their basis on the theory of the firm and the firm's motivation. This side of general economics, dealing with individuals or institutions in separation, is an indispensable part of the subject, but it is only a part. Side by side with it is macro-economics (the study of the economy as a whole). Macro-economics concerns itself with problems of investment, overall employment, the balance of payments, monetary policy etc. It looks at the results of the interlocking and interdependent relationships between the individuals and institutions making up the economy.

7.4.2 We have only to compare the tremendous fluctuations in employment and general business activity in the decades before the Second World War with the post-1945 situation of relative stability to see why modern macro-economics is of crucial importance. The abstract economic analysis of J. M. Keynes (see Bibliography, page 370) established the fundamental variables affecting the economy and their relationship one with another. The awareness of these basic relationships has enabled public administrators to understand the means of dealing with actual or potential imbalances in the economy, and as Professor Ely Devons has written of the 1930s (see Bibliography, page 370):

We ought no longer to expect the utter bewilderment, bafflement, perplexity and intellectual despair which was so characteristic of that period.

7.4.3　　The work of Keynes and the post-Keynesian theoretical economists can be thought of as the qualitative basis of macro-economics, telling us which variables should be changed in order to achieve a certain objective. Its weakness lies in the fact that little is said about the amount by which this or that variable should be increased or decreased. This weakness has been very apparent in the United Kingdom since 1945. Successive governments have tried their hands at striking a balance of action to overcome inflationary and deflationary tendencies in the economy, to strengthen sterling at times of monetary instability, and to improve an adverse balance of payments. Rarely has the balance been achieved. Instead, we have seen the phenomenon known as 'stop–go'. Pressures in various directions have been applied to prevent an inflationary situation getting out of hand, but these restraints seem sometimes to have been a little too severe and a loss of confidence has resulted, causing excessive contraction of the economy. Consequently measures have had to be adopted to restore confidence and a mild type of oscillation has appeared because of an inability to predict the precise results of a given quantitative change in the situation.

7.4.4　　The author does not want to give the impression that any blame should be levelled in the direction of politicians or civil servants for this failure; the problem is complex and cannot be solved overnight, but the econometrician is able to afford considerable assistance. If the relationship between the variables can be quantified it will probably be possible to predict the future repercussions of present changes, which not only helps in formulating corrective and remedial action for present ills afflicting the economy but can also facilitate planning for growth. If it is possible to influence the overall level of economic activity by altering the independent variables, the process can perhaps be reversed: let us prescribe a level of activity for the future and try to ascertain what must happen to the variables if the objective is to be achieved.

This is the essence of various attempts which have been made since the early 1960s to implement a planned growth rate for the economy of Great Britain (and indeed for the economies of many other countries). The seeds of long- and short-term planning, as developed in the U.S.S.R. during the inter-war years, have germinated not only in the communist bloc, but also in Asia and many parts of western Europe. The post-1945 era has seen a succession of nations producing five-year plans, setting targets which have in many cases been achieved.

7.4.5   Only for a relatively short period of time has Britain been formally committed to planning. Its first direct incursion into the field of five-year planning came with the establishment of the National Economic Development Council (N.E.D.C.) in the spring of 1962, the primary objective of which was to study the implications of a 4 per cent annual growth rate between 1961 and 1966. The conclusions of the N.E.D.C. (see Bibliography, page 370) were that

the achievement of an average rate of growth of 4% should not prove impossible. There are undoubtedly difficult problems to be tackled, the solution to which will call for changes in policies, arrangements and attitudes. A vital element will be the determination to succeed on the part of government, management and trade unions.

7.4.6   Similar conclusions were drawn in the 'National Plan', produced by the Department of Economic Affairs in October 1965 when considering the possibility of a 25 per cent increase in gross domestic product between 1956 and 1970. Both studies rest largely upon an assessment of growth potential by businessmen, trade associations, trade unions and government officials. Behind both there has nevertheless been an awareness of the more rigorous analytical methods being developed by applied economists throughout the world. The desire for an improvement in national welfare and stability has fostered wide interest in this aspect of econometrics and there has been close liaison in Britain between economists working at Cambridge University on one hand and the N.E.D.C. and government departments on the other.

7.4.7 *The Cambridge approach*

7.4.7.1 The Department of Applied Economics at Cambridge, under Professors R. Stone and A. Brown, has been working to produce a model of the British economy. We will first look at this project in a general way and then consider some of the analytical methods on which it is based.

The model is extremely complex and has been built up in such a way that it can be programmed for computer use. The importance of computer application is that it enables the model to be continually recomputed as information is corrected and brought up to date, and also enables the results of experimental changes in the data to be quickly obtained. Indeed, without modern computing facilities the calculations (involving six thousand coefficients divided among sixteen producing sectors of the economy) would be insuperable.

Two variations on the basic model are being considered at Cambridge, as J. M. Bates (see Bibliography, page 370) has explained:

(i) A behaviouristic projection of the U.K. economy in 1970, on the assumption that present attitudes and institutional forces remain essentially unchanged, or change in a similar way to the observed changes over the last decade or so,

(ii) a programmed model, which is intended to show the implications of increasing the growth of the U.K. economy by more than that experienced over the last decade.

The procedure used in the two models is fundamentally the same. Firstly, estimates of final demand in 1970 are made (in the form of consumers' expenditure, government expenditure and exports); these are estimated exogenously from time-series studies and cross-section analysis. Secondly, the required level of output from each of the industrial sectors is calculated from these final demands. Finally, the requirements of raw materials, capital and labour for the production of these levels of industrial output is ascertained. The procedure outlined appears to be straightforward, but in practice the achievement of the necessary aggregates requires very advanced techniques.

Let us now consider in a little more detail the second of the two models mentioned above, which has been described by the Department of Applied Economics, Cambridge (see Bibliography, page 370). Basically, the N.E.D.C.'s 4 per cent growth projection is adopted. The rate of growth has once more been deliberately accelerated in order to study its implications, and two different projections have been calculated. The first assumes a growth in private consumers' expenditure of 3·2 per cent per annum and the second a growth of 3·7 per cent per annum. Each of these has two versions. The first assumes a zero balance of payments in 1970 and the second a surplus of £200,000,000. It is apparent that the easiest of these four to realize will be the 3·2 per cent growth with zero balance of payments, whilst the most difficult will be the case of 3·7 per cent growth with a £200,000,000 balance of payments surplus.

7.4.7.2   The answers which the model gives are not perfect. The estimation of all the coefficients in the equations is obviously very difficult; it is of little use using the present coefficients (industrial technology will be more advanced in 1970 and consumer tastes will have changed) whilst the extrapolation of past trends will only be of use up to a certain point.

Whatever devices are used, there must be considerable doubt about the accuracy of the results achieved. Furthermore, all aspects of the study cannot be brought to a fruitful conclusion at the same time, and where work is still progressing interim assumptions have to be made which might prove to be unrealistic. As results in these areas become available, they can be fitted into the model and a re-calculation of resource requirements takes place.

Whatever the present reservations and imperfections, the fundamental method is sound and can enable certain objectives to be achieved. A change in some aspect of the economy, say an increase in the domestic demand for cars, can be followed through the system and all its implications examined. Resultant changes in the demands for inputs of labour, raw materials and capital can be evaluated together with the effect on imports, the balance of payments in general, distribution requirements and so on. With this information available decisions taken by central and local government, nationalized industries, private industries, trade unionists, and consumers will have a more objective background than is the case at the present time.

7.4.8 *Input–output tables*

7.4.8.1 We have talked in general terms about the methods used at Cambridge. We should now specify more definitely the analytical foundations upon which the model of the United Kingdom's economy has been constructed.

The first requirement of a planning model or programme is that it should possess internal consistency. The interdependent parts of the model must be co-ordinated in such a way as to make the whole feasible. There is no point in specifying an output level in a certain industry when there is no possibility of having a sufficient labour force possessing the necessary skills, just as it is unrealistic to indicate that all supplies of iron ore should be produced in this country when the ore deposits are insufficiently large.

Even bearing in mind this need for internal consistency in the plan, it is evident that there may be many ways in which the programme can be formulated. Which of these will be used depends on the objective. If we desire to maximize employment, one particular programme will be optimal; if we want to maximize national income or the economy's growth rate, then another may be the best. Thus, the best way of achieving an objective, the optimality of the programme, will be equally as important as the objective itself. In this section we shall concentrate on the problem of internal consistency, leaving the question of the optimal solution until later (7.5.5.4).

The analysis involved in establishing the internal consistency of a programme was first developed by W. Leontief in the U.S.A. It is based upon a study of the relationship between the inputs (labour, raw materials, fuel, machine tools, etc.) going into different sectors of the economic production and the outputs (finished products) of these same sectors. For this reason, it is called input–output analysis, or analysis of inter-industry flows or relations.

7.4.8.2   For studying these input and output flows round the economy, we distinguish a number of sectors; the division is largely arbitrary and depends upon the detail required. We may identify individual industries (civil engineering, wool textiles, motor vehicles, coal mining) or we may use broad categories of activity (consumer goods, consumer durables and dwellings, capital goods). In this outline the amount of detail is immaterial, so let us therefore consider n sectors, and denote the output of each of these per year $Q_1, Q_2, \ldots Q_n$. Some of the output of each sector may be used up in that sector (e.g. a motor manufacturer uses some of his own vehicles for transporting materials inside and outside the plant), some of the output will go to other sectors to form part of that sector's input, and some will be left for domestic consumption, export or stockpiling. Consider the first sector, with a total output Q_1. That part of the output which it uses itself we will call q_{11}. The first figure one indicates the producing sector and the second the sector of use. It follows that the output of sector 1 going to sectors 2, 3, 4 \ldots n will be shown by $q_{12}, q_{13}, q_{14} \ldots q_{1n}$. In general, the ith sector is the producing sector and the jth sector is the using sector. The amounts q_{ij} are the *intersector flows*. The surplus, that part not used as a means of further production, constitutes the final output or product and is denoted simply by q_i (for sector 1 it is q_1).

From this, we find the relationships

$$Q_1 = q_{11} + q_{12} + \ldots + q_{1n} + q_1$$
$$Q_2 = q_{21} + q_{22} + \ldots + q_{2n} + q_2$$
$$\cdot$$
$$\cdot$$
$$\cdot$$
$$Q_n = q_{n1} + q_{n2} + \ldots + q_{nn} + q_n$$

The total output of the ith sector is equal to the sum of the flows from the ith into the jth sectors ($j = 1, 2, 3 \ldots n$) plus the final product of the ith sector. Schematically, the set of n allocation of output equations is often put in the form of an input–output table or Leontief table, as shown below with an additional row (placed at the top) representing the total labour force Q_0 and the allocation of labour to the j sectors, so that q_{01} shows the amount of labour (man-days) required in the first sector; q_0 is the amount of labour unemployed or employed in non-productive activities such as government, teaching and the services.

Leontief or input–output tables

Total output	Intersector flows (physical units)						Final output
Q_0	q_{01}	q_{02}	q_{03}	$\cdot$	$\cdot$	$\cdot\ q_{0n}$	q_0
Q_1	q_{11}	q_{12}	q_{13}	$\cdot$	$\cdot$	$\cdot\ q_{1n}$	q_1
Q_2	q_{21}	q_{22}	q_{23}	$\cdot$	$\cdot$	$\cdot\ q_{2n}$	q_2
Q_3	q_{31}	q_{32}	q_{33}	$\cdot$	$\cdot$	$\cdot\ q_{3n}$	q_3
$\cdot$							
$\cdot$							
Q_n	q_{n1}	q_{n2}	q_{n3}	$\cdot$	$\cdot$	$\cdot\ q_{nn}$	q_n

The inherent weakness in a system designed round physical units of measurement is that although the rows in the Leontief table can be summed (being in the same units) this is not the case with the columns. The columns are made up of inputs into the ith sector from all the other sectors, and contain fuel in tons, gallons or kilowatts, raw materials in

Value of total output	Intersector flows (value units)						Value of final output
V_0	v_{01}	v_{02}	v_{03}	$\cdot$	$\cdot$	$\cdot\ v_{0n}$	v_0
V_1	v_{11}	v_{12}	v_{13}	$\cdot$	$\cdot$	$\cdot\ v_{1n}$	v_1
V_2	v_{21}	v_{22}	v_{23}	$\cdot$	$\cdot$	$\cdot\ v_{2n}$	v_2
V_3	v_{31}	v_{32}	v_{33}	$\cdot$	$\cdot$	$\cdot\ v_{3n}$	v_3
$\cdot$							
$\cdot$							
V_n	v_{n1}	v_{n2}	v_{n3}	$\cdot$	$\cdot$	$\cdot\ v_{nn}$	v_n
	m_1	m_2	m_3	$\cdot$	$\cdot$	$\cdot\ m_n$	
V	V_1	V_2	V_3	$\cdot$	$\cdot$	$\cdot\ V_n$	

tons, bushels, barrels or crates, and machinery of many different types and sizes. For this reason it is more convenient to convert the physical output table into a value output table by introducing the price p of the physical units; V_i will be the value of the total output of the ith sector, v_{ij} will be the value of the output of the ith sector used in the jth sector, and v_i will be the value of the surplus. Similarly, the units of labour will be expressed as the cost of labour. This gives:

$$V_i = Q_i p_i, \quad v_{ij} = q_{ij} p_i, \quad v_i = q_i p_i$$

The new table is shown schematically on page 337. We have included a further row denoting the profits, m_i, of the different sectors. This needs some elaboration.

If the items in each row are summed (excepting the profit component) we get the following equations:

$$C_1 = v_{01} + v_{11} + v_{21} + \ldots + v_{n1}$$
$$C_2 = v_{02} + v_{12} + v_{22} + \ldots + v_{n2}$$
$$\vdots$$
$$C_n = v_{0n} + v_{1n} + v_{2n} + \ldots + v_{nn}$$

Each of these expresses the total production costs of the sector C_i in terms of the costs of the means of production, v_{ji}, used in the ith sector (no matter from which other sector they originate) plus the cost of the labour used in the ith sector. Now V_i equals the value of the total output of the ith sector and C_i equals the total cost of producing that output, so that $V_i - C_i = m_i$ (the profits accruing to the ith sector).

From this, we can see that the sum of all the items in the columns (including profits) equals the value of the output:

$$V_i = C_i + m_i$$

We therefore get the following n equations

$$V_1 = v_{01} + v_{11} + v_{21} + \ldots + v_{n1} + m_1$$
$$V_2 = v_{02} + v_{12} + v_{22} + \ldots + v_{n2} + m_2$$
$$\vdots$$
$$V_n = v_{0n} + v_{1n} + v_{2n} + \ldots + v_{nn} + m_n$$

which are the cost equations. We now have two sets of equations for V_i. The first shows that the value of the total output of the ith sector is equal to the value of that part of the output used as a means of further production (inputs) plus the value of the surplus available for consumption etc. The second shows that the value of the output of the ith sector equals the value of the inputs used in the sector and received from other sectors plus the cost of the necessary labour force and the profits. This relationship between the equation of allocation of output and the cost equation is called the equation of intersector flow equilibrium.

We have established the importance of the equilibrium of flows within the economy to the internal consistency of the programme. We must now look at these flows in more detail.

7.4.9 *Coefficients of production*

7.4.9.1 It is evident that we have so far looked at the end result of the inter-sector allocation problem. We have said nothing about how much of the output of the ith sector must go to the jth sector. The amount of coal that will be used in the production of steel not only depends upon the total output of steel, but also upon the quantity of coal required to produce one ton of steel. We must know something of the technical conditions of production.

If four tons of coal are needed to produce one ton of steel, the ratio $4:1$ can be used as an indication of the technical conditions prevailing and this ratio expressed in a fractional form is called the technical coefficient of production. In general, the units of the output of the ith sector required in the jth sector divided by the total output of the jth sector equals the technical coefficient of production:

$$a_{ij} = \frac{q_{ij}}{Q_j}$$

These coefficients a_{ij} can be determined statistically from past data of inputs and outputs in each sector, or from engineering methods. In practice both may be used, the important thing being that from the above relationship we find

$$q_{ij} = a_{ij} Q_j$$

Substituting this result in the equation of the allocation of output we get

$$Q_1 = a_{11} Q_1 + a_{12} Q_2 + a_{13} Q_3 + \ldots + a_{1n} Q_n + q_1$$
$$Q_2 = a_{21} Q_1 + a_{22} Q_2 + a_{23} Q_3 + \ldots + a_{2n} Q_n + q_2$$
$$\cdot$$
$$\cdot$$
$$\cdot$$
$$Q_n = a_{n1} Q_1 + a_{n2} Q_2 + a_{n3} Q_3 + \ldots + a_{nn} Q_n + q_n$$

or

$$q_1 = Q_1 - (a_{11}Q_1 + a_{12}Q_2 + a_{13}Q_3 + \ldots + a_{1n}Q_n)$$

$$q_2 = Q_2 - (a_{21}Q_1 + a_{22}Q_2 + a_{23}Q_3 + \ldots + a_{2n}Q_n)$$

.
.
.

$$q_n = Q_n - (a_{n1}Q_1 + a_{n2}Q_2 + a_{n3}Q_3 + \ldots + a_{nn}Q_n)$$

From this we see that if the technical coefficients of production are known, then there are $2n$ unknowns,

$$Q_1, Q_2 \ldots Q_n \text{ and } q_1, q_2 \ldots q_n$$

If the total outputs Q_i are prescribed in the economic plan then we can find the final products of the sectors q_i; if the final products are given then the total outputs can be found; if some of each are given (n in all) then the other n can be found. As a general rule n of the unknowns must be set arbitrarily and the remainder will be determined uniquely from the technical coefficients a_{ij}.

Matrix of inter-sector flows (with three independent systems)

$a_{11}Q_1$	$a_{12}Q_2$					
$a_{21}Q_1$	$a_{22}Q_2$					
		$a_{33}Q_3$	$a_{34}Q_4$	$a_{35}Q_5$		
		$a_{43}Q_3$	$a_{44}Q_4$	$a_{45}Q_5$		
		$a_{53}Q_3$	$a_{54}Q_4$	$a_{55}Q_5$		
					$a_{66}Q_6$	$a_{67}Q_7$
					$a_{76}Q_6$	$a_{77}Q_7$

7.4.9.2   The methods of input–output analysis outlined above are the basis of the work carried out at Cambridge and elsewhere. We have considered it in a very simple form, but in practice it may be both necessary and expedient to divide the economy into sectors or geographical areas and deal with each independently. As an illustration of this, consider the Leontief table on page 340 in which some of the cells have zero values because some sectors use none or very little of the output of others. When this happens it is possible to see that the whole can be divided into independent parts, each of which may be solved in separation.

Again our outline has been based on a closed economy, whereas the Cambridge team have to contend with the problems and complexities of international trade and finance, so results will inevitably be slow in forthcoming. This aspect of applied economics is breaking new ground, but once established it can provide a major contribution to the planned development of the economy.

7.5   Operational research

7.5.1   Operational research (O.R.) has been defined by Churchman, Ackoff and Arnoff (see Bibliography, page 370) as

the application of scientific methods, techniques and tools to problems involving the operations of a system so as to provide those in control of the system with optimum solutions to the problems.

The key words in this definition are 'system' and 'optimum solutions'. O.R. is an aid in solving management's fundamental problem of decision making. It aims particularly at providing a quantified means of deciding how the separate but interconnected parts of an organization (system) should be co-ordinated in order to realize the best (optimum) results from the operation of the whole.

It seems that O.R. is concerned with measurement in management. The same, of course, can be said of industrial engineering, management accounting, organization and method, and work study. All of these are intended to improve the efficiency of the firm in different aspects of its operations, but there is nevertheless a real distinction between them and O.R. The importance of the scientific, financial and organizational side of industry cannot be stressed enough, but experts in these fields are mainly concerned with specific problems treated in isolation. The costing of a certain production procedure, the design of a new machine tool, and the improvement of the invoicing system make valuable contribution to the firm's operations, but they do not view the system in its entirety. The implications and repercussions of actions are not always followed through, and indeed will rarely be apparent to these specialists. This then is what sets O.R. apart: the O.R. man must view the whole system and not just separate components of it.

7.5.2   In establishing the purpose of O.R. we have also indicated its conceptual difference compared with econometrics, which in the main uses statistical techniques to provide empirical validity for the propositions of theoretical economics. O.R. has few if any of these theoretical laws on which a basis could be established: essentially it is a way of thought, incorporating the methods of many subjects, which is useful in solving practical problems. The very origin of O.R. illustrates this point. The Second World War required the planned transportation and strategically significant deployment of complex and varied equipment with its attendant personnel with the result that exponents of many subjects were brought together. The team approach of mathematicians, engineers, physicists, economists, psychologists etc. generated completely new methods of dealing with the problems of global war, including the production of raw materials quickly and efficiently. With the end of the war industry naturally maintained its link with these new methods, their development now being motivated by the desire for profits.

O.R. is thus the product of a need to solve actual problems; outside this context the techniques have no existence.

7.5.3   The methods of O.R. and econometrics are to a certain extent similar. Economic planning requires the formulation of the problem (the fundamental relationships of macro-economics), the establishment of an internally consistent mathematical model, the means of achieving an optimal solution of the model, and finally the testing of the model to consider its implications. The same procedure has applicability to O.R. The researcher first needs to take an overall view of the problem faced. He must analyse the system being studied and consider the objectives of the operation, bearing in mind the effect of changes on associated systems and the consequences accruing from possible alternative courses of action.

A mathematical model of the system can be built on the basis of this general appraisal. It may only be a partial representation of reality but as long as it produces accurate predictions it has value. The optimum solution of the model can be achieved either mathematically (requiring abstract analysis using the calculus and matrix algebra) or through the trial and error 'iterative' method, which is very suitable for computer application and simply involves trying different values of the variables and observing which produces the best results. The model can then be tested using past data to see whether it is in accord with reality, and simple procedures must finally be specified for those people who will implement the solution in the factory, plant or office.

7.5.4   We have mentioned the purposes and methods of O.R. Now we must consider four of the many techniques which can be employed to realize the objectives: linear programming, Monte Carlo, stock control and queueing. All four draw extensively on mathematics and statistics and the first two have very wide application throughout O.R. work.

7.5.5 *Linear programming*

7.5.5.1   Linear programming is the principal technique used to determine the best utilization of specified resources to reach a desired objective (for example the maximization of profits or output, or the minimization of costs). Whatever the objective is, there will normally be certain constraining conditions on the resources used, such as limitations on machine time, man-hours, storage capacity etc.; these constraints will be found in the following form:

  (i)   Machine A can be used not more than x hours per day.
  (ii)   At least y units of product M must be produced per week.
  (iii) The output of R, S and T cannot be negative.

In mathematical shorthand we get

  (i) $A \leqslant x$ (ii) $M \geqslant y$ (iii) $R \geqslant 0$, $S \geqslant 0$, $T \geqslant 0$.

As the name suggests, the system of equations expressing the desired optimization and the constraints will be in a linear form. It cannot be solved by the normal methods of simultaneous equations however, because of the inequalities present within the system. The new technique of linear programming has been developed to overcome this problem. Its methods use the principle of iteration: choosing from a set of solutions the best possible or optimal one(s).

7.5.5.2   By looking at a simple problem which is capable of solution using linear programming we can demonstrate the main features of the technique. A firm produces two products x and y, the unit profit on x being £2 and on y £1. Each product has to be passed through an acid bath which takes 2 hours 20 minutes to prepare, so that it only functions for 6 hours 40 minutes per shift; each product also needs machine time on special equipment that is in action for only 5 hours per shift, due to the need of regular re-setting, and finally there are only 1000 square feet of storage space available each shift.

Now x takes 4 minutes in the acid dip and y only 1 minute; both x and y

require 1 minute on the special machine; and x takes 2 square feet of storage space whilst y takes 5 square feet. Within this situation we want to know how much of x and y should be produced in order to maximize the profits of the firm.

We want to maximize the profits equation representing the fact that product x earns twice the profit of product y, i.e. maximize $2x+y$.

To start with we have 400 minutes of time in the acid bath, each unit of x needing 4 minutes and each unit of y 1 minute; this can be expressed as

$$4x+y \leqslant 400$$

which shows that the number of units of x and y which can be processed must result in a total utilization time of 400 minutes or less. Similar reasoning applies to machine time and storage space, i.e.

Machine time	$x+y \leqslant 300$
Storage space	$2x+5y \leqslant 1000$

7.5.5.3 *Graphical solution*

We can visualize these three constraining inequalities in a graphical form. Taking the first one, we find that if we only produce x during the shift then we will be able to process at the most 100 units; if we only produce y, then 400 units can be processed. Any mixture of the two can be found so long as $4x+y$ never exceeds 400. For instance, we can produce 75 units of x and 100 units of y, or 25 units of x and 300 units of y (fig. 87).

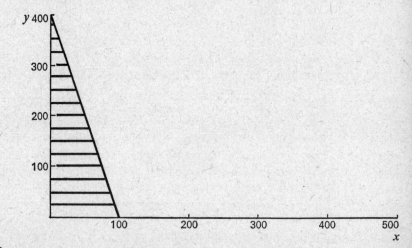

Fig. 87

The line in this diagram shows the maximum position only. We should not forget that we are dealing with an inequality in the form 'less than or equal to' ($\leqslant$) which means that while any point on the line represents a feasible production mixture of x and y, so also does any point in the shaded triangle of fig. 87. We do not necessarily have to utilize the whole of the time available.

An identical situation is present when you consider machine time and storage space. The shaded areas in figs. 88 and 89 show the feasible output arrangements of the two products with respect to the constraints.

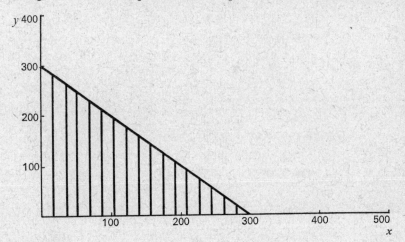

Fig. 88 Machine time.

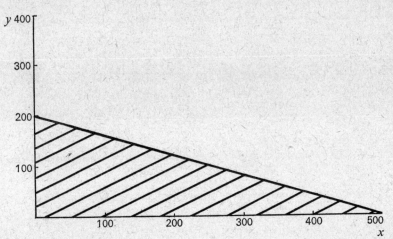

Fig. 89 Storage space.

When we combine these three diagrams, we find that only where the three sets of shading coincide are all the constraints satisfied (fig. 90).

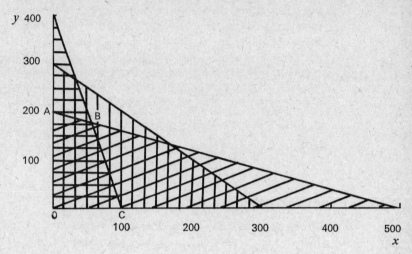

Fig. 90

Any point in the polygon *ABCO* represents a feasible solution, but we want to find the optimal feasible solution, that is, we want to produce amounts of *x* and *y* to yield the highest profit. To achieve this, we need to be at *A*, *B* or *C*; in this case our best point will be *B* where *AB* and *BC*

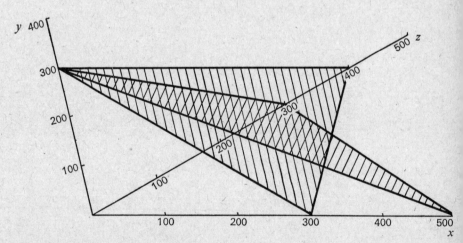

Fig. 91   Three-dimensional constraints.

intersect. At this point we will produce approximately 56 units of x and 178 units of y, giving a profit of £290 per shift. (The reader may care to calculate the profit at A or C or any other point on or in the area of feasible solution.) It should be noticed that we will have surplus machine time in this case as the point of optimal solution does not lie on the machine time line. The surplus can easily be found from

$$300-(56+178) = 66$$

so there will be 66 minutes when the machine is not utilized.

It is apparent that while this method of solution is possible where one is dealing with a mixture of two or three components (in this case products) as in fig. 91, the occurrence of four or more components makes it impossible to construct a diagrammatic representation without entering the realms of multi-dimensional geometry.

7.5.5.4 *The simplex method*

The iterative method can be employed where the graphical approach will no longer produce results. We shall look at the technique mechanically, without any indication of proof, and for the sake of simplicity the example solved in 7.5.5.3 will be used in this explanation.

We set out our problem in the following form:

Maximize $\qquad\qquad 2x+y$

Subject to $\qquad\qquad 4x+y \leqslant 400$

$\qquad\qquad\qquad x+y \leqslant 300$

$\qquad\qquad\qquad 2x+5y \leqslant 1000$

where $\qquad\qquad\qquad x \geqslant 0$

$\qquad\qquad\qquad\qquad y \geqslant 0$

To overcome the difficulty of the inequalities in the constraints we insert what is called a 'slack' variable. This is a convenient means of expressing that part of the various capacities (acid bath time, machine time and storage space) which may be unutilized; the result is

$$R = 400-4x-y$$
$$S = 300-x-y$$
$$T = 1000-2x-5y$$

where $\qquad\qquad R \geqslant 0$

$\qquad\qquad\qquad S \geqslant 0$

$\qquad\qquad\qquad T \geqslant 0$

We now set out these three equations plus the profit maximization equation in the matrix shown below.

		x	y
P		2	1
R	400	-4^*	-1
S	300	-1	-1
T	1000	-2	-5

The steps in the matrix solution are:

1. Choose the pivot element in this first matrix from the column which has the largest value at the top (in this case column x with a top element of 2).

2. Having decided in which column the pivot element will be found, divide each negative value in that column into the corresponding values in the first column, i.e. $\frac{400}{-4} = -100$, $\frac{300}{-1} = -300$, and $\frac{1000}{-2} = -500$.

The answer which is smallest in absolute terms (ignoring the sign) indicates the pivot element. In this case $\frac{400}{-4} = -100$ is the smallest and therefore -4 is the pivot element (marked with an asterisk in the matrix above).

3. Construct a new matrix plan in which R and x are interchanged:

		R	y
P	$^d 200$	$^c -\frac{1}{2}$	$^d \frac{1}{2}$
x	$^b 100$	$^a -\frac{1}{4}$	$^b -\frac{1}{4}$
S	$^d 200$	$^c \frac{1}{4}$	$^d -\frac{3}{4}$
T	$^d 800$	$^c \frac{1}{2}$	$^a -\frac{9}{2}$

The values of the elements in this new matrix will be found as follows:

(a) Replace the pivot element by its reciprocal (in the new matrix element $xR = -1/4$).

(b) The other elements in the pivot row are converted to the values by changing the sign and dividing by the pivot value, i.e. $\dfrac{-400}{-4} = +100, \ -\dfrac{(-1)}{-4} = -\dfrac{1}{4}.$

(c) The other elements in the pivot column are converted by simple division by the pivot value (no change in the sign in this case), i.e. $\dfrac{2}{-4} = -\dfrac{1}{2}, \ \dfrac{-1}{-4} = \dfrac{1}{4}, \ \dfrac{-2}{-4} = \dfrac{1}{2}.$

(d) The remaining elements are found by imagining a rectangular box in which the element concerned and the pivot occupy diagonally opposite corners. The new element is the old value minus the product of the other two corner elements divided by the pivot element, i.e. to find a new element value Ty the rectangular box will be

	y	
	-4^*	-1
	-1	-1
T	-2	-5

Ty in the new matrix will be

$$- 5 - \frac{(-1 \times -2)}{-4} = -4\tfrac{1}{2}$$

4. The new matrix is complete. We now repeat the whole procedure (1, 2 and 3) with the new matrix until all the product letters (x, y etc.) have been moved from the top of the matrix to the side. In our example, only one more matrix is required:

		R	T
P	$288\tfrac{8}{9}$	$-\tfrac{4}{9}$	$-\tfrac{1}{9}$
x	$55\tfrac{5}{9}$	$-\tfrac{5}{18}$	$\tfrac{1}{18}$
S	$66\tfrac{2}{3}$	$\tfrac{1}{6}$	$\tfrac{1}{6}$
y	$177\tfrac{7}{9}$	$\tfrac{1}{9}$	$-\tfrac{2}{9}$

We find that the first column gives us all the required answers: $55\frac{5}{9}$ units of x and $177\frac{7}{9}$ units of y will be produced, giving a profit of £$288\frac{8}{9}$ and leaving $66\frac{2}{3}$ minutes of machine time unused. The whole capacity of acid bath time and storage space will be utilized.

Once we start to consider a practical case where there may be twenty or thirty different products with possibly hundreds of constraints, it is apparent that the solution will only be found after very tedious arithmetical treatment. In fact it is most unlikely that the solution would be arrived at manually and it is just this sort of problem which is suitable for a computer; the programming involved is relatively straightforward and the answer can be found in a matter of minutes.

Maximizing profits is not the only application of linear programming. The technique in various forms has been and can be used in many fields, such as transportation in which the optimal patterns of rail and road transport starting from different places and serving different centres can be established using the 'transportation technique' (applicable wherever the requirements and resources are given in one kind of unit only). The 'dual' of the profit maximization solution enables one to consider the marginal productivity of inputs and the opportunity cost of their use. Baumol (see Bibliography, page 370) discusses these economic interpretations of the dual in some detail. Linear programming can be used to establish optimal mixes of raw materials for obtaining a given end product (as in the case of the oil or steel industries). Optimal purchasing policies and personnel placement are two further applications in the business world, and an almost limitless further list of commercial uses could in fact be made out, as Vadja, and Dorfman, Samuelson and Solow have shown (see Bibliography, page 370).

In addition linear programming has been used to establish optimal military strategies, for ascertaining the optimal diets at minimum cost in times of rationing and short supply, and in the field of econometrics input–output analysis.

In 7.4.9.1 we established that in the series of equations

$$Q_i = \overset{j=n}{\underset{i}{\Sigma}} a_{ij} Q_j + qi$$

we can arbitrarily set the final products q_i, and the sector outputs and intersector flows will be found uniquely from the technical coefficients of production. This results from the internal consistency of the model. What we did not specify is the level at which the final outputs should be set. If our objective is to maximize the national product, then we want to maximize Σq_i subject to $q_i \geqslant 0$.

Fundamentally, this is a problem for linear programming. We will not look at this particular problem in depth, but its obvious importance in the over-all analysis of planning should be emphasized.

7.5.6 *Queueing*

7.5.6.1 Queues of shoppers forming at supermarket pay-desks, a line of lorries waiting for unloading at the docks, or circling aircraft waiting to land at a busy airport are all fairly common phenomena. We are familiar with the idea of queueing. Do we, however, ask ourselves why a queue forms or what its consequences are? The general observation which we are likely to make is that there are either insufficient facilities for serving the queue or that those which are available are serving too slowly. Yet we have all seen the other side of the picture, where servers are idle because there is no one to serve. This everyday observation of what occurs illustrates the crux of the problem which O.R. specialists are faced with. On the one hand the formation of a queue can be very costly: shoppers faced with the prospect of waiting may take their custom elsewhere, lorries waiting to unload could be delivering the return payload, an aircraft waiting to land is consuming hundreds of gallons of expensive fuel and wasting the salaries of its highly paid crew. On the other hand the lack of someone to serve is equally costly. Although a supermarket cashier may be diverted to other work when there are no customers, this is unlikely to be a possibility when the server is a highly skilled specialist, such as an airport controller or a maintenance engineer. The problem, in fact, is to strike a balance between the cost of having a queue and the cost of having idle resources.

7.5.6.2 There would be no problem if the arrival of 'customers' and the service time of the customers were regular. If there is an arrival every three minutes and service takes $2\frac{11}{12}$ minutes, then the situation is satisfactory. This can and does occur. One only has to think of the production line in a car factory: the speed of the line is regulated in such a way that each man can just complete his particular operation on a vehicle before the next one arrives. In many situations, however, there is likely to be a chance element in both the arrival times and the service times, so all one can say is that there will on average be x arrivals per hour and the service takes an average of y minutes. When these circumstances pertain it is inevitable that sometimes there will be a queue and sometimes no queue at all. To evaluate the likelihood of either of these occurring and the costs involved we must first specify the nature of the problem in more precise terminology.

The system's input is a description of the way in which units arrive for service, usually in the form of a statistical distribution of arrivals. The service mechanism gives information about the number of service stations and the service policy. The queue discipline indicates in what order the queue is served, and the system's output describes the amount of service given from the standpoint of both quantity and time.

7.5.6.3   Taking a simple case, suppose that a gang of 6 men are employed on a building site unloading lorries bringing in bricks from different sources. The gang works and is paid in 4-hourly periods. On average 8 lorries arrive every 4 hours (2 randomly within each hour) and unloading a lorry takes exactly 20 minutes.

This gives

(i)   Input: 2 per hour (random)
(ii) Service mechanism: 1 service station
(iii) Queue discipline: first come, first served
(iv) Output: 3 per hour (regular).

If the lorries arrive in the morning at 08.05, 08.30, 09.05, 09.15, 10.10, 10.50, 11.12 and 11.30, we will get the following situation:

Lorry arrives	Unloading		Lorries waiting		Gang idle time
	Begins	Ends	Time	Number	
08.05	08.05	08.25	0	0	10[1]
08.30	08.30	08.50	0	0	15
09.05	09.05	09.25	0	0	0
09.15	09.25	09.45	10	1	25
10.10	10.10	10.30	0	0	20
10.50	10.50	11.10	0	0	2
11.12	11.12	11.32	0	0	0
11.30	11.32	11.52	2	1	8[2]
			12		80

If the service time had been increased to 30 minutes by reducing the size of the gang of labourers, then instead of 8 minutes idle time for the

[1] 5 minutes before first lorry arrives plus 5 minutes between end of unloading first lorry and arrival of second lorry.
[2] Time until completion of work period.

gang and only 12 minutes waiting time for the lorry we have the following:

Lorry arrives	Unloading		Lorries waiting		Gang idle time
	Begins	Ends	Time	Number	
08.05	08.05	08.35	0	0	5
08.30	08.35	09.05	5	1	0
09.05	09.05	09.35	0	0	0
09.15	09.35	10.05	20	1	5
10.10	10.10	10.40	0	0	10
10.50	10.50	11.20	0	0	0
11.12	11.20	11.50	8	1	0
11.30	11.50	12.20	20	1	0
			53		20

There are now 53 minutes when the lorries are waiting and 20 minutes when the gang is idle; in addition, the gang works 20 minutes of overtime. Assuming that a lorry standing idle costs 25 shillings per hour, that each labourer is paid 6 shillings per hour (with time and a quarter for time in excess of 4 hours), and that in the first case there were 6 labourers whilst in the second only 4, we get the following cost situation:

	Case I (20 minute service)	Case II (30 minute service)
Cost of waiting lorry	$\frac{12}{60} \times 25s. = 5s.$	$\frac{53}{60} \times 25s. = 22s. 1d.$
Cost of idle labour	$\frac{80}{60} \times 6s. \times 6 = 48s.$	$\frac{20}{60} \times 6s. \times 4 = 8s.$
Cost of overtime	0	$\frac{20}{60} \times 7s. 6d. \times 4 = 10s.$
	53s.	40s. 1d.

It is apparent that we have reduced the total cost of idle resources by increasing the service time. Although this is a very simple and somewhat unrealistic example, it does demonstrate the need to manipulate the various aspects of the system in order to strike a balance between the two types of cost.

7.5.6.4   Let us now take a rather more extensive view of the distinct parts of the queueing problem. The input or arrival distribution is often adequately described by the Poisson distribution (see Chapter 3) where $P(x) = \dfrac{\lambda^x e^{-\lambda}}{x!}$ expresses the probability of x arrivals during a given period of time. λ (lambda) is the arrival rate or the average number of arrivals per unit of time. Thus if the unloading example in 7.5.6.3 had had a Poisson arrival distribution the probability of 0, 1, 2, 3, 4, . . . lorries arriving in one hour would have been:

x	$P(x)$
0	$\dfrac{2^0 e^{-2}}{0!} = 0\cdot14$
1	$\dfrac{2^1 e^{-2}}{1!} = 0\cdot27$
2	$\dfrac{2^2 e^{-2}}{2!} = 0\cdot27$
3	$\dfrac{2^3 e^{-2}}{3!} = 0\cdot17$

Alternatively, the input can be expressed as a distribution of the time intervals between successive arrivals. An exponential distribution (derived from the Poisson distribution) describes the inter-arrival situation as long as the arrival distribution is Poisson. Using the exponential form we can find the probability of the time between two successive arrivals lying between two arbitrary limits which we set ourselves. This probability is found from

$$e^{-\lambda a} - e^{-\lambda b}$$

so that in our example (7.5.6.3) the probability of a 30 to 45 minutes delay between two arrivals is

$$e^{-2(0\cdot5)} - e^{-2(0\cdot75)} = 0\cdot15$$

Note that the arbitrary limits are measured in the same units as λ (in this case hours).

The main points about the service mechanism which we require to know are the number of service stations, and any restrictions on the amount of service which each is able to give. This latter fact is obviously going to influence the output circumstances, because if for instance a petrol station attendant is told to serve only petrol and oil and to leave radiator, battery and tyre checks to the motorists themselves, then the dispersion of the service time will be less than if the attendant can be asked to provide these as well.

The queue discipline may be in the straightforward 'first come, first served' form, as in a shop or cinema. Alternatively it may be random or 'last come, first served' (e.g. where components are dropped into a bin for further work by another machinist, the last ones dropped thus being nearer the top). In certain special circumstances there may be priorities allocated to the arrivals. A security firm moving large quantities of money to or from banks may have special arrangements for speedy collection or deposit to minimize the possibility of robbery.

Finally we must remember that the service time or output is just as likely to fluctuate as the input. An exponential distribution will generally be adequate to describe the output, μ being substituted for λ, to show the average number of complete services which can be carried out per unit of time.

7.5.6.5   Once the characteristics of the various sections of the system have been ascertained, a mathematical model of the whole can be constructed. From this we can estimate the average length of the queue, the average time spent before service, the probability of a queue length of a certain size, etc.

All these depend largely upon the fraction $\dfrac{\lambda}{\mu}$ (the utilization factor) which shows the proportion of time during which the service mechanism is being used, or the probability of a new arrival having to wait. The utilization factor is very important, because only if $\dfrac{\lambda}{\mu} < 1$ will the queue be controllable; as $\dfrac{\lambda}{\mu}$ gets closer to 1 so the average queue length will increase and once $\dfrac{\lambda}{\mu} \geqslant 1$ then the queue will grow *ad infinitum* since the service rate will be less than the arrival rate.

A reasonably accurate approximation of the system can be created if a simple statistical investigation of it has been carried out by observing the input and output pattern. We can then experiment with the controllable parts of the model, such as the number of service stations and the service time, in order to establish what improvement can be made to reduce the over-all level of cost and to bring the two types of cost into a more satisfactory form.

7.5.7 *Stock-control*

7.5.7.1   In some ways the difficulties of deciding what level of stock to hold are similar to the problems posed by queueing. A wholesale paint supplier has two factors to worry about. The first is how long he must wait for the supplies which he orders from the manufacturer, and the second is how quickly his stocks will be used up as orders come in from customers. The two factors together will determine just how much stock he is compelled to hold, and can be compared with the input, output and service mechanism side of queueing. The need is once again to balance costs. If the wholesaler carries too much stock he is tying up capital unnecessarily, and losing money by using space which could be valuably employed in some other way, risking deterioration of the product, and using labour on storage and general maintenance. However, if his stocks are so small that he runs out and cannot complete orders he may lose the business and the goodwill of the customer, with in some circumstances even the incurment of a penalty payment for non-delivery. A financial loss once more results.

Not only wholesalers are faced with these difficulties. A manufacturer producing for direct sale to customers will also have to hold stock, but in his case there is an added factor to take into account. He may not be producing one particular line continuously, so a batch will often be produced and held in stock; only when the stock level falls to a certain point will a further batch be produced. Under these circumstances, the manufacturer has to decide how much to produce or how long his production run should last, and his decision will largely be influenced by the cost of setting up the necessary machinery and production facilities. This is a third factor to be given consideration in the overall evaluation.

Two of these types of cost associated with the stock or inventory question can be ascertained without too much difficulty, the problem of fixing stock-holding costs and set-up costs being amenable to straightforward accounting. This cannot be said of the cost of losing an order: a penalty clause in a contract speaks for itself, but how does one measure goodwill? How does one add up the losses incurred when prospective buyers have been deterred by a bad reputation over delivery dates? It is very often impossible. Consequently in circumstances where this hidden cost may be very prevalent (a highly competitive market) more weight should be given to lessening the risk of run-out than would otherwise be the case.

7.5.7.2   The first difficulty we encountered in this general discussion of the stock-holding problem was that of variability in both the time required for stocks to be replenished and the demand for goods from stock. It is in this particular area that statistical techniques can most usefully be applied, as a D.S.I.R. study has shown (see Bibliography, page 370); let us illustrate this by considering a problem of demand.

A furniture firm producing bedroom suites finds from its records that over a period of one year the number of orders received each week has fluctuated considerably, as fig. 92 shows. Our first concern should be to

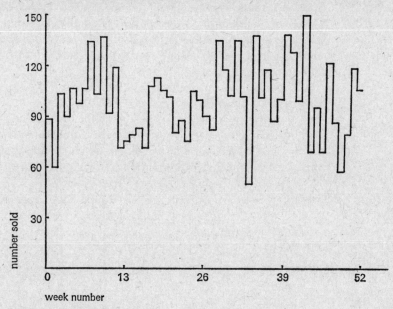

Fig. 92 Pattern of weekly orders.

discover whether there is any pertinent trend in sales over the year (e.g. seasonal pattern). In this case the situation appears to be completely random when the chronological approach is adopted, but if we group the size of weekly orders according to their frequency of occurrence we get the results shown below:

Number sold	Number of weeks
50–69	4
70–89	14
90–109	17
110–129	11
130–149	6
Total	52

This approximates to a normal distribution and a χ^2 test (see Chapter 6) shows that the difference between the actual and theoretical forms is not significant. We can conclude that the general pattern of weekly demand (of which one year's orders is a sample) has the characteristics of the normal distribution, and that these characteristics can be used to determine the risks of running out of stock when certain stock levels are maintained. This information will enable the O.R. man to prescribe a buffer stock level which will absorb the majority of this unpredictable variation in demand, and also the size and length of production runs (assuming no set-up costs).

We will not find only normal distributions describing situations of this type: we may be able to fit a binomial, a Poisson, a χ^2 or an exponential distribution, depending very largely upon the nature of the product and the methods and institutions of distribution and marketing. No matter which provides the best approximation, however, our quantitative conclusions concerning risk and stock levels will nevertheless still apply.

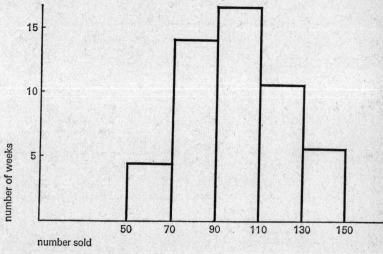

Fig. 93   Histogram of sales distribution.

It is evident that the same approach may be used when dealing with variability in the time (the lead-time) between the placing of an order by a wholesaler or a firm's store and the completion and delivery of the order by the manufacturer or production department. The splicing of the two together in cases where one requires to establish a stock level to minimize the risk of having a particularly high level of demand and a long lead-time is mathematically quite difficult. In this case a Monte Carlo experiment (see 7.5.8) may be quite useful.

7.5.7.3   So far an explicit treatment of the costs encountered in inventory problems has been left out, but we will now develop this side of the analysis by investigating the question of batch sizes. If the demand for a certain line and its output were constant, there would be no need to hold stock at all, because everything manufactured would be sold and delivered immediately. Once batches are produced, however, stocks have to be held.

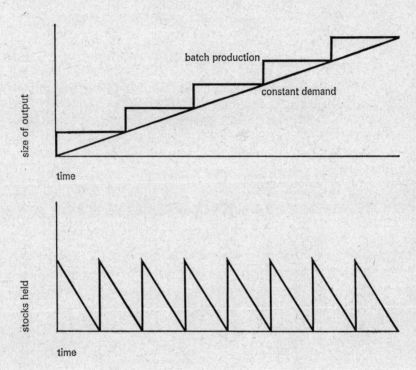

Fig. 94

In fig. 94 we show what happens when demand is constant but production is in batches. Suppose that a manufacturer is under contract to supply a customer with a total of Q units over a period of time T; the deliveries are to be at a constant rate (i.e. so many units per day/week/month) and deliveries must arrive on time. The manufacturer wants to minimize his costs, so he has to decide how often to produce batches and how much each batch should contain. If q is the batch size then Σq must be equal to Q

and the number of batches required is $\frac{Q}{q}$. The interval of time between the production of batches will be T (the time over which the contract runs) divided by the number of batches produced, i.e. $\frac{T}{Q/q}$ or $\frac{Tq}{Q}$.

Now if C_s is the set-up cost per batch and C_I is the inventory cost per unit stored per unit of time, we obtain the following relationships:

$$\text{Total set-up cost} = C_s \times Q/q$$

(the set-up cost per batch × the number of batches)

$$\text{Total inventory cost} = C_I \times \frac{q}{2} \times T.$$

(the inventory cost per unit × the average size of the inventory × the total period that the stocks must be held).

The manufacturer's total cost will be the sum of these two components:

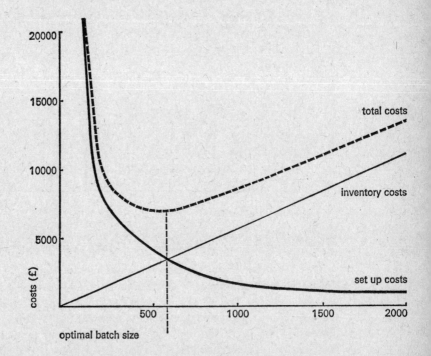

Fig. 95   Graphical solution for minimum total cost and optimal batch size.

$$C_T = \frac{C_s Q}{q} + \frac{C_I q T}{2}$$

If we consider an example where 10,000 gearbox castings have to be produced for a car manufacturer over 6 months, with a set-up cost of £200 per batch and an inventory cost of £2 per unit, we get the cost picture for different batch sizes shown in fig. 95.

Where total costs are at their lowest point we will have the optimal batch size: from the graph this is found to be approximately 575 castings. To get an exact figure, we need to know at what point the slope of the total cost curve is zero, and by using differential calculus we find that this point (and therefore the optimal batch size q_0) is given by

$$q_0 = \sqrt{\left(\frac{2QC_s}{TC_I}\right)}$$

In the example we get

$$q_0 = \sqrt{\left(\frac{2 \times 10{,}000 \times 200}{6 \times 2}\right)} = 577 \text{ castings.}$$

Now the time between batches has been defined as $\frac{Tq}{Q}$, but we have optimized q (above) so that the optimal interval between batches is

$$t_0 = \frac{T}{Q}\sqrt{\left(\frac{2QC_s}{TC_I}\right)} = \sqrt{\left(\frac{2TC_s}{QC_I}\right)}$$

giving $\sqrt{\left(\frac{2 \times 6 \times 200}{10}\right)} = 0{\cdot}346$ of a month or 7·5 working days in our example.

7.5.7.4   This brief discussion of inventory costs is naturally in its simplest form and should be extended for more difficult cases. Account can be taken of non-instantaneous production, where some of the batch is used up as produced and never forms part of the stock held; we can introduce a penalty clause factor, or the possibility of hiring additional storage capacity. The feasible modifications are limitless but the principles involved will always be in the form we have discussed.

7.5.8   *Monte Carlo*

7.5.8.1   As the name of the technique suggests, Monte Carlo is concerned with the random outcomes of specified situations. In just the same way as the individual throw of a die or spin of a roulette wheel will produce an unpredictable result, so the business situation is largely subject to chance elements. We have seen this in both queueing and stock-control: arrivals at a service line or the receipt of orders may well be random.

Because of this similarity we are often in the fortunate position of being able to simulate what would actually happen in practice by effecting modifications to our model. Tables of random numbers can be used to reproduce the unpredictable nature of the events in question: we may postulate the existence of extra service stations or faster service time in a queueing model and then operate and analyse the results of the system on paper, or we can ascertain the effect on a firm's inventory costs of building an extra warehouse. In all cases of this kind conclusions can be drawn without the necessity of actually installing and operating expensive equipment.

The two examples cited could be solved using Monte Carlo techniques. In fact, because they are relatively straightforward problems, they could and probably would be solved by direct mathematical analysis. There are circumstances, however, where the sets of equations describing a system are so complicated that they defy mathematical solution, or alternatively a system may be such that it cannot be described in a mathematical form at all; in either case the Monte Carlo technique can help to produce meaningful results and conclusions.

7.5.8.2 In 7.5.7.2 we mentioned that a stock control problem in which both the lead time and orders from stock are subject to variability was suitable for analysis by Monte Carlo methods. We will now illustrate the technique by dealing with a hypothetical example in this form.

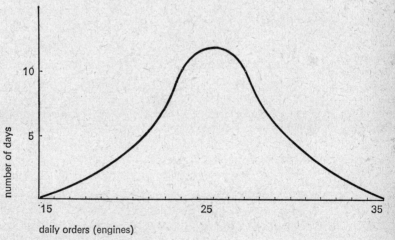

Fig. 96   Distribution of daily orders.

A main agent for a motor manufacturer tries to maintain sufficient stocks of engines (for a particular model of car) to avoid run-out. He finds from observation of 100 days that the daily orders have a normal distribution (fig. 96) and the lead times a binomial distribution (fig. 97). His

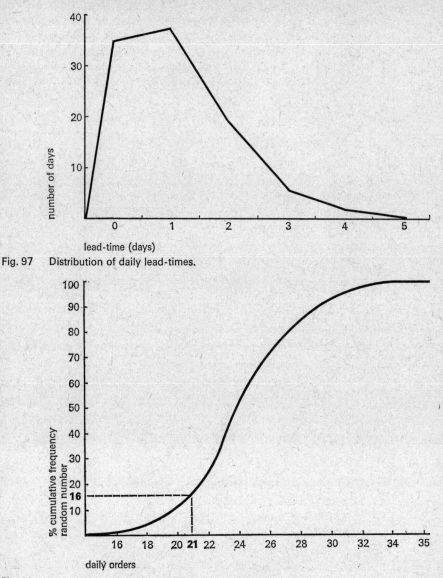

Fig. 97   Distribution of daily lead-times.

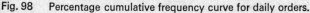

Fig. 98   Percentage cumulative frequency curve for daily orders.

363   Econometrics and operational research

policy is to maintain his stocks at approximately 50 engines and to do this he telephones an order to the manufacturer at the end of each day for as many units as have been sold. If these are delivered during the following morning, he considers the lead time to be zero. Under these circumstances we want to discover how often he will run out of stock and by how many engines. Obviously we cannot use random numbers simply to indicate the order sizes and lead times shown on the abscissae of the distributions in figs 96 and 97. We have to take into account the fact that some of these occur more often than others, and the best way of doing this is to construct a percentage cumulative frequency curve (figs. 98 and 99). The random

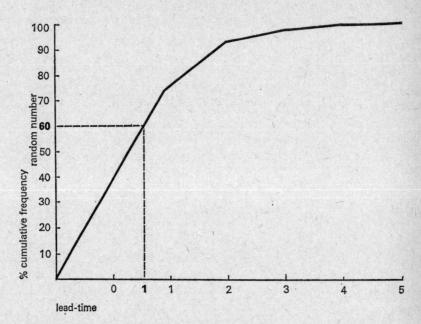

Fig. 99 Percentage cumulative frequency curve for lead-time.

numbers found from the table indicate the position on the percentage cumulative frequency axis and a horizontal line is drawn from this position to the ogive curve; a perpendicular is dropped from the point of intersection to the abscissa and the order size or lead time is read off. In fig. 98 the random number 16 gives an order of 21 and in fig. 99 the random number 60 gives a lead time of 1 day. The procedure is repeated for each random number.

We can now proceed to our Monte Carlo simulation:

Day	Opening stocks		Orders		End-of-day stocks	Run-out	Lead time	
			Random number	Quantity			Random number	Days
1		50	16	21	29	—	60	1
2		29	98	33	0	4	05	0
3	(21+33)	54	01	16	34	—	91	2
4		34	29	23	11	—	83	2
5		11	72	27	0	16	48	1
6	(16)	16	71	27	0	27	08	0
7	(23+27+27)	77	61	26	24	—	75	2
8		24	81	28	0	4	48	1
9		0	10	20	0	24	72	1
10	(26+28)	54	14	21	9	—	20	0
11	(21+20)	50	35	24	26	—	42	1
12		26	07	20	6	—	96	3
13	(24)	30	27	23	7	—	90	2
14		7	95	31	0	24	29	0
15	(31)	31	12	21	0	14	72	1
16	(20+23)	43	35	24	5	—	97	3
17	(21)	26	86	29	0	3	21	0
18	(29)	29	02	18	11	—	48	1
19		8	44	24	0	16	99	4
20	(24+18)	42	08	20	6	—	56	1
21		6	61	26	0	20	79	2
22	(20)	20	67	27	0	27	04	0
23	(27)	27	23	22	0	22	53	1
24	(24+26)	50	89	29	0	1	66	1
25	(22)	22	84	29	0	8	30	0
26	(29+29)	58	82	29	21	—	17	0
27	(29)	50	89	29	21	—	76	2
28		21	65	26	0	5	13	0
29	(26)	26	13	21	0	—	75	2
30	(29)	29	03	18	11	—	35	1
31		11	10	20	0	9	14	0

Day	Opening stocks	Orders		End-of-day stocks	Run-out	Lead time	
		Random number	Quantity			Random number	Days
32	(21+18+20) 59	23	22	28	—	03	0
33	(22) 50	35	24	26	—	13	0
34	(24) 47	42	24	26	—	47	1
35	26	67	27	0	1	99	4
36	(24) 24	91	30	0	7	07	0
37	(30) 30	37	24	0	1	24	0
38	(24) 24	07	20	3	—	36	1
39	3	92	30	0	27	76	2
40	(27+20) 47	00	16	4	—	41	1
41	4	08	20	0	16	79	2
42	(30+16) 46	67	27	3	—	46	1
43	3	24	23	0	20	21	0
44	(20+27+23) 70	65	26	24	—	77	2
45	24	52	25	0	1	48	1
46	0	32	23	0	24	66	1
47	(26+25) 51	54	25	2	—	51	1
48	(23) 25	95	31	0	6	92	3
49	(25) 25	93	30	0	11	62	1
50	0	19	22	0	33	78	2

The agent starts off with 50 engines. We subtract from the stock level the number sold during the day and record the end-of-day stocks. The re-stocking order to the manufacturer is then entered (in brackets) in the opening stock column for the day it will be received (found from the lead time). The end-of-day stocks are then placed in the following day's opening stock column and added to any orders which arrive that morning; If a stock-out occurs, we increase the next day's orders by the number short.

The simulation has been carried out over only 50 days and for this reason completely meaningful results cannot be obtained (as always, the validity of our conclusions will improve as the 'sample' size is increased). Nevertheless we are beginning to get a picture of what will happen in these circumstances. On 27 out of the 50 days the magnitude of the shortages was as follows:

Number short	Number of days
1–9	12
10–19	5
20–29	9
30–39	1
	27

On three occasions customers were kept waiting more than one day for engines, but in all of these cases the supplies were available on the second day after the order was placed. From the point of view of storage the opening stock exceeded 50 engines on seven days and of these only two had more than 60. The average opening stocks were 30 engines so that inventory costs were lower than might have been anticipated.

Evaluating the agent's policy of trying to maintain twice the average daily demand for engines is rather difficult. In fact, because of the variability in lead times and (particularly) demand he has fallen short of his objective, with the result that he has on average run out of stock almost every other day. He may not consider this to be too disastrous as customers have generally been subject to a delay of only one day and we assume here that no orders are lost. This may be true if the agent is the sole distributor in his area, but if he is not the picture may be very different, and it may be better to repeat the experiment with modifications to the policy. The stock-holding objective, viz. 50 engines, could be increased to reduce the number of stock-outs.

The implications of other modifications can also be explored by carrying out the simulation again. The agent could consider the possibility of re-ordering stock from the manufacturer only twice a week instead of daily if the initial investigation shows that the distribution of orders varies on different days: the earlier part of the week may have average daily sales of 35 engines, while on Thursday and Friday the figure is only 15. Factors of this type can easily be allowed for.

7.5.8.3   This example demonstrates the principle of Monte Carlo experiments, which have many variants and possess an adaptability that makes them a powerful tool in a wide range of circumstances. The fact that complex simulations can be programmed for computer operation is once again of great value, as the functioning of a complicated system over many months or even years can be reproduced in a matter of minutes or hours.

7.6 Discussion questions

7.6.1 *Econometrics*

(a) In what way might the results of a series of annual cross-sectional family expenditure surveys be used to estimate demand functions for broad categories of consumer goods?

(b) Which variables would you take into account and how would you treat them in attempting to estimate the demand for the following:

(i) Men's clothing
(ii) Bread
(iii) Ships.

(c) Would the market equilibrium points in the following circumstances be more likely to indicate demand, supply or mongrel relationships?

(i) The price and quantity per head of wheat sold in the U.S.A. between 1945 and 1965.
(ii) The price and sales of pig iron in the U.K. between 1850 and 1900.
(iii) The price and sales of washing machines in 1930 and in 1960.

Fully explain the reasons for your decisions.

(d) Why are demand studies particularly difficult where the product is manufactured by only one or a few firms?

(e) What categorization has been used in the family expenditure surveys in this country? What additional information do you consider would benefit the econometrician in studying demand?

(f) How would you estimate the present technical coefficients of production in the following cases:

(i) Labour used in the motor industry.
(ii) Coal used in producing gas.
(iii) Lime used in the production of sulphuric acid.
(iv) Cement used in house-building.

(g) In the Cambridge model of the British economy different types of imports are treated in different ways. What broad classifications of imports are relevant to a planning model and why?

(h) There are necessarily certain outside or exogenous factors over which the economic planner can have no control. What are these factors?

7.6.2 *Operational research*

(a) How does the cost minimization problem differ schematically from that of maximizing profits in linear programming? Illustrate your answer using the following example:

Two forms of raw material x and y cost respectively £A and £B per ton. L tons of x and M tons of y are required to produce 1 ton of a finished product C. In all, we require V tons of the finished product. In the same way, we want W tons of finished product D where N tons of x and O tons of y will be necessary to manufacture it.

(b) Discuss how linear programming can be used to minimize the size of a fleet of lorries delivering goods between two points. Indicate how you would set up the problem.

(c) Why does the probability of a queue vary more or less directly with the proportion of time that the service provided is in demand?

(d) Under what circumstances would you expect a customer's waiting time for service to be greatest?

(e) Consider how the service time in any waiting line situation with which you are familiar could be reduced.

(f) When dealing with patterns of demand from stock would it be conceptually better to distinguish two different families of theoretical distributions? Explain, giving examples.

(g) How would you illustrate the changing stock situation over a period of time in circumstances where demand is constant and

  (i) Some of the batch is used up while the rest is being produced (i.e. slow production),
  (ii) Regular stock-outs occur?

(h) How could Monte Carlo techniques be used to estimate the life distribution of a generator which is made up of four distinct components?

(i) What information would you require to carry out a simulation of the following water supply problem?

A city is supplied by a reservoir which is filled from bore holes, emergency supplies being obtainable from a neighbouring water authority. The demand is greater at the week-end than during the week. The managers of the water authority want to know whether they are ever likely to run out of water.

Bibliography

The following references may be consulted to obtain an exposition of findings and theories mentioned in the text. Those seeking to expand their knowledge of inductive statistics still further will find a list of suggested further reading on page 372.

Bates, J. M. (1962), 'Input–output problems in relation to projections and programming', *Input–Output Tables – Their Compilation and Use*, Akademiai Kiado (Budapest).

Baumol, W. J. (1965), *Economic Theory and Operational Analysis*, Prentice-Hall (2nd edn).

Churchman, C. W., Ackoff, R. L., and Arnoff, E. L. (1964), *Introduction to Operations Research*, Wiley.

Coutie, G. A., *et al.* (1964), 'Short-term forecasting', *Mathematical and Statistical Techniques for Industry* (I.C.I. monograph no. 2), Oliver & Boyd.

Croxton, F. E., and Crowden, D. J. (1960), *Applied General Statistics*, Pitman.

Brown, A., Department of Applied Economics, Cambridge (1965), *Programme for Growth*, no. 6 (ed. R. Stone), *Exploring 1970*, Chapman & Hall.

Devons, E. (1965), 'Economists and the public', *Lloyds Bank Review*, no. 77.

Department of Scientific and Industrial Research, Industrial Operations Unit (1963), *Stock Control: A Demonstration in the Cutlery Industry*.

Dorfman, R., Samuelson, P. A., and Solow, R. M. (1958), *Linear Programming and Economic Analysis*, McGraw-Hill.

Gregg, J. V., Hossell, C. H., and Richardson, J. T. (1964), 'Mathematical trend curves: an aid to forecasting', *Mathematical and Statistical Techniques for Industry* (I.C.I. monograph no. 1), Oliver & Boyd.

Keynes, J. M. (1936), *The General Theory of Employment, Interest and Money*, Macmillan.

Moroney, M. J. (1956), 'Safety in sampling', *Facts from Figures* (3rd edn), Penguin Books.

National Economic Development Council (1963), *Conditions Favourable to Faster Growth*, H.M.S.O.

National Economic Development Council (1964), *Report on the Growth of the Economy, March 1964*, H.M.S.O.

Schultz, H. (1928), *Statistical Laws of Demand and Supply with Special Applications to Sugar*, University of Chicago Press.

Schultz H. (1938) *The Theory and Measurement of Demand*, University of Chicago Press.

Vadja, S. (1960), *An Introduction to Linear Programming and Theory of Games*, Methuen.

Wold, H., and Juréen, L. (1953), *Demand Analysis: A Study in Econometrics*, Wiley/Almqvist & Wiksell.

Woodward, R. H., and Goldsmith, P. H. (1964), 'Cumulative sum techniques', *Mathematical and Statistical Techniques for Industry* (I.C.I. monograph no. 3), Oliver & Boyd.

Yule, G. U., and Kendall, M. G. (1950), *An Introduction to the Theory of Statistics* (4th edn), Griffin.

Suggestions for further reading

For an alternative view of sampling principles in the estimation and testing of hypotheses A. L. Edwards (*Statistical Methods for the Behavioural Sciences*; Holt, Rinehart & Winston 1964), B. C. Brookes and W. F. L. Dick (*Introduction to Statistical Methods*; Heinemann 1951) and M. Quenouille (*Introductory Statistics*; Pergamon 1950) should be consulted. These three works extend in differing ways the coverage given to the analysis of variance in this book and introduce the experimental sample designs on which this type of analysis is largely based. For a concise summary of the main principles underlying z, t and F tests both S. Siegel (*Non-parametric Statistics*; McGraw-Gill 1956) and C. A. Moser (*Survey Methods in Social Investigation*; Heinemann 1958) are to be recommended; the former is a most useful and comprehensive introduction to survey methods, covering all aspects of practical sampling problems clearly and readably. Although more ponderous in style, F. Yates (*Sampling Methods for Censuses and Surveys*; Griffin 1960, 3rd edn) is carefully written and can be read together with W. G. Cochran (*Sampling Techniques*; Wiley 1953) and W. E. Deming (*Sample Design in Business Research*; Wiley 1960); a detailed account of survey methods in commercial and business research is also included in the Deming volume.

M. J. Moroney (see Bibliography) provides a very sound introduction to statistical quality control and develops the methods of acceptance sampling extremely well. R. H. Woodward and P. H. Goldsmith (see Bibliography) give a thorough exposition of the principles and main applications of the various cumulative sum techniques, but for a book specifically on quality control J. M. Juran (*Quality Control Handbook*; McGraw-Hill 1962, 2nd edn) should be employed as the standard reference at an advanced level; F. E. Croxton and D. J. Cowden (see

Bibliography) on non-linear regression and correlation is a sound alternative for this topic and also gives very thorough coverage to the methodology of multiple regression and correlation analysis, although it is not quite so good on sampling theory. M. Budin (*Statistics for Economics and Administration*; Asia Publishing House 1962) gives many useful illustrations in developing multiple regression and correlation and the sampling-theory aspects of the two-variable case, and as long as the student spots the sometimes confusing but fairly obvious textual errors it is to be recommended. For the more mathematically inclined great benefit is to be derived from working carefully through the whole of the first part of J. Johnston (*Econometric Methods*; McGraw-Hill 1963) and some of the second part: if the reader wants to acquire a knowledge of the relevant matrix algebra for multiple regression analysis this book has few peers.

For the more advanced time series analysis we can return to Croxton and Cowden which, together with G. A. Coutie *et alia* (see Bibliography) and J. V. Gregg, C. H. Hossell and J. T. Richardson (see Bibliography) provides a comprehensive alternative view of mathematical trend curves and exponential smoothing. For a brief and elementary review of non-parametric methods the relevant chapter in P. G. Hoel (*Elementary Statistics*; Wiley 1960) is worth reading, but for a full technical understanding and clear perspective of this topic Siegel (see above) must be acquired: although some lack of continuity results from the manner in which the subject-matter of the book has been divided up, the text is nonetheless very workmanlike. B. H. Rivett and R. L. Ackott (*A Manager's Guide to Operations Research*; Wiley 1963) can be highly recommended as an introduction to the place and methodology of operational research, followed up at an introductory level by E. Duckworth (*A Guide to Operational Research*; Methuen 1964, 2nd edn) and at a more advanced level by C. W. Churchman, R. L. Ackott and E. L. Arnoff (*Introduction to Operational Research*; Wiley 1957) and G. M. F. di Roccaferrera (*Operational Research Models for Business and Industry; an Introduction to Quantitative Methods in Economics*; South Western/ Arnold 1965); these volumes will provide a full survey of operational research. On econometrics M. J. Brennan (*Preface to Econometrics*; South Western/Arnold 1962) provides a first-rate introduction, while O. Lange (*Introduction to Econometrics*; Pergamon 1962, 2nd edn) and L. R. Klein (*Introduction to Econometrics*; Prentice-Hall 1962) are interesting and clearly written follow-ups.

Appendix
Statistical tables

Table 1. The normal deviate

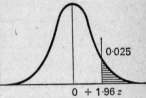

0·025

0 + 1·96 z

z		0	1	2	3	4	5	6	7	8	9
0·0	0	5000	4960	4920	4880	4841	4801	4761	4721	4681	4641
0·1		4602	4562	4522	4483	4443	4404	4364	4325	4286	4247
0·2		4207	4168	4129	4091	4052	4013	3974	3936	3897	3859
0·3		3821	3783	3745	3707	3669	3632	3594	3557	3520	3483
0·4		3446	3409	3372	3336	3300	3264	3228	3192	3156	3121
0·5		3085	3050	3015	2981	2946	2912	2877	2843	2810	2776
0·6		2743	2709	2676	2644	2611	2579	2546	2514	2483	2451
0·7		2420	2389	2358	2327	2297	2266	2236	2207	2177	2148
0·8		2119	2090	2061	2033	2005	1977	1949	1922	1894	1867
0·9		1841	1814	1788	1762	1736	1711	1685	1660	1635	1611
1·0		1587	1563	1539	1515	1492	1469	1446	1423	1401	1379
1·1		1357	1335	1314	1292	1271	1251	1230	1210	1190	1170
1·2		1151	1131	1112	1094	1075	1057	1038	1020	1003	9853
1·3	0·0	9680	9510	9342	9176	9012	8851	8692	8534	8379	8226
1·4		8076	7927	7780	7636	7493	7353	7215	7078	6944	6811
1·5		6681	6552	6426	6301	6178	6057	5938	5821	5705	5592
1·6		5480	5370	5262	5155	5050	4947	4846	4746	4648	4551
1·7		4457	4363	4272	4182	4093	4006	3920	3836	3754	3673
1·8		3593	3515	3438	3363	3288	3216	3144	3074	3005	2938
1·9		2872	2807	2743	2680	2619	2559	2500	2442	2385	2330
2·0		2275	2222	2169	2118	2068	2018	1970	1923	1876	1831
2·1		1786	1743	1700	1659	1618	1578	1539	1500	1463	1426
2·2		1390	1355	1321	1287	1255	1222	1191	1160	1130	1101
2·3		1072	1044	1017	9903	9642	9387	9138	8894	8656	8424
2·4	0·00	8198	7976	7760	7549	7344	7143	6947	6756	6569	6387
2·5		6210	6037	5868	5703	5543	5386	5234	5085	4941	4799
2·6		4661	4527	4397	4269	4145	4025	3907	3793	3681	3573
2·7		3467	3364	3264	3167	3072	2980	2890	2803	2718	2635
2·8		2555	2477	2401	2327	2256	2186	2118	2052	1988	1926
2·9		1866	1807	1750	1695	1641	1589	1538	1489	1441	1395
3·0		1350	1306	1264	1223	1183	1144	1107	1070	1035	1001
3·1	0·000	9676	9354	9043	8740	8447	8164	7889	7622	7364	7114
3·2		6871	6637	6410	6190	5977	5770	5571	5377	5190	5009
3·3		4834	4665	4501	4342	4189	4041	3897	3758	3624	3495
3·4		3369	3248	3131	3018	2909	2803	2701	2602	2507	2415
3·5		2326	2241	2158	2078	2001	1926	1854	1785	1718	1653

Table 2.   Distribution of *t*

Probability

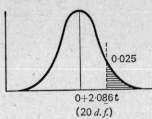

0.025

0+2·086*t*
(20 *d.f.*)

d.f	0·1	0·05	0·025	0·010	0·005
1	3·078	6·314	12·706	31·821	63·657
2	1·886	2·920	4·303	6·965	9·925
3	1·638	2·353	3·182	4·541	5·841
4	1·533	2·132	2·776	3·747	4·604
5	1·476	2·015	2·571	3·365	4·032
6	1·440	1·943	2·447	3·143	3·707
7	1·415	1·895	2·365	2·998	3·499
8	1·397	1·860	2·306	2·896	3·355
9	1·383	1·833	2·262	2·821	3·250
10	1·372	1·812	2·228	2·764	3·169
11	1·363	1·796	2·201	2·718	3·106
12	1·356	1·782	2·179	2·681	3·055
13	1·350	1·771	2·160	2·650	3·012
14	1·345	1·761	2·145	2·624	2·977
15	1·341	1·753	2·131	2·602	2·947
16	1·337	1·746	2·120	3·583	2·921
17	1·333	1·740	2·110	2·567	2·898
18	1·330	1·734	2·101	2·552	2·878
19	1·328	1·729	2·093	2·539	2·861
20	1·325	1·725	2·086	2·528	2·845
21	1·323	1·721	2·080	2·518	2·831
22	1·321	1·717	2·074	2·508	2·819
23	1·319	1·714	2·069	2·500	2·807
24	1·318	1·711	2·064	2·492	2·797
25	1·316	1·708	2·060	2·485	2·787
26	1·315	1·706	2·056	2·479	2·779
27	1·314	1·703	2·052	2·473	2·771
28	1·313	1·701	2·048	2·467	2·763
29	1·311	1·699	2·045	2·462	2·756
30	1·310	1·697	2·042	2·457	2·750
∞	1·282	1·645	1·960	2·326	2·576

Table 3. 5 per cent points of the *F*-distribution

$v_1=$	1	2	3	4	5	6	7	8	10	12	24	∞
$v_2=$ 1	161·4	199·5	215·7	224·6	230·2	234·0	236·8	238·9	241·9	243·9	249·0	254·3
2	18·5	19·0	19·2	19·2	19·3	19·3	19·4	19·4	19·4	19·4	19·5	19·5
3	10·13	9·55	9·28	9·12	9·01	8·94	8·89	8·85	8·79	8·74	8·64	8·53
4	7·71	6·94	6·59	6·39	6·26	6·16	6·09	6·04	5·96	5·91	5·77	5·63
5	6·61	5·79	5·41	5·19	5·05	4·95	4·88	4·82	4·74	4·68	4·53	4·36
6	5·99	5·14	4·76	4·53	4·39	4·28	4·21	4·15	4·06	4·00	3·84	3·67
7	5·59	4·74	4·35	4·12	3·97	3·87	3·79	3·73	3·64	3·57	3·41	3·23
8	5·32	4·46	4·07	3·84	3·69	3·58	3·50	3·44	3·35	3·28	3·12	2·93
9	5·12	4·26	3·86	3·63	3·48	3·37	3·29	3·23	3·14	3·07	2·90	2·71
10	4·96	4·10	3·71	3·48	3·33	3·22	3·14	3·07	2·98	2·91	2·74	2·54
11	4·84	3·98	3·59	3·36	3·20	3·09	3·01	2·95	2·85	2·79	2·61	2·40
12	4·75	3·89	3·49	3·26	3·11	3·00	2·91	2·85	2·75	2·69	2·51	2·30
13	4·67	3·81	3·41	3·18	3·03	2·92	2·83	2·77	2·67	2·60	2·42	2·21
14	4·60	3·74	3·34	3·11	2·96	2·85	2·76	2·70	2·60	2·53	2·35	2·13
15	4·54	3·68	3·29	3·06	2·90	2·79	2·71	2·64	2·54	2·48	2·29	2·07
16	4·49	3·63	3·24	3·01	2·85	2·74	2·66	2·59	2·49	2·42	2·24	2·01
17	4·45	3·59	3·20	2·96	2·81	2·70	2·61	2·55	2·45	2·38	2·19	1·96
18	4·41	3·55	3·16	2·93	2·77	2·66	2·58	2·51	2·41	2·34	2·15	1·92
19	4·38	3·52	3·13	2·90	2·74	2·63	2·54	2·48	2·38	2·31	2·11	1·88
20	4·35	3·49	3·10	2·87	2·71	2·60	2·51	2·45	2·35	2·28	2·08	1·84
21	4·32	3·47	3·07	2·84	2·68	2·57	2·49	2·42	2·32	2·25	2·05	1·81
22	4·30	3·44	3·05	2·82	2·66	2·55	2·46	2·40	2·30	2·23	2·03	1·78
23	4·28	3·42	3·03	2·80	2·64	2·53	2·44	2·37	2·27	2·20	2·00	1·76
24	4·26	3·40	3·01	2·78	2·62	2·51	2·42	2·36	2·25	2·18	1·98	1·73
25	4·24	3·39	2·99	2·76	2·60	2·49	2·40	2·34	2·24	2·16	1·96	1·71
26	4·23	3·37	2·98	2·74	2·59	2·47	2·39	2·32	2·22	2·15	1·95	1·69
27	4·21	3·35	2·96	2·73	2·57	2·46	2·37	2·31	2·20	2·13	1·93	1·67
28	4·20	3·34	2·95	2·71	2·56	2·45	2·36	2·29	2·19	2·12	1·91	1·65
29	4·18	3·33	2·93	2·70	2·55	2·43	2·35	2·28	2·10	2·10	1·90	1·64
30	4·17	3·32	2·92	2·69	2·53	2·42	2·33	2·27	2·16	2·09	1·89	1·62
32	4·15	3·29	2·90	2·67	2·51	2·40	2·31	2·24	2·14	2·07	1·86	1·59
34	4·13	3·28	2·88	2·65	2·49	2·38	2·29	2·23	2·12	2·05	1·84	1·57
36	4·11	3·26	2·87	2·63	2·48	2·36	2·28	2·21	2·11	2·03	1·82	1·55
38	4·10	3·24	2·85	2·62	2·46	2·35	2·26	2·19	2·09	2·02	1·81	1·53
40	4·08	3·23	2·84	2·61	2·45	2·34	2·25	2·18	2·08	2·00	1·79	1·51
60	4·00	3·15	2·76	2·53	2·37	2·25	2·17	2·10	1·99	1·92	1·70	1·39
120	3·92	3·07	2·68	2·45	2·29	2·18	2·09	2·02	1·91	1·83	1·61	1·25
∞	3·84	3·00	2·60	2·37	2·21	2·10	2·01	1·94	1·83	1·75	1·52	1·00

Table 3 *(continued)*. $2\frac{1}{2}$ per cent points of the F-distribution

$v_1=$	1	2	3	4	5	6	7	8	10	12	24	∞
$v_2=$ 1	648	800	864	900	922	937	948	957	969	977	997	1018
2	38·5	39·0	39·2	39·2	39·3	39·3	39·4	39·4	39·4	39·4	39·5	39·5
3	17·4	16·0	15·4	15·1	14·9	14·7	14·6	14·5	14·4	14·3	14·1	13·9
4	12·22	10·65	9·98	9·60	9·36	9·20	9·07	8·98	8·84	8·73	8·51	8·26
5	10·01	8·43	7·76	7·39	7·15	6·98	6·85	6·76	6·62	6·52	6·28	6·02
6	8·81	7·26	6·60	6·23	5·99	5·82	5·70	5·60	5·46	5·37	5·12	4·85
7	8·07	6·54	5·89	5·52	5·29	5·12	4·99	4·90	4·76	4·67	4·42	4·14
8	7·57	6·06	5·42	5·05	4·82	4·65	4·53	4·43	4·30	4·20	3·95	3·67
9	7·21	5·71	5·08	4·72	4·48	4·32	4·20	4·10	3·96	3·87	3·61	3·33
10	6·94	5·46	4·83	4·47	4·24	4·07	3·95	3·85	3·72	3·62	3·37	3·08
11	6·72	5·26	4·63	4·28	4·04	3·88	3·76	3·66	3·53	3·43	3·17	2·88
12	6·55	5·10	4·47	4·12	3·89	3·73	3·61	3·51	3·37	3·28	3·02	2·72
13	6·41	4·97	4·35	4·00	3·77	3·60	3·48	3·39	3·25	3·15	2·89	2·60
14	6·30	4·86	4·24	3·89	3·66	3·50	3·38	3·29	3·15	3·05	2·79	2·49
15	6·20	4·76	4·15	3·80	3·58	3·41	3·29	3·20	3·06	2·96	2·70	2·40
16	6·12	4·69	4·08	3·73	3·50	3·34	3·22	3·12	2·99	2·89	2·63	2·32
17	6·04	4·62	4·01	3·66	3·44	3·28	3·16	3·06	2·92	2·82	2·56	2·25
18	5·98	4·56	3·95	3·61	3·38	3·22	3·10	3·01	2·87	2·77	2·50	2·19
19	5·92	4·51	3·90	3·56	3·33	3·17	3·05	2·96	2·82	2·72	2·45	2·13
20	5·87	4·46	3·86	3·51	3·29	3·13	3·01	2·91	2·77	2·68	2·41	2·09
21	5·83	4·42	3·82	3·48	3·25	3·09	2·97	2·87	2·73	2·64	2·37	2·04
22	5·79	4·38	3·78	3·44	3·22	3·05	2·93	2·84	2·70	2·60	2·33	2·00
23	5·75	4·35	3·75	3·41	3·18	3·02	2·90	2·81	2·67	2·57	2·30	1·97
24	5·72	4·32	3·72	3·38	3·15	2·99	2·87	2·78	2·64	2·54	2·27	1·94
25	5·69	4·29	3·69	3·35	3·13	2·97	2·85	2·75	2·61	2·51	2·24	1·91
26	5·66	4·27	3·67	3·33	3·10	2·94	2·82	2·73	2·59	2·49	2·22	1·88
27	5·63	4·24	3·65	3·31	3·08	2·92	2·80	2·71	2·57	2·47	2·19	1·85
28	5·61	4·22	3·63	3·29	3·06	2·90	2·78	2·69	2·55	2·45	2·17	1·83
29	5·59	4·20	3·61	3·27	3·04	2·88	2·76	2·67	2·53	2·43	2·15	1·81
30	5·57	4·18	3·59	3·25	3·03	2·87	2·75	2·65	2·51	2·41	2·14	1·79
32	5·53	4·15	3·56	3·22	3·00	2·84	2·72	2·62	2·48	2·38	2·10	1·75
34	5·50	4·12	3·53	3·19	2·97	2·81	2·69	2·59	2·45	2·35	2·08	1·72
36	5·47	4·09	3·51	3·17	2·94	2·79	2·66	2·57	2·43	2·33	2·05	1·69
38	5·45	4·07	3·48	3·15	2·92	2·76	2·64	2·55	2·41	2·31	2·03	1·66
40	5·42	4·05	3·46	3·13	2·90	2·74	2·62	2·53	2·39	2·29	2·01	1·64
60	5·29	3·93	3·34	3·01	2·79	2·63	2·51	2·41	2·27	2·17	1·88	1·48
120	5·15	3·80	3·23	2·89	2·67	2·52	2·39	2·30	2·16	2·05	1·76	1·31
∞	5·02	3·69	3·12	2·79	2·57	2·41	2·29	2·19	2·05	1·94	1·64	1·00

Table 3 (continued). 1 per cent points of the F-distribution

$v_1 =$	1	2	3	4	5	6	7	8	10	12	24	∞
$v_2 = 1$	4052	5000	5403	5625	5764	5859	5928	5981	6056	6106	6235	6366
2	98·5	99·0	99·2	99·2	99·3	99·3	99·4	99·4	99·4	99·4	99·5	99·5
3	34·1	30·8	29·5	28·7	28·2	27·9	27·7	27·5	27·2	27·1	26·6	26·1
4	21·2	18·0	16·7	16·0	15·5	15·2	15·0	14·8	14·5	14·4	13·9	13·5
5	16·26	13·27	12·06	11·39	10·97	10·67	10·46	10·29	10·05	9·89	9·47	9·02
6	13·74	10·92	9·78	9·15	8·75	8·47	8·26	8·10	7·87	7·72	7·31	6·88
7	12·25	9·55	8·45	7·85	7·46	7·19	6·99	6·84	6·62	6·47	6·07	5·65
8	11·26	8·65	7·59	7·01	6·63	6·37	6·18	6·03	5·81	5·67	5·28	4·86
9	10·56	8·02	6·99	6·42	6·06	5·80	5·61	5·47	5·26	5·11	4·73	4·31
10	10·04	7·56	6·55	5·99	5·64	5·39	5·20	5·06	4·85	4·71	4·33	3·91
11	9·65	7·21	6·22	5·67	5·32	5·07	4·89	4·74	4·54	4·40	4·02	3·60
12	9·33	6·93	5·95	5·41	5·06	4·82	4·64	4·50	4·30	4·16	3·78	3·36
13	9·07	6·70	5·74	5·21	4·86	4·62	4·44	4·30	4·10	3·96	3·59	3·17
14	8·86	6·51	5·56	5·04	4·70	4·46	4·28	4·14	3·94	3·80	3·43	3·00
15	8·68	6·36	5·42	4·89	4·56	4·32	4·14	4·00	3·80	3·67	3·29	2·87
16	8·53	6·23	5·29	4·77	4·44	4·20	4·03	3·89	3·69	3·55	3·18	2·75
17	8·40	6·11	5·18	4·67	4·34	4·10	3·93	3·79	3·59	3·46	3·08	2·65
18	8·29	6·01	5·09	4·58	4·25	4·01	3·84	3·71	3·51	3·37	3·00	2·57
19	8·18	5·93	5·01	4·50	4·17	3·94	3·77	3·63	3·43	3·30	2·92	2·49
20	8·10	5·85	4·94	4·43	4·10	3·87	3·70	3·56	3·37	3·23	2·86	2·42
21	8·02	5·78	4·87	4·37	4·04	3·81	3·64	3·51	3·31	3·17	2·80	2·36
22	7·95	5·72	4·82	4·31	3·99	3·76	3·59	3·45	3·26	3·12	2·75	2·31
23	7·88	5·66	4·76	4·26	3·94	3·71	3·54	3·41	3·21	3·07	2·70	2·26
24	7·82	5·61	4·72	4·22	3·90	3·67	3·50	3·36	3·17	3·03	2·66	2·21
25	7·77	5·57	4·68	4·18	3·86	3·63	3·46	3·32	3·13	2·99	2·62	2·17
26	7·72	5·53	4·64	4·14	3·82	3·59	3·42	3·29	3·09	2·96	2·58	2·13
27	7·68	5·49	4·60	4·11	3·78	3·56	3·39	3·26	3·06	2·93	2·55	2·10
28	7·64	5·45	4·57	4·07	3·75	3·53	3·36	3·23	3·03	2·90	2·52	2·06
29	7·60	5·42	4·54	4·04	3·73	3·50	3·33	3·20	3·00	2·87	2·49	2·03
30	7·56	5·39	4·51	4·02	3·70	3·47	3·30	3·17	2·98	2·84	2·47	2·01
32	7·50	5·34	4·46	3·97	3·65	3·43	3·26	3·13	2·93	2·80	2·42	1·96
34	7·45	5·29	4·42	3·93	3·61	3·39	3·22	3·09	2·90	2·76	2·38	1·91
36	7·40	5·25	4·38	3·89	3·58	3·35	3·18	3·05	2·86	2·72	2·35	1·87
38	7·35	5·21	4·34	3·86	3·54	3·32	3·15	3·02	2·83	2·69	2·32	1·84
40	7·31	5·18	4·31	3·83	3·51	3·29	3·12	2·99	2·80	2·66	2·29	1·80
60	7·08	4·98	4·13	3·65	3·34	3·12	2·95	2·82	2·63	2·50	2·12	1·60
120	6·85	4·79	3·95	3·48	3·17	2·96	2·79	2·66	2·47	2·34	1·95	1·38
∞	6·63	4·61	3·78	3·32	3·02	2·80	2·64	2·51	2·32	2·18	1·79	1·00

Table 4. e^{-x}

x	0·00	0·01	0·02	0·03	0·04	0·05	0·06	0·07	0·08	0·09
0·0	1·0000	0·9900	0·9802	0·9704	0·9608	0·9512	0·9418	0·9324	0·9231	0·9139
0·1	0·9048	0·8958	0·8869	0·8781	0·8694	0·8607	0·8521	0·8437	0·8353	0·8270
0·2	0·8187	0·8106	0·8025	0·7945	0·7866	0·7788	0·7711	0·7634	0·7558	0·7483
0·3	0·7408	0·7334	0·7261	0·7189	0·7118	0·7047	0·6977	0·6907	0·6839	0·6771
0·4	0·6703	0·6637	0·6570	0·6505	0·6440	0·6376	0·6313	0·6250	0·6188	0·6126
0·5	0·6065	0·6005	0·5945	0·5886	0·5827	0·5769	0·5712	0·5655	0·5599	0·5543
0·6	0·5488	0·5434	0·5379	0·5326	0·5273	0·5220	0·5169	0·5117	0·5066	0·5016
0·7	0·4966	0·4916	0·4868	0·4819	0·4771	0·4724	0·4677	0·4630	0·4584	0·4538
0·8	0·4493	0·4449	0·4404	0·4360	0·4317	0·4274	0·4232	0·4190	0·4148	0·4107
0·9	0·4066	0·4025	0·3985	0·3946	0·3906	0·3867	0·3829	0·3791	0·3753	0·3716
1·0	0·3679	0·3642	0·3606	0·3570	0·3535	0·3499	0·3465	0·3430	0·3396	0·3362
1·1	0·3329	0·3296	0·3263	0·3230	0·3198	0·3166	0·3135	0·3104	0·3073	0·3042
1·2	0·3012	0·2982	0·2952	0·2923	0·2894	0·2865	0·2837	0·2808	0·2780	0·2753
1·3	0·2725	0·2698	0·2671	0·2645	0·2618	0·2592	0·2567	0·2541	0·2516	0·2491
1·4	0·2466	0·2441	0·2417	0·2393	0·2369	0·2346	0·2322	0·2299	0·2276	0·2254
1·5	0·2231	0·2209	0·2187	0·2165	0·2144	0·2122	0·2101	0·2080	0·2060	0·2039
1·6	0·2019	0·1999	0·1979	0·1959	0·1940	0·1920	0·1901	0·1882	0·1864	0·1845
1·7	0·1827	0·1809	0·1791	0·1773	0·1755	0·1738	0·1720	0·1703	0·1686	0·1670
1·8	0·1653	0·1637	0·1620	0·1604	0·1588	0·1572	0·1557	0·1541	0·1526	0·1511
1·9	0·1496	0·1481	0·1466	0·1451	0·1437	0·1423	0·1409	0·1395	0·1381	0·1367
2·0	0·1353	0·1340	0·1327	0·1313	0·1300	0·1287	0·1275	0·1262	0·1249	0·1237
2·1	0·1225	0·1212	0·1200	0·1188	0·1177	0·1165	0·1153	0·1142	0·1130	0·1119
2·2	0·1108	0·1097	0·1086	0·1075	0·1065	0·1054	0·1044	0·1033	0·1023	0·1013
2·3	0·1003	0·0993	0·0983	0·0973	0·0963	0·0954	0·0944	0·0935	0·0926	0·0916
2·4	0·0907	0·0898	0·0889	0·0880	0·0872	0·0863	0·0854	0·0846	0·0837	0·0829
2·5	0·0821	0·0813	0·0805	0·0797	0·0789	0·0781	0·0773	0·0765	0·0758	0·0750
2·6	0·0743	0·0735	0·0728	0·0721	0·0714	0·0707	0·0699	0·0693	0·0686	0·0679
2·7	0·0672	0·0665	0·0659	0·0652	0·0646	0·0639	0·0633	0·0627	0·0620	0·0614
2·8	0·0608	0·0602	0·0596	0·0590	0·0584	0·0578	0·0573	0·0567	0·0561	0·0556
2·9	0·0550	0·0545	0·0539	0·0534	0·0529	0·0523	0·0518	0·0513	0·0508	0·0503
3·0	0·0498	0·0493	0·0488	0·0483	0·0478	0·0474	0·0469	0·0464	0·0460	0·0455
3·1	0·0450	0·0446	0·0442	0·0437	0·0433	0·0429	0·0424	0·0420	0·0416	0·0412
3·2	0·0408	0·0404	0·0400	0·0396	0·0392	0·0388	0·0384	0·0380	0·0376	0·0373
3·3	0·0369	0·0365	0·0362	0·0358	0·0354	0·0351	0·0347	0·0344	0·0340	0·0337
3·4	0·0334	0·0330	0·0327	0·0324	0·0321	0·0317	0·0314	0·0311	0·0308	0·0305
3·5	0·0302	0·0299	0·0296	0·0293	0·0290	0·0287	0·0284	0·0282	0·0279	0·0276
3·6	0·0273	0·0271	0·0268	0·0265	0·0263	0·0260	0·0257	0·0255	0·0252	0·0250
3·7	0·0247	0·0245	0·0242	0·0240	0·0238	0·0235	0·0233	0·0231	0·0228	0·0226
3·8	0·0224	0·0221	0·0219	0·0217	0·0215	0·0213	0·0211	0·0209	0·0207	0·0204
3·9	0·0202	0·0200	0·0198	0·0196	0·0194	0·0193	0·0191	0·0189	0·0187	0·0185
4·0	0·0183	0·0181	0·0180	0·0178	0·0176	0·0174	0·0172	0·0171	0·0169	0·0167
4·1	0·0166	0·0164	0·0163	0·0161	0·0160	0·0158	0·0156	0·0155	0·0153	0·0152
4·2	0·0150	0·0149	0·0147	0·0146	0·0144	0·0143	0·0142	0·0140	0·0139	0·0137
4·3	0·0136	0·0135	0·0133	0·0132	0·0131	0·0129	0·0128	0·0127	0·0126	0·0124
4·4	0·0123	0·0122	0·0121	0·0120	0·0118	0·0117	0·0116	0·0115	0·0114	0·0113
4·5	0·0111	0·0110	0·0109	0·0108	0·0107	0·0106	0·0105	0·0104	0·0103	0·0102
4·6	0·0101									
4·7	0·0091									
4·8	0·0082									
4·9	0·0074									

Table 5. Distribution of χ^2

n	Probability													
	0·99	0·98	0·95	0·90	0·80	0·70	0·50	0·30	0·20	0·10	0·05	0·02	0·01	0·001
1	·0³157	·0³628	·0³393	·0158	·0642	·148	·445	1·074	1·642	2·706	3·841	5·412	6·635	10·827
2	·0201	·0404	·103	·211	·446	·713	1·386	2·408	3·219	4·605	5·991	7·814	9·210	13·815
3	·115	·185	·352	·584	1·005	1·424	2·366	3·665	4·642	6·251	7·815	9·837	11·345	16·268
4	·297	·429	·711	1·064	1·649	2·195	3·357	4·878	5·989	7·779	9·488	11·668	13·277	18·465
5	·554	·752	1·145	1·610	2·343	3·000	4·351	6·064	7·289	9·236	11·070	13·388	15·086	20·517
6	·872	1·134	1·635	2·204	3·070	3·828	5·348	7·231	8·558	10·645	12·592	15·033	16·812	22·457
7	1·239	1·564	2·167	2·833	3·822	4·671	6·346	8·383	9·803	12·017	14·067	16·622	18·475	24·322
8	1·646	2·032	2·733	3·490	4·594	5·527	7·344	9·524	11·030	13·362	15·507	18·168	20·090	26·125
9	2·088	2·532	3·325	4·168	5·380	6·393	8·343	10·656	12·242	14·684	16·919	19·679	21·666	27·877
10	2·558	3·059	3·940	4·865	6·179	7·267	9·342	11·781	13·442	15·987	18·307	21·161	23·209	29·588
11	3·053	3·609	4·575	5·578	6·989	8·148	10·341	12·899	14·631	17·275	19·675	22·618	24·725	31·264
12	3·571	4·178	5·226	6·304	7·807	9·034	11·340	14·011	15·812	18·549	21·026	24·054	26·217	32·909
13	4·107	4·765	5·892	7·042	8·634	9·926	12·340	15·119	16·985	19·812	22·362	25·472	27·688	34·528
14	4·660	5·368	6·571	7·790	9·467	10·821	13·339	16·222	18·151	21·064	23·685	26·873	29·141	36·123
15	5·229	5·985	7·261	8·547	10·307	11·721	14·339	17·332	19·311	22·307	24·996	28·259	30·578	37·697
16	5·812	6·614	7·962	9·312	11·152	12·624	15·338	18·418	20·465	23·542	26·296	29·633	32·000	39·252
17	6·408	7·255	8·672	10·085	12·002	13·531	16·338	19·511	21·615	24·769	27·587	30·995	33·409	40·790
18	7·015	7·906	9·390	10·865	12·857	14·440	17·338	20·601	22·760	25·989	28·869	32·346	34·805	42·312
19	7·633	8·567	10·117	11·651	13·716	15·352	18·338	21·689	23·900	27·204	30·144	33·687	36·191	43·820
20	8·260	9·237	10·851	12·443	14·578	16·266	19·337	22·775	25·038	28·412	31·410	35·020	37·566	45·315
21	8·897	9·915	11·591	13·240	15·445	17·182	20·337	23·858	26·171	29·615	32·671	36·343	38·932	46·797
22	9·542	10·600	12·338	14·041	16·314	18·101	21·337	24·939	27·301	30·813	33·924	37·659	40·289	48·268
23	10·196	11·293	13·091	14·848	17·187	19·021	22·337	26·018	28·429	32·007	35·172	38·968	41·638	49·728
24	10·856	11·992	13·848	15·659	18·062	19·943	23·337	27·096	29·553	33·196	36·415	40·270	42·980	51·179
25	11·524	12·697	14·611	16·473	18·940	20·867	24·337	28·172	30·675	34·382	37·652	41·566	44·314	52·620
26	12·198	13·409	15·379	17·292	19·820	21·792	25·336	29·246	31·795	35·563	38·885	42·856	45·642	54·052
27	12·879	14·125	16·151	18·114	20·703	22·719	26·336	30·319	32·912	36·741	40·113	44·140	46·963	55·476
28	13·565	14·847	16·928	18·939	21·588	23·647	27·336	31·391	34·027	37·916	41·337	45·419	48·278	56·893
29	14·256	15·574	17·708	19·768	22·475	24·577	28·336	32·461	35·139	39·087	42·557	46·693	49·588	58·302
30	14·953	16·306	18·493	20·599	23·364	25·508	29·336	33·530	36·250	40·256	43·773	47·962	50·892	59·703

For larger values of n, the expression $\sqrt{2\chi^2} - \sqrt{2n-1}$ may be used as a normal deviate with unit variance, remembering that the probability for χ^2 corresponds with that of a single tail of the normal curve.

Table 6. Table of critical values of r_s, the Spearman rank correlation coefficient

N	Significance level (one-tailed test) 0·05	0·01
4	1·000	
5	0·900	1·000
6	0·829	0·943
7	0·714	0·893
8	0·643	0·833
9	0·600	0·783
10	0·564	0·746
12	0·506	0·712
14	0·456	0·645
16	0·425	0·601
18	0·399	0·564
20	0·377	0·534
22	0·359	0·508
24	0·343	0·485
26	0·329	0·465
28	0·317	0·448
30	0·306	0·432

Table 7. Table of critical values of W in the Kendall coefficient of concordance

k	n 3	4	5	6	7	Additional values for $n=3$ k	W
Values at the 0·05 level of significance							
3			64·4	103·9	157·3	9	54·0
4		49·5	88·4	143·3	217·0	12	71·9
5		62·6	112·3	182·4	276·2	14	83·8
6		75·7	136·1	221·4	335·2	16	95·8
8	48·1	101·7	183·7	299·0	453·1	18	107·7
10	60·0	127·8	231·2	376·7	571·0		
15	89·8	192·9	349·8	570·5	864·9		
20	119·7	258·0	468·5	764·4	1158·7		
Values at the 0·01 level of significance							
3			75·6	122·8	185·6	9	75·9
4		61·4	109·3	176·2	265·0	12	103·5
5		80·5	142·8	229·4	343·8	14	121·9
6		99·5	176·1	282·4	422·6	16	140·2
8	66·8	137·4	242·7	388·3	579·9	18	158·6
10	85·1	175·3	309·1	494·0	737·0		
15	131·0	269·8	475·2	758·2	1129·5		
20	177·0	364·2	641·2	1022·2	1521·9		

Table 8.   Table of critical values of ν in the runs test

Given in the bodies of table (a) and table (b) are various critical values of ν for various values of n_+ and n_-. For the one-sample runs test, any value of ν which is equal to or smaller than that shown in table (a) or equal to or larger than that shown in table (b) is significant at the 0·05 level.

(a)

n_+ \ n_-	2	3	4	5	6	7	8	9	10	11	12	13	14	15	16	17	18	19	20
2											2	2	2	2	2	2	2	2	2
3					2	2	2	2	2	2	2	2	2	3	3	3	3	3	3
4				2	2	2	3	3	3	3	3	3	3	3	4	4	4	4	4
5			2	2	3	3	3	3	3	4	4	4	4	4	4	4	5	5	5
6		2	2	3	3	3	3	4	4	4	4	5	5	5	5	5	5	6	6
7		2	2	3	3	3	4	4	5	5	5	5	5	6	6	6	6	6	6
8		2	3	3	3	4	4	5	5	5	6	6	6	6	6	7	7	7	7
9		2	3	3	4	4	5	5	5	6	6	6	7	7	7	7	8	8	8
10		2	3	3	4	5	5	5	6	6	7	7	7	7	8	8	8	8	9
11		2	3	4	4	5	5	6	6	7	7	7	8	8	8	9	9	9	9
12	2	2	3	4	4	5	6	6	7	7	7	8	8	8	9	9	9	10	10
13	2	2	3	4	5	5	6	6	7	7	8	8	9	9	9	10	10	10	10
14	2	2	3	4	5	5	6	7	7	8	8	9	9	9	10	10	10	11	11
15	2	3	3	4	5	6	6	7	7	8	8	9	9	10	10	11	11	11	12
16	2	3	4	4	5	6	6	7	8	8	9	9	10	10	11	11	11	12	12
17	2	3	4	4	5	6	7	7	8	9	9	10	10	11	11	11	12	12	13
18	2	3	4	5	5	6	7	8	8	9	9	10	10	11	11	12	12	13	13
19	2	3	4	5	6	6	7	8	8	9	10	10	11	11	12	12	13	13	13
20	2	3	4	5	6	6	7	8	9	9	10	10	11	12	12	13	13	13	14

(b)

n_+ \ n_-	2	3	4	5	6	7	8	9	10	11	12	13	14	15	16	17	18	19	20
2																			
3																			
4				9	9														
5			9	10	10	11	11												
6			9	10	11	12	12	13	13	13	13								
7				11	12	13	13	14	14	14	14	15	15	15					
8				11	12	13	14	14	15	15	16	16	16	16	17	17	17	17	17
9					13	14	14	15	16	16	16	17	17	18	18	18	18	18	18
10					13	14	15	16	16	17	17	18	18	18	19	19	19	20	20
11					13	14	15	16	17	17	18	19	19	19	20	20	20	21	21
12					13	14	16	16	17	18	19	19	20	20	21	21	21	22	22
13						15	16	17	18	19	19	20	20	21	21	22	22	23	23
14						15	16	17	18	19	20	20	21	22	22	23	23	23	24
15						15	16	18	18	19	20	21	22	22	23	23	24	24	25
16							17	18	19	20	21	21	22	23	23	24	25	25	25
17							17	18	19	20	21	22	23	23	24	25	25	26	26
18							17	18	19	20	21	22	23	24	25	25	26	26	27
19							17	18	20	21	22	23	23	24	25	26	26	27	27
20							17	18	20	21	22	23	24	25	25	26	27	27	28

Answers to examples

Chapter 1

1.19.1   (a) 0·0256   (b) $\left(\dfrac{5}{12}\right)^x, x \geqslant 11$ (c) (i) $\dfrac{842}{1331}$ (ii) $\dfrac{9}{121}$

      (d) 0·421   (e) 0·0475   (f) 0·8; 0·25

1.19.2   (a) $26^3 \times 999 = 17558424$ (b) 86   (c) 864

      (d) $10! = 3628800$ (e) 56

1.19.3   (a) 0·00001301

      (b) Probability of successive samples with 4, 6 and 3 defective springs = 0·000152. Expected number of defective springs = 2 per sample. The process is therefore out of control.

      (c) 0·06   (d) 0·0178

      (e) (i) 2·4 per cent   (ii) At least 1536 pints   (iii) 793–1307 pints

      (f) P (not more than 70 per cent leaving) = 0·1635

      (g) 0·0608

1.19.4   (b) $\sigma_{\bar{x}} = £31·86$ (c) $n = 1359$

      (d) Between 2·22 million and 2·52 million readers

      (e) 99·54 per cent

      (f) Approximately £13 19s. 0d.; none over all, although two students wanting 4s. 6d. meals could not be served.

      (g) 15

Chapter 2

2.11.1   (a) $\bar{x} = 20·32$ years; $s = 1·836$ years; $z = 7·41$ (highly significant)

      (b) $\bar{x} = 6·245$ hours; $s = 3·136$ hours; for $\alpha = \beta$ critical value = 6·0 hours. Reject H_0.

(c) Alloy A: $\bar{x} = 609 \cdot 2$ lb.in.^{2}; $s = 39 \cdot 3$ lb.in.^{2}
Alloy B: $\bar{x} = 618 \cdot 25$ lb.in.^{2}; $s = 34 \cdot 0$ lb.in.^{2}
$z = 2 \cdot 466$ (significant at 5 per cent level, but not at 1 per cent level)

(d) Decontrolled: $\bar{x} = £93 \cdot 25$; $s = £73 \cdot 09$ (last class interval £100–£300
Council: $\bar{x} = £57 \cdot 15$; $s = £25 \cdot 45$ (last class interval £100–£250)
$z = 4 \cdot 37$ (significant)

(e) $\beta = 0 \cdot 18$ or 18 per cent. Accept $H_0 : \pi = 0 \cdot 54$

(f) $z = -0 \cdot 56$. Accept H_0
Increase in sample size reduces the standard error so that $z = -5 \cdot 6$, which is significant; reject H_0.

(g) $z = 2 \cdot 15$. Therefore reject $H_0 : \pi_1 = \pi_2$ at 5 per cent level (not at 1 per cent level), i.e. a higher proportion express full approval.

2.11.2 (a) With mathematics: $\bar{x} = 59 \cdot 67$; $s^2 = 144 \cdot 93$
Without mathematics: $\bar{x} = 59 \cdot 15$; $s^2 = 301 \cdot 1156$
Therefore $F_{(\text{calc.})} = 2 \cdot 08$. For $d.f.$ 25 and $d.f.$ 23 significant at 5 per cent level but not at 1 per cent level.
Assuming $\sigma_1^2 = \sigma_2^2$
$\sigma_{\bar{x}_1 - \bar{x}_2} = 4 \cdot 258$. Therefore $t_{(\text{calc.})} = 0 \cdot 122$ (one-tail test).
Not significant, so accept $H_0 : \mu_1 = \mu_2$
Assuming $\sigma_1^2 \neq \sigma_2^2$
$t_{(\text{calc.})} = 0 \cdot 124$, 46 $d.f.$
Not significant, so accept $H_0 : \mu_1 = \mu_2$

(b) New process: $\bar{x} = 3683 \cdot 3$; $s^2 = 197666 \cdot 67$
Old process: $\bar{x} = 2933 \cdot 3$; $s^2 = 63333 \cdot 33$
$F_{(\text{calc.})} = 3 \cdot 121$, which is not significant so assume $\sigma_1^2 = \sigma_2^2$
$\sigma_{\bar{x}_1 - \bar{x}_2} = 282 \cdot 21066$, therefore $t_{(\text{calc.})} = 2 \cdot 6576$
$t_{0.05} = 2 \cdot 36$, $t_{0.01} = 3 \cdot 5$ for $6+3-2 = 7$ $d.f.$
Reject $H_0 : \mu_1 = \mu_2$ at 5 per cent level but not at 1 per cent level.

(c) (i) $H_0 : \sigma_A^2 = \sigma_B^2$
$s_A^2 = 8 \cdot 2$, $s_B^2 = 2 \cdot 875$, $F_{(\text{calc.})} = 2 \cdot 85$, which is significant at a 5 per cent level but not at a 1 per cent level.
(ii) $H_0 : \sigma_A^2 = \sigma_C^2$
$s_C^2 = 4 \cdot 118$, $F_{(\text{calc.})} = 1 \cdot 99$, which is not significant at a 5 per cent level.
(iii) $H_0 : \sigma_B^2 = \sigma_C^2$
$F_{(\text{calc.})} = 1 \cdot 43$, which is not significant at a 5 per cent level.

(d) $F_{(\text{calc.})} = 7 \cdot 53$ for 12 $d.f.$ and 3 $d.f.$
$F_{0.05} = 3 \cdot 49$, $F_{0.01} = 5 \cdot 95$
Therefore reject $H_0 : \mu_A = \mu_B = \mu_C = \mu_D$

Chapter 3

3.9.1 (c)

| | Male | | Female | |
Age	Working class	White collar class	Working class	White collar class
Under 16	175	75	175	75
16–65	420	180	420	180
Over 65	105	45	105	45
	700	300	700	300

Sample size: 2000

(d)

	Constant sampling fraction (sample size)	Variable sampling fraction (sample size)
Urban areas		
Primary	170	75
Secondary		
Non-selective	116	102
Selective	60	66
Rural areas		
Primary	96	190
Secondary		
Non-selective	42	46
Selective	16	21
	500	500

3.9.2 (a) $\bar{\bar{x}} = 2000$, $\bar{R} = 22$

Mean chart	Range chart
U.A.L. = 2016·55	U.A.L. = 56·54
U.W.L. = 2010·56	U.W.L. = 42·46
L.W.L. = 1989·44	L.W.L. = 6·38
L.A.L. = 1983·54	L.A.L. = 2·20

$\sigma = 10·68$, therefore $6\sigma = 64·08 < 100$ tolerance in specification.

(b) $\bar{P} = \dfrac{1}{10} = 0 \cdot 1$

    U.A.L. $= 0 \cdot 164$; eliminating sample number 4:
    U.W.L. $= 0 \cdot 142$, $\bar{P} = 0 \cdot 096$
    L.W.L. $= 0 \cdot 058$ giving
    L.A.L. $= 0 \cdot 036$

    U.A.L. $= 0 \cdot 158$
    U.W.L. $= 0 \cdot 138$
    L.W.L. $= 0 \cdot 054$
    L.A.L. $= 0 \cdot 034$

(c) $\bar{P} = 0 \cdot 032$, $np = 0 \cdot 64$

    U.A.L. $=$ between $\dfrac{4}{20}$ and $\dfrac{5}{20}$

    U.W.L. $= \dfrac{3}{20}$

    Lower line $= 0$

(d) Nothing.   Satisfactory.

Chapter 4

4.16.1   (a) $\log y = 1 \cdot 9831 - 0 \cdot 2244x$
       or $y = (98 \cdot 18)(0 \cdot 5965^x)$
       $r_{\log y,\, x} = -0 \cdot 984$
   (b) $\log y = 2 \cdot 3948 - 1 \cdot 5682 \log x$
       or $y = (248 \cdot 2)(x^{-1 \cdot 5682})$
   (c) $y = 133 \cdot 313682 - 0 \cdot 595019x + 0 \cdot 0037204x^2$
       $r_{y,\, x,\, x^2} = 0 \cdot 888$
   (d) $y = 223 \cdot 407 - \dfrac{10885 \cdot 398}{x}$

4.16.2   (a) $y_1 = 57 \cdot 230 + 0 \cdot 4768x_2 - 0 \cdot 0243x_3$
   (b) (i) $r_{12.3} = 0 \cdot 9666$, $r_{13.2} = -0 \cdot 9703$
      (ii) $b_{12.3} = 1 \cdot 3289$, $b_{13.2} = -0 \cdot 4609$, $a_{1.23} = 2 \cdot 8425$
      (iii) $R_{1.23} = 0 \cdot 9747$
   (c) $b_{12.34} = 1 \cdot 3220$
      $b_{13.24} = -0 \cdot 7632$
      $b_{14.23} = 0 \cdot 8883$
      $\beta_{12.34} = 0 \cdot 66100$
      $\beta_{13.24} = -0 \cdot 22896$
      $\beta_{14.23} = 0 \cdot 53298$

	x_2	x_3	x_4	*Total*
Direct effect	0·43692	0·05242	0·28407	0·77341
Indirect effect				
$x_2 x_3$	−0·10594	−0·10594		−0·21188
$x_2 x_4$	0·24661		0·24661	0·49322
$x_3 x_4$		−0·10165	−0·10165	−0·20330
Net effect	0·57759	−0·15517	0·42903	0·85145

4.16.3   (a) $t_{(calc.)} = 1\cdot700; t_{0.05} = 1\cdot725$ (one-tail); not significant
          $Z_1 = 0\cdot51366$
          $Z_2 = 0\cdot39973$
          $\sigma_z = 0\cdot343$
          $z_{(calc.)} = 0\cdot332; z_{0.05} = 1\cdot96$ (two-tail); not significant

    (b)   (i) $b = 0\cdot9610, a = 4\cdot8421$

        (ii) $t_{(calc.)} = 50102; t_{0.05} = 1\cdot860$ (8 *d.f.*, one-tail); significant, accept $H_0 : \beta > 0$

        (iii) $t_{(calc.)} = 0\cdot00207$; not significant

        (iv) Confidence interval for mean predicted value (95 per cent confidence) $= 16\cdot6418$ to $21\cdot8724$
             Confidence interval for predicted value (95 per cent confidence) $= 10\cdot7117$ to $27\cdot8025$

        (v) 95 per cent confidence interval; 0·5452 to 0·9700

    (c) $F_{(calc.)} = 29\cdot861; F_{0.01} = 9\cdot33$ (1 and 12 *d.f.*); therefore c is very significantly greater than 0.

    (d) $F_{(calc.)} = 1\cdot139; F_{0.05} = 4\cdot15$ (1 and 33 *d.f.*); therefore $b_{13.2}$ is not significant.
        $F_{(calc.)} = 253\cdot327; F_{0.01} = 7\cdot48$ (1 and 34 *d.f.*); $b_{12.3}$ is highly significant.

Chapter 5

5.7.1   (a) $\left. \begin{array}{l} \log y_t = 2\cdot9185 + 0\cdot02408 x_t \\ \text{or } y_t = (828\cdot8)(1\cdot057^{x_t}) \end{array} \right\}$ Origin 1953–4, unit $\frac{1}{2}$ year or 6 months

    (b) $y_t = 104\cdot8228 - 1\cdot5909 x_t - 0\cdot5186 x_t^2$ (origin 1959, unit 1 year)

    (c) $y_t = 97\cdot892584 - 0\cdot026270 x_t + 0\cdot099758 x_t^2 + 0\cdot010782 x_t^3$ (origin 1933, unit one year); $1950 = 179\cdot248$

    (d)   (i) $\log y_t = 1\cdot7379 - (1\cdot2128)(0\cdot8175^{x_t})$
          or $y_t = (54\cdot69)(0\cdot06127^{0\cdot8175^{x_t}})$

(ii) $\dfrac{1}{y_t} = 0.000013104 + (0.034704)(0.6734^{x_t})$

(iii) $y_t = 1498.9438 - (1241.9703)(0.7864^{x_t})$

(iv) $y_t = 94.9625 - (84.9645)(0.8189^{x_t})$

(e) Parabola, log parabola, Gompertz or logistic

Chapter 6

6.11.1 (a) $\chi_{(\text{calc.})}^2 = 7.415$; $\chi_{0.05}^2 = 5.99\,(2\,d.f.)$; $\chi_{0.01}^2 = 9.21\,(2\,d.f.)$
Reject H_0 at 0.05 but not 0.01 level.

(b) $\bar{x} = 3.945$; $s = 0.469$; $\chi_{(\text{calc.})}^2 = 1.607$; $\chi_{0.05}^2 = 7.81\,(3\,d.f.)$
Accept H_0, normal distribution.

(c) $\chi_{(\text{calc.})}^2 = 9.707$; $\chi_{0.05}^2 = 19.675\,(11\,d.f.)$
Accept H_0, Poisson distribution.

(d) $\chi_{(\text{calc.})}^2 = 8.988$; $\chi_{0.05}^2 = 3.84\,(1\,d.f.)$; $\chi_{0.01}^2 = 7.88\,(1\,d.f.)$
Significant, reject H_0; binomial distribution.

(e) $\chi_{(\text{calc.})}^2 = 16.03$; $\chi_{0.05}^2 = 3.84\,(1\,d.f.)$; $\chi_{0.01}^2 = 6.63\,(1\,d.f.)$
Highly significant, reject H_0.

(f) $C = 0.2282$; $C = 0.2724$

6.11.2 (a) $\chi_{(\text{calc.})}^2 = 1.286$; $\chi_{0.05}^2 = 3.84\,(1\,d.f.)$
Not significant; accept $H_0 : M_1 = M_2$

(b) Critical Region

Old process	Σx_1	New process	Σx_2	$\Sigma x_1 - \Sigma x_2$
5329, 4900, 4859, 4740	19828	3562, 2730, 2610, 2583	11485	8343
5329, 4900, 4859, 3562	18650	4740, 2730, 2610, 2583	12663	5987

Also -5987 and -8343

Actual difference $= 17552 - 13761 = 3791$, therefore not significant.

(c) $H_0 : \pi > 0.9$; $H_A : \pi < 0.9$
Critical value 0.8, $p = 0.75$; reject H_0 at 5 per cent level

6.11.3 (a) $r_s = 0.873$; $r_{s_{0.05}} = 0.564$; $r_{s_{0.01}} = 0.746$
Significant at both 5 per cent and 1 per cent levels

(b) $W = 0.840$

6.11.4   (a) $n_+ = 11; n_- = 13; v = 10$
          Not significant, randomness accepted.
      (b) $n_+ = 6; n_- = 12; v = 2$
          Critical values of $v = 3$ and 11; $v = 2$ falls in region of rejection. There-
          fore H_0: Random series rejected and we accept time dependence.

Index

Studies in Applied Statistics

Statistics now plays a significant part in many different fields: technology, the behavioural, biological and physical sciences, management
and government. Each volume of *Studies in Applied Statistics* explains
statistical methods in relation to a particular subject. The required techniques are described carefully and clearly, and are not obscured by
unnecessary mathematical theory.

Statistics for the Social Scientist: 1 Introducing Statistics

K. A. Yeomans
This introductory text starts early: it revises some useful school algebra
and makes clear for the non-mathematician the grammar of statistics,
including the use of such terms as mean, standard deviation, correlation
and index number.

Contents

1 The mathematical basis of statistics
2 The arrangement and presentation of data
3 Index numbers in theory and practice
4 Two-variable linear regression and correlation
5 The analysis of time series

Statistics for Technology

Christopher Chatfield
Provides a sound knowledge of statistical knowledge to meet the
demands created by the steadily increasing use of statistical methods in
engineering and applied science. The mathematics is kept as simple as
possible.
The book is in three parts. The first part introduces the ideas and
simple ways of analysing data. The second part explains the theory. The
third part deals with applications to experimental design and analysis,
quality control and life testing. It includes many topics not previously
brought together in one book.

Other Penguin Education Titles on Statistics

Statistics for the Teacher

A. C. Crocker

An introduction to statistics for use by the teacher-in-training, to assist him in understanding the frequent references to statistics in his reading or practical work. It is written in a simple, attractive style and assumes very little previous mathematical knowledge whilst covering a wide range of statistical topics including correlation, significance, item analysis and the reliability of tests.

Basic Statistics in Behavioural Research

A. E. Maxwell

This book, written to provide medical students on a postgraduate course in psychiatry with some initial understanding of the statistical terminology and elementary techniques, will be useful to any student of the behavioural sciences who wants a simple introductory course on the principles of experimental design and data analysis.

The author takes account of the fact that many of his readers will have forgotten their school mathematics.